CULTURAL CODE

CULTURAL CODE

Video Games and Latin America

Phillip Penix-Tadsen

The MIT Press
Cambridge, Massachusetts
London, England

This book was set in Gentium Plus by Toppan Best-set Premedia Limited. Printed and bound in the United States of America.

Library of Congress Cataloging-in-Publication Data is available.

ISBN: 978-0-262-03405-0

10   9   8   7   6   5   4   3   2   1

CONTENTS

ACKNOWLEDGMENTS

This book would not have been possible without the enormous support of the many friends, colleagues, game designers, and fellow gamers who provided their encouragement and feedback at various points in this project's development. I wish to acknowledge their contributions, though I of course take full responsibility for the final contents of the book.

First and foremost, I am thankful to my wife and my rock, Rebecca, for her unwavering encouragement. *Cultural Code* would not exist without her immeasurable support throughout its development, as well as the motivation she has provided for me in every way since long before research on this project began. Likewise, my daughters Josie and Roxy have given me the inspiration to take games seriously, never more so than when I get to play and discuss their favorite video games with them.

There were four other people in particular who were indispensable to the gestation of this book. My longtime friend and early gaming partner Matt Harrington sparked the initial idea that led to *Cultural Code* when he recommended that I play *Red Dead Redemption*, telling me that it made him want to go to Mexico—since that time there's been no turning back on my road to cultural ludology. Rachael Hutchinson, my colleague in foreign languages as well as game studies at the University of Delaware (UD), has provided thoughtful feedback and support throughout this process as well as helping to inspire this book with her own insightful research on games and culture. Miguel Sicart has not only provided a model for nuanced and thoughtful game studies scholarship on difficult topics, he also was instrumental in nurturing this project in its proposal phase, providing invaluable feedback and support for which I will be forever grateful. And finally, Gonzalo Frasca's pioneering work on ludology and groundbreaking game design have provided me with continued inspiration, making him the spiritual and conceptual godfather of this work, which I can only hope will live up to the standards he has set.

Over the past several years I have presented work from or related to *Cultural Code* at a number of conferences and institutions, and I am thankful to all those who provided feedback on those occasions. I am especially grateful for invitations to give lectures on games from my colleagues Melissa González at Davidson College, Manuel Olmedo and the Romance Language graduate students of Villanova University, and Michael Solomon at the University of Pennsylvania. Likewise, I am indebted to those who have invited me to join their conference panels and thus provided me with a forum for a fruitful exchange of ideas, including Osvaldo Cleger, Craig Epplin, Tania Gentic, Matthew Bush, Paige Rafoth, and Laura M. Herbert. I am also thankful to those colleagues who shared panels with me or provided feedback at these presentations, or both, including Bram Acosta, Daniel Chávez, J. Andrew Brown, César Barros, Rafael M. Montes, Mark Sample, Kyra A. Kietrys, Brian Price, Justin Read, Rebecca Biron, Luis Duno-Gottberg, and John D. Riofrio.

This project was also nurtured by my colleagues in Latin American literary and cultural studies who reviewed the book proposal and other parts of the text, as well as my colleagues in game studies who spoke with me about the book at various stages of its production. The former group includes my PhD thesis advisor and longtime mentor and friend Carlos J. Alonso, as well as my colleagues and friends Sam Steinberg, Dierdra Reber, Nicolas Poppe, and once again Justin Read and Craig Epplin. The latter group includes Steven E. Jones, Judd Ruggill, and Mia Consalvo, as well as those with whom I had the pleasure of sharing time at game studies conferences, among them Albith Delgado, Saúl González, Luiz Ojima Sakuda, Ivelise Fortim, Rogelio Cardona-Nivera, and Alyea Sandovar. Finally, I am thankful to the MIT Press and in particular my editor Douglas Sery for his continued support of this project, which was instrumental in bringing it into being.

At the University of Delaware I have found support from many individuals, especially my colleagues in the Game Studies Research Group, Rachael Hutchinson, Juliet Dee, Daniel Chester, Troy Richards, Siobhan Carroll, and Jenny Lambe. I am also thankful to the staff of Morris Library, particularly Meghann Matwichuk, Megan Gaffney, and Nico Carver. The students in my Spanish and Latin American studies capstone seminar on new media also provided the testing ground and valuable feedback about various aspects of this book. I am also grateful to my colleagues in Languages, Literatures, and Cultures, especially my colleagues Persephone Braham and Cynthia Schmidt-Cruz in contemporary Latin American literary and cultural studies, as well as Deborah Steinberger for conducting the department's faculty research workshop. Likewise, I am thankful to the entities at UD that have provided financial support in the form of grants, including the College of Arts and Sciences, the Department of Languages, Literatures, and Cultures, and the Interdisciplinary Humanities Research Center.

I am also extremely grateful to all of the Latin American game industry and game studies contacts who have provided their insights and shared their work. I am especially thankful for the work of Luis Wong, Eduardo Marisca, and Jochen Siess and their insights regarding various aspects of the book. I also wish to thank all of the game designers and developers who have allowed me to use images of their work or provided feedback on this project, or both, including

Gonzalo Frasca, Daniel Benmergui, Coco Fusco and Ricardo Dominguez, Rafael Fajardo, Jessica Irish, Juan Pablo "Pex" Pison, Ariel and Enrique Arbiser, and the many, many others whose work graces the pages of this book.

Last but definitely not least, I would like to thank all of those friends and family members who have not only provided me with support over the years but have also been a part of my formative experiences as a gamer. These include first and foremost Ryan "The Brain" Brannon, Ben Daigneau, Jon Finley, Uri Garcia, and everyone from my longtime video game gang The Zone in Kent, Ohio, as well as the Jessie Avenue gaming corridor, where I spent countless hours of my childhood plugging away at Nintendo and Intellivision games with Jamie Stillman, Matt Harrington, Ron Wesley, and Kevin Walter, among others. I am indebted to my parents, Tom and Frankie Tadsen, for many things—among them buying an Atari 2600 and playing it with my sister and me for many hours during our youth. Likewise, my grandparents Shirley and Lester Anderson helped open me up to gaming by providing a Magnavox Odyssey to entertain my cousins and me on our visits (a console that I'm not sure they ever played themselves). And finally, I wish to acknowledge the gaming friends and archivists whose conversations and insights have fueled me over the past few years, including Josh Finnell, Tom Pulhamus, Philip Swift, Joshua Sabin, Diego Domínguez, Meghan McInnis-Domínguez, Marcus Vinicius Garrett Chiado, and Carl Larson.

Cultural Code has been helped along by these and many others who have contributed their time, thought, financing, feedback, companionship, and encouragement. This book is dedicated to them.

INTRODUCTION: TOWARD A CULTURAL LUDOLOGY

Video games and culture have specific uses for one another. Since the first personal computers and home game consoles hit worldwide markets in the late 1970s, interactive games have come to serve a growing array of purposes for human culture, while game designers have developed increasingly complex ways of incorporating cultural context into their products. Today, in Latin America and across the globe, games are put to use for a broad array of social, political, and economic purposes, and are becoming an ever more ubiquitous element of daily life. Apart from being played, games are being referenced, reviled and regaled, polemicized and politicized, monetized and monumentalized, and otherwise converted into cultural currency with increasing frequency. For video game designers worldwide, meanwhile, culture functions as a resource that can be utilized to meaningfully impact the player's experience. Both static code and subjective play have been shown to contribute to the process of meaning creation in games. But culture also comes into play, not only due to the particularities of the social contexts in which video games are produced and consumed, but also through symbolic, environmental, and narrative elements that contribute to meaningful in-game experiences. Therefore, this book uses a twofold approach to unpack the complex relationship between video games and culture, looking first at how culture uses games, and then at how games use culture.[1]

The objective of this book is to bring together the critical vocabularies of game studies and Latin American cultural studies in order to offer the first synthetic theorization of the relationship between video games and culture, based on analysis of both in-game representations and the real-life economic, political, and societal effects of games. By focusing on the specific but enormously diverse region of Latin America, the book offers the keys to unlocking the intricate relationship between video games and culture today. Given the complexity of this relationship, game scholars have noted the inherent need for a multifaceted and interdisciplinary approach,[2] in order to overcome the conceptual oversimplification that can lead to misunderstandings about video games' role as cultural products and as portrayals of culture. Due to the intrinsic interdisciplinarity of the questions this book examines, it is necessary to clarify certain concepts that might seem elementary to an expert audience, either in Latin American cultural studies or in game studies, but that may not be clear to those who examine games or culture from other perspectives. Therefore I do my best to explain with clarity and precision the basic concepts that are incorporated into the book's critical methodology, to help make its arguments meaningful to as many audiences as possible.

For game studies, this book's unique focus on Latin America reveals how video games and culture affect one other on a global level, inside as well as outside of the dominant commercial markets. Too frequently, analysis of new media and culture suffers from critical tunnel vision, focusing only on the world's wealthiest nations to the detriment of our understanding of the unique ways in which media products are appropriated and reappropriated in diverse cultural contexts throughout the globe. In light of recent theoretical discussions of the ways games make meaning either through the procedural rhetoric set in place by a game's preprogrammed rules or through the unpredictable activity of play, culture remains an underexplored "third level" of signification in video games. Other regional game scholars have argued that it is problematic when "socio-cultural differences and contextual specificities are elided or neglected in 'global' studies of games," highlighting the need for "a comprehensive mapping of the socio-technological, socio-cultural, techno-nationalist and economic dimensions" of games' meaning "as both a new media and a social phenomenon."[3] This book undertakes a related endeavor, seeking to deepen and diversify our understanding of culture within the field of game studies by providing a preliminary mapping of the cultural history of video games in Latin America, as well as a critical guide to the history of Latin American cultural representation in video games.

For Latin American cultural studies, the book offers a portrayal of the complex relationship between games and the region's cultures over several decades of development. Latin Americans (like all gamers) approach games first and foremost as players, and this book demonstrates how unique local practices, playing habits, and software and hardware adaptations throughout the region reflect a diverse and expanding population of gamers that crosses all socioeconomic sectors of society. At the same time, Latin America is home to a host of cultural contexts that have been portrayed in video games since the onset of the medium, from the ancient ruins explored in *Pitfall!* (Activision 1982), *Tomb Raider* (Eidos 1996), and *Uncharted: Drake's Fortune* (Sony 2007) to the paramilitary war zones of *Contra* (Konami 1987), *Just Cause* (Eidos 2006) or *Call of Duty* (Activision 2003), making the region key to understanding the history of in-game cultural representation. Today, Latin America's growing contributions to game design, production, and consumption are pushing it from the margins toward the center of the gaming world, all of which makes the region an ideal model of the shifting cultural terrain on which games operate in twenty-first-century global society.

A new type of interdisciplinary methodology is required in order to analyze the relationship between games and culture, and therefore I offer this project as an example of what I refer to as "cultural ludology." Conceptually, this is a reference to Uruguayan game theorist and designer Gonzalo Frasca's usage of the term "ludology" to refer to "a discipline that studies games in general, and video games in particular," focusing on the specific coded mechanisms at work in games.[4] Some have seen Frasca's approach as a recapitulation of the "history of twentieth-century *literary* formalism, with 'the game itself' replacing the New Critics' 'text in itself,'"[5] or have even accused the ludologists of being "backdoor" formalists following a current of "technological determinism."[6] Others, however, more sympathetically accept Frasca's explanation that his concept of ludology was never intended as a closed system aimed at studying game mechanics in isolation.[7] In this sense, this book is in solidarity with the ludologists' drive to define games as unique forms of expression, always paying careful attention to how games' coded software produces meaning. However, my analysis departs from an inward focus on "the game itself" by examining the multiple ways that culture impacts the meaning of video games. Cultural ludology focuses on the analysis of video games as such, attending to the myriad ways culture is incorporated into game mechanics, but at the same time recognizes the signifying potential of the cultural environment in which games are created, designed, manufactured, purchased, played, and otherwise put to use.

What Is a (Video) Game?

But before getting into greater specifics about the potential for examining the relationship between Latin America and video games from the standpoint of cultural ludology, we must clarify some basic questions, beginning with the concept of the *game* in general, and the *video game* specifically. It is worth noting that many scholars prefer to use the terms "electronic game" or "computer game" rather than "video game" because these labels more accurately reflect the nature of games that are not always entirely or even partially visual—take for example *Papa Sangre* (Somethin' Else 2010), a survival horror "audio game" set in a Mexico-based "land of the dead," which players navigate on their mobile devices by responding to sound cues transmitted to their headphones. Exceptions such as this aside, I prefer the term "video game" simply because it is the most commonly used terminology for the medium among the general populace, and the one that feels most natural to me as a lifelong video gamer. But prior to arriving at a more precise definition of the *video game* it is essential to define the *game*.

Scholars generally trace the origins of the formal academic study of games to Dutch historian Johan Huizinga's 1944 work *Homo Ludens: A Study of the Play Element in Culture*. Huizinga grouped games along with rituals as activities that take place outside of ordinary life, defining play as "a stepping out of 'real' life into a temporary sphere of activity with a disposition all of its own."[8] Huizinga coined the term "magic circle" to describe the isolated, hallowed spaces used for rituals and games.[9] This concept was generally upheld by Roger Caillois in his 1958 work *Man, Play and Games*, wherein he describes "the game's domain" as "a restricted, closed, protected universe: a pure space,"[10] while asserting that "[n]othing that takes place outside this ideal frontier is relevant"[11] to the experience of play.

With the advent of electronic games and especially online games, the concept of a separate and sealed "magic circle" for gameplay has come increasingly under fire. Edward Castronova has redefined the magic circle as a "membrane," noting that "we find human society on either side of the membrane, and since society is the ultimate locus of validation for all of our important shared notions—value, fact, emotion, meaning—we will find shared notions on either side as well."[12] In *The Meaning of Video Games*, Steven E. Jones notes that "almost any successful game exists in a system of many worlds, only some of which are strictly story-worlds but all of which … add to the sum total of the game's universe."[13] This interplay between the game world and the real world is reiterated by Celia Pearce, who cites "leakages between play, imagination, and real life," arguing that rather than a singular and discrete magic circle "it may be more useful to think of clusters of intersecting and overlapping magic circles within the larger constellation of networked play spaces, which we might call the 'ludisphere,' which exists in the larger frame of 'real life.'"[14] Contemporary critics like Castronova, Jones, and Pearce highlight the ways "real life" enters into the gaming experience and vice versa, both in the values the player brings to the arena of play and the increased interpenetration of "reality" and "gamespace." Reality enters the game experience when players voice-chat with their real-life companions while playing online games, post videos of their gameplay to YouTube, or communicate about the games they play in online forums or offline conversations. Meanwhile, the increasing presence of games in everyday life is evidenced by skyrocketing global software and hardware sales as well as the increasing diversification of electronic games, which are now played more frequently on social networks or mobile devices than on traditional game consoles, making the distinction between "real life" and "gamespace" ever more tenuous.[15]

Since classical definitions of games were insufficient for characterizing the unique nature of video games, scholars from a range of disciplines have created new definitions particular to the experiences of electronic gaming. Some early studies of video games' meaning, like Janet H. Murray's *Hamlet on the Holodeck*, sought to hold the developing medium to literary standards of greatness, though many within game studies were quick to defend games from any literary, filmic, or otherwise borrowed critical methodologies. In volume 1, issue 1 of the academic journal *Game Studies*, Markku Eskelinen has a bit of fun at the expense of those who would seek to "colonize" games for their own already-existing disciplines, arguing: "Outside academic theory people are usually excellent at making distinctions between narrative, drama and games. If I throw a ball at you I don't expect you to drop it and wait until it starts telling stories. On the other hand, if and when games and especially computer games are studied and theorized they are almost without exception colonised from the fields of literary, theatre, drama and film studies."[16] Espen J. Aarseth, considered by many the godfather of game studies, reflects similar incredulity in a rhetorical question-and-answer dialogue with himself: "Are games texts? The best reason I can think of why one would ask such a crude question is because one is a literary or semiotic theorist and wants to believe in the relevance of one's training."[17] Rather than attempt to fit games into already existing analytical categories, these early ludologists suggested, what was needed was a bona fide effort to define games in terms of the uniqueness and particularities of the medium.

This is easier said than done—even some of the most convincing ways of defining games rely heavily on analogy and metaphor. Game designer and critic Eric Zimmerman highlights games' unique signifying context by explaining that, within a game of football, the ball itself is not a formed and sewn piece of leather, but "a special object that helps me score," one with "very specific rules about who can touch it, when, where, and in what ways,"[18] a demonstration of how an object whose meaning is superficially familiar takes on a transformed significance in the context of gameplay. For his part, Frans Mäyrä likens gameplay to a musical performance or dance, a nonlinguistic but nonetheless meaningful experience whose significance cannot be fully articulated in words: "An immersed player can be engaged with the game for hours on end, and yet it is hard to tell precisely what the actual meaning of game is for this player. Hands may be locked to the game controls, there are movements and maybe sometimes (conscious or involuntary) sounds, but even when interviewed, a player is rarely able to verbalize very well the exact quality of gameplay experience. The internal experience can be rich and multidimensional, and yet hard to communicate precisely."[19] Trying to explain what a video game is "about" is akin to explaining what an orchestral performance is "about"—they are both nonverbal, yet meaningful, experiences. The impossibility of verbally communicating a video game's meaning further demonstrates how games differ from traditional linguistic texts, even if we have only succeeded in supplanting one not-quite-accurate analogy for games (text) with another (music).

Beyond these analogical descriptions of *how* games make meaning, some scholars have offered important insights into *what* makes a game, many of them schematizing their definitions in terms of a precise number of characteristics: for Jesper Juul, there are six,[20] while for Aarseth there are only three—namely, "(1) rules, (2) a material/semiotic system (a gameworld), and (3) gameplay."[21] Alexander R. Galloway supplants Aarseth's semiotic system with an objective, describing a game as "an activity defined by rules in which players try to reach some sort of goal."[22] Meanwhile, gamification evangelist and TED Talk superstar Jane McGonigal says that any true game has four traits, "*a goal, rules, a feedback system*, and *voluntary participation*."[23] These definitions all coincide on several points, and their disconnects speak to each author's unique approach and examples. All of them cite the presence of *rules*, which in terms of video games means the basic coded operations of the software and related functions assigned to player actions (in a sense, the *goal* element suggested by Galloway and McGonigal could be considered a component of the overall *rule* system). Likewise, all of these definitions cite gameplay or active participation by a player as a fundamental element in defining a game and understanding its meaning, along with a specific game world, feedback system, semiotic system, or combination of these.

The prevailing scholarly definition of video games, therefore, takes all of these qualities into account: they are virtual spaces that cross over with real life; they are contexts for the creation of nonverbal experience; and they are signifying systems in which meaning is generated through the coordination of coded rules and player performance. My own definition of games as meaning-making systems builds upon the examples cited previously by adding the consideration of *cultural context* into the ways games' meaning is made: Video games are activities with rules that take place in a specific semiotic system and create meaningful experiences for the player in relation to the cultural context in which they are played as well as the cultural scenarios they portray.

What Is (Latin American) Culture?

For the purposes of this book, "culture" is taken to have a double meaning. My aim is to examine both the specific ways that *culture*—in this case a synonym for "human society"—uses games, and the ways that games use *culture*—condensed into the form of representative symbolic, environmental, or narrative elements used to characterize a specific group of people. This second sense of culture is a bit more complex, and traces its origins to contemporary cultural studies and particularly to certain trajectories in Latin American studies. A significant critical current within contemporary Latin American cultural studies represented by scholars like Néstor García Canclini, Beatriz Sarlo, George Yúdice, and Jesús Martín-Barbero examines culture in terms of the way it is negotiated through media technologies. In *Consumers and Citizens* García Canclini succinctly sums up the philosophical underpinnings of this critical trajectory, asserting that "[t]he exercise of citizenship has always been associated with the capacity to appropriate commodities and with ways of using them."[24] He would later note that culture "does not take place only within an ethnicity, it does not even take place within a nation, but rather globally, crossing borders, opening up national and inter-ethnic barriers and making it so that each group can stock itself with very different *cultural repertoires*."[25] Yúdice, for his part, has noted the inseparability of video games from other commercial media in twenty-first-century Latin America,[26] and his work is central to the characterization of culture as something whose meaning is always defined within some context of negotiation. It is in this sense that culture can be converted into a resource or commodity, translated into exchangeable tokens with relational and situational value. In looking at the ways games use Latin American culture, I adopt this view of culture as an impermanent and constantly changing resource, one that holds different meanings depending on the context of its transmission and reception.

This relational definition of culture has its roots in a critical discussion that began with the initiation of the discipline of cultural studies under the Frankfurt School of philosophy. In the 1963 essay "Culture Industry Revisited," Theodor W. Adorno suggests that culture not only is represented through the products of the cultural industries, it also is supplanted by these products and their representative illusions: "The colour film demolishes the genial old tavern to a greater extent than bombs ever could: the film exterminates its imago. No homeland can survive being processed by the films which celebrate it, and which thereby turn the unique character on which it thrives into an interchangeable sameness."[27] Adorno's sentiment is echoed in Walter Benjamin's discussion of the work of art's loss of its "aura" in the age of mechanical reproduction, which "substitutes a plurality of copies for a unique existence."[28] Adorno and Benjamin are true to their school's view of cultural production: at the same time that they elevate the cultural status of popular media like film, for example, by making it the subject of their philosophical explorations, they do so ultimately in order to condemn it and other forms of media as the tools of hegemony. Fredric Jameson, in calling for on scholars "to reach out into the expanded realm of production to map its effects"[29] in order to grasp how culture is integrated into the commodity system of late capitalism, expands upon the Frankfurt School's tradition. Like his precursors, Jameson sees himself as denouncing culture's commodification while highlighting cultural politics as "the primary space of struggle" in contemporary society.[30] But even if it is not his primary goal, Jameson's call to "map the effects" of an extended realm of cultural production marks a change in critical perspective, an effort to supersede a critique that begins and ends with the condemnation of media.

With the advent of the "network society," to borrow Manuel Castells's terminology, the need for a paradigmatic shift in theoretical approaches to culture gains urgency. A quarter century ago, Anthony Giddens spoke of *disembedding* social systems through the mechanism of the "symbolic token," or "media of interchange which can be 'passed around' without regard to the specific characteristics of individuals or groups that handle them at any particular juncture."[31] A few years later, philosopher Pierre Lévy spoke of the "anthropological object," a symbolic object that "traces a situation, bears with it the field of a problematic, the knot of tensions or psychic landscape of the group."[32] Video games are full of symbolic tokens and anthropological objects rooted in Latin American cultural iconography, from the Mexican Day of the Dead, to the pyramids of the Mayan, Aztec, and Incan empires, to historical scenarios of conquest, colonization, and revolution. And for the reasons explained previously, such objects must not be taken as transparent in their meaning, or as having the same meaning in a video game that they would have in the "real world," or in another historical or cultural context.

Interactivity is an essential element of the way culture is represented in contemporary society, a fact that Arjun Appadurai observed in 1996, when he characterized the circulation of culture in terms of "ethnoscapes" that no longer consist of static, familiar anthropological objects, but rather are profoundly interactive in nature.[33] That same year, Castells spoke of contemporary culture in terms of "real virtuality," explaining that "[l]ocalities become disembodied from their cultural, historical, geographic meaning, and reintegrated into functional networks, or into image collages, inducing a space of flows that substitutes for the space of places."[34] Like Appadurai, Castells emphasizes the integration of the real and the symbolic, through networked and interactive flows of cultural meaning outside of national boundaries. As a region comprised of some twenty different Spanish and Portuguese-speaking nations (among which dozens of indigenous languages are also spoken), Latin America today is an area of great diversity, meaning that an extensive array of cultures and subcultures exist within what we might call "contemporary Latin American culture."

In the two decades since these foundational concepts regarding the relationship between new media and global culture were established, Giddens's disembedded symbolic tokens, Lévy's deterritorialized anthropological objects, Appadurai's ethnoscapes, and Castells's real virtuality have gained increasing conceptual relevance as mechanisms for analyzing cultural signification in media consumed on the screens of today's tablets, smartphones, personal computers, and televisions. In his pioneering work *The Language of New Media*, theorist Lev Manovich explains that media in general can be thought of as consisting of two distinct layers—the "cultural layer" and the "computer layer"—with the cultural layer including elements like story, plot, dramatic tone, and point of view, as opposed to the computer layer's "computer language and data structure."[35] In sense, then, we can think of culture as a "layer" of signification that relates to the already-existing social patterns and norms of the individual player, as well as a foundational layer to the making of video game meaning by game designers with their own cultural backgrounds. Mäyrä defines culture as "a *system of meaning*,"[36] which means video games require familiarity with how cultural signifiers are integrated into game mechanics and the player experience, pointing to why James Paul Gee refers to gaming as "a new *literacy*."[37] In the present analysis I bring my own game literacy to bear on an examination of culture's contributions to meaning both within and around games, integrating Manovich's systematic categorization of the cultural and computer layers into an examination of the cultural meaning of games.

Therefore, in analyzing how games use culture, I define culture in terms of the tokens, symbols and other devices that are employed in the context of specific semiotic systems (including but not limited to video games) in order to represent characteristics attributed to a group of individuals. This definition of culture recognizes its commodified and negotiated nature, while also accounting for the contrasting meanings that culture can take on depending on the semiotic systems and interpretive contexts in which its signification is generated. Mäyrä offers a final point of reflection on the importance of context for games' meaning, noting that "all games have their uses, and only when situated within such contexts of play do they derive their meaning."[38] It is in the spirit of identifying these "uses" that link games to culture that I turn now to a review of historical purposes for play in Latin America.

Games and Latin American Culture: A Brief History of Uses

This book is predicated on the idea that video games and culture have specific uses for one another, and that their relationship is most clearly understood in terms of these uses. Games have served multiple purposes for human culture in general, and in Latin America specifically, since long before the advent of video games. A cursory glance at some of the major events of Latin American history reveals a longstanding tradition of using games for a variety of socio-cultural purposes. The *Popol Vuh*, a compendium of orally transmitted Mayan beliefs first transcribed and published in the sixteenth century, describes a culture that used games primarily for the purposes of leisure or play, albeit one whose players' motivations differ fundamentally from those of today's gamers. The *Popol Vuh* presents gaming as a form of ceremonial negotiation, a system of communication between earth and the heavens. The central story of the hero twins Hunahpú and Xbalanqué highlights the values of strategy, dexterity, and cunning, both in game and out of game, focusing largely on their skills in the ceremonial *juego de pelota* or ball game. When the arrogant lords of Xibalbá scheme to kill the twins because of their noisy game playing in the ball court, the twins use their playing skills to trick the ruling lords into demanding their own sacrifice. Once the twins succeed in vanquishing Xibalbá, they ascend to the heavens, where one becomes the sun and the other the moon.[39]

Centuries later, video game designers the world over show a sustained fascination with this mythical environment: several early games focus specifically on the iconography and environments of the Mayan world, including *The Mask of the Sun* (Broderbund 1982), designed by the Slovakian firm Ultrasoft and *Quest for Quintana Roo* (Telegames 1983), designed by Texas-based Sunrise Software; Lara Croft spends a significant portion of her time exploring the mythical temple of Xibalbá in *Tomb Raider: Underworld* (Eidos 2008); and recently two separate groups of Guatemalan game designers have created interactive electronic versions of the Mayan ball game. One of them, *Mayan Pitz* (Calidá 2013), adapts episodes from the Popol Vuh into the simplified format of a "casual" game, defined as "games that are easy to learn to play, fit well with a large number of players and work in many different situations," including games for

Figure 0.1
Mayan Pitz (Calidá 2013)

play on social media and portable devices[40] (see figure 0.1). *Mayan Pitz* is an iPad, iPhone, and iPod app aimed at a young audience, which was translated into the major Mayan dialects of Guatemala thanks to support from the country's Ministry of Culture.[41] The second of these reimagined versions of the Mayan ball game is the highly ambitious *Pok ta Pok* (Lion Works 2012), which incorporates a high degree of historical detail into its environments (including the mythical Xibalbá as well as real-world ball court sites like Chichén Itzá, Palenque, Teotihuacán, and Tenochtitlán), characters (a veritable pantheon of Mesoamerican gods including Tláloc, Cuauhtémoc, and Xóchitl) and indigenous cultures (not only the Maya but other ball-playing civilizations like the Aztecs, Olmecs, Zapotecs, and Teotihuacanos)[42] (figure 0.2). Both of these Guatemalan-designed video games demonstrate that culture, when meaningfully incorporated into game design, can significantly impact the player experience. One way these games' designers get culture "right" is by making it more than just part of the narrative or visual embellishment of the setting: as was the case for the Maya, the ball game holds cosmic significance in these video games, as they reflect the alternately destructive and productive Mayan view of play by putting the player through a continual process of failure and success, cataclysmic end and glorious rebirth.

Figure 0.2
Pok ta Pok (Lion Works 2012)

By a measure that far exceeds even the enormous popularity and cultural significance of today's major video games, play was utterly fundamental to the Mayan way of looking at the world—indeed gaming was the very source of the sun and the moon, which were converted into trophies awarded to the best players in Mayan legend. The Maya clearly did not conceive of play as an activity separated from "real" life, or secluded to an imaginary or magic circle. This is not to say that play was anything less than magical—indeed, for the Maya the game arena itself was the portal between the human world and the world of the gods, the enchanted court where kings competed with immortals to steer the direction of the universe. But the Maya's magical space of play is just the opposite of Huizinga's isolating magic circle, demonstrating the fundamental interplay between the game world and the real world as well as the impossibility of separating one from another.

Games and play were also of great significance to the other major indigenous groups of the Americas, including the Aztec and Incan empires. In 1577 Fray Bernardino de Sahagún published his *General History of the Things of New Spain*, a compendium of knowledge on Aztec culture penned by indigenous scribes under Sahagún's editorial supervision. One particular chapter of this codex is dedicated to the pastimes of the royalty and nobility, and describes the dice-like betting game *patolli* as well as *tlachtli*, a variation on the Mesoamerican ball game that, the text notes, was previously played for cosmic and spiritual purposes, but had

Figure 0.3
Patolli, as depicted in Bernardino de Sahagún's *General History of the Things of New Spain*, 1577

come to be regarded as sport or as a competitive supplement to warfare[43] (figure 0.3). Another period text by Francisco López de Gómara highlights the social role of play when describing how, shortly after the arrival of conquistador Hernán Cortés and his armed contingent, Aztec ruler Moctezuma II took the Spaniards out to a ball game: "Other times Moctezuma would go to the *tlachtli*, which is the ball court. [...] Moctezuma took the Spaniards to this game, and he showed great joy at seeing it played, just as much as he liked seeing them play their cards and dice."[44] Here, play is a public spectacle, an opportunity to see and be seen and a chance for Moctezuma to do some high rolling in front of his Spanish guests (and vice versa). And indeed, the stakes were high: the prizes for the winners of these games included gold beads and jewelry, precious stones, rare feathers, extravagant garments, lush textiles, loads of cacao, cornfields, homes, and slaves.[45] In contrast to the Maya, who saw games as a means of negotiating with the spiritual realm, the Aztecs viewed games as a recreational pastime for noble lords, a spectacular form of creative leisure that they went to great ends to achieve. Games were a mark of social status for the Aztecs as well as an opportunity to show power, wealth, and privilege, demonstrating how games' meanings can be contextually redefined by the ways they are put to use.

Figure 0.4
Felipe Guaman Poma de Ayala, *First New Chronicle and Good Government*, 1615

The Inca, too, had rigidly defined roles for games and play in society, using them for the purposes of persuasion and negotiation in a range of contexts. Chronicler Felipe Guaman Poma de Ayala dedicates significant attention to the subject in his exhaustive history of Incan culture before and after the Spanish conquest, *First New Chronicle and Good Government*, completed in 1615. Those familiar with the history of the conquest of the Americas will recall that in November of 1532, the Spanish *conquistadores* Francisco Pizarro and Diego de Almagro imprisoned Incan leader Atahualpa, who promised them the unfathomably exorbitant ransom of a large room filled with gold and silver to the height of his raised hand, and that in spite of his aston-ishing fulfillment of this promise, Pizarro ordered Atahualpa's public execution after eight months in Spanish captivity. In his introduction to the chapter on "The Imprisonment and Execution of Atahualpa Inka," Guaman Poma offers insight into how the Incan leader passed the time during his imprisonment: "Atahualpa, being imprisoned, conversed with Don Fran-cisco Pizarro and Don Diego Almagro and with the other Spaniards and he played with them in the game of chess which they call *taptana*. And he was a very peaceful prince and he contented himself in this way with the Christians."[46] The episode highlights another use of games for historical Latin American cultures, that of negotiation and diplomacy through playful compe-tition. The *taptana* board—which can be seen between Atahualpa and an armed Spanish guard in one of the hundreds of drawings by the author that accompany Guaman Poma's text—is the literal and figurative site for power negotiations between Atahualpa and the Spanish, the staging ground for a final attempt by the Incan leader to save himself through the persuasive power of play (figure 0.4). Ultimately, the real-life Atahualpa is of course engaged in a losing game, due to the fact that his opponents refused to observe the rules of competition.

An opposing form of persuasion dominates the other references to games and gaming in the *First New Chronicle*. Though Guaman Poma first mentions games in the context of ritual celebration, noting that they are played in times of condoned leisure such as April, the month celebrating Inka Quilla,[47] he also cites some of the same games—*challco chima, riui, uayro ynaca*, and *pichica*—in several later sections dedicated to the dangers of social vices. Not unlike the present-day pundits who decry controversial video games as signposts of cultural decline, Guaman Poma sees gaming as responsible for problems including social disorder, public drunkenness, the mixing of castes, and crimes against God and humanity:

> These principal chiefs are enormous cheaters and liars and idlers. The only thing they have is their vice of being continuously drunk and on coca from their tribute. And they teach one another to play cards and dice like the Spaniards, chess, *hilancula, chalco chima, uayro, ynaca, riui, pampay runa, yspital, uayro ynaca* [games]. The Spaniards play with mestizos, mulattos and blacks and with Yanacona and Curaca Indians. And along with them, they get drunk and kill one another and rob the poor at the same time. And they do offense to the service of God and your Majesty, and they do evil and harm to the Indians and the poor, and bring the destruc-tion of this realm with their drunkenness.[48]

Guaman Poma establishes a contrasting dynamic of pleasure and vice, celebratory ritual and social conflict, painting games as both the source and the potential solution for societal problems. While for Atahualpa, playing *taptana* represents a symbolic battle of the wits at the same time as it serves to mete out time during his real-life imprisonment, for the rest of Incan society Guaman Poma suggests games are a temptation that, if not treated with respect and moderation, could lead to the decline of civilization.

Taking a step back, we can see that the first recorded cultures in Latin America established certain paradigms for game usage that endure to this day. For the Maya, games were integral to day-to-day life and necessary for maintaining the balance between the living world and the world of the gods, revealing multiple and intersecting purposes for *play*. The Aztecs used games as a forum for public self-aggrandizement and competitive performance, as well as a means of social and economic advancement; for the Aztecs, games' primary function was their productive *potential*. Finally, the Inca used games as a means of political negotiation as well as, in Guaman Poma's particular case, a sort of moral commodity used to substantiate claims of cultural degradation. In the former, negotiation occurs through games, while the latter represents a use of games in order to persuade an audience, both demonstrations of how games can be used for *persuasion*. Thus, the indigenous practices of play in the region now known as Latin America provide a foundational model for the first half of this book's examination of how culture uses games for the purposes of play, persuasion, and potential.

However it is important to remember that since these early episodes, the relationship between Latin American culture and games has continued to develop and change, as is evident in the region's cultural production over the last century. One of the most important Latin American authors of the twentieth century, Argentine short story writer, essayist, and poet Jorge Luis Borges, has become a favorite of new media scholars due to the interplay between his texts and other theoretical and philosophical tendencies. Borges's works are not only filled with references to actual games (such as chess) but also themselves consist of literary games played between author and reader by way of text. Each of Borges's characteristic stories and essays establishes its own "world," with its own set of rules guiding the physical and metaphysical possibilities that exist therein. These games of logic are frequently couched in referential prose that cites invented authorities and speaks to the interconnectedness of textual experiences in a way that is startlingly poignant in light of today's network societies. Murray characterizes the Borges short story "The Garden of Forking Paths"—and more specifically, an invented work described within this story, the "infinite book" of Ts'ui Pen, in which "all possible outcomes occur; each one is the point of departure for other forkings"[49]—as "the quintessential multiform narrative"[50] as well as "a book that has the shape of a labyrinth that folds back upon itself in infinite regression,"[51] a conceptual prototype for later forms such as hypertext media. Manovich sees the Internet as a version of Borges's "On Exactitude of Science" (a story that describes a map with a 1:1 size ratio to the territory it represents) with the difference that in the case of the Internet, "the map has become larger than the territory."[52] Aarseth cites Borgesian labyrinths as a precursor to what he defines as "ergodic literature,"[53] while to Gordon Calleja, who begins his book *In-Game: From Immersion to Incorporation* with the epigraph "The world will be Tlön,"[54] Borges's texts offer a useful reminder of the lack of tenable divisions between fiction and reality, or between the "real world" and gamespace. However,

Nick Montfort suggests that these analogies between a mid-twentieth-century author and new media should not be taken too literally, being that in reality "Borges was no hacker."[55] These constant references to Borges from game studies and new media scholars offer a subtle reminder of the underexplored relationship between Latin American cultural production and scholarship on new media.

Aside from Borges, there are many authors whose works play games, but few have ever done so more literally than the 1963 novel *Hopscotch*, written by another Argentine literary giant of the twentieth century, Julio Cortázar. The novel, which from its very title suggests the centrality of games and play, starts by outlining the rules by which the text should be approached: specifically, the reader may (1) choose to read the novel directly through from chapter 1 to chapter 56, ignoring a series of 99 "expendable" chapters situated after the main body of the novel; (2) read the novel in the order proposed by the author, which requires the reader to actively follow the instructions at the end of each chapter, leading to a multicursal narrative told through fragments with juxtaposed and contrasting content and styles; or (3) approach the novel in any other way she or he sees fit.[56] *Hopscotch* is named after a game, set up as a game, and guided by a rulebook fit for a game, which is why Montfort—who himself once created a hypertext fiction version of Cortázar's story "House Taken Over"—sees *Hopscotch* as a "hypertext novel (in codex form)"[57] as well as a "book-length antecedent to the Choose Your Own Adventure genre of popular fiction and video games."[58] In terms of its stylistic innovation and playful experimentation with literary structure, *Hopscotch* further demonstrates the infiltration of games into unexpected corners of (Latin American) culture.

In Latin American visual arts, the concept of the "active viewer" has fueled an enduring tradition of creative expression. Mexican muralist David Alfaro Siqueiros and others emphasized this concept in the written manifesto that accompanied the monumental 1933 mural work *Plastic Exercise*, explaining that the work's design was guided by the logical route to be taken through and amid the work by a "dynamic spectator."[59] This idea was radicalized by two other groups of modern artists from Latin America. The first were the Venezuelan kineticists Jesús Rafael Soto, Carlos Cruz-Diez, and Julio Le Parc, whose works require the spectator to physically move about in space in order to perceive the illusion of movement created by the optical play of the various elements employed in their three-dimensional sculptures, environmental works, and prints. The Brazilian Neoconcretists also emphasized the role of the spectator in the active generation of meaning in their participatory, experiential works. These included Lygia Clark's *bichos* or "bugs," foldable metal sculptures that could be manipulated by the spectator and displayed in any number of arrangements, as well other works by Clark like her *Sensorial Masks*; Hélio Oiticica's *Parangolés*, frocks made out of inexpensive everyday materials like burlap and plastic sheeting made to be worn by Samba dancers during Carnaval celebrations; and Lygia Pape's *Divider*, an enormous cloth sheet with holes cut throughout it, through which participants poke their heads and move about as one enormous organism. Works such as these anticipate the emergence of a dynamic *spect-actor* (to borrow a term from Brazilian playwright and theorist Augusto Boal)[60] that in many ways resembles the contemporary gamer—these artists' works require active participation in order to construct their basic content, and cannot be observed statically but must be experienced in order to be understood. Like video games or the analogous orchestral performance described earlier, these works are nonlinguistic occurrences that nonetheless constitute substantial signifying experiences for their participants, paving the way for a sea change in the dynamics of spectatorship and active participation in mediated meaning making in the twenty-first century.

A deepening relationship between Latin American film and video games can also be seen in both the content and aesthetics of recent cinema in the region. One example of this crossover is the work of Argentine composer Gustavo Santaolalla, perhaps best known internationally for his back-to-back Oscar-winning scores for Ang Lee's film *Brokeback Mountain* (2005) and Alejandro González Iñárritu's *Babel* (2006), but who more recently has won acclaim for his first original score for a video game, the envelope-pushing survival thriller *The Last of Us* (Sony 2013). Likewise, directors who use video games as part of their films' content demonstrate the broader impact of games on culture. A prime example is Fernando Eimbcke's 2004 film *Duck Season*, in which two teenage boys, left home alone in their Mexico City apartment, order pizza and play Xbox, eventually embarking on a voyage of self-discovery from the comfort of their own home (figure 0.5). Although the film's minimalist, black-and-white aesthetics bear little resemblance to many games' dazzling graphics, video games are nonetheless a ubiquitous element of *Duck Season*'s plot and visual framing, which frequently centers on shots from the perspective of the monitor as the boys engage the frame with greater or lesser intensity depending on their engagement in the games. Like Tenoch Iturbide, Diego Luna's character in Alfonso Cuarón's *Y tu mamá también* (2001), the protagonists of *Duck Season* whittle away their days playing video games, offering a reminder of the pervasiveness of games in the everyday life of many in today's Latin America, bolstering their symbolic utility for the region's filmmakers.

Though Jay David Bolter has noted that by and large, filmmakers and production companies "have been conservative when it comes to what they regard as the defining practices of camera work, continuity editing, and the temporal flow of the visual narrative,"[61] several standout examples from Latin America help demonstrate video games' growing impact on film. Guillermo del Toro's 2006 film *Pan's Labyrinth*, for example, adopts a game-like narrative structure based on *progression*. Juul describes progression in this sense as "the historically newer structure that entered the computer game through the adventure genre" in which "the player must perform a predefined sequence of events" in order to achieve a predetermined objective.[62] In *Pan's Labyrinth*, the protagonist, Ofelia, passes through what we could consider a series of "boss

Figure 0.5
Duck Season (dir. Fernando Eimbcke, 2004)

battles" with monsters (both human and supernatural), shootouts in the forest, encounters with fascist enemies and valiant heroes, and tasks that allow her to "level up" in her quest. "It is characteristic of progression games that there are more ways to fail than to succeed,"[63] and this is also the case in the precarious and dangerous fantasy world that del Toro creates in *Pan's Labyrinth*. Though del Toro himself has yet to produce or direct a full video game title, he has shown sustained interest in the medium, working on projects such as *P.T.* [*Playable Teaser*] (Konami 2014), a horror thriller set in a recursive corridor that was used to announced a subsequently canceled installment in the series of survival horror games that began with *Silent Hill* (Konami 1999).

Alfonso Cuarón, a Mexican contemporary of del Toro's whose films also offer aesthetic nods to games, has made movies that could certainly be described in terms of the structure of progression explained earlier, as a series of predetermined challenges that the protagonist must overcome. Such is the case of three of his most well-known films, *Gravity* (2013), *Y tu mamá también,* and *Children of Men* (2006). All three of these movies featured the same director of photography, Emmanuel Lubezki, who won back-to-back Academy Awards for cinematography on *Gravity* and González-Iñárritu's *Birdman* (2014). In one of the most notable sequences of *Children of Men*, Lubezki's camera follows the protagonist, played by Clive Owen, for an uninterrupted shot that lasts nearly seven minutes, as he wends his way through battlefields and buildings in ruin, seeking his objective. In this scene, the spectator sees the protagonist walking at a distance from the camera, much like the third-person perspective seen in many video games, from *Grand Theft Auto* (Rockstar 1997) to *Tomb Raider*. At one point in this scene, blood spatters the camera's lens, an effect that (intentionally or not) visually references the aesthetics of games like *Call of Duty*, where players also frequently find the "lens" of their visual readouts spattered with blood.

A more wholehearted embrace of video game aesthetics can be found in Chilean director Alicia Scherson's fantastical film *Play* (2005). The film opens with shots of the protagonist, Cristina, playing *Street Fighter II* (Capcom 1991) in Santiago's historical *Juegos Diana* arcade, her eyes glued to the screen, fingers expertly tapping away at the grid of buttons adjacent to the joystick. In the film, Cristina is an active gamer that spends a lot of time in the local arcade, and her gaming gradually begins to bleed over into real life. In a memorable sequence that mixes Cristina's game-based fantasies with the film's reality, she comes to the rescue of a child being chastised by her mother, engaging the mother in a battle complete with *Street Fighter* graphics, health meter, and sound effects (figure 0.6). The film is also about a different sort of play, Cristina's role-play in which she is pretending to be someone else, her public performance akin to taking on an avatar. Above and beyond examples of video games that directly adapt films like the 1982 Atari games *E.T.* and *Raiders of the Lost Ark*, as well as films that adapt video games

Figure 0.6
Play (dir. Alicia Scherson, 2005)

like the movies *Lara Croft: Tomb Raider* (2001) and *Need for Speed* (2014), video game aesthetics are increasingly being transferred into other media like film through a process referred to as remediation. Bolter and Richard Grusin define "remediation" as the manner in which new media "refashion older media and the ways in which older media refashion themselves to answer the challenges of new media,"[64] a process that is clearly visible in films like Scherson's *Play*, which incorporates video games on the level of content as well as aesthetics.

There are many other examples of the crossover between video games and other cultural spheres in Latin America, including museum exhibitions on video game design in Colombia and Argentina,[65] and a 2013 performance in which the Costa Rican national Symphony Orchestra, under the baton of Puerto Rican conductor Emanuel Olivieri, enchanted the capacity crowd with the soundtracks of popular game series like *The Legend of Zelda* (Nintendo 1986), *Super Mario Bros.* (Nintendo 1985), and *Final Fantasy* (Square Enix 1987).[66] Across centuries and in diverse contexts, games have been put to use for leisure, spiritual communication, political negotiation, lively competition, cultural caché, and a variety of other sociocultural purposes. The examples in this section and further cases of crossover between video games and other spheres of cultural production throughout Latin America today drive home the ways in which games and culture can be useful to one another. This symbiosis between games and culture is an apt starting point for a consideration of how game studies and Latin American cultural studies can be useful to one another from a critical and methodological point of view.

Why Latin America(nism) Matters to Game Studies

The field of game studies needs more cultural perspective. In spite of a growing body of groundbreaking scholarship on the subject, the relationship between games and culture deserves further exploration. This critique has been around since the onset of the discipline—Tom Boellstorff, in the inaugural issue of the academic journal *Game Studies*, noted "the relative absence of feminist, political, economic, queer, and other theories of culture in videogame analysis," adding that a lack of critical terminology for studying the subject obfuscates the ways that "games can act as contexts for culture."[67] Tara McPherson echoes this critique, blaming "scant attention to the dialectics of race" in studies of new media for "unwittingly producing a body of theory that cannot understand the generative role forms play in the reproduction of racialised (if not racist) epistemologies and aesthetics."[68] With regard to the analysis of cultural representation in video games, David Golumbia argues that "[p]art of what is so unconvincing about the new media literature is that it fails so often to address real examples of digital media."[69] Larissa Hjorth further emphasizes the pedagogical need for multiculturalism in game studies: "Through investigating a context outside the well-known and frequently cited locations such as the U.S., students can gain a clearer understanding of the complex ways in which games reflect social, cultural, economic and political spaces."[70] While the video game industry is often described in global terms, it is important to pay attention to the ways cultural context affects video game meaning, especially in areas outside the globally dominant markets.

These critiques call for research that will bring increased cultural perspective to game studies, which is one of the primary objectives of this book. It also responds to the calls of scholars like Mäyrä, who argues in *An Introduction to Game Studies: Games and Culture* that "[t]here appears to be a dialectic in more recent games related research, oscillating between work that focuses either only on games, or only on play behavior or its various cultural contexts, whereas it would be very valuable to see how these two are interrelated."[71] Synthetic, interdisciplinary work on culture and games is especially urgent given the increasing role that new media have in shaping cultural attitudes and identities. In today's cultural environment, as Imma Tubella has argued, "the role of the mass media is clear as an instrument for creating an image of the collective identity for insiders and for outsiders, and in doing so, they contribute to the construction of the identity itself," which means for Latin America that video games are not only shaping the way the world thinks of the region, but the way Latin Americans think of themselves. This is a point that film scholar Stuart Hall made regarding cinema back in 2000, when he spoke of "identity as constituted, not outside but within representation; and hence of cinema, not as a second-order mirror held up to reflect what already exists, but as that form of representation which is able to constitute us as new kinds of subjects, and thereby enable us to discover who we are."[72] And if cinema was able to provide a space of representation and identification that affected our ideas of who we were, interactive games have intensified this effect. Correspondingly, we need critical work that examines Latin America as both a context of development and consumption of new media, as well as a region that is frequently represented therein.

Though there is still much work to be done in analyzing the relationship between new media and Latin American culture, a number of pioneering scholars have laid the groundwork for the analysis of this relationship. For example, recent studies have offered economic and historical assessments of Latin American hardware and software development, such as in Yuri Takhteyev's *Coding Places: Software Practice in a South American City*, about development firms in Rio de Janeiro, Brazil, as well as Anita Say Chan's *Networking Peripheries: Technological Futures and the Myth of Digital Universalism*, which examines multiple initiatives to "network" contemporary Peru. Others have tackled the technopolitical dimensions of the relationship between Latin American culture and new media technologies, such as Eden Medina's *Cybernetic Revolutionaries: Technology and Politics in Allende's Chile*, about Project Cybersyn, a 1970s-era

government-sponsored computer engineering venture designed to achieve a utopian economic balance in Chilean society, or Cristina Venegas's *Digital Dilemmas: The State, the Individual,
and Digital Media in Cuba*, which examines the relationship between political power and digital information sharing in contemporary Cuban culture. The 2013 anthology *Gaming Globally:
Production, Play, and Place* also represents a significant contribution to the analysis of gaming
across cultures, including snapshots of game development and consumption in Brazil and
Argentina; likewise, the 2015 anthology *Video Games around the World*, which includes chapters
on Argentina, Brazil, Colombia, Mexico, Peru, Uruguay, and Venezuela, makes major contributions to the critical analysis of video games' impact in Latin America. In addition to following
the trails blazed by examples of recent scholarship such as these, this book builds upon existing
ethnographic[73] and anthropological[74] analyses of gaming communities as well as entering the
scholarly discussion of popular media's significance in Latin American culture in particular[75]
and on cultural representation in new media in general.[76] Together, these wide-ranging analytical approaches have paved the way for the development of a cultural history of gaming and
new media in Latin America, a task that I aim to push forward in the chapters that follow.

Likewise, there is an important and growing body of scholarship on the subject of cultural
representation in new media that has helped establish the foundation for the present analysis. Game scholars frequently speak of the ways embodiment, personification, or immersion
into a character and environment impact the player experience. Anthony Sze-Fai Shiu argues
that in "securely suturing the first-person views of the action and the user-controlled, real-
time speech of the video game character," games create scenarios "where the player's control over virtual embodiment demands critical decisions concerning subjective investments
in the games' scenarios and narratives,"[77] meaning that players do not only imagine themselves as characters of diverse cultural backgrounds, they also can be called upon to make
subjective decisions that are informed by cultural identity among myriad other factors. Lisa
Nakamura, however, warns of the dangers of this type of "identity tourism that allows a player
to appropriate an Asian [or another] racial identity without any of the risks associated with
being a racial minority in real life."[78] Nakamura coined the term "cybertype" to characterize
"the distinctive ways that the Internet propagates, disseminates, and commodifies images of
race and racism,"[79] taking a critical perspective toward what she refers to as "the globalizing
Coca-Colonization of cyberspace and the media complex within which it is embedded."[80] Like
Nakamura, Christopher McGahan's *Racing Cyberculture* suggests that the idea of "racelessness"
in new media is a "presumably inadvertent concession to white racial hegemony" based on the
"radically false" claim that online denizens are free "to volitionally choose the ethnoracial (or
'postethnoracial') identities according to which they will be socially recognized."[81] With regard
to the games industry, Dean Chan offers a similarly critical outlook, stating that attempts to
diversify the software trade by recruiting personnel of different cultural backgrounds may

represent a well-intentioned step in the right direction toward a more diverse video game industry, but that "it is no guarantee of the consequent creation of more equitable racialized representations."[82] Critiques such as these make clear the need for attention to the ways cultural background and context can affect the circulation of meaning in new media products like video games.

Where, then, might we turn in search of a greater variety of ethnic, racial, and cultural representations in the world of video games? For one, we must not focus only on the most stereotypical or negative cultural representations in games, but also examine "genuine attempts to transcend the simplifying patterns of representation in video games."[83] Certainly, there are still too few games featuring Latin American protagonists and characters with depth. But at the same time, the video game medium is ripe with opportunities for significant cultural (and intercultural) experiences. As Manovich once asserted, with the increasing availability of new media technology throughout the world, "cultural possibilities that were previously in the background, on the periphery, come into the center,"[84] creating opportunities for novel ways of examining and experiencing culture. Jonathan Dovey and Helen W. Kennedy have argued that new media provide "both the opportunities for the articulation of outsider identities and also the means through which existing normative meanings around gender and race are circulated,"[85] and to be certain, games offer powerful tools for experiencing things that are foreign to the player's daily existence, as well as for challenging—and not just upholding—cultural stereotypes and misconceptions. This is why Latin America—and Latin Americanism—can make such a significant contribution to our understanding of the relationship between video games and culture. Latin America matters to game studies because it offers a testing ground for the examination of the complex relationship between games and culture, as well as a pathway toward greater cultural perspective for the discipline.

Why Video Games Matter to Latin America(nism)

Turning to the other side of the coin, we must ask from the perspective of Latin American cultural studies, what is the value of studying video games, whether as a form of creative and economic production or as a medium for cultural representation? There are several answers to this question, and a number of critical discussions have taken up topics related to new media circulation in "peripheral" regions of technological development, revealing the paradoxical centrality of the so-called periphery to an understanding of how new media impact culture on a global scale. This is why recent scholarship has pointed to the need to look to the "wrong places" to understand how technology impacts culture at the periphery as well as the center,[86] and called for "greater emphasis to the historical context in which the relevant technologies and technological practices have developed and devoting attention to key moments in the development of the discourses that have surrounded them."[87] For cultural studies, an analysis of video games can exemplify the ways in which products of "global" media are transformed by local and regional practices particular to the multiple markets in which games circulate.

This means unearthing previously underexamined connections between games and culture, though in one sense, Latin American game studies could be considered an existing discipline. After all, some of the pillars of contemporary Latin American cultural studies—Sarlo, García Canclini, and others—have touched on the relationship between video games and culture, while some of the most important tenets of ludology as a nascent discipline were established by Frasca, a theorist and game designer from Uruguay. And indeed, scholars from game studies and cultural studies have convincingly analyzed many of the games that I discuss in this book, from *Tomb Raider* to *Grand Theft Auto*. But up to now these games haven't been studied as games about Latin America, and the contributions of Latin American cultural studies scholars haven't previously entered into dialogue with the broader field of game studies. This critical intersection is my own project's point of departure.

A prime example of the underexplored connections between game studies and Latin American studies is the scholarly production of contemporary Argentine cultural critic Beatriz Sarlo. Her seminal 1994 work *Scenes from Postmodern Life* was a forerunner in noting the impact of video games on culture in Latin America, specifically in Argentina. Though Sarlo's analysis of video games focuses mostly on the subculture of gamers in the "seedy" environment of the video arcade, she offers some truly groundbreaking observations about the nature of games as interactive experiences, anticipating later work on embodiment and incorporation by games scholars such as Calleja. In *Scenes from Postmodern Life*, Sarlo examines the essentially active and subjective nature of gameplay, noting that "[p]layers learn little if they submit to a video game as if it were but a television program with a little more interactivity,"[88] and offering a thorough examination of the video game as a non-narrative form of expression: "The medium contains a set of repetitions organized into cycles that demand a performance whose truth is not to be found in any confrontation between characters, but rather in the duel between player and machine. In this sense the classic video game produces a non-narrative plot, composed of an encounter between physical actions and their digital consequences."[89] Sarlo also broke ground more recently by taking the cultural context of gaming into account in her 2009 study *La ciudad vista*, noting the contrast between the dazzling virtual spaces explored in a cybercafé and the impoverished shantytown in which the business was situated. For Sarlo, gamers play video games because they find in them "an imaginary heterotopia, a unique place where actually existing streets are replaced, for an hour's time, with an arrangement of virtual space that is more attractive," and certainly this type of virtual tourism is a primary motivator for many gamers.[90]

For his part, García Canclini cites video games as a factor in the "dissolution of national and regional identities" in his 1995 work *Consumers and Citizens*, asserting that along with other information technologies, they have brought on "effects on the reconstitution of identities" through "cultural engineering" in ways that merit further study.[91] In his 2001 work *Hybrid Cultures*, García Canclini reiterates the centrality of examining the ways global media produced in economically dominant areas reflects the culture of economically developing ones, noting that "[t]here continues to be inequality in the appropriation of symbolic goods and in access to cultural innovation, but that inequality no longer takes the simple and polarized form we thought we would encounter when we were dividing every country into dominant or dominated, or the world into empires and dependent nations."[92] Indeed, today we understand the flows of international capital as well as the representation of culture on a global level to be more than just a top-down transmission from the centers of production.

Social theorist Martín Hopenhayn also engages the multilateral nature of globalized cultural exchange, calling globalization "a mass-mediated but also a 'mass-mestizo,' hybridizing phenomenon,"[93] while Martín-Barbero describes contemporary cultural exchange in terms of "a new mode of relation between symbolic processes—which constitute the cultural—and the forms of production and distribution of goods and services."[94] These multilateral movements of cultural objects, symbols, and experiences still have yet to be examined in a way that reflects on the complex systems at work when cultural meaning is created, coded, and contextually unpacked by the player of a video game.

Cultural identity is certainly impacted by the consumption of mass media, but this is also not the only way of looking at the relationship between media and culture. Gareth Williams suggests that scholars like García Canclini, who focus on culture's circulation in commodified form, "ultimately maintain thought, social existence, and the freedom of expression purely within the realm of consumer identification, market-based choice, and the limits of neoliberal hegemonic thought."[95] Williams ultimately suggests that García Canclini's own consumerist obsession, like the critique it accompanies, is a sign of the political and economic times in 1990s neoliberal Latin America. Shirin Shenassa criticizes García Canclini's approach for upholding "a clear division between actors and technologies which, in turn, leads to an inability to sufficiently take into account the ways in which media develop and the ways in which people make use of them."[96] Another aim of the present study is to offer an integrated analysis of the relationship between actors and technologies, the type of material cultural studies that critics like Shenassa see as lacking in existing scholarship.

This book looks at games both in terms of their self-contained mechanisms of meaning making and in terms of the ways that meaning is transformed through its circulation within different geographical and cultural contexts. This study is also in line with a more hemispheric cultural studies perspective, examining the way that video games—many of the most popular of which are produced in the United States—circulate within the Americas but outside of the United States. The call for greater deterritorialization of [(Latin) American] cultural studies has been echoed time and again in recent discussions. Performance theorist Diana Taylor called for "remapping the Americas" and "reconfiguring cold war area studies into hemispheric studies,"[97] highlighting the significant impact that Latin American culture has on the meaning of cultural objects. Such assertions have inspired works like Heidi Tinsman and Sandhya Shukla's *Imagining Our Americas: Toward a Transnational Frame*[98] and José David Saldívar's *Trans-Americanity*,[99] which focus on the fundamentally interconnected aspects of cultural experiences across the Americas. These efforts reflect a recognition of García Canclini's observation that, "in times of globalization there is not just the 'Americanization' of the world"[100] but a "highly heterogeneous cultural space"[101] in which identity is continually negotiated, not unidirectionally imposed.

My own perspective is that of a US-born specialist in contemporary Latin American cultural studies, seeking to bring my own research and experiences across North, Central, and South America into an integrated examination of the cultural meaning of video games, a fundamentally global form of media. In that sense I am asking myself some of the questions posed by cultural critic John Beverley, who describes his own scholarship as "a conscious reinvestment in my own problematic and always deferred identification with the United States," and asks, "[w]hat would it mean then to pose the question of the United States 'desde Latinoamérica'— that is, from my own investment in Latin America and Latin American radical politics and criticism—instead of, as I have been doing for so many years, posing the question of Latin America *from* the United States?"[102] Though I cannot lay claim to Beverley's considerable history of impactful scholarship, I take inspiration from his work in my own attempt to look at a form of media born of US culture, from a perspective fundamentally informed by my investment in Latin American culture.

In this introduction, I have attempted to lay the groundwork for what I have referred to as cultural ludology, that is the analysis of the relationship between culture and video games, both in terms of the use of games by the broader culture for politics, economics, leisure, and other pursuits, as well as the use of culture by video games in the form of iconography, playable environments, and linguistic and narrative elements. It is no longer enough to study games in the isolation of the magic circle, nor can we look at contemporary culture without an awareness of the way it circulates through media networks, and therefore cultural ludology is an urgent necessity. Video games are being converted into cultural currency for an ever-increasing array of purposes throughout Latin America and the globe. In light of this fact, cultural ludology seeks to define the ludic value of culture from a game development and gameplay perspective, as well as examining the myriad ways ludic products are used by cultures today. With these objectives in mind, I offer this book as an initial step toward a cultural ludology.

Structure of the Book

This book is divided into two halves, part I: "How Culture Uses Games" and part II: "How Games Use Culture." Each chapter in these two sections focuses on a specific "use" that culture has for games, or vice versa; the chapter titles are not intended to cover each and every aspect of the relationship between games and culture in a comprehensive or encyclopedic manner, but rather provide umbrella categories that are useful for exploring some of the many manifestations of this relationship. The three chapters of part I comprise a cultural history of Latin American gaming, analyzing diverse game-related practices across the region from the onset of the video game medium to the present day. Chapter 1, "Play," focuses on the diverse practices of play in contemporary culture, and in Latin America specifically. It begins with a conceptual analysis of video game play, examining the embodied experience of gameplay as well as looking at player motivations including exploration, discovery, and acquisition. Next, the chapter explores the preliminary history of video game play in Latin America, as reflected through the practices of game marketing, consumption, and distribution throughout the region. Finally, chapter 1 surveys the state of play in contemporary Latin America, cutting through demographic myths to reveal how a surprisingly diverse population of gamers throughout the region is acquiring real-life experiences through the practice of play.

Chapter 2, "Persuasion," focuses on the ways games are put to use toward ideological and intellectual ends in Latin American culture, examining how games are commodified in order to stimulate players intellectually as well as to politically persuade the public at large. On the one hand, there are those examples that fall under the conventional categorizations of "serious" or "persuasive" games that aim to challenge the player as much on an ideological level as on the level of gameplay. On the other hand, video games are increasingly used for "persuasive" ends unrelated to gameplay, most notably when they are used by public figures to stoke the fires of political controversy. This chapter examines both games' increasingly significant status as political commodities and the unique possibilities for meaningful ideological inquiry opened up by the medium.

The final chapter in the first half of the book, "Potential," focuses on the creative and economic possibilities opened up by video games in Latin America. First, it explores the history of video game production and the birth of the Latin American game industry, looking at early examples of regional game design as well as the obstacles these games' producers had to overcome. Practices such as software modification paved the way for regional game development, and today game jams, design competitions, incubation programs, and cultural policy are transforming the creative ecosystem of the Latin American game industry. Chapter 3 concludes with a survey of the many trajectories being followed by current regional game designers, from the big budget console titles referred to as "AAA" games to increasingly ubiquitous casual games.

The second half of the book focuses on "How Games Use Culture," examining in-game cultural representation from an array of popular titles set in the region by examining three dimensions of meaning making in games, one per chapter: "Semiotics," "Space," and "Simulation." In other words, part II explains how culture, broken down to its constituent sound elements, visual iconography, and other signs, is used to create meaning in video games. Chapter 4, "Semiotics," examines the signifying systems of video games in relation to other semiotic domains, as well as analyzing the specific signifiers of Latin American culture that are frequently used in game design. Following this overview, the chapter focuses on two particular symbolic repertoires from Latin American culture seen in games of different genres throughout the history of the medium, namely the iconography of Mexican Day of the Dead celebration and the culturally coded environmental space of the Brazilian *favela*, or shantytown. Chapter 4 concludes with an explanation of how this array of cultural signifiers creates meaning in video games' particular semiotic domains.

Chapter 5, "Space," examines the spatialization of culture in video game environments. After reviewing the different roles of landscape, setting, and environment as spatial models, the chapter focuses on particular ways that culture is incorporated into gamespace. The chapter examines the sonic and spatial ways that culture is conveyed through game design, including the use of foreign language dialogue, ambient effects, and music to convey cultural context. Next, chapter 5 turns to an examination of three paradigmatic models of Latin American gamespace—the recursive space of exploration-based action/adventure games, the isometric perspective of management simulations and other "god games," and finally, the open world environment of so-called "sandbox" games—in order to demonstrate the ways that the spatial model employed in a given video game can affect its capacity for portraying culture.

The final chapter, "Simulation," examines the ways cultural meaning is conveyed procedurally and algorithmically through game mechanics. This chapter explores the overarching importance of games' tone as well, looking at the relative weight of realism, verisimilitude, and parody on the production of video game meaning. Delving into sticky ethical questions from video games' relationship to imperialism to the representation of race in games, chapter 6 aims to take the discussion of cultural representation in games beyond narrative and symbolic interpretations, demonstrating how culture is coded into the very structures for meaning making particular to video games.

I   HOW CULTURE USES GAMES

1 PLAY

The spirit of playful competition is, as a social impulse, older than culture itself and pervades all life like a veritable ferment. Ritual grew up in sacred play; poetry was born in play and nourished on play; music and dancing were pure play. Wisdom and philosophy found expression in words and forms derived from religious concepts built up on play-patterns. We have to conclude, therefore, that civilization is, in its earliest phases, played. It does not come *from* play like a babe detaching itself from the womb: it arises *in* and *as* play, and never leaves it.

Johan Huizinga, Homo Ludens (1944)[1]

Play is and has always been a core element of human civilization. Therefore when we ask how contemporary culture uses games, we must necessarily begin with a discussion of their primary use: play. Why does the player play the game? Games act differently than other media, and they allow us to act differently. Moreover they make meaning differently, and they teach differently, by offering experiences unlike those we encounter in day-to-day life. In order to analyze the relationship between play and human civilization, a discussion that in many ways begins with Huizinga, this chapter starts with a theoretical examination of the motivating forces of gameplay. Next, it reviews the historical contexts of video game consumption and play in Latin America, concluding with a survey of player demographics and sales data that reflect the way games are played in the region today. Put another way, this chapter discusses *why* Latin American players play games, *how* and *where* they play them, *when* they began playing them in different formats, *who* is playing today, and *what* games they play.

Players are motivated by a number of factors, among them the desires to explore a novel environment, to discover unforeseen situations, and to acquire knowledge and experience. Therefore we will look first at how the acts of exploration, discovery, and acquisition are both core elements of the gameplay experience and also concepts with longstanding and significant connotations within the historical and cultural contexts of Latin America. The latter half of the chapter offers a preliminary social history of video gaming in the region, discussing how electronic games first came to impact Latin American culture, and how their uses and significance have been transformed over more than three decades of development.

Play is a contextual concept, one that takes on different meaning in different situations. The term "play" can refer both to a universal element of human culture and to gameplay, a particular way of interacting with electronic media. It fulfills "the ludic function"[2] of providing leisure and an alternative to other forms of daily routine, but at the same time play itself can often be a daily routine. For Roger Caillois, like Huizinga before him, play was an essential element of culture. In his 1958 work *Man, Play and Games*, Caillois argues that games in the modern world "are now merely tolerated, whereas in the earlier society they were an integral part of its basic institutions, secular or sacred. At that time, to be sure, they were not games, in the sense that one speaks of children's games, but they already were part of the essence of play."[3] The increasingly pervasive presence of games in the daily lives of people worldwide—and in Latin America in particular, as this chapter will show—can be seen as a renaissance in games' centrality to culture, a re-suturing of play to civilization to allow us to once again conceive of culture *in* and *as* play.

Gameplay as Embodied Performance

In what ways is playing a video game unique from playing another sort of artifact? After all, Roland Barthes conceived of reading as a type of multivalent play that involved a relational exchange between reader and text: "'Playing,'" Barthes argues in *Image, Music, Text*, "must be understood here in all its polysemy: the text itself *plays* (like a door, like a machine with 'play') and the reader plays twice over, playing the Text as one plays a game, looking for a practice which re-produces it, but, in order that that practice not be reduced to a passive, inner *mimesis* (the Text is precisely that which resists such a reduction), also playing the Text in the musical sense of the term."[4] So if the reader is already a player who both enacts the text and performs its meaning in an act equivalent to playing an instrument, is it really any different to be a "player" of a text by Cervantes than to be a player on the chivalric battleground of a video game?

The substantial difference in the case of video game play lies in the relationship between the player and the game software and hardware, and the requirement of the subjective exercise of player agency in order to produce meaning. This is why some game scholarship characterizes play as "an act of appropriation of the game by players."[5] Murray, for example, focuses on the importance of the "interactor" in generating games' meaning, and of player agency in determining the course that meaning will take: "The interactor, whether as navigator, protagonist, explorer, or builder, makes use of this repertoire of possible steps and rhythms to improvise a particular dance among the many, many possible dances the author has enabled. [...] The interactor is not the author of the digital narrative, although the interactor can experience one of the most exciting aspects of artistic creation—the thrill of exerting power over enticing and plastic materials. This is not authorship but agency."[6] Murray's interactor finds its conceptual parallel within Latin American cultural studies in Néstor García Canclini's *internauta* ("internaut," a portmanteau of "internet" and "astronaut"), "a multimodal actor that reads, watches, listens and combines diverse materials derived from reading and public spectacles."[7] This type of play is an essentially active experience on many levels, requiring what Manovich refers to as "cognitive multitasking," or "rapidly alternating between different kinds of attention, problem solving, and other cognitive skills."[8] Understood in this way, play is a fundamentally subjective experience, and games are dependent on player input in order to create meaning.

Indeed many critics see interactive play as the foundation of ludic signification, above and beyond coded rules and game mechanics. For example, Galloway argues that video games only "come into being when the machine is powered up and the software is executed; they exist when enacted."[9] From this viewpoint, a game's meaning is uniquely dependent upon play—unlike a painting or a television program, no matter how active a spectator they may necessitate, a game requires action to access its content as well as its meaning, implying a mental as well as a physical effort. With his concept of "incorporation," Gordon Calleja builds on earlier articulations of "immersion" as an essential element of the gameplay experience, noting that "the core experience of digital gameplay requires active engagement and input from players," and that "[p]layers do not merely consume a pre-established piece of media, but instead are active participants in the creation of their experience through interaction with the underlying code during gameplay."[10] Like Galloway and Murray, Calleja is quick to note that play is not the *only* element in the creation of video game meaning, nor does it exist in isolation, but rather it requires an interaction between player *and machine*, between active participant and active software, in order to create meaning.

To unlock the meaning of video games, players must engage in a reciprocal and interactive exchange with the game's hardware and software. This is what Martti Lahti refers to as "the corporealization of the experience of playing,"[11] explaining that video games "commodify our cyborg desires, our will to merge with and become technology."[12] And we merge with technology in multiple senses when playing video games, engaging in an active sensorial performance that is dependent on a collaborative performance by the machine. Galloway observes, "[p]eople move their hands, bodies, eyes, and mouths when they play video games," but machines can also "act in response to player actions as well as independently of them."[13] Adopting Philip Agre's term "grammars of action," Galloway continues, "[v]ideo games create their own grammars of action; the game controller provides the primary physical vocabularies for humans to pantomime these gestural grammars. But beyond the controller, games also have their own grammars of action that emerge through gameplay."[14] These "grammars of action," like the grammars of languages, are not just static sets of rules but a structure that is transformed by subjective use. By engaging in a pas de deux with the coded restrictions and affordances of the game software, the player merges with the technology of the video game in the act of meaning creation referred to as gameplay.

Thus play is performance, and performance, like play, implies action. In linguistic philosophy, J. L. Austin theorized the grammatical *performative*, an utterance that *does something* rather than just express or describe it, as is the case of performative speech acts such as marrying, promising, or betting.[15] John Searle added that it is not the word or sentence that constitutes the basic unit of linguistic communication, but rather the "production of the token in the performance of the speech act."[16] Thus all expressive acts require some type of participatory engagement in order to produce meaning. Performance is the essence of meaning making, which takes on a different character depending on context. Feminist theorist Judith Butler refers to gender itself as "a corporeal field of cultural play,"[17] adding a resistant dimension to this definition by observing that, "[i]n its very character as performative resides the possibility of contesting its reified status."[18]

There are several ways video game players take advantage of this resistant capacity of play, including what we could refer to as counter-play (playing against the established rules or intended routes of the game), as well as game modification (alteration of the programmed software code to enhance the gameplay experience) and (condoned or uncondoned) cheating. It is important to remember that players play games in whatever way they find pleasing for their own purposes at the time of playing, and this can produce results that go beyond the original intent of a game's designers. As Mia Consalvo argues, cheating "constitutes players asserting agency, taking control of their game experience," or "going beyond the 'expected activity' in the game."[19] Reading Consalvo through Butler, we might say that players who cheat or otherwise enhance their gameplay experience are exercising resistant agency through corporeal play, manifesting through performance the possibility of resisting the status of game rules as the bases of ludic meaning. In this way, the possibility of counter-play highlights the indeterminate nature of games' meaning prior to the engagement of a player agent.

Therefore video game experiences, which draw upon subjective decision-making and the use of cognitive skills on the part of the player, are not just make-believe. They are situations encountered through what Gee refers to as embodied action—that is, "action actually carried out in the game world or simulated in your mind,"[20] leading to authentic and meaningful experiences. Theorists define performance as "ritualized behavior conditioned/permeated by play."[21] In her own definition of performance, Diana Taylor echoes the importance of "embodied practice," stating that it "offers a way of knowing" in the form of "a practice that brings together what have historically been kept separate as discrete, supposedly freestanding, ontological and epistemological discourses."[22] Performance takes place in the user's interactions with multiple forms of media, but it is a particularly useful theoretical frame for understanding video games as a nonlinguistic, multivalent means of acquiring experience through embodied performance.

Exploration, Discovery, and Acquisition in Video Game Play

Why do we play games? For one, they allow us to do things differently than we can in other contexts of our day-to-day lives. They also allow us to experience success and failure, to be emotionally and intellectually stimulated, and to test our skills against other players, human and artificial. In games, as Murray has suggested, "we have a chance to enact our most basic relationship to the world—our desire to prevail over adversity, to survive our inevitable defeats, to shape our environment, to master complexity, and to make our lives fit together like the pieces of a jigsaw puzzle."[23] Even more than in their daily lives, games allow players to be masters of their own domains, offering a personally tailored experience unlike any other. Some game critics and designers have even gone so far as to conclude that "reality is broken," and that adapting the strategies of games to our real lives is the way to fix it.[24]

Games not only allow us to *do* things that we cannot do in the rest of our lives, they also allow us to *go* to places and times that we could not otherwise experience, a phenomenon sometimes referred to as "virtual tourism." This phenomenon is also not strictly limited to games—Richard Schechner notes that "Brazilians watching reruns of *Seinfeld* or Americans watching a *National Geographic Special* (or any number of programs on the Discovery Channel) are virtual tourists," along with those who "experience the far away" on the web.[25] However it has been argued that "digital games became popular because they transported our imaginations to the places represented on screen,"[26] and the video game medium is indeed uniquely suited to virtual tourism. In a video game, I can embody the character of Adéwalé, an eighteenth-century African slave turned Caribbean pirate who finds himself shipwrecked near Port-au-Prince in the *Freedom Cry* downloadable content (DLC) pack for *Assassin's Creed IV: Black Flag* (Ubisoft 2013), being transported into another time, place, and body and discovering something about each as I play.

The themes of exploration, discovery, and acquisition have a long history worldwide, but in Latin America they irrevocably call to mind a historical legacy of seafaring expeditions, conquering forces, forced colonization, and genocide. In addition to its immeasurable historical, cultural, and demographic impact, the history of colonialism has profound effects on the way

Latin America is portrayed in video games, making the region's indigenous empires and colonial administrations one of the most frequent tropes for in-game representation. Because of their environmental nature, video games "are particularly adept at facilitating spatial exploration that enables players not only to project their imagination into the represented landscapes but also to traverse them,"[27] and many contemporary games feature open-world exploration in place of (or in addition to) a linear narrative. Unlike the "forced exploration" of arcade games, where play time was tightly limited in order to encourage players to plunk ever more of their coins into the machine in order to extend their gameplay experiences, exploration in video games played on home consoles, computers, and other personal gaming devices "tends to be unforced, and the player is free to navigate as quickly or slowly as he desires."[28] Thus players of open-world games set in Latin America such as *Just Cause* or *Mercenaries 2: World in Flames* (EA 2008) are free to spend all their time exploring their environment if that is how they wish to play the game, without fear of the conventional ticking clock or the dreaded arcade death sentence, "Game Over."

The thrill of exploration in video games, above and beyond the "tourist moments" they provide,[29] is consistently cited as one of the primary motivations for video game play. In their exemplary 2006 work *Tomb Raiders and Space Invaders: Videogame Forms and Contexts*, Geoff King and Tanya Krzywinska underline the importance of exploration as a motivator of play: "Exploration and the sense of presence that results from the creation of sensory immersion in the gamescape can also be central to the accomplishment of gameplay tasks in many games. [...] Even where exploration is closely linked to the pursuit of goals or missions that advance the player through game levels, for example, it can include scope to move more freely within and through a variety of on-screen landscapes, a pleasure that can be indulged for its own sake."[30] In this sense, players of the game *Red Dead Redemption* (Rockstar 2010) are rewarded for their exploration whether they choose to: (1) follow the sanctioned path of exploration by guiding John Marston through the twists and turns of the Mexican Revolution; (2) engage in open-world exploration, taking in the sights and sounds of a simulated early twentieth-century borderland region between the United States and Mexico; or (3) exercise "counter-play," wandering the outer boundaries of the game world, and using trial-and-error interactions with the environment and other nonplayer characters (NPCs) in order to seek out the limitations of the game's algorithm (figure 1.1). Each of these types of exploration offers its own benefits to players, depending on their own unique motivations for play.

Discovery is the reward for exploration, and it takes multiple forms in video games. Alison Gazzard contrasts rewards of environment and rewards of exploration, defining the latter as "rewards that allow players to move along paths that have now been unlocked in the gameworld."[31] While rewards of environment place more obstacles and puzzles in front of the player, exploration in this sense can offer its own compensation, with the player benefitting simply by

Figure 1.1
Red Dead Redemption (Rockstar 2010)

discovering and opening up new space in the game world. Gee's "Discovery Principle" asserts that games best enable players to learn when "[o]vert telling is kept to a well-thought-out minimum, allowing ample opportunity for the learner to experiment and make discoveries,"[32] again highlighting the importance of this aspect of the player experience. Indeed, many video games rely on a process of exploration and discovery to establish the basic parameters for gameplay—the player learns the rules to most current games not by consulting a written manual, but through trial-and-error gameplay. Gee describes this process as "probing the world" by "doing something" and then "reflecting in and on this action and, on this basis, forming a hypothesis; reprobing the world to test this hypothesis; and then accepting or rethinking the hypothesis."[33] By and by, the space explored becomes space inhabited, familiar to the player through sensorial memory. In his work on the process of incorporation, Calleja explains this process in succinct detail:

> During the first few hours of playing a new digital game, you adapt yourself to the game's mechanics, physics, and rules. You take the first uncertain steps in the unexplored spaces, experiment with running, jumping, leaning around corners. The boundaries of character creation are prodded and initial strategies of virtual world domination are formed. In geographically rich game worlds, you're likely to explore the first areas slowly and thoroughly, until you form a cognitive map of the layout of the world, country, region, or city. [...] Later, when the controls are second nature to you, and the environment of the game has become a familiar space for you to move within, you find yourself feeling as though you exist within the world. You become accustomed to your digital manifestation of self.[34]

This explanation allows a clear visualization of the process I am describing here in terms of exploration, discovery, and acquisition. The player prods the boundaries of the game's mechanics while *exploring* thoroughly. Eventually the player makes *discoveries* that enable mapping and control over the game environment. And last but definitely not least, the player *acquires* a sense of self and an ability to interact and exist within the game world. It is in this final stage of the process of gameplay that the player, in a fluid interaction with the now-well-explored gamespace, can make truly significant acquisitions of skills and knowledge through precisely rehearsed interactions with the game software.

I speak of the acquisition of skills and knowledge in video games not in terms of learning exact combinations of buttons for executing cliffhanging maneuvers off the coast of Panama in *Uncharted: Drake's Fortune* or figuring out the most efficient solutions to the block puzzles in *Angry Birds Rio* (Rovio 2011), though these are indeed meaningful achievements that enable the player to advance and excel. However, I am speaking of the ways that we can gain real knowledge, and real experience, from gameplay. Scholarship on games and education roundly confirms that knowledge is gained as players interact with games requiring critical thinking. Mark Prensky enumerates several of the benefits derived through strategic gaming, including "real-life lessons" on cause-and-effect relationships, long-term winning versus short-term gain, second-order consequences, complex system behaviors, counterintuitive results, and the value of persistence.[35] Moreover, there is a "huge amount of *cultural* learning that goes on in video and computer games," including the acquisition of "cultural metaphors and images to use in describing the real world," as well as real and valid experiences with the concept of cultural relativity: players "learn that on one planet, in one society, in one world you can't do X, even though it may be perfectly normal in their own world," a lesson that can have a real-world impact on the players' way of comprehending cultures other than their own.[36]

These are the types of *acquisitions* that gamers make in their gameplay, above and beyond their numerous in-game trophies and tokens. Furthermore, significant knowledge is transmitted through play, leading to the possibility of increasing cultural literacy, at least in part, through gaming. Several recent examples from Latin American game designers highlight the way meaningful knowledge can be transmitted—didactically or passively—through gameplay, and I will focus on three particular cases to illustrate this form of ludic acquisition. First, there is the Uruguayan game developer Trojan Chicken, whose games *D.E.D.* (Trojan Chicken 2010) and *1811* (Trojan Chicken 2011) focus on teaching national history, geography, and related subjects to the country's schoolchildren. The second is the Mexican game studio Immersion Games (now Larva Game Studios), which was responsible for designing a game touted as the first-ever multiconsole title ever to be developed entirely in Latin America, the wrestling game *Lucha Libre AAA: Héroes del Ring* (Konami 2010). Finally, I will discuss the form acquisition takes in

Papo & Yo (Minority 2012), an imaginative take on the adventure/puzzle game genre that is the brainchild of Colombian designer Vander Caballero.

Games transfer knowledge and experience to their players, some more consciously than others. Some game designers, like those working at Trojan Chicken, an independent game studio located in the Uruguayan capital of Montevideo, develop games specifically for educational purposes. Trojan Chicken has created several of these edugames, including *D.E.D.* and *1811* as well as their puzzle/role-playing game (RPG) series *Cazaproblemas* (*Puzzlehunters*, Trojan Chicken 2011), with support from the government's Plan Ceibal, an ambitious "One Laptop per Child" initiative aimed at fostering the real-life rewards of "digital equality" and technological advantage for Uruguayan students[37] (figure 1.2). *D.E.D.* is a mystery-solving game in which players in their first years of primary school can find and collect clues in order to solve crimes related to important objects of national cultural heritage (figure 1.3). The player uses a magnifying glass to pick out clues that will lead to the identification of a thief who has stolen an object of national heritage. Much of the fun in the game is in discovering clues, compiling pieces of information, and tracking down the suspect in high-speed chases. But these playful mechanics transmit important lessons, in this case important enough for the Uruguayan government to

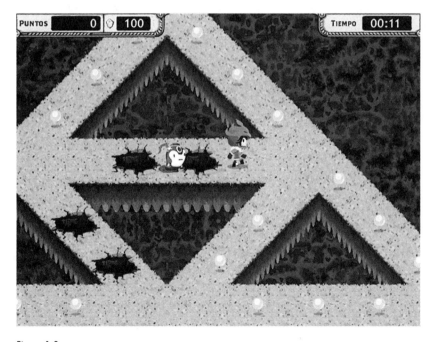

Figure 1.2
Cazaproblemas (Trojan Chicken 2011)

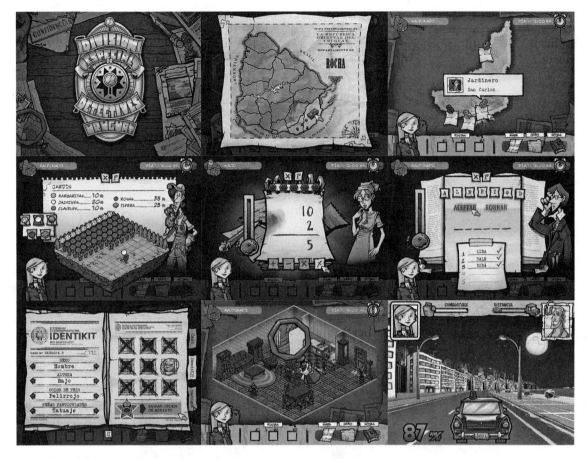

Figure 1.3
D.E.D. (Trojan Chicken 2010)

promote them on the digital desktop of every student in the nation. *1811*, like its sequel *1812* (Trojan Chicken 2015), is a free-roaming RPG in which older primary and high school students learn about the nation's independence movement through firsthand interaction with NPCs whose dialogue and activities round out the game's cultural contextualization of early nineteenth-century Uruguay (figure 1.4). The games use a variety of conventional and novel game scenarios in order to convey lessons on national geography, history, and ecology, giving educators the opportunity to see content related to their classes disseminated to students through an appealing interface, and allowing students to acquire substantial cultural knowledge.

At first glance it might be difficult to see the relationship between clearly pedagogical games like *1811* and *D.E.D.* and a game on *lucha libre*, Mexico's national variation on professional

[Franciscano] Fray Tomás siempre quiere ayudar a indios y esclavos. Seguramente esté junto a varios de ellos.

Figure 1.4
1811 (Trojan Chicken 2011)

wrestling. But on the level of acquisition—again, the end result of a process of exploration and discovery—they do indeed relate. While we might not expect a pro wrestling game to disseminate significant knowledge related to culture, it can be shown that in many ways, *Lucha Libre AAA: Héroes del Ring* does precisely that. Released internationally in October of 2010, *Lucha Libre AAA* was a collaboration between developers in Mexico, Colombia, and Brazil and, as noted earlier, was advertised as the "the first Latin American game to be built ground-up for next generation console platforms"[38] (figure 1.5). The game's contextualization of lucha libre goes beyond the iconography of wrestling masks (though this is by no means overlooked!) in order to thoroughly portray the cultural traditions surrounding this Mexican cultural phenomenon. The player is introduced to the sport's "hero/villain" binary of "rudos" vs. "técnicos"; receives a historical contextulization of *luchadores* dating back to 1930s through documentary footage narrated in Spanish or English; can play characters based on real-life wrestlers with personal histories, bios, and background information; and hears the crowd taunting wrestlers in authentic Mexican slang, along with familiar commentators who chime in with taglines such as "¡Este sí comió pozole!" ("This guy ate his pozole today!").

Cultural lessons can be transmitted in humorous ways, and this by no means diminishes the potential impact of that knowledge for the player. Indeed, generating culturally contextualized

Figure 1.5
Lucha Libre AAA: Héroes del Ring (Konami 2010)

knowledge was one of the express goals of the game's Mexican publisher, Slang, as its then-director Federico Beyer has explained. Beyer suggests that explosive growth in the Latin American gaming population is leading to an ever-expanding need for games "that deliver Latin authenticity—culturally relevant content for the Hispanic community," a niche that represents a "huge opportunity" for game designers and publishers to "transcend borders" and make cultural products with a global impact.[39] With *Lucha Libre AAA*, Beyer explains, "[o]ne of the key things is that we're sharing something Hispanic, which is fun and culturally relevant for the video game," and therefore it is important to get the details right: "If you grab a certain luchador, pick up a certain luchador in our title, you will do *la hurricanrana, el columpio, la de a caballo*. You will do that sort of lucha libre moves. You will wrestle in venues such as the Teotihuacan Pyramids. You will wrestle in the gym called *El Panamericano*, which is in Mexico City in Pepito. You will wrestle obviously in the arenas in which the big shows are held."[40] While other US-based wrestling game franchises have occasionally included famous *luchadores* like Rey Misterio on their rosters, adding in a handful of signature moves and taunts, the level of cultural specificity in *Lucha Libre AAA* is ultimately its most groundbreaking characteristic. Even more than the way it enhances the wrestling game genre, then, *Lucha Libre AAA* represents a break with convention by offering the player an opportunity for the acquisition of contextualized cultural knowledge through the process of play.

Not only can players acquire factual knowledge and cultural context in video games, more and more they are finding ways to use video games to seek new answers to age-old problems.

Figure 1.6
"Monster" in *Papo & Yo* (Minority 2012)

My final example here is *Papo & Yo*, a game from Colombian designer Vander Caballero's Montreal-based studio Minority Media, initially released for exclusive download on the PlayStation
Network in 2012, and later for Mac OS X, Windows, and Linux.[41] *Papo & Yo* operates on two
essential levels: on one level, it is an puzzle game in which the protagonist, a young Afro-
Brazilian boy named Quico, must use the architecture of the surrounding favelas in order to
advance through a series of environmental challenges. On another level, however, the game
is a departure from the norm for the video game medium: it is also an allegory for a childhood under the control of an alcoholic father, with Quico attempting to negotiate a loved one's
addiction through the parental placeholder of Monster, another of the game's main characters
(figure 1.6). Over the course of the game, Quico slowly learns to let go of his struggle to find a
cure for Monster's addiction, coming to accept that he can only do so much, and that addicts
must find it within to solve their own problems. These are enormously ambitious psychological and emotional lessons to transmit in the form of a video game, which is what makes *Papo
& Yo* so powerful in affectively transmitting cultural experience and knowledge through play.

Papo & Yo represents a fresh gameplay experience, but more than that, it offers a glimpse
of another horizon for gameplay: the potential use of video games for therapeutic purposes.
Mark Griffiths notes that therapists have been using video games "as therapy in sessions with
their young patients" for decades, and that play itself has been used in therapy since the work
of Anna Freud and Melanie Klein in the 1920s and 1930s.[42] Griffiths reports several examples of

positive therapeutic effects derived from video game play, explaining that video games "have been shown to help children undergoing chemotherapy, children undergoing psychotherapy, children with particular emotional and behavioral problems (ADD, impulsivity, autism), individuals with medical and health problems (Erb's palsy, muscular dystrophy, burns, strokes, movement impaired), and the elderly," and noting that games have been found particularly effective in enhancing the moral development of youth in distress.[43] These potential benefits of video games are very real, and they were also a part of what Caballero intended in creating *Papo & Yo*, a game based on lessons learned in his own childhood. Seeking to share that personal knowledge with a broader population, he set about designing the mechanics and narrative tools necessary for transmitting a meaningful affective experience to the player on the theme of addiction while still keeping in place the ever-important factor of an enjoyable and compelling experience of play.

Games like *D.E.D.* and *1811, Lucha Libre AAA*, and *Papo & Yo* represent the unique visions of designers from throughout Latin America, working in distinct contexts with diverse goals. However each also exemplifies how games can offer their players acquisitions in the form of real-world knowledge and experience, unlockable through the processes of exploration and discovery. Today, the pedagogical and therapeutic potential of the video game medium seems greater than ever. And even still, the objectives of exploring new territories, discovering new experiences, and acquiring knowledge have been driving players to play video games since the onset of the medium. Having reviewed the very real motivations that explain *why* gamers play games in Latin America as well as elsewhere, I will now turn to a historical overview of *when* and *how* games have been played in the region, from their introduction in the public sphere to the contemporary era of their increasing ubiquity.

A Preliminary Cultural History of Video Game Play in Latin America

When and how did Latin American gamers start playing video games? The history of video gaming in Latin America has yet to be written down in any comprehensive manner. In a region characterized by a great deal of cultural, political, and economic diversity, one must take into account the exceptionality of each unique national context as well as the presence of multiple subcultures of gamers from different socioeconomic backgrounds within each country, all of which makes it very difficult to arrive at generalizations about the social history of video games in Latin America. Too frequently, we simply accept outdated characterizations of the global south as a massive technological backwater, strictly on the downside of the "digital divide" between hi-tech haves and have-nots, when the reality of technological acquisition and usage in Latin America tells a much more nuanced tale.

Latin American gamers consume and play games in ways that reflect diverse and idiosyncratic regional subcultures within the gaming community. With regard to global and local gaming, Larissa Hjorth has noted that "each location adopts and adapts particular types of games and gameplay that reflect the specificities of the place and its associated techno-culture."[44] Documenting the history of Latin American gaming allows us a glimpse of how games circulate beyond the primary markets in the United States, Europe, and Asia that dominate scholarship on the subject. There are glimpses of this type of media history in some recent critical, historiographical, and documentary work—such as Mexican cultural critic Héctor Óscar González Seguí's research tracing the first quarter century of video game history in Mexico; Marcus Vinicius Garrett Chiado's history of early 1980s video game culture in Brazil; Daniel Madrid and Jonathan Valenzuela's 2013 documentary *Chile Game*, which surveys the early development and recent transformations in game consumption and production in Chile; or the exemplary research on the development of Peruvian gaming and game development communities in Eduardo Marisca's "Developing Game Worlds: Gaming, Technology and Innovation in Peru." Though the tradition of electronic gaming in Latin America spans but a few decades, it has undergone enormous transformations during that time, perhaps none more concentrated than those that have taken place in the past five to ten years. More archival work is necessary to produce a truly wide-ranging history of gaming in the region. However, enough historical data and criticism exist at present to allow for the development of a preliminary cultural history of video gaming in Latin America.

Computer games first arrived to the Latin American region in the late 1970s, in the form of coin-operated arcade machines exported to major urban centers by US-based game companies including Atari.[45] Thus early video gaming in Latin America, like elsewhere in the world, was a social experience centered on standalone games in bars, restaurants, and shopping centers. By the mid-1980s, businesses dedicated to the importation, assembly, marketing, and sale of video game machines began to appear in major cities throughout the region, and by the early to mid-1990s, in the case of Mexico, "machine assembly companies popped up, that put together the games with monitors, cabinets with buttons and joysticks, as well as motherboards,"[46] a level of diversification which reflected a robust arcade game industry in the region during this period.

Practically at the same time as the first arcade games were appearing, home game consoles began to gain traction in Latin America, taking the gaming experience—at least in part—from the public into the private sphere. The first game consoles were the products of the "invisible importation" of individuals traveling abroad and bringing back consoles that were not yet officially exported to Latin American markets, another factor that makes the history of gaming in the region uniquely difficult to trace.[47] Marisca explains how games first began arriving in Peru "hidden under layers of clothing in the suitcases of tourists or expats that were visiting their families in the country, who quickly discovered that a game that was sold abroad for between

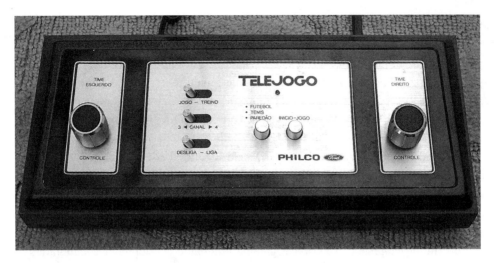

Figure 1.7
The *Telejogo* game console

US$30 and $50 could easily be placed on the local market for double the price, or more."[48]
This regional practice of individualized importation of game hardware and software has arisen
largely from cultural, political, and economic factors common among many Latin American
countries, particularly in the early days of home video game technology. Marisca recalls some
of these factors, noting that in early-1990s Peru, "there were no official distributors for brands
like Nintendo or Sega, as there was no market to take advantage of: the Peruvian economy at
the start of the 1990s was in such grave condition that the idea of a local market for consoles
and games was almost laughable."[49] Most of the game industry's heavy hitters would not officially enter the Latin American market until much later, and their absence had begun to create
a substantial void in the regional video game market.

It wasn't long before local modifications and unique consoles began to pop to fill this void,
such as the *Telejogo*, a 1977 modification of the home *PONG* console marketed in Brazil by US
radio and television giant Philco (then Ford Philco)[50] (figure 1.7), or the Argentine *Telematch*,
which "was basically a bare-bones clone of the Magnavox Odyssey (1972), which had been
stripped down [of] its accessories and from many of its games"[51] (figure 1.8). One peculiar detail
of the Telematch stands out as an early form of cultural localization of video game hardware
and software: the console "was hacked to include two extra knobs for controlling a brand new
game not included in the original Odyssey" that was unique to the Telematch; that game was
"*Soccer*, a *PONG*-like game with two paddles in which one paddle represented a player and the
other the goalie. Goalkeepers were controlled by the extra knobs."[52] Including a soccer game as
part of the Telematch console package in Argentina is typical of the way game companies seek

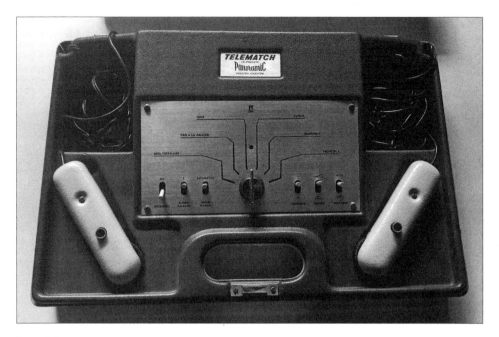

Figure 1.8
The *Telematch* game console

to generate marketing appeal by adapting their products for cultural relevance. As with arcade games, Atari was one of few major game industry players to stoke the fires of this wave of in-home gaming in Latin America, taking on aggressive ad campaigns in which they marketed their machines as a kind of "in-home competitor" against whom players could test their skills. In a memorable and ironic 1980s ad campaign in Brazil, for example, Atari marketed its home video gaming system as "O inimigo No. 1 da família brasileira," or "The Number One Enemy of the Brazilian Family" (figure 1.9).

However, the largest explosion in home gaming in Latin America over the course of these first decades of video game technology came with the success of the Nintendo Entertainment System (NES), released worldwide in 1987.[53] Even more significant in Latin America (a market ignored by Nintendo at the time) was the advent of Chinese-made clones of the NES, going by names such as the *Creation* and the *Family*.[54] The advent of CD-ROM-based gaming with the console generation of the first Sony PlayStation in 1994 signaled a further tidal change in Latin American gaming, as software piracy was facilitated and became more widespread than ever, though it had indeed taken place with previously existing game technologies.[55] The rising popularity of video games led to repercussions in other areas of society as well, inspiring experts in Latin American popular culture like García Canclini to comment on the increasing impact of

Figure 1.9
Brazilian advertisement for Atari, early 1980s

"home computer access to video games,"[56] and compelling Martín-Barbero to remark upon "an omnipresent compulsive need for microcomputers, VCRs, video games and videotext not only in the capital cities but in the provincial towns" as well, throughout the region.[57] At the same time, popular gaming magazines had begun to pop up in the region with pioneers like *Mundo Atari* in 1987, and carried through by the highly successful national issues of the magazine *Club Nintendo* published in Mexico from December 1991 to June 2015, and in Chile from 1992 through 1999[58] (figure 1.10). The inaugural issue of the Mexican version symbolically portrays Mario's arrival by parachute alongside the Angel of Independence, the iconic monument on Mexico City's main promenade, el Paseo de la Reforma, signaling the dawn of a new era in terms of video games' relationship with Latin America.

In the early years of video games' presence in Latin America, enduring patterns of play were established. By the turn of the millennium, González Seguí was able to assess a quarter century of gaming history in Mexico, offering insights with sustained relevance a decade and a half later. The first is that, in Mexico just like in the rest of Latin America and across the globe, video games are an established part of young people's lives, with nine out of ten Mexicans playing video games in their youth by the year 2000.[59] González Seguí's second conclusion discounts any overly rigid notion of a "digital divide" leaving Latin Americans out of

Figure 1.10
Club Nintendo (Mexico), vol. 1, no. 1, December 1991

the gaming equation: video games have been disseminated among all socioeconomic strata; moreover, "there are few significant differences among users" of different economic classes, and the "small variations found are not conclusive, even with detailed statistical observations."[60] Socioeconomic status did not have a significant impact on intensity or attitudes of gamers with regard to video games, though González Seguí notes that there is something of a technological lapse in the way software and hardware are consumed by gamers of different economic backgrounds: "On the one hand, there is an elite of young people that continually update their hardware and games, but on the other hand, for example in El Platanal, a small village in Michoacán, video games arrive already installed on consoles that just need to be plugged in to an electrical socket, and they stay that same way for years."[61] The results of this two-tiered market system have certain benefits for game manufacturers and consumers alike, with game companies gaining access to high-paying customers as well as "secondary centers of consumption" where they can sell "self-contained packets with games considered obsolete in first-level markets," allowing consumers to access games at a low price while enabling small local business owners to find subsistence by dealing in technology overlooked by the dominant market.[62] All of these factors lead González Seguí to conclude that for the Latin American public at the turn of the millennium, video games constituted "agents of cultural and educational change with enormous geographical reach and individual penetration, made invisible by the cover of their commercial quality."[63]

Nevertheless, a number of factors have impeded the expansion of first-run video game hardware and software in Latin America in recent years, the first of which is the historically high cost of imported entertainment technology in many countries throughout the region. Today, for example, "Mexicans appear to pay 30–60 percent more than their American counterparts for legally purchased (non-pirated) software and hardware just about across the board,"[64] while in Peru "a current-generation game console can cost upwards of $600."[65] And depending on the year and the national context, that price hike can actually be significantly steeper. Take the PlayStation 4 console, introduced in 2013 at US$399 in the United States, £349.99 in the United Kingdom, and €399.99 in the rest of Europe. In Brazil, the release price was equivalent to US$1,840, a more than 450 percent increase on the US introductory price. In this particular instance, Sony's general manager for Latin America blamed Brazil's heavy importation taxes for two thirds of the difference and distributor costs for another 22 percent of the sales price,[66] highlighting some of the impediments that have historically driven corporations away from the region, in turn reducing the chances for legal video game hardware and software consumption in Latin America.

Perhaps not surprisingly in light of these factors, piracy is another of the major reasons gaming history is so difficult to trace in Latin America. Frasca has suggested that piracy is partially to blame for the slow takeoff of the game design industry in Latin America as well, though he notes that this dynamic is changing because of online distribution and increased access to the market for small designers on the mobile market.[67] The prevalence of pirated software is another factor that makes it difficult to estimate levels of video game consumption with any precision, as it is widely accepted that a much greater number of illegal copies of games have been sold on the black market or freely distributed than purchased as legal copies on store shelves in Latin America. In Chile, an estimated two of every three games in the average gamer's inventory are pirated copies.[68] Thirty-nine percent of the respondents to a 2010 survey of Colombian gamers had purchased an illegally pirated video game within the prior month "with no remorse,"[69] given their few available alternatives. Indeed, the local and global circumstances that drive prices beyond the reach of the average consumer have sparked a range of black market game sellers across the region, from street vendors with blankets covered in Xbox games, to small-town game stores featuring some major game series and used titles, to shopping center-style clearing houses of pirated wares in urban centers. Luis Wong describes one of the latter locales, Lima's Polvos Azules or Blue Powders, as "the place where poor and rich gamers go to find the latest games," a store "where you can buy all sorts of illegal merchandise," including clothing, music, and video games.[70] Polvos Azules houses "16,000 square meters and more than 1,000 sellers of stuffed animals, T-shirts of metal bands, acoustic guitars and action figures of wrestlers, among other things," and unlike your average street stall, the store offers a well-illuminated and secure environment for the consumer, with each stand featuring a large LCD screen where players can try games before buying them.[71] Surprisingly, Wong notes, at Polvos Azules "most of the PlayStation 3 and Xbox 360 games are between $62 and $67, almost the same as in the US," which goes against what we might expect of a pirated software marketplace. However, these games still come as a substantial discount to the consumer, considering that official copies can cost upward of $100 on Lima's department store shelves.[72] Today this consumer landscape is slowly changing, with local video game distributors working with game publishers and designers to circulate their products securely with payment options tailored to gaming audiences in different countries throughout Latin America. But in spite of these efforts, it remains the case that Latin America's gaming history cannot be fully understood without accounting for the complex role of piracy.

The cybercafé—known in different countries by a variety of names including *cabina*, *cibercafé*, *cyber*, *locadora*, *sala de juegos*, and *vicio*—is another factor with a unique role in expanding the Latin American gaming audience, as well as making it more difficult to trace through conventional sales statistics (figure 1.11). The cybercafé is a socio-commercial institution with a particular history of prominence in the region for a number of reasons. First and foremost, of course, is the question of economics. Unlike video arcades in many parts of the world, the Latin American cybercafé has historically been a small-scale operation in which a single owner will purchase several game consoles and monitors, as well as his or her own selection of game software, then rent out gameplay time to the consumer by the hour, or by the minute. The regional prevalence of the cybercafé has been driven by the fact that, as we have seen, game hardware and software represent significant expenses for the average consumer, especially for the populations of developing countries faced with heavy taxation on imports that dramatically increase consumer prices. Furthermore, the rate of the average Internet connection in some parts of the region is relatively low, with several Brazilian cities making the list of the ten slowest worldwide with average rates of 65Kbps (versus the average US rate of around 600Kbps).[73] This means that a business owner capable of offering access to a reliable and fast Internet connection in addition to the latest consoles and games at a reasonable rate makes them accessible to an exponentially larger number of players than the sales numbers for hardware and

Figure 1.11
A Brazilian *locadora* focused on Atari games, late 1970s

software reflect. While a cybercafé owner may purchase a single (licensed or unlicensed) copy of a given game, dozens or even hundreds of players who visit the cybercafé might end up playing that same copy of the game, demonstrating how the number of game players and consumers in Latin America can far exceed sales statistics.

Partially as a result of the cybercafé's prominence, gaming in Latin America has sustained a longer history as a phenomenon centered on social interaction than it has in the United States and elsewhere. Rather than the hardcore solitary US gamer who holes up for days alone in a room, many Latin American gamers play with one another in a space that is not made for playing games in isolation, but rather is a "hub for social activity, where players can hang out together, talk about games, and actually play with their friends," forming group relationships that can significantly impact the popularity of a given game in the region.[74] Pedagogical scholar Viviana Celso characterizes the role of cybercafés in Latin America as fundamentally social in nature as well, defining them as "public spaces where children and young people meet, where their practices as online gamers are circulated and socialized."[75] Celso sees cybercafés as "transparent, regulated and controlled spaces where encounters among strangers take place, spaces of transience and permanence, of communication and disconnection,"[76] highlighting the parameters within which this particular institution has hosted the development of gaming communities throughout Latin America. Marisca recalls that in early-1990s Peru, where cyber-cafés are known as *cabinas*, "[p]laying in cabinas became popular enough that it got its own verb ("cabinear") and would become a regular activity even for kids who did have access to the hardware at home," driving the young populace into shared spaces with "the gaming machines in a darkened back room, with graffitis and player nicknames all over the walls and black light-ing defining the ambience."[77] Again, these spaces were about more than just commerce, they were the forum for the development of a local gaming subculture, some of whose members would eventually figure among the first generations of regional game designers. As Marisca elaborates, "[t]he knowledge transmission that was taking place in the cabinas and vicios began to articulate into strong community ties over time, as people who patronised individual establishments would become acquainted with each other through play, and hierarchies would form based on skill and dexterity. The communities that formed around cabinas and vicios, in turn, became over time the foundation for teams and leagues of competitive play, with teams establishing their home base and their training regime around a specific cabina often receiv-ing support from operators who would allow them to pull training all-nighters at a discount."[78]

Above and beyond its role as a democratizing market force spreading game access far beyond the reach of official sales data, the cybercafé is a shared space that has fostered the develop-ment of a community of gamers, game developers, and game industry professionals across Latin America. This helps to demonstrate the way local cultural factors—including political and economic impediments to importation, a lack of official presence from major game cor-porations, widespread availability of pirated software, and the prevalence of the cybercafé as an economic and social institution—have shaped the historical development of video gaming in the region.

The State of Play in Contemporary Latin America

So, what are Latin American gamers playing now, and what effects is gameplay producing throughout the region? Today, play is beginning to hold a new significance in Latin America, and gamer demographics in the region are trending toward an ever more inclusive proportion of the population. Performance artist Guillermo Gómez-Peña has observed cultural transfor-mations in Latin America and elsewhere resulting from the profound impact of an increase in games and other interactive technologies: "Audiences are increasingly having a harder time just sitting and watching passively a performance, especially younger audiences. They've been trained by television, Supernintendo [*sic*], video games, and the internet to 'interact' and be part of it all, whatever 'it' may be. [...] Given this epistemological shift, artists and art institutions are pressured to redefine our own epistemological relationship with our public."[79] And this is not just a phenomenon to be decried, but rather a social reality reflecting a time of transition from an episteme based upon representation to one based upon interaction, as Gómez-Peña accurately characterizes the present era. These circumstances call for an increasingly nuanced conceptualization of the gamer, or what Miguel Sicart refers to as "a player that is morally aware and capable of reflecting upon the nature of her acts within the game world."[80] And Latin America's thriving and increasingly diverse populace of gamers exhibits a growing tendency to rely on technology distributed through official channels, particularly when supported by local economic legislation favorable to game consumers and producers.[81]

Cultural context has a significant impact on the meaning conveyed by video games. King and Krzywinska note that play "is always shaped by, and appears within, particular cultural contexts, even if these are often largely implicit and kept in the background," adding that such "contexts are often quite broadly framed, particularly in games designed for something close to a global marketplace, although particular types of games and game content are sometimes favoured in one place more than another."[82] Indeed, the same message can be received differently within a different cultural context, and therefore we must consider what it means for games to be played within different economic, political, and social circumstances. This is particularly crucial because, as García Canclini has argued, contemporary identity is established vis-à-vis global and local criteria: "subject identities are now formed in interethnic and international processes, among the flows produced by technologies and multinational corporations, globalized financial exchanges, repertoires of images and information created to be distributed throughout the planet by the cultural industries."[83] Media shape who we are, and who we think we are, and therefore "[t]oday we imagine what it means to be a subject not just from the standpoint of the culture in which we were born, but from an enormous variety of symbolic repertoires and behavioral models,"[84] among which video games are gaining increasing prominence.

Latin American communities of play have come about in different contexts and for diverse reasons, as exemplified in the preceding discussion of the cybercafé. Today's gaming communities are generally more likely to interact online than they are in real life. Javier Jerjes Loayza describes the process of community formation among Latin American online gamers, explaining that "[l]ittle by little the networks are timidly put together, thanks to some gamers inviting Spanish speakers from elsewhere in Latin America to their networks when they meet them while playing," resulting in local and dispersed communities of gamers throughout the region.[85] Playing among a community of like-minded players who share one's language and nationality can substantially enhance the experience of gameplay: once gamers can compete and interact with a shared community, they "are no longer searching for success before the mirror of their television, they are searching for an existential proclamation before a global ludic audience."[86] And the place of play is only the first of several observable transformations in the demographics of Latin American gaming today.

The current regional population of gamers is diverse and varied, including players of all ages, sexes, and socioeconomic classes and representing a vast array of ethnic, racial, national, and linguistic backgrounds. In all, market data indicate that there are currently some 185 million active gamers in Latin America, or about one third of the overall regional population, a gaming populace that is expected to grow to nearly 230 million by 2017.[87] Keeping in mind the sustained significance of factors like the cybercafé and software piracy in spreading access beyond traceable sales figures, we can assume that the number of Latin Americans actually playing video games (and not just buying them on the official market) is in reality much higher than these estimates. It is estimated that out of those 185 million statistically active gamers, 104.5 million are *paying* gamers that spend a monthly average of US$2.67 on games.[88] This is roughly consistent with other data, for example those indicating that about 60 percent of Brazil's 48.8 million gamers regularly spend some amount of money on or in games. These statistics from Brazil, a nation ranked eleventh globally for game revenues, are also a reminder of the existence of a great number of gamers who spend no money at all on gaming, opting for free versions of online games, social games, and mobile applications. Increasingly, Latin American gamers are diversifying the types of screens and platforms that they use for gaming as well—in Brazil, over 45 percent of gamers play social/casual games, while only one-third of gamers play either on TV/game console or on PC/Mac computer.[89] Other figures more emphatically reflect the recent expansion of the mobile gaming sector, estimating that 70 percent of Brazilian gamers play games on their mobile devices.[90] The demographics of Latin American gamers are generally shifting toward greater inclusion, with a growing proportion of female gamers and an increasing average player age as well. Brazilian gaming experts place their audience anywhere between 5 and 60 years of age, with the 13-to-35-year-old range being the most prevalent.[91] A 2010 Colombian survey found an average age of twenty-three and a prevalence of male students among the 200 gamers polled, among whom 35 percent owned a home video game console and 5.8 percent had acquired a new console within the preceding year.[92] The same survey also found a shift in cultural attitudes surrounding video games among parents, with 72 percent saying they considered games to be helpful to the development of skills and stimulation of creativity and 68 percent of parents saying they prefer to have their children at home playing video games rather than out in the street.[93] Likewise, an average of 14 out of 16 Brazilian gamers who are parents report playing frequently with their children.[94] Such local data help to outline some of the overall shifts taking place within the Latin American gaming community, whose demographic contours continue to rapidly expand and transform.

The genres and game series most popular among Latin American gamers vary considerably among different national audiences, making it difficult to arrive at many sustainable generalizations. However, at least insofar as official sales data is representative of the reality of gaming in the region, it is possible to reach several conclusions. First, many popular games and series including *Call of Duty*, *Halo* (Microsoft 2001), *Metal Gear Solid* (Konami 1998), *God of War* (Sony 2005), *League of Legends* (Riot 2009), and *Final Fantasy* (Square Enix 1987) sell at virtually the same rates of popularity in Latin America as in the rest of the world.[95] Player preferences vary depending on national and local context, but blockbusters are blockbusters anywhere you look. Still, cultural differences in game preferences between national contexts are observable and verifiable. In 2014, Brazil's most popular PC/console game genres were, in order: action/ adventure, strategy, racing, shooter, sports, and fighting (with simulation, arcade, dance/ movement, and card games scoring lower).[96] Relative to US consumers, then, Brazilian players show a much higher predilection toward racing and action/adventure games, while US gamers trend more heavily to the shooter and strategy genres,[97] demonstrating the ways that cultural context can have a measurable impact on the experience of gaming. Konami's Latin American Director Erik Bladinieres observes that hockey and NFL football games that perform well in Canada or the United States, perhaps predictably, do poorly in Latin America.[98] Meanwhile, there has been an all-out regional war between the two major soccer game franchises: *Pro Evolution Soccer* (Konami 2001), a top-20 title in the United States, was consistently the top-selling game in Latin America for many years running, but has lost that title to *FIFA* (EA 1993) for the past several installments.[99] As a typical illustration of official console game preferences in the region, the top three games sold in the relatively small Paraguayan market in 2012 were *FIFA 12* (EA 2011), *Pro Evolution Soccer 2012* (Konami 2011), and *Call of Duty: Black Ops II* (Activision 2012).[100]

Rapid shifts in platforms and genres also make it more difficult to map the terrain of Latin American gaming. Over the course of the early 2010s, the game industry has experienced great diversification in the region as well as globally, with a high concentration on the growing market segment of casual games rather than traditional console and personal computer titles. Brazil is the top-ranked country in the Western world in social network gaming, with 36 percent of the country's Internet population playing at least once a week.[101] Not coincidentally, Brazil is also home to Latin America's largest social gaming publisher, Mentez, which has offices in Miami, São Paulo, Bogotá, and Mexico City, and draws 22 million active users per week with games on Orkut, the Google-owned social network that is Brazil's most popular, with games ranging from the farm simulation *Colheita Feliz* (*Happy Harvest*, Mentez 2009) to the tourist-oriented city management simulator *Cidade Maravilhosa Rio* (*Marvelous City Rio*, Mentez 2011). Gamers are consuming these types of "freemium" and "free-to-play" web games with increasing voracity, along with game applications available for several different mobile operating systems. Globally, the mobile gaming segment grew 35 percent from 2012 to 2013, while console gaming actually fell 1 percent.[102] Global mobile gaming revenues totaled more than US$17 billion in 2013, with the mobile market segment projected to bring in as much as US$40 billion annually by 2017.[103] In Latin America alone, mobile games are estimated to have brought in US$510 million in 2014, showing 60 percent growth relative to the previous year, with the average paying mobile player spending US$0.74 per month on games and a regional mobile gaming population of 148 million players (just about on par with North America's 152 million mobile gamers).[104] Casual games represent the segment with the greatest growth over the past several years in Latin America and across the globe.

This boom in casual game consumption has gone hand in hand with a skyrocketing rate of access to mobile web technology supported by cellular networks in the region that began with the launch of the region's first 3G licenses in 2007, which brought substantial new audiences of Latin American gamers online.[105] This revolution in wireless Internet technology represents a major change for the digital consumption of cultural products in Latin America. Today, mobile phone services have become the predominant means of communication throughout Latin America and the Caribbean,[106] partially as a result of active efforts by the "regional duopoly" of wireless providers Mexico-based Telmex subsidiary América Móvil and Spain's Telefónica Móviles to expand their consumer base.[107] Mobile subscriptions now outpace land lines in the region by a factor of more than 4 to 1: out of every 100 inhabitants in the region, there are 22 fixed phone lines, 90 mobile phone subscriptions, 7 broadband subscriptions, and 12 personal computers (the respective numbers for OECD countries—the major economies measured by the Organization for Economic Cooperation and Development—are 44, 115, 54, and 54). "Regional frontrunner" countries including Brazil, Chile, Uruguay, Costa Rica, and Mexico "are roughly on par with the typical OECD country," however in poorer economies such as those of Nicaragua or Guatemala, "even the highest income brackets have very limited access to ICTs [information and communication technologies] at home (and sometimes negligible levels, as in the case of the Internet)."[108] The Inter-American Development Bank (IDB) speaks of a "*geographic* digital divide" between broadband Internet access in major cities and rural areas within a given country, exacerbated by a lower level of purchasing power among inhabitants of rural areas, the lack of technological infrastructure, and the higher cost of providing service to sparsely populated regions.[109] Narrowing this divide is one of the major policy objectives the IDB advocates. Likewise, there are major gaps in the penetration of technology in different national and regional contexts throughout Latin America—Internet access in schools, for example, ranges from 96 percent of students in Chile to only 9 percent in Guatemala,[110] meaning that it is important to examine local factors in determining the level of access of a given population.

Above and beyond profit margins, there are major motivations for improving broadband Internet access. In fact, Rubén López-Rivas and Antonio García Zaballos tie broadband penetration to increases in gross domestic product, worker productivity, and employment, estimating that "in Latin America and the Caribbean, on average, a 10 percent higher broadband penetration is associated with 3.19 percent higher GDP, 2.61 percent higher productivity and 67,016 new jobs."[111] Likewise, the push to increase Internet availability through mobile technology is radically transforming the experience of play as well as the demographics of gamers in the region today. In Brazil, for example, from 2000 to 2013 the number of Internet users increased more than twentyfold, from 5 million to 104 million; another way of saying this is that while there were fewer than *three* Internet connections per 100 people in Brazil in 2000, by 2007 that rate was over 30 per 100, and since then has continued to grow dramatically, topping 50 Internet connections per 100 people in 2013.[112] Demographic transformations are beginning to show up in sociological data sets regarding gaming in Latin America as well, such as research conducted in the southern Brazilian city of Santa Catarina in 2001 and 2011, in which more than five thousand public high school students between the ages of fifteen and nineteen years were polled about their media consumption habits. The results of this decade-long study clearly demonstrate "a decrease in the prevalence of TV watching and an increase in the use of computers/videogames."[113] Specifically, the prevalence of watching TV for more than two hours a day *decreased* 15 percent over ten years, while the prevalence of using computers/video games for more than two hours a day *increased* more than 20 percent in the same period, and in both genders.[114] Thanks in part to growing access to the Internet and mobile technologies, gaming is now a daily part of life in Latin America, and its prevalence is on the rise.

Likewise, in twenty-first-century Latin America, it should not be assumed that a low level of income or rural location necessarily translates to a complete lack of access to information technology. In *Communication Power*, Manuel Castells estimates that "over 60 percent of the people on this planet have access to wireless communication in 2008, even if this is highly constrained by income," noting that "studies in China, Latin America and Africa have shown that poor people give high priority to their communication needs and use a substantial proportion of their meager budget to fulfill them."[115] Indeed, even after discounting for factors that impede access to game technology, the Latin American video game market is booming, with revenues climbing in double and triple digits annually throughout the region.[116] According to one source, the region saw 600 percent growth in the rate of game downloads from 2009 to 2011 alone,[117] while estimates appraising the size of the Latin American market for "virtual items" by themselves (those goods and services purchased within games that offer a temporary subscription, upgrade, or quantity of virtual currency) at more than US$600 million for 2014.[118] Ever more, people worldwide are driven to connect, plugging into global and local flows of information using communication technologies and devices, as these patterns of media consumption demonstrate.

Today there is no longer any doubt about the vitality and legitimacy of the Latin American video game market, with gamers buying software and hardware in massive proportions. Estimates place 2014 Latin American game revenues at US$3.3 billion, and project massive growth toward US$5 billion in annual regional game sales by 2017.[119] Seven Latin American countries are in the global top fifty countries in terms of revenue (Brazil, Mexico, Argentina, Colombia, Chile, Venezuela, and Peru), together accounting for over US$3 billion in annual revenue. Brazil alone generates more than US$1 billion in game sales annually, placing it just outside the top ten worldwide.[120] Other Latin American nations lie closer to the bottom of the rankings—out of 100 countries surveyed, Cuba, Guatemala, Paraguay, and El Salvador were ranked 87, 91, 95, and 96, respectively—and even still, each of these nations boasts a gaming population in the range of two to four million, and each generated over US$10 million in game revenues in 2014.[121] Perhaps even more important, Latin America is one of the major growth regions in terms of global game sales, which means its market potential is skyrocketing. Research has shown that countries with the lowest share in the games market have the highest level of growth in online population as well as gross domestic product (Panama and Paraguay are examples).[122] Accordingly, the Latin American games market saw massive 11 percent year-on-year growth from 2012 to 2013, while the North American market produced seven times as much revenue, but grew only 2 percent from the previous year.[123] The regional rate of growth climbed yet again the following year, with a total compound annual growth rate of nearly 14 percent for Latin America as a whole in 2014, partially accounted for by astronomic growth among sectors like tablet gaming, whose revenues grew 61 percent over the preceding year.[124] When those in the game industry think of Latin America today, they think less about piracy and digital divides, and more about profits and double-digit growth.

Conclusion: Next Generation Play

As the data presented in this chapter clearly demonstrate, interactive play is gaining increasing prevalence in contemporary Latin America. This heightened level of play in the region, combined with increased access to the Internet, represents a major potential source of cultural change in coming years. Castells argues that we have not fully learned to exploit "the possibilities created by the new multimodal, interactive communication system," which "extraordinarily reinforce the chances for new messages and new messengers to populate the communication networks of society at large, thus reprogramming the networks around their values, interests, and projects."[125] More and more, a growing populace of Latin American gamers that crosses all socioeconomic levels and geographic regions is reinforcing its own messages and communicating its values and interests through online play. This level of voluntary participation represents one of the great benefits of play to be harnessed. As Jane McGonigal argues, the drive to visit "*autotelic* space—spaces we visit for the pure enjoyment of it" is a powerful force that can be measured in terms of "participation bandwidth," or the "individual and collective capacity to contribute to one or more participatory networks."[126] Harnessing this potential into an "engagement economy" is a more and more realistic possibility in Latin America today, thanks to a decades-long expansion in the social prevalence of play.

Video games are impacting Latin American culture in increasingly visible ways, showing great promise for future expansion. The game convention known as the Brasil Game Show or BGS began in 2009 and drew around four thousand attendees; by 2014 the expected attendance was over a quarter million, among them representatives from virtually every major developer, distributor, and publisher in the global games industry.[127] Other spheres of society are raising alarms about the explosive growth of the medium in Latin America—for example, the Nicaraguan Ministry of Health claims that one in five children aged thirteen to eighteen in the country is "pathologically addicted to video games."[128] But a great many more are finding new opportunities in an increasingly impactful medium, including the advent of gaming as a professional competitive sport. The US-based Major League Gaming rolled out their first international franchise in 2014, partnering with Brazilian entertainment company Grupo Águia to create Major League Gaming Brasil, "a franchised partner of the competitive gaming network aimed specifically at the expanding South American game market."[129] Even earlier, though, there were many Latin American gamers interested in representing their region, their country, their city, or their local group of gamers in major international game competitions. In preparation for the 2011 Electronic Sports World Cup, Bolivian gamers in the cities of Cochabamba, La Paz, and Santa Cruz competed in elimination tournaments that drew hundreds of participants and thousands of spectators, with the champions receiving an all-expense paid trip to Paris for the grand finale.[130] In 2014, the fighting-game-centered Evolution Championship Tournament (EVO) also attracted interest from Latin American gamers, including a delegation of nine Panamanian competitors in *Ultra Street Fighter IV* (Capcom 2014),[131] as well as four Puerto Rican medalists whose work (and play) was admired by some 1.7 million attendees.[132] Video game play is a ubiquitous element of life for a great many Latin Americans today, and its prominence is expanding in previously unforeseen manners.

Regardless of the other purposes to which they are put and irrespective of the other types of potential they possess, games are first and foremost products of play. This means that it is important to take account of who plays video games in Latin America, and in which circumstances. On one hand, there are the players, a rapidly changing population of gamers in Latin America and worldwide, whose demographics are shattering conventional concepts of who plays video games and what they play. On the other hand, there are the material conditions of play in Latin America, which necessitate particular attention to regionally significant factors in how games are consumed, phenomena that serve to expand game access in the region beyond the scope of official economic data on video game consumption practices. In a sense, the aim of this chapter has been to bring us back to its starting point, the epigraph in which Huizinga reminds us of the inseparability of culture and play, since civilization "arises *in* and *as* play, and never leaves it."[133] While play has always been significant to human culture, an examination of the specific functions and practices of play in contemporary Latin America demonstrates that play is not only universal but also irreducibly local and contingent on the specificity of culturally contextualized practice and performance. Today, the connection between play and culture is being renewed and reinterpreted ever more vigorously, as can be observed in innumerable ways and in contexts throughout the Latin American region. This is, in a sense, a return to the original state of culture as Huizinga described it, a phenomenon inseparable from play itself.

While play is the primary motivator for the engagement between culture and games, it is by no means their only use. When video games attract broader public attention, particularly in the spheres of politics and the mass media, it is frequently due to concerns that have little relation to gameplay itself. This chapter is primarily concerned with two "persuasive" uses that contemporary culture has for games, both in Latin America and worldwide: First, when used as sensationalistic news fodder or publicly denounced by politicians, video games are divested of their ludic meaning and converted into political currency, as in the case of the controversies surrounding games in Mexico, Venezuela, and Cuba discussed in the first half of this chapter. Second, there are those video games that have been alternatively labeled "serious" or "persuasive" games due to their nature as intellectual statements designed to provoke thoughtful reflection above and beyond their commercial or recreational uses. Games have been used for ideological critique, pedagogy, and political parody throughout the history of the medium. The latter half of the chapter examines avant-garde projects produced by Latin American game designers and artists whose work demonstrates that video games are not only fit for raising controversy but also ripe for repurposing by activists, offering an alternative vision of what video games are capable of in Latin America in terms of ethics, politics, and persuasion.

Games and Persuasion in Public Discourse

Politicians and the mass media frequently depict video games as exceptionally dangerous cultural products, and it is important to understand the motivations underlying such characterizations as well as their ramifications in the public sphere. Juul refers to the tendency to view video games with a particularly critical or prejudicial eye as "videogame exceptionalism,"[1] while Bolter and Grusin argue that video games "come under attack precisely because they remediate the two genres (film and television) that American society has come to regard as immediate and therefore potentially threatening."[2] Christopher A. Paul has suggested that a focus on controversial games may lead to particular insights about what makes them so threatening, as well as noting that "[a]nalyzing video games requires reaching beyond the games themselves to examine how they are discussed by those who play them and those who do not."[3] Paul points to a fundamental paradox of video games' meaning: Unlike the discussion of literature, in which the opinions of "those who do not" read books would be summarily disregarded, with video games we must take into account how their de facto meaning can be shaped by the opinions of individuals with little or no firsthand gaming experience.

This is what I refer to as the political commodification of video games, though the phenomenon of cultural commodification is not unique to this medium. In his 1963 essay "Culture Industry Reconsidered," Adorno explains how a cultural product can be impacted by the reduction and repurposing of the constituent elements of its meaning, a process through which "important individual points, by becoming detachable, interchangeable, and even technically alienated from any connected meaning, lend themselves to ends external to the work," a description which helps explain the way games' meaning can be reduced and instrumentalized within public discourse.[4] In the United States, the so-called "Columbine theory" of game analysis—that is, the suggestion that "games plus gore equals psychotic behavior"[5]—has been criticized as dominating public discourse on the subject of games to the detriment of other, more nuanced perspectives. The *Grand Theft Auto* (*GTA*) series is a quintessential example, as Judd Ruggill and Ken S. McAllister explain: "Anyone who has read a newspaper or watched the nightly news since the turn of the millennium knows that the *Grand Theft Auto* series has been made infamous by a largely non-game-playing popular press that has reduced this suite of complex, big-budget games—each containing dozens of hours of play and a host of intricate, interconnected stories—to the headline 'Video Game Allows Kids to Solicit Prostitutes, Run Them Over, Get Their Money Back.'"[6] Much of the meaning of video games is conveyed within the mass media and political discourse by way of a methodology that isolates their most spectacular (and morally, politically, or culturally objectionable) elements, exaggerates the significance of these elements relative to the overall experience of the game in which they appear, and finally channels the power of the public response to this operation into support for an underlying agenda.

In Latin America as elsewhere, video games frequently enter into broader cultural discourse when they become convenient to other strategic political or economic interests. Rather than the "Columbine theory"—which refers to the 1999 Colorado high school shooting perpetrated by alienated teens who were also avid gamers—in the Latin American context we might rightfully conceive of a "*Mercenaries 2* theory" within political discourse, in reference to EA's 2008 game *Mercenaries 2: World in Flames*. This game, a moderately popular success on the mainstream market, would come to be associated with the most sociopolitically impactful video game controversy to date within the region, resulting in a wide-reaching 2011 Venezuelan censorship law that banned scores of video games from circulation in the country.

The specific controversies examined in this chapter have arisen in part because of the well-evidenced tendency on the part of designers of video games (and military-themed games in particular) to use storylines set in contemporary and historical geopolitical hotspots—including Revolution-era Cuba, contemporary socialist Venezuela, and drug war-afflicted Mexico. Matthew Thomas Payne has observed that games frequently feature "combat that unfolds in authentic theaters of war, both historic and those 'ripped from today's headlines,'" which is one way game designers create a compelling context for confrontation.[7] When these headlines center on sensitive political issues, they naturally touch on raw nerves among certain segments of the Latin American public and political spheres. But in each of the cases examined here, it can be seen that games are used rhetorically by public figures pursuing their own political agendas—that is, as the technological scapegoats of moralistic and ideological discourse—in a manner unrelated to the meaning these games generate through gameplay. The specific types of erasures and distortions necessary to make games politically expedient are revelatory of the underlying ideologies of those that employ them as political commodities.

Video Games and Political Controversy in Latin America

Political controversies have arisen around games in a number of different circumstances throughout Latin America, with telling similarities and differences in legislators' responses to games in each case. For Mexico, ludic representation is certainly nothing new, since early titles like the 1982 computer games *Aztec* (Datamost) and *The Mask of the Sun*, or the 1984 Atari games *Montezuma's Revenge* (Parker Brothers) and *Quest for Quintana Roo* incorporated the iconography of the Maya and Aztec cultures into their digital environments, formulating what would be one of the most enduring tropes of Latin American culture in the realm of electronic games. It probably wasn't until the Super Nintendo/Sega Genesis title *Urban Strike* (EA 1994) that Mexico was rendered in a video game not as a setting steeped in ancient culture, but as a modern society, albeit strictly as the backdrop to a military airstrike by helicopter (figure 2.1). *Urban Strike*, the third game in EA's helicopter shoot-'em-up *Strike* series following *Desert Strike: Return to the Gulf* (1992) and *Jungle Strike* (1993), was set in a then-futuristic 2001. The game's Mexico mission, set among the military barracks of an army fortress and a nearby town, is replete with architecture that signifies Mexican culture through colonial adobe structures with red tile roofs, and at the same time stands out as an advance in game mechanics, since the player can use the helicopter's weapons to destroy the architectural structures in the game. The responsiveness of its environment set *Urban Strike* apart from the earlier titles in the series, and at the

Figure 2.1
Urban Strike (EA 1994)

same time paved the way for a new Mexican cultural trope in video games, that of the unstable neighbor to the south of the United States in a dystopian futuristic military scenario.

Video game representations of Mexico as a setting for military intervention have surged in recent years, occasionally igniting controversy within Mexican politics. The day after the release of *Tom Clancy's Ghost Recon: Advanced Warfighter 2* (Ubisoft 2007), mayor Héctor Murguía of Ciudad Juárez asked legislators to block its sale, calling the game despicable, xenophobic, and harmful to children.[8] Similar controversy arose surrounding the release of Ubisoft's *Call of Juarez: The Cartel* in 2011, when the state legislature of Chihuahua unanimously approved an official request for the game to be banned nationwide.[9] On one hand, it is understandable that local legislators would object to games in which their people are characterized as criminals and cannon fodder more often than not. On the other hand, this is video game exceptionalism in political practice. Other forms of media, like film, television, and literature have long depicted the hardships of human existence, including gritty realism torn from the news stories of their times. Likewise, there are established traditions in the representation of the drug war in Mexican cultural production, from the *narcoliteratura* of writers like Élmer Mendoza, to the *narcocorridos* of bands like Los Tigres del Norte or Los Buitres de Sinaloa, to recent films like *El infierno* (Luis Estrada 2010), *Miss Bala* (Gerardo Naranjo 2011), and *Saving Private Pérez* (Beto

Gómez 2011). What is it, then, that makes games like this so particularly notable, and objectionable, to politicians?

Call of Juarez: The Cartel was developed by the Polish firm Techland and published by Ubisoft, the Montreal-based software giant. It is the third game in the series, after the original *Call of Juarez* (Ubisoft 2006) and its prequel, *Call of Juarez: Bound in Blood* (Ubisoft 2009). Unlike the previous titles in the series and the latest entry, *Call of Juarez: Gunslinger* (Ubisoft 2013), all of which are first-person shooter (FPS) games set in the Old West, *The Cartel* took on the setting of the contemporary US-Mexico border in the midst of an expanding drug war. There is no shortage of evidence in the game to support claims that it is xenophobic—despite its ostensible focus on "The Cartel," characters of Mexican origin play only tangential and one-dimensional roles in the game. As the playable team of US authorities fights largely on their own country's territory against the encroaching violence of a politically connected cartel, the team members gun down countless Mexican affiliates, all of whom respond with redundant and basic expletive phrases in Spanish: "¡Puta madre!," "¡Puta!," "¡Hijo de puta!," "¡Chinga tu madre!" In the game's subtitles, nameless characters are merely referred to as "Mexican," as in this exchange: "Mexican: I hate it down here, it smells all funky and shit." "[Another] Mexican: Are you sure that's not you?" And while the playable protagonist Eddie Guerra is one of relatively few Latino protagonists in the history of video games, his cultural depth does not go far beyond his biographical background in East LA or the inflection of his dialogue with the occasional "*ese*" or Spanglish phrase: "The enemy of my enemy is my *carnal*."

There are, however, elements of contemporary reality in the game that contribute to a unique portrayal of border geography and culture in the present day, particularly the ways *Call of Juarez: The Cartel* simulates border militarization. Throughout the game, US government officials push for a frontal military invasion of Mexico, citing increasing threats to national security. Through Fox News-like cable news reports that play during the cutscenes between missions, we hear the perspective of the politicians that inhabit this particular gamespace. Early on, we learn that Attorney General Joseph B. Reynolds is weighing military action in Mexico: "We will seize their drugs, freeze their assets, and hang 'em high like the outlaws they are! This is war! We have declared war on the Mendoza cartel!" His perspective is amplified by archconservative senatorial candidate Ron Lindsay, who in a Glenn Beck-like bluster calls for the United States to go beyond prosecuting criminals in its territory and to actually enact a full-scale military invasion of its southern neighbor. This fictitious militarization has real-world roots: at least as far back as 1999, Claire F. Fox was already referring to the government's "stepped-up presentation of the US-Mexico border region as a 'staging area' for 'war games.'"[10] In the present day, the US government is using "the philosophy of 'low-intensity wars'"[11] by patrolling the border with drone aircraft and generating an increased presence along what Fernando Romero/Lar has called the "Hyperborder." Romero/Lar notes that in 2008 there were more American Border Patrol agents than there were American soldiers in Afghanistan,[12] leaving little doubt as to the reality of border militarization today.

Games like *Call of Juarez: The Cartel* create speculative fiction by incorporating details of actual geopolitical conflicts, using topical poignancy to generate interest in their games. From its title to its pre-release announcements calling the drug cartels "the new outlaws" and running the slogan, "Welcome to the new wild west," it would appear that the marketers of *Call of Juarez: The Cartel* sought to raise public ire, generating some sales in the process.[13] If so, they ultimately succeeded in the former, but failed at the latter. The shift from the Old West to Mexico's contemporary drug war put the game in countless headlines prior to its release. A general shock permeated reports that noted that in the year prior to the games release, some six thousand people had been killed in drug-related violence in Ciudad Juárez.[14] Others celebrated the advent of such controversy, saying, "[b]ring on the virtual violence. Maybe then we'll pay attention to the real thing."[15] As noted earlier, Mexican congressional representatives called upon the country's Department of the Interior to ban the game altogether from circulation in Mexico. But in spite of its pre-release attention, it quickly flailed once it was on the market, racking up an aggregate rating of 45/100 from gaming site Metacritic. It ultimately sold around half a million copies in an expanding market in which successful video game titles measure their sales in tens of millions.[16] In this sense, *Call of Juarez: The Cartel* is most of all an example of how the political significance of some games can be disproportionate to their actual social or economic impact.

Mercenaries 2: World in Flames is comparable in this sense—while it was a moderately successful release for its publisher EA, selling just over two million console and PC copies worldwide, its impact within the political arena came to outweigh its significance as a playable game, particularly with regard to Latin America. This is due to opposition to the game from one of the most polarizing political figures of the early twenty-first century, Venezuelan president Hugo Chávez, who held office from 1998 until he succumbed to cancer in 2013. Chávez took issue with the representation of Venezuela, and in particular of its socialist leadership, in a game designed by California-based Pandemic Studios, who had also developed the previous game *Mercenaries: Playground of Destruction* (LucasArts 2005). *Mercenaries 2* situates the player as a Swedish soldier of fortune named Mattias Nilsson (voiced by actor Peter Stormare) at war in a fictionalized Venezuela whose government has recently been toppled by a military coup that installs fictional politician Ramón Solano as the civilian leader of the new government (figure 2.2). Solano pontificates on the need to nationalize the nation's petroleum reserves while in reality pursuing his own economic gains, sparking violent conflicts between different sectors within the game, including a CIA-funded mercenary force, the private security agency of Universal Petroleum (the foreign-owned company looking to maintain its stake in the country's oil in spite of the coup), and the guerrilla organization known as the People's Liberation Army

Figure 2.2
Mercenaries 2: World in Flames (EA 2008)

of Venezuela. These factions do battle in what is doubtlessly the most thorough rendering of Venezuela's geography in video game form to date, including the cities of Caracas, Maracaibo, Mérida, Cumaná, and Guanare, the areas of Amazonas and Isla Margarita, and several unspecified locales in the Venezuelan countryside. Overall, the game's tone is reminiscent of a satirical and ironic comic book in which nothing is taken too seriously and political metaphors are mixed without any consistent narrative thread that would indicate a sustained commentary on real-world affairs. However, little time passed before this game—despite a relative lack of success in terms of sales and critical reception—produced major effects in the real world.

Sensing critical overtones in the game's depiction of national politics, members of Chávez's Patria Para Todos (PPT) party began to denounce the game publicly as a threat to national security, characterizing its designers as "doing the work of Washington in order to drum up support from Americans for an eventual operation to overthrow Chávez."[17] Before long, president Chávez himself took up the subject, offering his evaluation of the game on his weekly "Aló Presidente" television program: "What about those games they call PlayStation. ... Poison! There are even games about killing, that teach you to kill, kill, kill. Once they even made one with my own face. Yes, that's right, you had to kill Chávez, seek out Chávez to kill him, bombarding cities, dropping bombs. A PlayStation. What's that? Ah, it's capitalism! Planting the seeds of violence in order to sell more weapons."[18]

Chávez's characterization of the game's plot was widely accepted and used as evidence by politicians and journalists alike, though in actuality, Chávez is never mentioned in *Mercenaries 2*.[19] This did not stop legislators from condemning video games at large as teaching children to be violent, and before long they found success in their political maneuvering, approving in December 2009 new legislation titled the "Law for the Prohibition of Bellicose Video Games and Bellicose Toys," which makes it a legal requirement for each and every video game sold in Venezuela to "promote respect for life, creativity, healthy entertainment, camaraderie, loyalty, teamwork, respect for the law, comprehension, tolerance, understanding between people and the spirit of peace and brotherhood," in addition to assigning fines of more than US$100,000[20] and mandating a three-to-five year prison sentence to any individual importing, manufacturing, selling, or renting games that fail to meet these requirements.[21] Moreover, "Article 8: Destruction" stipulates that the Venezuelan government is responsible for destroying the offending materials, a task that was then carried out as a public spectacle by operatives who literally steamrolled controversial toys and video games (figure 2.3). Within a short time, the Venezuelan model was duplicated elsewhere: Panamanian politicians proposed their own "Law prohibiting bellicose or violent games and toys" in 2011[22] and Chile drafted legislation placing legal restrictions on the circulation of violent video games in 2014.[23] Venezuelan game designers complain the law has crippled the national industry at a time when many other Latin American administrations are looking to enhance their countries' game production.[24] By politically distorting the dimensions of a game that one Venezuelan writer has ironically

Figure 2.3
Venezuelan officials steamroll "bellicose games and toys," June 2010

labeled "the most controversial video game that no one ever played,"[25] all while characterizing the game's intended audience as juvenile and its political implications as transparent, Chávez and his supporters succeeded in legislating far-reaching censorship that eliminates creative freedoms in the country under the guise of confronting capitalist imperialism.

But how did *Mercenaries 2* really depict Venezuela? To begin with, this was not the first (nor is it likely to be the last) representation of Venezuela to appear in video game form: over the course of the early 2000s a kind of fictionalized representation of Chávez's Venezuela was practically a trope among military games. The plot of *Tom Clancy's Rainbow Six 3: Raven Shield* (Ubisoft 2003) revolves around a covert operation by the US government to assassinate the fictitious Venezuelan president Juan Crespo after he attempts to create an international oil crisis and benefit from it by jacking up prices to the United States. The futuristic tactical role-playing game *Front Mission 4* (Square Enix 2004), set in 2096, involves an allied international invasion of Venezuela after its rogue leader breaks away from the international diplomatic organization known as the United States of the New Continent (USN). Just six months before the release of the controversial *Mercenaries 2* came *Conflict: Denied Ops* (Eidos 2008), which revolves around a CIA operation to take out the fictional regime of General Ramirez, a petroleum-nationalizing maverick seeking to take control of the country after internal divisions have left it polarized and embattled. To greater or lesser extremes, all of these games create a fictional rendering of certain tendencies of the Chávez administration as well as the interventionist pretensions of the United States. So why did *Mercenaries 2* garner special attention from the regime?

Like the other military-themed games discussed in this chapter, *Mercenaries 2* attempts to create a sense of realism by including references to real-world political circumstances, albeit through the lenses of fictionalization and parody. Pandemic Studios, the creators of the game, have stated that they "always want to have a rip from the headlines" and that they focus specifically on geopolitical situations where "a conflict doesn't necessarily have to be happening, [but] it's realistic enough to believe it could eventually happen."[26] Matthew Colville, the lead writer for *Mercenaries 2*, explains in an interview with Venezuelan journalist Gregory David Escobar that when the design team heard of the denunciations of the game as propaganda, "we never thought anyone in Venezuela could take that seriously," asserting that the decision to set the game in Venezuela was made for creative and artistic reasons.[27] On the one hand, there are elements of this fictitious environment that seem to match up with real-life Venezuela under Chávez: for example, Solano is a vociferous leader who seeks to use Venezuela's oil reserves as the basis for making the country into a "South American super power," while pro-Solano pedestrians shout out, "¡Viva Solano! ¡He is Bolívar reborn!," referencing not only the enduring legacy of Venezuelan national hero Simón Bolívar but also Chávez's self-fashioning as the leader of a new movement that took the Liberator's name, his Bolivarian revolution. On the other hand, the game is clearly a parody, with a tone closer to a Hollywood action movie than a realist documentary. Indeed, for those who have played *Mercenaries 2*, it is difficult to imagine it being seriously characterized as a "justification of imperialist aggression,"[28] much less part of a "campaign of psychological terror,"[29] in the words of two different Venezuelan congressional representatives. It would be much easier, in fact, to substantiate the opposite reading: the game is not an endorsement but a critique of US interventionism.

For one thing, the player of *Mercenaries 2* is not in fact playing a game of US intervention: on the contrary, as the title indicates, the protagonist belongs to a force of mercenaries for hire. Indeed, not one of them is American: Nilsson is Swedish, his main radio dispatcher is Australian, his helicopter pilot Ewan is Irish, the mechanic Eva Navarro is Venezuelan, and the jet pilot is an inebriated Russian. The player fights for all (fictitious) sides in this struggle as well—the first missions support Universal Petroleum, but quickly give way to jobs for the People's Liberation Army of Venezuela and other factions. There are also numerous indications of the game's critical stance toward the neo-imperialist efforts of the international governments and corporations portrayed in the game. First, there is the actual written information provided to the player—for example, Universal Petroleum, the game's version of a Texas-based multinational oil giant, is described as having "made a deal with the Venezuelan Government 50 years ago. In the decades since, U.P. made billons of dollars from the arrangement." If this wasn't plain enough, late in the story the CEO of Universal Petroleum directly tells the player, as the mercenary Nilsson, that the corporation has "been screwing the Venezuelans out of their oil." US imperialism, corporate greed, and disrespect for Venezuela are not the hidden truths of this game, but rather the superficially evident elements of its parodic framework.

However, nobody in the Chávez administration seemed especially interested in examining how *Mercenaries 2* worked on a ludic level—it was more politically efficacious to use the game in other ways. But when Chávez denounced the game for devaluing Venezuelan lives, he failed to note that the game in fact does place a value on those lives: they are worth $5,000 apiece. At first blush, this reduction of a human life to a monetary value may seem absurd and dehumanizing. But understood within a ludic system of logic, this $5,000-per-life price tag actually has a profound functional impact on the meaning of human life in the game. To comprehend this, we must take into account that *Mercenaries 2* is essentially a "skinned" version of the open-world genre defined by the *Grand Theft Auto* (*GTA*) series.[30] This means that *Mercenaries 2* and *GTA* not only share their genre and basic scenario (both are open world third-person shooters in which the player can hijack vehicles and take on missions to make money) but also their fundamental game mechanics, including the manner in which missions are presented to the player as multiple tangentially interrelated options within an expansive and responsive world, as well as elements such as the health meter, damage to vehicles, and transportation physics.

Given its provenance in the genre defined by *Grand Theft Auto*, there is an important departure from generic convention in *Mercenaries 2* that Chávez failed to take into account. In the GTA games, players receive no monetary penalty for running down or shooting pedestrians unless they are caught by the police doing so—on the contrary, most of their victims will leave behind some money to award their aggression, meaning that NPC murder is a profitable enterprise in the GTA universe. In *Mercenaries 2*, on the other hand, protection of the population is incentivized early on when rebel leader Marcela Acosta offers "a big bonus not to injure any civilians," after which the player is fined for each civilian casualty incurred. By imposing a significant monetary penalty on players who show wanton disregard for the lives of the game's NPCs, *Mercenaries 2* actually forces the player to veer from the norm for this genre, and into a less sociopathic relationship to the game's NPCs by design. From a game-literate perspective, then, Venezuelan lives are actually worth much more in *Mercenaries 2* than a veteran gamer might expect. This is one of many indications that what games mean for political discourse is frequently quite the opposite of what they mean for their players.

Chávez was by no means the only national leader in Latin America to take on the video game industry in recent years. Former Panamanian dictator Manuel Noriega, who remains in prison for human rights violations, attracted headlines when he sued Activision, the publisher of the 2012 game *Call of Duty: Black Ops II*, alleging that they illegally used his image and likeness in a defamatory manner.[31] Though the case was dismissed, it is evidence of the increasing relevance and immediacy of video games, for gamers and politicians alike. Noriega's case, which dealt with a Latin American head of state who was also a known political enemy of the United States suing the publishers of *Call of Duty*, had echoes of another major political controversy, this one surrounding the depiction of Cuban leader Fidel Castro in Activision's 2010 release *Call of Duty: Black Ops*.

Like so many geopolitical hot spots, Cuba has a relatively lengthy history of representation in video games. Prior to its appearance in *Call of Duty: Black Ops*, the era of the Cuban Revolution has served as the backdrop of games since the arcade action shooter *Guerrilla War* (SNK 1987), whose original Japanese title was *Guevara*, and which followed the exploits of Ernesto "Che" Guevara and the forces of the Cuban Revolution as they proceed to overthrow dictator Fulgencio Batista. For the North American release of this Japanese title, the name was changed, the dictator and island setting made generic, and the protagonist of Guevara swapped for a US soldier. The Cuban Revolution also provided the setting for games such as the real-time strategy PC game *Cuban Missile Crisis: The Aftermath* (G5 Software 2005) and the open-world action-adventure adaptation of *The Godfather II* (EA 2009). Post-revolutionary Cuba is also a favored setting for games portraying US interventions, international intrusions, and criminal activity, including flight simulator *A-10 Cuba!* (Activision 1996), hit Nintendo 64 James Bond adaptation *Goldeneye 007* (Nintendo 1997), real-time strategy titles *Command & Conquer: Red Alert 2* and *3* (EA Games

2000, 2008), action driving game *Driver 2: Back on the Streets* (Infogrames 2000), the *Island Thunder* expansion pack for the tactical shooter *Tom Clancy's Ghost Recon* (Ubisoft 2002),[32] and the PC real-time strategy game *Act of War: High Treason* (Atari 2006). Along with ancient Mexico, the Spanish colonies, and the Amazon jungle, revolutionary and post-revolutionary Cuba represents one of the most frequent scenarios for the portrayal of Latin American culture in video games.

So what was it that made *Black Ops* unique? For one, unlike some of the controversial games discussed in this chapter, it was a widely played international success. While *Call of Juarez: The Cartel* sold around half a million copies and *Mercenaries 2: World in Flames* topped out at just over two million, *Call of Duty: Black Ops* set a new global record for the most successful release of a media product in history, and has sold more than thirty million copies worldwide to date. Noting the game's broad dissemination and appeal, the Cuban government interpreted *Black Ops* as an attack on national sovereignty, declaring on the state website Cubadebate that "[w]hat the US government was unable to achieve for more than 50 years, it is now trying to reach through virtual means," by requiring players to assassinate Fidel Castro in a game that is "without a doubt, entertainment for psychopaths."[33] While questioning the mental stability of the millions of global players of *Black Ops* might overstep the bounds of reason, in this case the government gets the facts right, at least in part: the objective of very first mission in *Black Ops* is indeed to "Find and kill Castro," an operation that the player attempts to carry out against the backdrop of the US-supported 1961 Bay of Pigs Invasion. In the mission, the player, in the role of a soldier named Woods, and his partner Mason enter the innermost rooms of the Castro compound, where a *Matrix*-like slow-motion effect kicks in, a final handful of soldiers are killed, and the protagonists proceed into the final bedroom (Woods: "Ready to make history?"), where Fidel Castro is located with a scantily clad female companion. He uses her as a human shield, but Mason fires a single bullet, which spurs an "angels singing" effect and more slow-motion, for a gruesome and graphic close up of Castro apparently getting assassinated by a bullet through the head. Woods (and thus the player) goes on to realize that it was a setup, that Castro knew of the plan and the individual assassinated was actually a stand-in, and we see the "real" Fidel handing the agent over to a military officer, saying (in English), "Do with him what you wish, general. He is my gift to you, in honor of our new relationship. Just … make sure that he suffers." This cues cutscene footage of the real-life Fidel Castro and Nikita Khrushchev and newsreel film of a summit between Cuba and the Soviet Union, as Mason is taken to a Soviet internment camp.

This is the basic thrust of the *Black Ops* storyline relating to the Cuban government, however Cuban culture is in fact much more richly represented through gameplay than in this narrative reduction. At least as many players spend their time playing *Call of Duty* online multiplayer mode as they do playing the offline story mode,[34] and this is significant because four of the fourteen multiplayer maps in *Black Ops* are situated in Cuba (Crisis, Villa, Firing Range, and Havana) meaning that more than 25 percent of the time that many players spend in the game is time spent in a virtual Cuba. There is also a playable Cuban military faction known as "Tropas" and a force of Cuban military contractors known as "OP-40," all of whom speak in untranslated Spanish in the game: "¡Tirando granada!," "¡Explosivo fuera!," "¡Cambiando cargador!," "¡Muerto confirmado!," "¡Enemigo a la vista!," "¡El blanco cayó!," "¡Cúbreme, que estoy recargando!," "¡Me han pegado!," "¡Tirando explosivos!," "¡Coño!," "¡Médico!," "¡Contacto!," "¡Enemigo!," and so on. Many of these phrases are divided into interchangeable groups (for example, "¡Cayó el enemigo!" and "¡Muerto confirmado!," both of which confirm an enemy fatality)—if the player watches the replay of her death immediately following her demise, the character killing her will not repeat the same phrase he said originally, but the next phrase in line for that function. The portrayal of Cuban culture in *Black Ops* pertains to the particularities of *Call of Duty* as a semiotic system, including linguistic as well as audiovisual signs that lead the player to reach several conclusions regarding Cuban culture: (1) Cuba is a revolutionary state, (2) prior to the Revolution Cuba was a decadent tourist playground, (3) Cuba was central to the Cold War confrontation between the United States and the Soviet Union, and (4) Cuba is defined by its tropical ecology, topography, and cultural production. Each of these messages provides potentially meaningful insights into Cuba's history and national identity, however, the Cuban government paid no attention to these procedural and semiotic representations of culture in its condemnation of *Black Ops* according to essentially narrative criteria.

It is understandable that games portraying the attempted assassination of Cuba's real-life leadership, requiring the overthrow of a fictionalized Venezuelan socialist leader, or trivializing the very real violence sweeping across Mexico today would raise the ire of politicians in these respective nations. Ethics do not disappear altogether within the game world, though they are contextualized differently. As Sicart asserts in *The Ethics of Computer Games*, "[e]mptying games of ethical reflection in their design and using unethical content for its shock value as a marketing resource means not only devaluing the possibilities of games as a means of expression, but also making products that are unethical objects."[35] Some of the content in the games at the heart of the political controversies discussed here is indeed ethically questionable, though it is important to remember that just how exactly ethics operate in these games is very much a question, rather than a foregone and transparent conclusion. The simplifications and distortions required to condemn these games in the press and to pass legislation censoring them show how video games are commodified in the political sphere, being utilized for political saber rattling rather than understood as unique cultural products with their own systems of signification.

Perhaps this is why the 2013 game *Gesta Final* (*Final Feat*), published by Cuba's Joven Club de Computación y Electrónica (JCCE, Youth Computation and Electronics Club), a computer science initiative supported by the national Ministry of Communications, is so groundbreaking

Figure 2.4
Gesta Final (JCCE 2014)

(figure 2.4). In *Gesta Final* the player embodies one of several unnamed bearded revolutionaries and, according to the JCCE's leadership, allows them to identify with the history of the Cuban Revolution.[36] Players of the first-person shooter act as members of the eighty-two-soldier contingent that disembarked from the yacht *Granma* and whose surviving members ultimately defeated the Batista regime, passing through five major in-game battles along the way: "El Desembarco" ("The Debarkation"), "Bautismo de Fuego" ("Baptism by Fire"), "La Plata," "El Uvero," and "Pino del Agua II" (all three names of locations of actual battles in the revolution).[37] JCCE spokesperson Haylin Corujo clarifies that the game was not designed as a direct response to the controversy stirred up by *Black Ops II*'s portrayal of Cuba, explaining, "We aren't responding to any other game. What's important for us is for young people to learn while playing."[38] Regardless, *Gesta Final* represents a truly novel approach: instead of simply rejecting games as the tools of capitalism that use violence to poison the minds of the youth á la Chávez, the government supported the development of a violent video game that also happens to teach the values of the Cuban Revolution.

In other words, rather than condemn or attempt to ban video games based on their violence or alleged imperialist bias, the makers of *Gesta Final* sought to produce the type of game that they think *should* be played about the Cuban Revolution. This exemplifies the potential for

Latin American game designers to take control of the ludic message on their own cultures and national histories. Controversies surrounding video games continue to be politically productive, and therefore their reductive but persuasive use by public figures is bound to continue. But meanwhile today's game designers, critics, and players are looking beyond this trivializing realm of political posturing and poisonous PlayStations, using games not only for entertainment but also as a means of confronting ideological issues through gameplay.

Persuasive Game Design in Latin America

Discussions of "persuasion" in game studies refer more often than not to a trajectory in game design that focuses on challenging the player intellectually or ideologically through gameplay, rather than simply providing recreation. The use of game design toward persuasive ends enjoys a long history both in Latin America and globally, even if in general, as Bogost notes, the rhetorical power of games "has gone untapped because the market has focused primarily on entertaining players, rather than engaging them in important topics."[39] Looking at the industry as a whole, it is hard to argue with this point. However, there are of course other possible uses for the tools that the industry has created, a fact that independent designers have long exploited toward unconventional ends. As García Canclini observes, "[t]he exercise of citizenship has always been associated with the capacity to appropriate commodities and with ways of using them," and for years Latin American game designers have been using the video game medium in unexpected and unconventional ways.[40] Many such games are technically modest by comparison to the mass-market AAA titles discussed earlier in this chapter, their designers opting for small-scale web games, interactive narratives, and playable Flash animation projects that use simple design mechanics to create ideologically compelling experiences through gameplay.

Designing ethically challenging games means creating a friction that causes the player to question the causes and effects of the actions undertaken in the game world. Sicart argues that for ethically transformative gameplay to be possible, "there has to be a contradiction between what to do in terms of gameplay, and the meaning and impact of those actions, both within the gameworld and in a larger cultural setting."[41] Moreover, the types of ethically challenging actions included in games will not necessarily be more effective if they are "cleaned up" or rid of the gruesome details of the violent acts they contain: "If anything, ethical gameplay should *increase* cognitive friction, forcing a split between the actions of the reactive agent and their interpretation by the reflective agent."[42] Sicart draws upon Bogost's notion of *procedural rhetoric*, defined as "the practice of persuading through processes in general and computational processes in particular," or "a technique for making arguments with computational systems and for unpacking computational arguments others have created."[43] By setting up a series of procedures that require the player to advance along a path of predetermined steps, games can on the one hand create a logical correspondence that offers the player an experience of believability and verisimilitude, in which the game is perceived as consistent with or further endorsing the player's own life patterns. On the other hand, the manipulation of these same techniques to increase "cognitive friction" in the player can serve to create a meaningful dissonance between the player's real-world ethics and functional understanding of the game's mechanics. This means that persuasive games function in the way that they do because they place the player in an ethical conflict between their own desires as a real-world moral being, and their operational understanding of what actions will lead to a successful outcome within the game. So how, exactly, do Latin American game designers go about creating ethical crises for their players?

Uruguayan critic and game designer Gonzalo Frasca is not only an early proponent of game studies as an academic discipline, he is also a prominent figure in the history of serious game design. Frasca has designed several "newsgames" centered on current events in geopolitics, and coined the term "video games of the oppressed" to describe the potential of using the medium as a tool for liberation, building upon Brazilian educational philosopher Paulo Freire's *The Pedagogy of the Oppressed* (1968) and playwright and drama theorist Augusto Boal's concept of "The Theater of the Oppressed."[44] Frasca's most notable attempts at this sort of game design were produced in his *Newsgaming* series, which aimed to "use games and simulations to analyze, debate, comment and editorialize major international news" with simple playable scenarios designed for use with Adobe Flash Player.[45] The first, *September 12th: A Toy World*, was produced in 2003 as a response to the US-led global "war on terror," while the second, *Madrid*, was put together within a day as a timely but enduring response to the March 11, 2004 Al Qaeda bombing of a number of passenger trains in Spain. Each of these games offers a paradigmatic model of ludic persuasion.

September 12th begins with a concise explanatory introduction: "This is not a game. You can't win and you can't lose. This is a simulation. It has no ending. It has already begun. The rules are deadly simple. You can shoot. Or not. This is a simple model you can use to explore some aspects of the war on terror." Alongside these explanations are two preparatory sketches for the characters who populate the simulation: one is labeled "Civilians," and features a family of three individuals in head-to-toe Islamic *hijab* and tunics. The other character is labeled "Terrorist," and in addition to a tunic and keffiyeh, holds a submachine gun. In the sketch as in the game itself, the differences between civilians and terrorists are subtle. Once the player clicks Start, the visuals of the simulation, which has been at work in the background, are revealed: the player observes a *Where's Waldo*-like world of tiny animated figures circulating busily and swiftly in an unnamed Middle Eastern city lined with buildings of varying sizes, bazaars,

Figure 2.5
September 12th (Newsgaming.com 2003)

fountains, vendors' stands, and palm-shaded plazas (figure 2.5). An aiming reticule replaces the player's mouse arrow, so that the only manner of interacting with the simulation is through the manipulation of the targeting system: pushing the reticule to the right or left extreme extends the player's view in that direction up to a finite point, meaning the reticule is a navigational tool as well as a ballistic mechanism.

Eventually, of course, nearly all players of *September 12th* will be tempted to click. When they do, after a brief pause that functionally allows for the targeted population to shuffle around and rearrange, a rather imprecise cruise missile rockets down from the sky, striking roughly in the area where the player aimed. The strike will usually kill several individuals, perhaps some terrorists (they are around 10 percent of the population initially circulating), and almost certainly several civilians. When they die, others begin to assemble and mourn at the bomb site, the visceral wails of the victims' relatives contributing to an impactful affective experience. Then the twist occurs: the characters that have gathered to mourn the victim begin to flash and transform, changing from their original civilian selves into an exponentially expanding population of terrorists. Each time the player aims to take out a single terrorist, he in fact ends up creating many more terrorists. The more missiles the player fires, the higher the percentage of terrorists circulating among the population. The buildings will eventually be reconstructed, and with the passing of time between missile attacks the number of terrorists in the population begins to thin out, but they will never disappear altogether. As Sicart notes, "*September 12th* makes a powerful ethical statement: the only way of surviving this game is not playing it ... but not playing it means letting those simulated terrorists 'live.'"[46] This is a simulated world in which there is no way to win, one can only *lose less*. And from the start, the best thing a player can do is simply to do nothing at all, meaning the procedural rhetoric of *September 12th* functions in a manner antithetical to the heroic triumphalism one generally expects of the medium.

Unlike many small-scale web games, *September 12th* has indeed garnered a significant amount of critical attention. The game is one of Bogost's primary case studies in *Persuasive Games*, and he has spoken of it elsewhere as an example of the fact "that games can be noteworthy rhetorical devices."[47] Bogost sees the procedural rhetoric of the game as providing a set of apparent rules, affordances, and possibilities that in fact do not deliver on their promises: "In *September 12th*, the rules depict the impossibility of achieving a goal given the tools provided [and] the represented procedural system fails to perform the services it alleges to provide."[48] Patrick Crogan sees this built-in failure as a way of addressing the complicity of the video game medium in the military-entertainment complex, "a reflective meditation on this backstory of military history and on its adoption in war game simulation practices that are now widely disseminated in commercial and amateur war game models."[49] Doubtless, *September 12th* is meant to problematize the role of technology in contemporary drone-dominated conflicts like those in Afghanistan and Iraq. Toward that end, it puts the player in control of the death and destruction in order to produce the kind of cognitive friction discussed earlier: the actions required by the game's rules are at odds with the outcome and do not produce the desired result, leading the player to a questioning of the underlying logic of using military intervention to eliminate opposition.

Frasca's next game, *Madrid*, went in an even less conventional direction, using peaceful protest against violence as the context for gameplay. This Flash animation game features a group of some twenty visible demonstrators gathered at a candlelight vigil, each one wearing a t-shirt featuring the name of a city that has been victim to terrorist violence (New York, Baghdad, Oklahoma City, Tokyo, Beirut, Paris, and Buenos Aires) and holding a candle with a flickering yellow flame (figure 2.6). The initial instructions, written in both Spanish and English, tell the player to "Click on the candles and make them shine as bright as you can," and as she does so a light meter at the bottom of the screen traces her progress toward the goal. As soon as the player has clicked on a candle's flame, it momentarily burns big and bright, then almost immediately begins to diminish until it becomes a barely lit flicker. As the player attempts to keep all twenty candles lit, the difficulty of keeping the flame alive becomes ever more apparent. If the procedural rhetoric of *Madrid* had not made it clear enough that the game is about the importance of remembering the lives of the victims and keeping alive the hope for a future

Figure 2.6
Madrid (Newsgaming.com 2004)

free of fear of violence, the message that the player reads each time she loses is a strong reinforcement: "Debes seguir intentándolo. You have to keep trying." *Madrid* is about the importance of the living keeping their commitment to nonviolence alive, a notion that is harmonious
with the content of the game, a candlelight vigil to remember the victims of terrorist violence
in Spain. In these two simple but thoughtfully designed games, Frasca establishes important
patterns for successful ideological game design that others have tried to reproduce, including
straightforward rules, a simple player interface, and coordination of content and mechanics in
order to create alternating experiences of friction and coherence.

Other politically and ideologically challenging games have resulted from collaborative
efforts combining game design, pedagogy, and community building. These include games that
seek to subvert generic norms for the use of violence in video games like *This War of Mine* (11
bit 2014), a survival-strategy PC game in which the player acts as a civilian attempting to survive within a war zone rather than the conventional video game soldier, or *NarcoGuerra* (2013),
a turn-based strategy iOS and Android app game developed by the UK firm Game the News,
which goes against conventional military shooter games about the drug war by focusing on the
difficulty of balancing the interests and demands of the multiple forces at work in the war for
control over Mexico's territory among cartels, government agencies, and citizens (figure 2.7).
Games such as these challenge our expectations of violence in video games in order to raise
important sociopolitical concerns in a complex yet playable manner.

The 2002 online Flash animation game *Tropical America* shares these other examples'
unique focus on examining and enhancing the player's understanding of history: it was

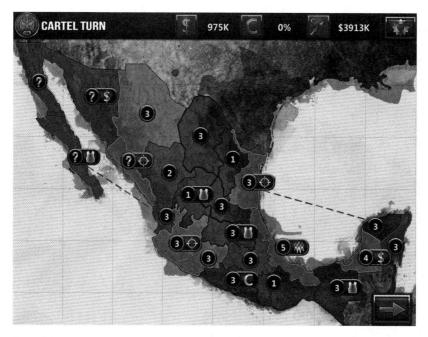

Figure 2.7
NarcoGuerra (GameTheNews 2013)

produced as a component of an after-school violence prevention program in a 90-percent-Latino public high school in Los Angeles, California, where the student population consisted primarily of first- and second-generation immigrants from El Salvador and elsewhere in Central America. The project that led to the development of *Tropical America* was spearheaded by OnRamp Arts, an organization that produced new media projects in collaboration with local high schools, youth, and artists, which received support from a US Department of Education media literacy grant to address youth violence.[50] *Tropical America* was intended in part to provoke reflection on the role of violence in society, but in this case it went beyond that initial goal by seeking to enhance students' knowledge of the cultural heritage that many of them shared as individuals recently displaced from their homelands. In the words of the project's description, "wanting to find a new and compelling way to connect young people to their history, OnRamp artists decided early on to create a database of historical texts, imagery and resources that would exist as a parallel web site to the online game."[51] This information was compiled under the guidance of *Tropical America*'s coeditor, Los Angeles-based Colombian media artist Juan Devis, who culled material from a play he had previously written to create a series of lectures on key episodes from Latin American history. Students used these

lectures as the basis for creating an index of symbolic iconography to parallel the historical processes and relationships they sought to describe in the game, then collaborated with
Mexican visual artist Artemio Rodríguez to produce the game's visual aesthetic.[52] As a result,
Tropical America has the look of a black-and-white woodcut print, an expressive genre with
a long history of use toward politically activist ends in Latin America. The game's aesthetic
is especially evocative of the work of early twentieth-century Mexican print artist José Gua-
dalupe Posada, which provided the basis for the Taller de Gráfica Popular (TGP), or People's
Graphic Workshop, whose members circulated sociopolitical critique through the woodcut
prints they produced in Mexico from the 1930s through the 1960s. *Tropical America*'s aesthetic
nod to this tradition suggests an affinity for the use of a simple and accessible interface in
order to convey messages with the clarity of a highly simplified form, illustrating historical
inequalities in black and white.

Though it requires the player to make decisions that affect the outcome of gameplay, *Tropical America* has such a strong concentration on narrative that it could be described as much
as an interactive fiction (to use Montfort's term)[53] or a form of "ergodic literature" (to use
Aarseth's)[54] as it could be a video game. The game begins when the player chooses between
playable protagonists Juan and María, after which the player is positioned as the lone survivor
of the real-life 1981 massacre of El Mozote, a small village in El Salvador, looking for clues as
to why this event came to pass. Against the backdrop of automatic gunfire and screams, the
opening passages of *Tropical America*'s narrative offer an elliptical explanation that parallels
the insecurity and confusion of the situation portrayed:

> They stormed into town early in the morning.
> There were 30 or 40 of them. They had machetes and guns.
> They were asking questions.
> I didn't know who they were, or why they came.
> We were all forced to line-up in the main plaza.
> My mom and I were taken into the church.
> They closed the door and everything was dark.
> When I opened my eyes, I was the only one left.
> I was scared, so I ran. I ran as fast as I could.
> There was a strange smell in the air, the smell of gunpowder, burning wood, rotting flesh.
> I'm afraid to go back but I need to know what happened.
> Who did this to my family and me?
> Who destroyed my town?
> What am I supposed to do now?[55]

From this point, *Tropical America* unfolds as a quest narrative in which the player searches
for an explanation for the atrocities introduced at the beginning. In this sense, the quest ultimately ends when the player is introduced to Rufina Amaya, the real-life sole survivor of the

December 1981 El Mozote massacre. However, the game also aims to take on topics such as cultural identity through diaspora, historical inequalities, and the contemporary structures of hegemony. As Henry Jenkins elaborates in his analysis of *Tropical America*, the player explores "some five hundred years of the history of the colonization of Latin America, examining issues of racial genocide, cultural dominance, and the erasure of history."[56] This is achieved through the completion of four different quests that will lead to the attainment of natural elements that symbolize the stages of the learning process through which the player progresses: corn, sugar, melon, and grapes.

The four quests in *Tropical America* follow different trajectories that bridge vast expanses of history and geography. The "corn" quest begins in the Mayan temple of Bonampak, then takes a somewhat less foreseeable turn, leading to an encounter in 1990s Chiapas, Mexico, in which the Zapatista National Liberation Army (EZLN) conjures the memory of their namesake, revolutionary hero Emiliano Zapata (figure 2.8). In the "melon" quest, the player attempts to deliver a melon along with a letter to Charles V, King of Spain and Holy Roman Emperor, but is derailed by parallel journeys to meet with either La Malinche or Tupac Amaru. In the "grapes" quest, the player must feed Christopher Columbus with native vegetables and fruits (he loves avocados), then encounters Sor Juana Inés de la Cruz in her colonial Mexican convent followed by a series of encounters with victims of torture and disappearance at the hands of the Latin

Figure 2.8
Tropical America (OnRamp Arts 2002)

American military regimes of the 1970s and 1980s. The "sugar" quest begins in the indigenous Taíno island territory that would soon receive its colonial name of Hispaniola. The player walks down a beach as three indigenous men pass by in their canoes, against the backdrop of the *Niña*, *Pinta*, and *Santa María* anchored in the bay. The player must produce an indigenous word like "canoe" from his inventory (it recognizes only words mentioned within the game, such as maize, avocado, and chocolate, but not other words derived from native languages such as chile or tomato), after which he is rewarded with a gold nugget.

This complex fabric of historico-cultural referentiality is put to an array of different uses throughout *Tropical America*, in an overall effort to interrogate the historical roots of contemporary violence and relationships of power. Indeed there is plenty of violence in *Tropical America*, but not exactly of the standard video game variety: first and foremost, violence is represented at an institutional level. The player is reminded time and again of historical and present inequalities through the game's discourse and gameplay. Spaniards are represented as violent (slapping María without provocation) and conniving (offering her "beads, mirrors and sugar" in exchange for her gold—a reference to the actions undertaken by members of Columbus's first expedition to the New World). Torture is enacted as punishment for participation in virtually any sort of subversive behavior in the game. Retribution for this institutionalized violence is the other side of this coin in the game: in one scenario, the player must cut the mustaches off the corpses of all the Spanish conquistadors to keep as trophies; in another, she must throw rocks at the heads of angry soldiers threatening her with bayonets. Though player agency has some effects in *Tropical America*, instances of violence are generally fixed elements of the game's narrative. For example, whether the player chooses to offer her gold to the Spaniard or not in the "Sugar" quest, the Spaniard will draw his sword and demand it. The player has no choice but to offer it, and is rewarded some sugar cane in return. Likewise, if the player decides to stay behind at the sugar mill and work for nothing rather than seeking justice for the indentured servants working there, she immediately dies of small pox as the screen flashes, "¡Perdiste! YOU LOSE!" At another point, the player must choose between five forms of torture at the hands of the Spanish colonial authorities: beating, asphyxiation, electric shock, burning, or stretching (figure 2.9). But it all comes out the same: the screen goes black and the words "(censored/censurado)" appear over the sonic backdrop of the avatar being tortured until finally being tossed out of the chamber by the Spanish guards. Nonetheless, there are other points in the narrative of *Tropical America* in which the player's decision will affect the trajectory by selecting between one of two possible trajectories, exercising player agency. For example, when the player must decide whether to (1) take on a career as a slave trader or (2) attempt to help a traveling seaman create a new business empire, choosing the former will lead to participation in a rebellion against the slave's owners, while the latter leads to a storyline taking place in contemporary Havana.

Figure 2.9
Tropical America (OnRamp Arts 2002)

Thus even when developed expressly as pedagogical tools, ideologically charged video games like *Tropical America* can be seen to employ complex systems of signification whose messages resist reduction to their narrative elements. It is the player's experience of the violence that gives it meaning as she clicks on each Spaniard's corpse in order to cut off his mustache, or chooses self-flagellation over a reading of Sor Juana's poetry. Whether gruesome or tongue-in-cheek, the game shows how even something as infinitely controversial as video game violence can be redeployed in unexpectedly revelatory ways by those willing to reexamine the potential of the medium as opposed to using it as a political commodity.

The 2005 Tijuana-San Diego-based art event inSite 05 included a number of other unique and ideologically challenging games that, like *Tropical America*, emerged out of the cross-pollination among spheres including video game design, social activism, pedagogy, academic analysis, and the visual arts. This transnational art fair was the fifth installment since inSite began in 1992 as a series of events focused on public art related to the specific context of the border region.[57] Contributions included public installations, performance-based works, and electronic works, among which were three very curious video games set along the US-Mexico border. Together these games exemplify Osvaldo Cleger's assessment that video games about border crossing "can be effectively *persuasive* in the way they manage to create computational representation of the experience of migrating, and its associated consequences, independently of

Figure 2.10
Turista Fronterizo (Ricardo Dominguez and Coco Fusco 2006)

the legal or illegal status of such displacements."[58] The first of these games, *Turista Fronterizo*, "a virtual journey through the San Diego-Tijuana borderlands,"[59] is an ironic and humorous border-themed electronic variation on *Monopoly* designed by the Cuban-American performance artist and theorist Coco Fusco and Mexican-American media artist Ricardo Dominguez (figure 2.10). Claire Taylor has rightly characterized *Turista Fronterizo* as an interrogation of the socioeconomic inequalities of border life that encourages the user to compare and contrast the experiences of characters from different sides of the border and different walks of life.[60] The player of *Turista Fronterizo* must choose between four playable avatars, each with a particular national origin, occupation, and form of transportation. Two of them are from the United States: El Gringo Poderoso, a 47-year-old binational businessman who drives a Lexus sedan, and La Gringa Activista, a 30-year-old anthropology student who drives a VW bug. The other two avatars are from Mexico: El Junior, described as a 25-year-old "huevón" ("lazy ass") who drives a Mercedes G500, and La Todológa [*sic*], a 23-year-old who does whatever work she can find and rides public transportation. Depending on the choice of player the game proceeds (almost) entirely in either English (for the US characters) or Spanish (for the Mexican characters).

Turista Fronterizo's characters' identification with their material possessions and income is indicative of the game's take on the border region, which problematizes privilege based on socioeconomic class as well as nationality. For example, El Gringo Poderoso spends lavishly but profits nonetheless: at Qualcomm Stadium, he takes a Japanese executive to the Chargers Game, spending $500 but scoring a big deal for his company. He also travels freely: at the San Ysidoro Border Checkpoint, he takes the Fast Lane but must shell out $200 to insure his Lexus; at the Castillo del Mar Hotel resort, he is told to "Have a second honeymoon. Spend $1,500." Naturally, the Gringo Poderoso is politically influential as well: at the Mexican Consulate, he is told to "Meet with consul to negotiate the sale of public land in Ensenada to US companies. Spend $300 on lunch." He is an international high roller whose privileges have a cost, but one with little impact as $100 police bribes and $1,000 fees to bring the nanny's children across the border barely make a dent in his $300,000 starting balance. Meanwhile the Gringa Activista skimps and scrapes by on a $10,000 total budget, though she still uses her money in ways that indicate her cosmopolitanism and her comfortable economic origins: she spends $100 on medicine at Farmacia Revolución to save her mother some cash, or bails out a Brazilian friend who forgot her green card, costing her $200 at the Campo Base Detention Center. Her other expenses are focused on supporting her political causes, regardless of where she might find herself: at the Bambi Club, she researches an article for Mother Jones on teenage sex slavery, spending $100 on drinks to get the bartender to chat; at Qualcomm Stadium, she spends another $100 on photocopies in order to "Hand out flyers to Mexican workers." Some of her costliest acts fall under "Nightmares," which along with "Dreams" are *Turista Fronterizo*'s equivalents of *Monopoly*'s taxes and utility bills on the one hand, and "Community Chest" and "Chance" on the other. One of the Gringa Activista's "nightmare" outcomes results from her attempt to take photographs of a maquiladora, which lands her in "La Cárcel" (labeled "Mexican Jail!" on the board played by the US characters), while her participation in a meeting to plan a protest is discovered by undercover police, leading again to her incarceration and a costly $1,000 fine. Nonetheless she also enjoys the status provided by her outwardly perceptible US nationality: when she lands on the Castillo del Mar Hotel, her outcome reads, "Hide your VW, pretend you're a guest and sip free margaritas on the beach, ¡órale!"; at the Fashion Valley Mall, she pastes stickers against worker exploitation in the Nordstrom's bathroom, but spends $100 there to avoid looking suspicious. Politically, the Gringa Activista is powerless and somewhat clueless, but she nevertheless remains economically unburdened.

Like the US characters, the Mexican protagonists of *Turista Fronterizo* are affected as much by their nationality as by economic and social factors in the game. El Junior, the quintessence of overprivileged upper-class Mexican "fresa," leads a life that in many ways is closer to that of the Gringo Poderoso than it is to either his compatriot La Todológa or the Gringa Activista, though he starts out with $50,000, one sixth of the budget enjoyed by the Gringo Poderoso (which is still five times that of the Gringa Activista). He tosses his money around by spending

$200 on "porquería" ("garbage") when he takes out his "cuates" ("homies") in Chula Vista to see the Chargers, $100 on a few tequilas and a striptease at the Bambi Club, or $250 for a bottle of perfume to earn the forgiveness of his "jefita" ("shorty"). In terms of his freedom of movement, El Junior experiences few obstacles: at the San Ysidoro Border checkpoint he hides his weed and crosses without raising suspicion; his trunk is searched by the Border Patrol but they fail to check his pockets, so he moves on. El Junior lacks the clout of the Gringo Poderoso, and in one of his "Nightmare" outcomes he is confused with a drug trafficker and has to pay $500 to the Policía Judicial for proper documentation of his identity, but he is still politically connected, able to complain to a cousin who works for the government when the smell of the Basurero del Tecate dump begins to get in the way of his trips to the beach with lovers, or to clear the way for his plan to build the nightclub of his dreams. In some ways, he is as much a "border tourist" as the Gringa Activista or any of the others, attending a conference at the Mexican Consulate on the history of tequila, but at the same time he is set apart by his relatively high level of purchasing power. La Todológa, meanwhile, is the representative of the economic underclass in *Turista Fronterizo*, starting out with a miniscule budget of $1,000 (less than one third of 1 percent of the Gringo Poderoso's money, a fiftieth of El Junior's, and only 10 percent of the Gringa Activista's). Her actions generally focus on finding odd jobs that provide tiny contributions to her income: at the Castillo del Mar Hotel she earns $10 working in the kitchen, while at the Fashion Valley Mall she makes $100 washing dishes and at the San Diego Convention Center she earns another $100 working on the cleaning staff. La Todológa's border tourism, like most of her existence, is penny-pinching: when she visits La Huerta for Day of the Dead, she spends just $1 on the public transportation to get there, though when times are tough, she will pay some criminal elements $400 to get her across the border overnight. Her familial and social responsibilities also generate significant expenses: she has to pay $100 to cover health costs for a cousin who got lung cancer from living close to the dump, and spends $50 on medicine after her boyfriend is beaten during a strike against a Hyundai sweatshop (losing all money causes the player to lose the game). Perhaps the most notable aspect of La Todológa's life is its precariousness—her very existence hangs in a balance controlled by the whims others: accused of stealing from a hotel guest where she works, she is incarcerated without further ado; when she reports to the police after having been robbed, she ends up in jail herself; when a coyote tries to turn her into a sex slave and cross the border, she loses her life savings in an attempt to escape. Because of the way it reflects the impact of privilege and nationality by providing different outcomes to the same set of circumstances depending on the attributes of the avatar being played, *Turista Fronterizo* rewards players who wish to find out how the other half lives, so to speak, by doing a bit of border tourism themselves, offering the player critical insights through the use of humor and a highly replayable and contrasting set of game dynamics.

Like *Turista Fronterizo*, media artist and scholar Rafael Fajardo's *Crosser* (2000) and *La Migra* (2001) use familiar gameplay mechanics—rather than the *Monopoly* board, the former is based on the arcade classic *Frogger* (Konami 1981), the latter *Space Invaders* (Taito/Midway 1978)—to problematize questions of personal and national security revolving around border crossing. Rita Raley explains that Fajardo's games "stage the scene of border crossing as one of collision detection"[61] through gameplay dynamics, though the procedural rhetoric these games employ has yet to be fully explored. In *Frogger*, the goal is to reach a row of secure lily pads; in *Crosser*, the stated objective is to "Get to the green card on the other side to pursue the American dream." *Crosser*, like its ludic archetype, consists of a series of rows of mobile obstacles whose movement restricts the player's progress from their starting point (the lowest playable area of screen space) to the destination (the highest playable area). In the original *Frogger*, there are a total of thirteen rows that the player must cross in order to get to the destination. Three of these are free of obstacles or threats: the starting row, the middle row (which offers the player a halftime respite after crossing the highway and prior to crossing the river), and the destination, the final row of lily pads. On the road, there are five more rows of different vehicles, and in the river there are five rows of logs, turtles, and alligators. *Crosser* operates on a relatively reduced scale, with seven traversable rows of space. Two are free of moving obstacles: the starting point on the Mexican side of the border, where the protagonist is surrounded by humble but colorful abodes and a series of prickly pear cacti, and the destination border checkpoint (figure 2.11). Floating down the river on the Mexican side of the border there are two threats: a gnarly log similar to those in *Frogger* as well as a rather unconventional obstacle, an X-eyed corpse in gang member garb (a plaid shirt buttoned only at the top over a white t-shirt, matching red cap, green fatigue pants, and shiny white sneakers). On the US side of the river there are two further items, floating kittens with their still-sharp and flailing claws, and abandoned rubber tires. Once the player makes it across the river in *Crosser*, she gets no respite as in *Frogger* but immediately faces the highway, replete with three more rows of threats: first, a squad of Border Patrol agents on foot, then a lane of the authorities' vehicles, and finally a stream of helicopters zooming overhead. In *Frogger*, the player goes from a precarious state to one of security, making her way home. In *Crosser* the topography is reversed, with the player starting out in the relative comfort of home, then having to cross the river and the highway in order to reach the goal, which instead of a secure lily pad is the looming monolith of a government visa office.

Fajardo's *La Migra* uses an interface virtually identical to that of *Crosser* but reverses the player's perspective: this time, the player's avatar is a Border Patrol vehicle that seeks to imprison, deport, or otherwise put a stop to those attempting to cross the border. Whereas the spacecraft in the original *Space Invaders* fired laser beams to destroy the descending aliens, the Border Patrol vehicle in *La Migra* launches handcuffs (figure 2.12). If the cuffs strike people

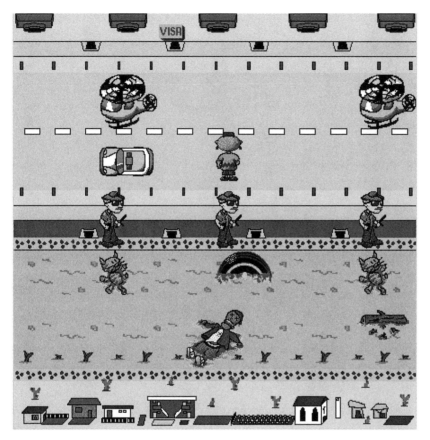

Figure 2.11
Crosser (Rafael Fajardo 2000)

crossing from the Mexican side of the border before they get to the United States, they bounce off and the character's progress continues. If they strike their target on the US side of the border, they redirect the NPC's trajectory toward an office entry labeled "Deportees" on the lower extreme of the map. The NPC then passes through the door on the US side of the border, reappears through a door marked "Repatriar" ("Repatriation") on the Mexican side, and goes right to crossing once again, creating a continual challenge for the player-as-Border Patrol agent. Should the agent become exasperated and want to do away with some of the crossers, he will have to run them down with the car, which leaves a bloody corpse in the road that is not only symbolically significant but has a ludic impact as well, as the bodies in the street restrict the movement of the Border Patrol vehicles. Like Frasca's *September 12th*, *La Migra* has no win condition: the player can only postpone losing for so long before the stream of individuals becomes

Figure 2.12
La Migra (Rafael Fajardo 2001)

too much to control given the increasing number of bodies serving as obstacles. The procedural rhetoric of *Crosser* and *La Migra* makes their message quite clear: the apparent solutions of border security and deportation do little to stymy the demand for illegal border crossing. Violent measures by the Border Patrol, meanwhile, not only make the exercise and legitimation of their own authority more difficult but also fail to address the root causes of undocumented immigration. Though the two games position players on opposite sides of the immigrant/border patrol divide, they procedurally lead toward a similar ideological critique.

Games used to persuade their players ethically and ideologically, such as the ones designed by Frasca, Dominguez and Fusco, OnRamp Arts, and Fajardo examined in this section, use retro game mechanics and basic graphics in order to make statements that are anything but simplistic. Thoughtful game design can use conventional practices for unconventional ends, persuading the player to make unexpected discoveries about the nature of violence and warfare through gameplay. These game designers also remind us that video games can capably and stirringly take on serious themes such as global terrorism and the so-called war on terror, the legacy of colonialism, civil war in El Salvador, the dangers of undocumented border crossing, and socioeconomic inequalities. Moreover, they do this in quirky and sometimes humorous ways that function harmoniously with game mechanics, evidencing how games can use an appealing and familiar interface and still provoke serious contemplation from players.

Conclusion: Beyond Persuasive Games

The importance of persuasion has been recognized in game studies for some time, but an examination of the ways games are used persuasively in contemporary culture signals a need to bring new materials, cultural contexts, and conceptual frameworks to bear on the discussion of persuasion. Bogost establishes the theoretical basis for this discussion in *Persuasive Games* by arguing: "We must recognize the persuasive and expressive power of procedurality. Processes influence us. They see changes in our attitudes, which in turn, and over time, change our culture. As players of video games and other computational artifacts, we should recognize procedural rhetoric as a new way to interrogate our world, to comment on it, to disrupt and challenge it."[62] In this chapter I have attempted to follow Bogost's lead by examining the procedural rhetoric of persuasive games like *Tropical America*, *Turista Fronterizo*, *Crosser*, and *La Migra*. These games further evidence Bogost's assertion that no game can be adequately interpreted strictly on a narrative basis, and that the procedural mechanics of gameplay hold enormous sway over the meaning created within the interactive environment of a video game.

But for better or for worse, there are other important ways that video games are used to persuade. As evidenced by the political controversies in Mexico, Venezuela, and Cuba examined in this chapter, games represent an increasingly valuable form of cultural currency even when isolated from their procedural meaning and used as political commodities. In the most drastic of cases, this has resulted in sweeping censorship measures and encroachments on intellectual freedom, such as those passed into Venezuelan law under Hugo Chávez. In the best of cases, though, it has occasioned thoughtful responses and genre-redefining takes on game design from Latin American designers seeking to take control of their country's ludic image, as with the Cuban designers of *Gesta Final*. Ever more, video games are being used to stir controversy and effect real-world changes, and it is therefore crucial to examine the ways games are used in public discourse and what effects they can produce. Analyzing games like *Call of Duty: Black Ops* and *Mercenaries 2* in terms of their depiction by public figures as well as gameplay allows us to see the ways in which reductive portrayals of games within political discourse differ fundamentally from the procedural meaning that games create for their players.

Video games are complex procedural objects that can persuade through the activation of self-contained semiotic systems. But games are also cultural commodities, and as such they can be used as instruments of persuasion even—or especially—when their meaning is divorced entirely from that which is conveyed through gameplay. The political posturing employed when video games are discussed in the public sphere must also be interpreted in terms of its own procedural rhetoric, bringing to light the disconnections and distortions frequently employed to make video games politically useful commodities. Games are being used in more and more ways today, and the analysis of video game meaning must now turn beyond the internal procedures and rhetorical devices of game design in order to understand just how persuasive games can be for contemporary culture.

3   POTENTIAL

This chapter examines how video games are used in Latin America for the purpose of their creative and economic potential. In other words, it explores the history of game development in countries throughout the region, as well as surveying the state of game production in Latin America today. While a generation ago there was virtually no infrastructure to support the region's burgeoning community of game designers and programmers, opportunities for game development, publishing, distribution, and related fields of production are expanding rapidly. This expansion is the result of a number of factors seen in cases across Latin America, including an increase in public policy initiatives in support of national game industries, the development of new advanced degree programs in game-related disciplines at institutions of higher education, the implementation of game industry incubator projects, and the growth of a supportive and nurturing community of game developers and designers through game expos, industry events, and professional collaboration. Using the conceptual model provided by the convergence of factors that propelled the Latin American Boom in literature of the 1960s and 70s, I argue that a series of adaptations and evolutions within the regional game industry have come together to create the ideal conditions for a twenty-first-century Latin American Boom in video game design and development. Though speaking of a "Boom" of this type could seem hyperbolic, anachronistic, or far-fetched to experts in Latin American literary and culture production, it should not. To be sure, the determining conditions of the Latin American Boom—a period when the popularity of novelists like Gabriel García Márquez, Carlos Fuentes, Mario Vargas Llosa, and Julio Cortázar skyrocketed, making them international celebrities—differ considerably from the conditions surrounding contemporary game design and development in Latin America. However there are similarities worth exploring as well, and an informed understanding of the multiple factors that brought about the original Latin American Boom illustrates how a dynamic combination of elements can produce a whole that is greater than the sum of its parts.

Experts in Latin American literature acknowledge that the Boom was the result of more than just the talent of its most well-known authors, and this recognition began when these novelists' works first hit the market. In his personal memoir of the period, Chilean novelist José Donoso emphasizes that the Boom was not only defined by a number of high-quality novels from throughout the region, but was also shaped by political events like the Cuban Revolution along with the influences of publishers, journal editors, literary prize juries, agents, and critics, and above all by the accusations of the Boom's detractors.[1] With the benefit of several decades of critical distance, Raymond Leslie Williams was able to clearly synthesize the strands contributing to the Boom, which he describes as "the result of the fortunate confluence of numerous individuals, institutions, and circumstances, among them the literary agent Carmen Balcells, the appearance of a brilliant translator (Gregory Rabassa), the Cuban Revolution, publishers Harper and Row in the United States and Seix Barral in Spain, the rise of international Latin Americanism as an academic discipline, and the publication of the literary magazine *Mundo Nuevo* in Paris."[2] For Jean Franco, the Boom represents all of this and also an exercise in exoticism, with its characteristic magical realism constituting "an appropriation of racial difference" and "an invigorating bath in Latin American originality" that made the movement so attractive to regional and international audiences alike.[3] Descriptions such as those of Donoso, Williams, and Franco highlight the extent to which the Latin American Boom consisted of strands of influence from many different sectors of society that came together to produce an explosive socioliterary phenomenon.

Today, a new confluence of conditions is setting the stage for another period of explosive growth, this time in game design. Again, this should not seem altogether surprising to those familiar with the subject. Several years ago, Aarseth predicted a global boom in "game auteurism" in the 2010s, anticipating games with unique visions "that emerge from strong, talented individuals as a conscious reaction to an industry where production costs, 'sequelitis' and licenses dominate the field."[4] In recent years, press and industry sources across Latin America have referred to rapid growth in the burgeoning game industry precisely as a "boom,"[5] and Argentina's Ministry of Economic Development cites the growth in the popularity of casual games as the basis for "the boom in the sector [of game design] over the past several years."[6] Like the Latin American Boom in literature, this explosive growth in game development and design is the result of a number of intertwining factors: a global consumer base, support from international organizations, enterprises, and individuals, widespread prominence in the news media and among communities of interest, translation and localization efforts to gain exposure in new markets, and a shared investment in the region's political and creative future. Though the contemporary context is of course different than the situation of Latin America's novelists a half century ago, knowledge of the multitude of factors that contribute to explosive growth in the field of cultural production helps illustrate the very real meaning of *potential* with regard to the future of Latin American game development.

Obstacles and Affordances to Latin American Game Design

The history of game development in Latin America is remarkably rich, especially when one takes into account the number of significant obstacles that the region's game designers have had to overcome in order to bring their work to light. Chief among these obstacles are: (1) lack of official support and governmental incentives for the game industry; (2) scarcity of education and training programs in software and game design; (3) widespread "digital poverty,"[7] especially in rural areas, and slow development of national and regional audiences; (4) a shortage of experienced game designers capable of providing guidance to younger startups; and (5) the demand to adapt local practices to global expectations. Unlike those working in game and software production centers like Silicon Valley or Montreal, Latin American game designers have historically produced their work in an atmosphere of relative isolation, with most early developers in the region working with small groups of friends, family, and associates and figuring out the process of putting games together from scratch.

And in spite of these obstacles, the region has produced the type of creative output that demonstrates the particular affordances pertaining to Latin American game design. Distance from the centers of the game industry may partially account for creative and outside-of-the-box game design such as the surreal gamescapes of *Zeno Clash* (2009) (figure 3.1) and *Rock of Ages* (2011) from Chile's ACE Team, or *Mr. Patch* (2014), a pioneering game by Paraguayan designer Gabriela Galilea that uses eye-tracking technology to provide sufferers of strabismus with ocular exercises that ultimately help correct their condition.[8] Breakthroughs like these provide a vision of what the Latin American game design industry can be, if we pay attention to focal points like those identified by Marisca in his analysis of the Peruvian game industry, including "building a critical mass of developers and studios, increasing the quality of their production and process and engaging international markets, and raising the industry's visibility and public profile in the local context."[9] Indeed, these tendencies will be of increasing importance to regional game development in the near future.

As Latin American game development has come into existence over the last several decades, it has been enabled by affordances including: (1) unique creative visions working both inside and outside of conventional cultural motifs; (2) the support of a community of like-minded game designers through events like game jams as well as more or less formally arranged creative collaborations; (3) the rise of casual games as a major focus in the global games industry along with an increasingly large local gaming audience; (4) a growing presence of industry

Figure 3.1
Zeno Clash (ACE Team 2009)

incubators and events designed to assist startup designers in getting on their feet; and (5) increasing efforts by policymakers to incentivize and promote the game design industry as an area of major economic potential. Together, these factors have contributed to the development of a vibrant and flourishing game industry that is operating in every single country in Latin America today, though taking full advantage of this potential will require considerable expanded efforts in the coming years.

When it comes to global industries like game design, it is frequently assumed that the common culture of the industry defines its development more significantly than national or regional contexts. Martín-Barbero has suggested that the circulation of contemporary cultural products has created transnational "cultures without territorial memory, or where place takes second place."[10] And even while the practices of these deterritorialized subcultures—the global culture of the game industry being one example—can be considered placeless, they are nonetheless determined in other ways by national context. The nation remains a significant frame for looking at game design because of crucial factors determined at the national level: each country has independent taxation and trade policies, educational and industrial infrastructure, and economic impediments and incentives for software development. This means that the way a given governing administration defines the country's posture toward the game industry can significantly impact the development of the creative industries at the national level, above and beyond the tendencies reflected in regional or global data.

An analysis of new media production in Latin America offers innumerable insights on the ways global cultural industries are developed at the local level. In his exploration of software development in the "wrong place" of Rio de Janeiro, Brazil, Takhteyev builds on Giddens's concept of *disembedding*, explaining that the cultural assumptions inherent in practices and knowledge produced at the dominant "centers" are simply expected to be incorporated into the development of those practices by "peripheral actors."[11] In Takhteyev's words, "central actors can 'disembed' their knowledge using the simplest strategy available, leaving others the hard work of reembedding it at the periphery."[12] Practices at the periphery, on the other hand, must be "actively disconnected" from the local context in order "to make reembedding at the center a trivial task," and therefore the needs of local users are subordinated to global norms.[13] Moreover, as Hjorth has explained, by "investigating a context outside the well-known and frequently cited locations such as the US," we can gain an appreciation of how each location within the global games industry incorporates particular practices specific to its own local technoculture.[14] Marisca also highlights the significance of national context in his exploration of how "[s]pecific national game industries have grown out of various entanglements with parallel or overlapping industries," juxtaposing the Peruvian industry's "informal and experimental origins" to the US industry's roots in computer science or the Japanese industry's roots in the local toy and animation industries.[15] These analyses allow us to perceive the impact of national and cultural factors on game development, showing how the seemingly "leveled" playing field of the globalized software industry is in fact quite asymmetrical.

Latin America's place within the geography of the global game industry is shifting rapidly, bringing about an expansion in the creative and economic potential of video games throughout the region. After winning the Nuovo Award for his simple yet innovative game *Storyteller* (2008 alpha, 2012 beta) at the Independent Game Festival in San Francisco in 2012, Argentine designer Daniel Benmergui offered a note of inspiration to his fellow Latin Americans in the game industry: "I'm sorry about this, English speakers," Benmergui explained, "but, quiero mandarle un saludo a todos los hermanos latinoamericanos e hispanoparlantes para que sepan que, digamos, estoy yo acá, entonces, acá puede estar cualquiera. ¡Incluso nosotros!" ("I'd like to send a shout-out to all my Latin American and Spanish-speaking brothers and sisters so that they know that, you know, I'm here, so anyone could make it here. Even us!")[16] Benmergui's speech was a nod to the substantial but often overlooked Latin American presence in the game industry, a recognition of the region's impact on the field of game design as a whole. He was awarded for the creative potential displayed in *Storyteller* and his other games (figure 3.2). These include *Today I Die* (2010), a Flash animation game that requires the player to rearrange

Figure 3.2
Storyteller (Daniel Benmergui 2012)

Figure 3.3
Today I Die (Daniel Benmergui 2010)

Figure 3.4
I Wish I Were the Moon (Daniel Benmergui 2008)

the words within a poem in order to change the game's tone and narrative from a dark and melancholy to bright and hopeful (figure 3.3), as well as *I Wish I Were the Moon* (2008), in which the player generates a series of simulated dramatic scenarios through manipulation of simple graphic *sprites*, or functional animated objects (figure 3.4). Benmergui's award-winning games demonstrate how an increasingly robust Latin American game industry is making its presence known on the global stage.

There are those within the game industry who believe that such a thing as a "Latin point of view" exists, but few would express it in such a simplistic manner. Colombian journalist Nicolás Rueda argues that representing one's cultural perspective does not mean just making games about the drug trade or other well-worn national themes: "It's not about making games that portray a particular version of reality, just the opposite. It's about using everyday life in Latin America to infuse a game with its own style."[17] Rueda's argument will surely ring true with anyone who has read "The Argentine Writer and Tradition" by Jorge Luis Borges, which proclaims that "either being Argentine is an inescapable act of fate—and in that case we shall be so in all events—or being Argentine is a mere affectation, a mask."[18] Borges's essay is a declaration of war on the literary nationalists who "pretend to venerate the capacities of the Argentine mind but want to limit the poetic exercise of that mind to a few impoverished local themes, as if we Argentines could only speak of *orillas* and *estancias* and not of the universe."[19] This struggle between national flavor and universal relevance is certainly nothing new, but it is taking on different dimensions in light of the particular demands faced by contemporary Latin American game designers.

Like Benmergui in his acceptance speech, some Latin American game designers produce their work at least in part to emphasize the growing potential for regional game design. This reflects a desire to support and build the region's game industry, as well as to declare a national presence on the global territory of game development. In such an environment, local and global concerns can compete for priority. For example, when developing *Breach* (2014), a multiplayer tower defense game for Android and iOS, Puerto Rican studio Space Rhino Games set out with a "100 percent Puerto Rican" development plan, but had to turn to assistance from New York in order to secure sufficient funding to complete the project—due in part to factors beyond their control, including investors' negative perceptions regarding industry talent in Puerto Rico.[20] Still other designers use national culture as the foundation for their games' content, like Peru's Pariwana Studios, whose designers explain that their aim is to produce games that travel "from Peru to the world" by "using Peruvian cultural heritage as our main asset."[21] So in spite of an enduring perception of the video game industry as a phenomenon of global homogenization, there are still many who maintain the importance of looking at their portion of the game design industry as particularly Puerto Rican, Peruvian, or Latin American.

Game designers, of course, must always work with forms of cultural representation that are abstracted from the realities to which they allude, and this invariably involves a process of simplification and reduction. But there are different ways of portraying culture in video games, depending on the decisions made by game designers according to their expectations of their products' audience. It is not the same to represent national culture in a game designed primarily for national consumption—say, the Argentine card game simulator *Truco* (Ariel and Enrique Arbiser 1982; to be discussed further), which is loaded with in-jokes and a vast array of cultural signifiers—as it is to represent national culture in a game designed primarily for international consumption, for example *Brasil Quest* (Embratur 2012), a casual game sponsored by the Brazilian Tourism Board that was developed to introduce a global gaming audience to the twelve host cities of the 2014 World Cup, reducing those cities to their most globally recognizable icons. Many of the games that most successfully represent traditional cultural motifs do so with an eye to their own national audience as at least part of the potential consumer base, compelling their designers to "keep it real" for the in crowd as well as outsiders. These games succeed where others have failed because they treat culture not as "something static and clearly bound, with precise beginnings and ends" but as "messy and permanently under redesign, in constant collision and articulation with other cultures."[22] Examples include games like those highlighted in Marisca's study, *Inka Madness* (Magia Digital 2013) and *Guacamelee!* (Drinkbox 2013), as well as *Lucha Libre AAA: Héroes del Ring*.

But at the same time, there is a strong current of game design that eschews the local in favor of the universal, making games that are Latin American in spite of, rather than because of, their content. Examples abound, and include the aforementioned *Zeno Clash*, a surreal fantasy-world first-person fighting game for consoles and PCs, or *Kingdom Rush* (Ironhide 2011), a fantasy-themed castle-defense mobile game replete with tiny ogres, knights, and flying dragons (figure 3.5). The latter has proven an enormous commercial success for Uruguay's Ironhide Studios, which got its start with *Clash of the Olympians* (2010) (figure 3.6) and has since released the successful sequels *Kingdom Rush: Frontiers* (2013) and *Kingdom Rush: Origins* (2014) (figure 3.7). On their surface, games like these would seem to have little to do with Latin America—their designers, like Borges, see the universe as their workshop. This has both cultural and economic implications, as developers choose between universal appeal and local specificity for a number of reasons. Bolivian designer Carlos Olivera expressly sought to reach US and European

Figure 3.5
Kingdom Rush (Ironhide 2011)

Figure 3.6
Clash of the Olympians (Ironhide 2010)

audiences with *Hooligan Alone* (Island of the Moon 2014), in which the player sneaks around as a rival soccer fan avoiding trouble from opposing hooligans and officers of the law while traversing riots in the opposing team's home neighborhood. Olivera explains that his Bolivian design team focused on quality, design, and presentation in order to make it an appealing export, modifying game design according to the anticipated expectations of that external market.[23] In this way, to paraphrase Takhteyev's argument regarding software production at the periphery, game designers operating in Latin America are required to produce work disembedded from their cultural environment, while embedding into their practices the norms defined in the centers of the creative industries. Clearly, Latin American games like *Hooligan Alone* or *Kingdom Rush* do not need to show any "local color" or "Latin flavor" in order to be Latin American. Content notwithstanding, these are Latin American games due to the context of their design and the origins of their designers, and they are also demonstrations of how culture shapes game development at every turn.

Though innovative game design has existed in Latin America virtually since the onset of the video game medium, it has generally lacked visibility and critical mass. As recently as 2002, Jairo Lugo, Tony Sampson, and Merlyn Lossada argued that there was "little opportunity to create an indigenous games industry" in Latin America, concluding that it was "improbable

Figure 3.7
Kingdom Rush: Origins (Ironhide 2014)

that the region would have the opportunity to offer its own version of *Space Invaders*—as the television did with the *telenovelas*—because the market and the industry have already been colonized and the economic actors appear to be from another planet."[24] The passing of several years and a growing corpus of documentation on game design in Latin America show us that by the time of that article's publication, there were already a great many hackers, programmers, and game designers actively at work on these types of projects in the region. However, the authors' cautious conclusion is understandable from the standpoint of an economic environment characterized by 1990s neoliberal free trade agreements like NAFTA, which allowed the game industry and a vast array of other sectors of the business world to expand their manufacturing operations into Latin America, particularly in the US-Mexico border region. This is what Lugo et al. are referring to when they explain how companies like Microsoft and Nintendo have developed "a manufacturing-marketing model for video games in Latin America based on local assembly-lines, located in 'special' economic areas where the main components were shipped from abroad with very little added value from the local industrial community," in a scheme "widely described in Latin America as the model of *Máquilas*,"[25] regional terminology for sweatshop manufacturing and assembly facilities aimed at increasing corporate bottom lines through outsourcing designed to exploit inexpensive foreign labor.

Over a decade later, the Latin American game industry is becoming less about máquilas and more about monetization. Estimated annual revenues for 2014 topped US$1 billion in Brazil and Mexico, respectively making them the eleventh and fourteenth highest-ranked nations in the globe for game revenues, in a region that produced over US$3 billion in total sales.[26] Official industry data from Mexico, one of the region's largest video game producers as well as consumers, reflect the scope of recent transformations: from 2004 to 2011, the Mexican national video game industry experienced average annual growth of 17.1 percent.[27] Phenomena like these are indicative of a sea change in the Latin American game industry over the past decade or so, making it necessary to reexamine the complex and varied terrain of regional game development, as Lugo himself would later suggest by calling for "a more nuanced analysis" that "attends to the specificities of Latin America's diverse media systems and their relation to global trends."[28] Indeed, since 2002 even foreign corporations like Microsoft, Sony, and Apple have begun to shift their operations in the region, increasing efforts to produce gaming consoles and consumer electronics for regional consumption rather than strictly for exportation to the United States and Europe. When Microsoft decided to start manufacturing 17,000 Xbox 360 consoles per week in Brazil in 2011, the company's primary focus was to make its products more attractive to local consumers: Xbox console prices dropped 40 percent in Brazil, subscription prices for Xbox LIVE were slashed, and the Xbox Kinect bundle brought the brand's motion-sensing technology to the Brazilian market for the first time.[29] This allowed the company to bring the price for an Xbox 360 down to R$799 (US$425), which in spite of being one of the console's highest price points worldwide, put Microsoft at a significant sales advantage over the PlayStation 3 and Wii, which were introduced at R$1,399 and R$999 (US$750 and US$535) respectively. These changes reflect a growing interest from the mainstream games industry in exploiting the potential sales base of Latin American console gamers, who now number nearly 200 million.[30]

Though each country's situation is distinct, the Argentine case is in many ways typical of the challenges and accomplishments of burgeoning national game industries in the region, illustrating the characteristic transformations that game design in Latin America has undergone over the past decade or so. Some seventy small- to medium-sized game design firms are currently operating in Argentina, creating 800 jobs and generating a combined US$90 million in annual revenues.[31] Between 2006 and 2008 alone, the proceeds of the Argentine national game industry increased by nearly 350 percent, while employment in the field rose more than 150 percent.[32] This meteoric growth has begun to stabilize but still indicates the development of a strong national industry—from 2009 to 2010, proceeds and employment levels both grew an additional 40 percent.[33] As in other Latin American cases, game development is undertaken with an eye to the global market and the industry is heavily concentrated in the country's major urban center: three out of every four Argentine game design firms focus on foreign markets, and nearly nine out of ten are based in the capital city of Buenos Aires.[34] In 2010, some 70 percent of the games produced by Argentine designers were web games, with only about one in fifty titles produced for nonportable game consoles.[35] In terms of publication and distribution, many firms aspire to one day market their games directly to consumers, using the typical monetization strategies of free-to-play apps, which rely on in-game purchases and upgrades. However the prohibitively high amount of capital necessary to market a game directly to consumers means that most Argentine game designers (nearly four out of every five) make games that will either be sold to advertising agencies or second-party publishers.[36] Likewise, only one fifth of the games produced in Argentina are their authors' own intellectual property, and nearly 90 percent of the national industry's proceeds come from third-party services offered to foreign game publishers and advertising firms.[37]

On the whole, the Argentine national industry is growing steadily in the twenty-first century, but it faces significant challenges, which by and large are typical of other regional cases. Argentine game designers face a scant internal market that is deeply impacted by a high incidence of software piracy, a resultant high level of dependency on foreign markets, and elevated turnover and mortality rates for small firms—40 percent of companies surveyed in 2006 had ceased to exist by 2009—as well as scarcity of financing and capital for foreign travel and project development.[38] More than half of the country's design firms were established within the five years prior to data collection, and many of them stress the need to increase sustainability in the national industry in the years to come.[39] However even in the face of these challenges, the Argentine game industry's level of growth has been remarkable. While most Argentine industries have declined in earnings over the past several years, video games have enjoyed sustained growth that has also increased job offerings in peripheral industries like music production, design, animation, and software engineering.[40] The advent of casual games and online gaming is a boon to the national industry as well, with access to touch-screen mobile devices and social media increasing significantly nationwide.[41] Government policy has also encouraged the industry by offering game designers legal protection for their intellectual property, reducing income taxes, offering business financing, and eliminating fiscal barriers to exportation.[42]

The transformations to Argentina's national game industry, as well as its challenges and successes, are mirrored in cases across Latin America, with notable variations and exceptions. The typical national game industry in the region today is largely concentrated in the nation's capital, shows increasing signs of health and sometimes surprising rates of growth, but remains dependent upon foreign markets and outsourcing rather than direct sales of unique intellectual property. Governmental policy and corporate support are increasing the Latin American game industry's sustainability, but it still faces high rates of turnover. Casual games are booming and audiences are expanding and diversifying as a result, but fighting piracy and building a sustainable national audience remain major concerns for national game industries. These factors provide a basic snapshot of the Latin American game industry today, but they do not reveal the historical roots of that industry. In order to fully understand the current state of affairs, we must go back to the origins of Latin American video game development.

Software Modification and Independent Game Development

As noted previously, the early history of game design in Latin America is sparsely documented and requires considerable effort to reconstruct, even partially. Various countries in the region have undergone successive waves of video game design starting by the early 1980s, but few enduring design firms were able to stand the test of time until the first decade of the twenty-first century. The early examples of Latin American game design that can be identified offer insights into the ways the region's up-and-coming software engineers and game designers were adding their own cultural perspectives into their games. A quintessential example is the 1982 game *Truco* by the Argentine nephew-and-uncle design team of Ariel and Enrique Arbiser (figure 3.8). A digital version of a popular traditional card game, *Truco* has been identified by the Argentine Video Game Association (ADVA) and other sources as the first commercial video game ever created in Argentina, and possibly in all of Latin America.[43]

In addition to using a card game beloved by the national audience, *Truco* appealed to Argentine players through the incorporation of local language and wordplay—it was perhaps most beloved by its audience for the way it incorporated the poetic national version of "trash talk" into gameplay, including taunts such as, "Si no me convidas con Cerveza, por lo menos ofreceme un Envido." ("If you're not going to get me a Beer, at least give me a Bluff") and fragments of the popular rhymes used by players of Truco, including, "Pa' pintar una pared/ Tuve que usar mameluco,/ y pa' ganarle a Usted/ tengo que hacerle algún truco" ("To paint a room/ it was the coveralls I picked/ and to beat you/ I'm going to have to pull a trick"), "Tengo apuro por ganar y no quiero padecer, Truco te voy a cantar para poderte vencer" ("I don't want to suffer and I'm in a rush to win, So I'll just call out 'Trick' and thus I'll do you in"), and "Un gaucho bajó del cielo/ en un plato volador,/ al pasar junto a una vaca,/ Real Envido le gritó" ("A gaucho on a flying saucer/ came down from the sky/ when he passed by a cow/ Royal Bluff he cried"). Best of all, when the player wins, the game's readout announces, in an ironic play on the human–machine interface, "Yo perdí ... es cierto/ pero puse calor humano ... / y vos

Figure 3.8
Truco (Ariel and Enrique Arbiser 1982)

parecías una fría máquina" ("I lost ... it's true/ but I gave human warmth ... / and you were as cold as a machine").

The Arbisers were pioneers in Argentine game design, going on to publish a number of other games from the early 1980s on in spite of the many limitations they faced. These not only included technical specs such as the limited RAM for memory and execution of design elements—they could only use three colors in addition to the background color at the time they wrote the program for *Truco*, for example—but also the difficulties presented by widespread unauthorized circulation of their work in the form of multiple pirated versions of *Truco* that were published and distributed at different points in the game's history.[44] Though their trajectory is singular and shows the way that each game corresponds to the particularities of its national context, similar pioneering cases were popping up in other countries throughout Latin America over the course of the 1980s into the early 1990s.

Like many early game developers, Brazilian electronics firm Tectoy (founded in 1987) made its business in part by adapting imported games like *Phantasy Star* (Sega 1991) and *Street Fighter II* for the national market. *Mônica no Castelo do Dragão* (*Monica in the Dragon's Castle*, 1991) was a modification of *Wonder Boy in Monster Land* (Sega 1988), in which "a neutral Wonder Boy was replaced by Mônica, a very popular and charismatic Brazilian comic character."[45] In addition to adapting and localizing games, Tectoy was also the contractual manufacturer and distributor of Sega hardware in Brazil, giving the Japanese game company an official foothold in South America and allowing it to control 75 percent of the official Brazilian video game market by 1995,[46] far ahead of the international leader Nintendo, whose initial entry to Brazil had not come until 1993.[47] Tectoy was successful enough that they not only produced games for the national consumption but also exported localized versions of games to other growing South American markets. One example is the 1989 game *Chapolim x Dracula. Um Duelo Assustador* (*Chapulín vs. Dracula: A Frightening Duel*), a port of the game *Ghost House* (Sega 1986) that Tectoy had localized by replacing the protagonist with the famous Mexican television character Chapulín Colorado, also wildly popular in Brazil.[48] This sort of localization was an early outlet for the creative potential of game programmers in Brazil and elsewhere in Latin America, paving the way for the major cultural localization efforts of the global game market today.[49]

The case of Peru, like other national examples, parallels these Argentine and Brazilian models in significant ways. Marisca traces the roots of Peru's game industry to an early venture in *advergaming*, the 1987 game *Aventuras D'Onofrio*, developed by a local software firm for a promotion that allowed players to acquire the game by collecting and trading in ice cream wrappers.[50] But it is a collective known as the Twin Eagles Group, or TEG, that both Marisca and Luis Wong cite as the founding fathers of Peruvian game design in their respective academic and journalistic work on the subject. TEG, which was active between 1989 and 2013, started when sixteen-year-old Lobsang Alvites returned to Peru after a stint studying in Italy, where he had been impressed with the way an indie development scene had arisen "by creating demos and intros and distributing modified software done by hackers," leading him to wonder, "Why not do the same in Peru?"[51] TEG was a grassroots effort built from the ground up, with group members learning to "crack" and copy imported games by reverse-engineering software in order to manipulate its source code: "They observed how the software functioned on the level of memory in order to deduce how the changes they made to the running software altered the results on the screen, and then they assembled modifications like these until they got the desired result."[52] Eventually, Marisca notes, "[t]heir *cracking* started to get creative."[53] One example of this creative initiative is *Fútbol Excitante* (*Exciting Soccer*, 1997), a modification of the Super Nintendo game *International Superstar Soccer* (Konami 1995). *Fútbol Excitante* "was modified to include the teams and players of the local soccer league, which was of course well beyond the range of Konami's interest, but which made the game much more interesting for the local market than the nonmodified alternatives"[54] (figure 3.9). Thus *Fútbol Excitante* is an example of the ways the culturally rooted preferences of local designers and gamers have long affected regional video game development practices.

Figure 3.9
Fútbol Excitante (TEG 1997)

TEG also produced a number of other modified versions of existing games, including the first Peruvian game ever published and released to the European and US markets, *Gunbee F-99* (APC & TCP 1998), a vertical shooting game to which the TEG team had added a level full of references to Peru's geography and history.[55] They also produced an erotically themed Tetris mod called *Samba de Oruga* (*Caterpillar Samba*, 2003), which they self-published and circulated as a unique version of pay-as-you-wish shareware they called *pollada-ware*, or *chicken party-ware*, in reference to a Peruvian type of potluck dinner[56] (figure 3.10). The latter was made in an

Figure 3.10
Samba de Oruga (TEG 2003)

attempt to pay legal fees incurred in a dispute over the political parody *The King of Peru 2* (2001), a fighting game in which the player chooses from a selection of characters including presidential candidates Alejandro Toledo, Alan García, and Alberto Fujimori. TEG had partnered with a local publisher, but that publisher was also deeply involved in local game piracy and turned to selling pirated copies of *King of Peru 2* without TEG's permission, ultimately contributing to the group's dissolution.[57]

Like Brazil's Tectoy as well as many independent game designers, TEG got their start in Peru through the practice of software modification, pointing to the need for a more nuanced critical understanding of this phenomenon, whose complexity exceeds the limiting label of piracy. The concept of software modification, or *modding*, refers not only to software piracy but also "to various ways of extending and altering officially released computer games, their graphics, sounds and characters, with custom-produced content," which "can also mean creating new game mechanics and new gameplay levels (maps) to the point where the original game transforms into a completely new title."[58] Commercial piracy is just one way that the practice of software modification has impacted the history of regional game development, and an often-misunderstood one at that. Piracy implies economic opportunism on the part of the pirating entrepreneur, but it has arisen historically from a lack of viable commercial opportunities as major game manufacturers either ignored Latin America as a potential market, or saw their products' prices rise to prohibitively high levels due to high importation taxes. And in countries without the kind of established software development industry that might allow competent programmers a viable outlet for their craft, the environment was ripe for the development of creative products using the tools at hand, even if those tools consisted of software published by another party.

Should we be surprised, then, by the way Latin American game designers frequently used products created by others as a basis for their own production? No and yes. Jenkins sees modding as an example of "grassroots convergence" in which modders "build on code and design tools created for commercial games as a foundation for amateur game production," arguing that on the one hand "it should be no surprise that much of what the public creates models itself after, exists in dialogue with, reacts to or against, and/or otherwise repurposes materials drawn from commercial culture."[59] But on the other hand, and particularly in the Latin American context, we should be surprised that *any* type of software development was possible at this early stage given the obstacles in its way. The presence of significant pockets of modders throughout Latin America "gave the local community important opportunities while faced with the absence of formal circuits and consolidated industries."[60] In this way, modding has provided an education in software engineering through hands-on experience as well as access to a community with shared interests and knowledge.

In fact, rather than simple theft of intellectual property, I would argue that software modification is more accurately characterized as an act of "counterconsumption," to use Alberto Moreiras's term for "a particular mode of relation to consumption from within consumption" that involves "the preservation of a sort of residual subject sovereignty or local singularity."[61] Though software modification is fundamentally linked to practices of consumption, its relationship to those practices operates beyond the traditional norms of commercial exchange. Indeed many mods, such as those circulated by TEG in Peru, were made without concern for financial gain: true to their roots in Lima's community of Commodore 64 programmers, "TEG states that they did not receive any profit whatsoever (although on occasions they charged in order to compensate for the effort invested) and they incentivized the distribution of their software through the then-novel Bulletin Board Systems (BBS) and 'copy parties' organized by the group itself, where visitors could bring their own 5" floppy disks and take away copies of the latest software *cracked* by the group."[62] Similarly but in a different context, when Ecuadorian game designer Estefano Palacios recalls his start in game design at age fourteen, he remembers focusing not on the potential for profit but on the support of a community that fed upon a mutual interest in the inner workings of computer software and hardware: "We were just hacking our way, machete-style, through our own code … trying to get cool experiences with the simplest tools."[63] These types of counterconsumptive practices show a greater concern for the nurturing of the software development community, a stand-in for absent national game-design infrastructure, than for profiting personally or as a business. It has been noted that modding is a social activity in more than one sense, one in which the modder can exercise agency by authoring a new artifact, as well as contributing to a collaborative effort by a network of enthusiasts with shared interests.[64] In this sense, the "modding scene" itself, along with the software development community it nurtured, can be seen as the most significant products of the history of software modification practices prevalent in Latin America.

Both licensed mods like *Chapolim x Dracula* and unlicensed mods like *Samba de Oruga* or *Fútbol Excitante* represent an effort to culturally recontextualize games in order to increase their appeal for a specific consumer base. Nowadays, the game industry overall has come to embrace this type of modding, recognizing it as beneficial rather than harmful to its commercial interests and therefore opening up to ways of blurring the boundary between player and creator by encouraging the development of user-produced content.[65] As Jenkins has explained, "the modding process may prolong the shelf life of the product, with the modding community keeping alive the public interest in a property that is no longer necessarily state-of-the-art technologically."[66] In this way, modding benefits the game's publishers by providing a continual stream of content that keeps interest in their product alive, with little to no additional effort on their part.

Within the Latin American context, the phenomenon known as *MVP Caribe* (2007) offers a clear example of how modding can create this "prolonged shelf life" effect. The game is a modification of *MVP Baseball 2005* (EA 2005), which was publisher EA Sports' final entry in the baseball simulator series prior to the transfer of licensing for Major League Baseball video games to 2K Sports, after which *MVP Baseball 2005* seemed destined to fade into the repetitive history of sports game sequels. But then something unforeseen occurred: it was picked up by a community of mostly Venezuelan modders (with some help from Mexico and the Dominican Republic) who set to creating a "full conversion mod" of the game, one in which the entire content of the game is transformed in order to create a new overall experience for players.[67] In the case of *MVP Caribe*, this meant programming in a great deal of culturally and regionally specific content: "28 national baseball teams—the 16 participants of WBC [World Baseball Classic] 13 with their accurate uniforms, plus 12 teams that played in the tournament's qualifying round,"[68] as well as thirty real-life stadiums from Mexico, Puerto Rico, the Dominican Republic, Venezuela, and Cuba, each one introduced by renowned professional baseball announcer Oscar Soria, who agreed to do the voiceover work for free based on the mod's positive reputation in the world of Mexican professional sports.[69] Since it was first released in October 2007, *MVP Caribe* has been updated continually through collaborative volunteer efforts by the modding community that puts it together, with painstaking detail going into the accuracy of rosters and uniforms. The game has become popular enough to be considered the "unofficial national baseball video game in countries like the Dominican Republic, Venezuela, and Mexico," and has even earned official endorsements from the Venezuelan Professional Baseball League (LVBP) and the Mexican Pacific League (LMP).[70] In this way, *MVP Caribe* is representative of the massive potential for growth in Latin American game development.

Modding has had a major impact on Latin American game design, with projects like those described giving way more recently to local versions of globally popular casual games like *Flappy Quetzal* (Carlos Villagrán 2014) and *NicaBird* (Ninfusds Estudio 2014), two recent mods from Guatemalan and Nicaraguan designers, respectively, of the simple but addictive independent hit *Flappy Bird* (Dong Nguyen 2013) (figure 3.11). Notably, the makers of *Flappy Quetzal* and *NicaBird* distributed their work for free, highlighting a desire to contribute to a growing sense of potential in their national game industries, whether by "showing Guatemalans that programming is easy and that, if you want to do it, you can,"[71] or by demonstrating "that if we put our heads together, we Nicaraguans can do great things."[72] In the absence of sustained national game industries and the nurturing community of experienced designers, modding has provided a practical outlet for Latin American game developers as well as building the necessary networks of experience and collaboration for the eventual establishment of independent game

Figure 3.11
Flappy Quetzal (Carlos Villagrán 2014)

development companies. Software modification has historically been, and remains today, a significant starting point for a game industry that has contributed to an increasing body of collective professional experience and thus enhanced the industry's sustainability in the region.

Nurturing the Creative Ecosystem of the Latin American Game Industry

Given the creative potential that can be observed in the tradition of Latin American software modification, it is understandable that one of the longstanding goals of the region's developers has been the establishment of a sustainable professional community in game design and publishing. While most countries in the region are still in the process of nurturing the type of "technology, entrepreneurship and innovation ecosystems"[73] necessary for sustaining an enduring game design industry, interest in professionalization efforts is increasing among industry insiders and has even been expressed by high-ranking politicians. After having served two terms as president of the Dominican Republic, Leonel Fernández now concentrates in part on defining the country's "digital agenda," including the creation of incentives for the video game industry, emphasizing the need for games and simulations with "national content."[74] Martín-Barbero highlights the role of public policy in fostering the creative and economic potential of cultural production in the global economy, explaining that "cultural identity will continue to be narrated and constructed in new media and audiovisual forms, but only if the communications industry is held accountable to cultural policies capable of accounting for what the mass media take from, and do with, the everyday culture of the people."[75] Across Latin America today, legislators are taking positive steps toward the development of policies designed to foster growth and stability in the region's game industry, while game designers are putting the medium to use for an expanding array of purposes.

And indeed, governmental support—in the form of cultural policy designed to promote and protect the region's game producers—is an integral part of the formula for the consolidation of a sustainable and robust game industry in Latin America. Other factors include the establishment of a "game design culture" through a number of institutions of varying levels of formality—for example, game jams and design competitions offer young designers a chance to develop and showcase their skills, while state-run and private incubator and accelerator programs help bring out the full potential of fledgling startups. From Mexico to the Southern Cone, the number and quality of academic programs dedicated to software and game design has begun to increase in recent years as well, which along with official promotion of the industry through policy, publicity, and support for development will help to further establish the region's potential for game development.

Glimmers of a twenty-first-century boom in Latin American game design began to appear in the late 1990s and early 2000s, when the region's developers gained sufficient footing to achieve sustainability. As in other phases of development, these included, on the one hand, companies that focused on exportation and the global audience by adopting universally familiar cultural themes in games such as *Druids, the Epic* (2002), designed by Costa Rican game studio Teleport Media for Irish publisher CPoint Entertainment, or the internationally popular *Regnum* series, a massive multiplayer online role-playing game (MMORPG) from Buenos Aires-based NGD Studios. NGD established a presence relatively early on in Argentina, its founders now having produced a twenty-year body of work that includes *Regnum* (1995), *Regnum 2* (1996), and *Pentagon* (1998), as well as their first entry into the MMORPG genre, *Argentum Online* (2001), and their breakthrough worldwide hit *Regnum Online* (2007). On the other hand, there were studios producing games explicitly set in contexts particular to their national cultures such as the Argentine titles *Fútbol Deluxe* (Evoluxion 2004), a soccer management simulation that parlayed the nation's fervor for *fútbol* into one of Argentina's first major commercial successes, and *Malvinas 2032* (Sabarasa 1999), a turn-based strategy game in which the player commands future Argentine forces in an effort to take back the Falkland Islands from the British. *Malvinas 2032* was Sabarasa's first entry into the video game market, and the firm has since gone on to work on a broad range of projects including the Wii singing game *Atrévete a soñar* (*Dare to Dream*, Televisa 2011), the Nintendo DS title *SpongeBob Skate & Surf Roadtrip* (THQ 2011), and the iOS, Android and DSiWare game *Save the Turtles* (Sabarasa 2012) (figure 3.12). Studios such as these demonstrated that regional game design held serious potential for success on a global level.

The Brazilian developer Devworks Game Technology, founded in 1999, is another pioneering firm that has stood the test of time. Devworks also offers a clear snapshot of the transforming dynamics and recent changes in focus for the region's game industry. Having begun with console games that were published by Tectoy for the Sega Master System and Sega Mega Drive such as *A Ponte* (*The Bridge*, 2003) and the turbo elephant racing game *Corrida da pesada* (*Heavy Racing*, 2003), Devworks designers were working simultaneously on the development of the dozens of online and casual games that now dominate the company's attention. These included Devworks's own version of the card game *Truco* (2003), in this case one that "uses the Truco rules from Brazil," and which also set the record for most-downloaded game in Brazil when the company began freely distributing it for compatible mobile phones.[76] Today, Devworks produces dozens of online games as well as mobile games for the four most popular cellular platforms in Brazil, demonstrating the shifting dynamics of the game industry that can be observed across the region.

Another important trend contributing to the professionalization of the Latin American game industry is a growing number of gaming-related events, which are drawing ever-larger crowds throughout the region. These include major showcases like Argentina's EVA

Figure 3.12
Malvinas 2032 (Sabarasa 1999)

(Exposición de Videojuegos de Argentina) and industry conferences like Mexico's DEVHR and Brazil's SBGames. Events like these are not only opportunities for the industry's major players to seek out talent and peddle their wares, they also showcase innovative and unique work in video game design from Latin America. An example is independent game designers Hernán Sáez and Máximo Balestrini's *NAVE* (2012), a retro arcade shooter in a 200-pound arcade cabinet that brought back "the glorious showoff days of the arcade" and drew hordes of devotees as one of the main attractions at EVA 2013.[77]

Sponsored design competitions and game jams, events in which teams work to create a game from concept to realization in a given period of time (often twenty-four, forty-eight, or seventy-two hours), are also on the rise throughout the region. Marisca notes that game jams are "an extremely important institution for the local industry" due to the fact that they constitute a "foundational alternative infrastructure that simultaneously addresses many of the challenges the industry faces, learning being one of the main ones."[78] Game jams are nurturing the creative ecosystem for the regional game industry by providing budding designers with an opportunity to interact and work with others with more experience in the field, and offering a unique set of circumstances in which technologies and knowledge are circulated freely among mutually supportive participants. Today, game jams and sponsored design competitions are appearing across Latin America. A 2014 game jam held in San Juan, Puerto Rico, attracted dozens of contestants who worked together to successfully create eight games, but comments from the event's participants suggest that its most important impact was its contribution to

Figure 3.13
Coca Kolector (Bujllai 2013)

the growing sense of possibility for the Puerto Rican game design community.[79] Other types of design competitions have also led to opportunities for the development of original concepts, such as the Bolivian game *Coca Kolector* (Bujllai 2013), in which the player, as president Evo Morales, must work through obstacles and dodge threats while collecting as many coca leaves as possible (a nod to Morales's past as a coca cultivator and union organizer for his fellow *cocaleros*) (figure 3.13). The game was the result of an internal competition at a national university that provided designers with funding for publication of their final product.[80] Throughout the region, and especially in those places where the talent and enthusiasm of the game design community exceeds the capacity of the local educational and industrial infrastructure, game jams and design competitions are making meaningful contributions to the training of a future generation of professional designers.

Incubators and accelerator programs also have an increasingly significant impact in Latin America. In some cases these incubation programs—which are designed to enable game design startups to find firm footing and solid prospects for a future in the industry—are supported by government and civic organizations, while in other cases they are private endeavors sponsored by large corporations prominent in the global game industry. As Marisca observes, software startups in the region have been fighting for visibility by staking claims to their own entrepreneurship communities modeled after Silicon Valley, including "Lima Valley, Santiago Valley, Montevideo Valley, Palermo Valley (Buenos Aires), the 'Brazilian Silicon Valley' (Campinas), Suma Valley (Guadalajara), Bogota Valley," and others.[81] Many of these initiatives are supported not only by game designers (and marketers) themselves, but by governmental entities. The state-funded accelerator program Start-Up Chile has provided seed funds to nearly one hundred tech startups in Santiago, and inspired other governments to take on similar initiatives including Start-Up Peru, Incubar in Argentina, and iNNpulsa in Colombia.[82] Likewise, since 2007 the Mexican government has promoted the work of the incubation company Juego de Talento, whose main goal is to promote the incorporation of Mexican talent into the global games industry while increasing the number and quality of developers in the country. Juego de Talento's first game development contest in 2008 received more than one hundred entries, from which the top ten were selected to collaborate with the incubator. A year later, with a contest centered on the theme of Mexican history in light of its approaching bicentennial of independence, Juego de Talento would receive entries from more than four hundred teams, a demonstration that the program was achieving its goal of creating a "critical mass" of industry talent in Mexico.[83] These state-run and hybrid public/private programs have helped nourish the talent pool of the game industry in the region in recent years, cultivating the potential of the regional game design community.

In addition to state-funded incubator or accelerator programs in Latin America, there are those financed by well-known multinational corporations from the gaming world, like Sony and Square Enix. Sony began to talk about its Latin American incubation program in 2008,[84] two years into the main-market lifespan of the PlayStation 3 (PS3), but still well in advance of the official Latin American regional release of the console in 2014.[85] The program aimed to bring regional game design talent into the fold of the Sony brand by giving qualified applicants a development toolkit to advance their technical knowledge of the hardware and development of software for the PlayStation Portable (PSP) and PS3,[86] at the same time bolstering Sony's credentials as a supporter of independent game design talent. The program has supported the development of several games to date, the first of which, the platform puzzler *Monster Bag* from Chilean studio IguanaBee, was released by Sony in April 2015. A tiny group of six individuals based in Santiago, Iguanabee found success by working closely with Sony's program for two years, but the company is quick to highlight the need for opportunities for game development in Chile as well as the substantial talent base that awaits such breakthroughs.[87] Other games developed in Sony's incubation program include *Fenix Rage* (Reverb Triple XP 2014), a fast-paced 2D platform/puzzle game designed by the three-person team at Costa Rica's Green

Figure 3.14
Fenix Rage (Reverb Triple XP 2014)

Lava Studios (figure 3.14), and *To Leave* (Sony 2013), "a puzzle-platformer about a boy trying to escape a city that seeks to drain him dry" created by an independent game development studio called Freaky Creations in Guayaquil, Ecuador[88] (figure 3.15).

After Sony opened a game development lab in collaboration with the Ecuadorian Escuela Superior Politécnica del Litoral (ESPOL) in 2012, several interested students formed a game design club and pitched each other ideas until settling on the concept for *To Leave*, which Sony eventually agreed to distribute through its digital platform.[89] While it is still in its early stages, Sony's incubation program presents one potential model for developing the Latin American game industry through the establishment of projects that are mutually beneficial to regional game designers and multinational game publishers alike. Though they are contractually tied to publication through Sony's PlayStation Network as part of the program, participants gain not only exposure for their products but also significant experience in developing polished games with the potential for success on the global market. Other companies have begun to follow in Sony's footsteps, most notably Japanese game publisher Square Enix, which launched its first Latin America Game Contest in 2012. Square Enix sees Latin America as a potential hotbed of design talent, and the company is particularly interested in those designers prepared to take "Latin American cultural references" to a global audience in their games.[90]

Figure 3.15
To Leave (Sony 2013)

A blend of initiatives from the public and private sectors is nurturing Latin America's potential for game development across the region today. Governmental entities are enabling national industries by offering financial incentives to game designers and publishers and, more important, by developing the educational infrastructure for a sustainable workforce. Likewise, governmental agencies are providing support in less direct ways, such as when the Bogotá Chamber of Commerce sponsored the public gallery exhibition "Video Games Made by Colombians" in summer 2014.[91] Along with these state initiatives, private corporations have begun to pay more attention to the region, contributing to the professionalization of the video game industry in Latin America through programs designed to nurture the region's abundant talent. As a result, video game development is alive and well in Latin America today, growing and diversifying in a number of directions.

Trajectories in Latin American Game Design

A broad spectrum of game design practices are taking place across Latin America today, with developers working with a variety of platforms, technologies, and game genres, each with different objectives and audiences in mind. Therefore it is important to avoid monolithically reducing the design traditions of countries throughout the region to a single moniker such as "Latin American game design" without accounting for the diverse range of creative visions and design methodologies that fall under this umbrella. The focus of this section is to help distinguish and enumerate some of the many types of game development work taking place in Latin America today, emphasizing the expanding potential for regional game production. Together, examples from a variety of genres and frameworks including newsgames and political parodies, educational games, advergames, outsourced games, independent games, casual games, and games from Latin American designers working abroad evidence the diversity of game development practices in the region today.

To begin with, the use of games for social critique has a longstanding tradition in Latin American game design. As discussed in chapter 2, it was Frasca that coined the term "newsgames" to describe games that respond to real-world events through gameplay in a way that is meant to provoke critical reflection. A number of other Latin American designers have also used games to respond critically to real-world situations and events, creating simulations that help process the complicated effects of real-world trauma. One example is Salvadoran designer Sergio Arístides Rosa, who was inspired by the violence around him to create *Enola* (Domaginarium 2014), a horror-themed game that uses violence to discomfort rather than gratify the player (figure 3.16). In a similar vein, Venezuelan designer Ciro Durán designed the game

Figure 3.16
Enola (Domaginarium 2014)

Nación Motorizada (*Motorized Nation*, 2012) after he was robbed on a Caracas highway, as a type of "intellectual vengeance" that transformed his victimization into something more meaningful than just "one more" random and unpunished crime[92] (figure 3.17). In *Nación Motorizada*, the player must drive a car down the highway and "survive the constant harassment of the motorbikes that are chasing" her vehicle by knocking the attackers off their bikes, offering a vindictive social critique of the crime problem in Caracas in the form of a simple Flash animation

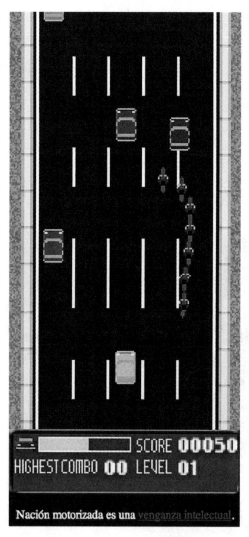

Figure 3.17
Nación Motorizada (Ciro Durán 2012)

Figure 3.18
La Mordida (LEAP 2014)

web game.[93] Others have used the newsgame format to lampoon the headlines of the moment using simple mechanics and satirical caricatures of newsmakers. Take, for example, *La Mordida* (*The Bite*), a game that was developed by Peruvian studio LEAP Games within days of one of the biggest stories of the 2014 World Cup in Brazil, when Uruguayan forward Luis Suárez famously bit the shoulder of his competitor, Italian defender Giorgio Chiellini (figure 3.18). The bite went unseen by the game's referees but was caught from several angles in high definition by the television cameras, making it a global subject of water cooler discussion in the days that followed. LEAP game developers took advantage of this moment of public visibility to launch their game, in which the player controls a biting Suárez as he attempts evade the referee's gaze, chomping away for as long as possible on the shoulder of Chiellini.[94] Games like these are also a chance for small developers to get the word out about their more ambitious projects, such as LEAP's 2015 release for the PlayStation Portable, *Squares* (figure 3.19). Like the Internet memes circulated through social media and the tweeted jokes about this event and others, games like *La Mordida* represent an attempt to be humorously provocative as well as a novel way of communicating *around* a world event through electronic media.

Political parodies are an even more common form of satirical newsgame. Games that poke fun at candidates for public office are being produced far and wide, even in countries without

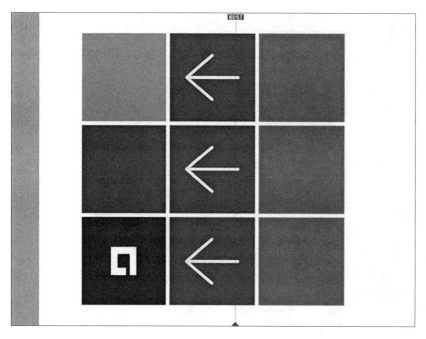

Figure 3.19
Squares (LEAP 2015)

a major national industry or significant game design infrastructure. After Paraguayan congressional representative Carlos Portillo was questioned in an interview about a number of allegedly false college degrees on his résumé as well as his professed fluency in English, he responded by saying, "My name is Charlie," then struggled to count to ten in English, forgetting the number five. Again, the Internet meme machine was quick to pick up on this event, taking advantage of the deep divide between the politician's public self-representation and the reality revealed in the interview in order to produce playful parodies. Within a short time, a video game parody had appeared as well: in *Portillo el Tontillo* (*Portillo the Little Fool*, Groupweird 2014), the player guides an avatar featuring a cut-and-paste image of the candidate's face as he tries to duck under and leap over the books flying his way—each time the politician comes into contact with a book, he loses a point, marked by a countdown in broken English, "te, nai, ..."[95] (figure 3.20). The low-fi aesthetics and simplistic gameplay mechanics of *Portillo el Tontillo* are characteristic of political parodies and other newsgames, which are often quickly compiled in response to recent or ongoing events, the comic timing of the parody's release ultimately taking precedence over complexity or replay value.

Similar examples of political parodies can be found throughout Latin America. In the Panamanian game *Carrera Presidencial 2014* (*Presidential Campaign 2014*, Cerdipuerca Studios 2013),

Figure 3.20
Portillo el Tontillo (Groupweird 2014)

the player chooses from caricatures of real-life candidates in the country's presidential elections, then attempts to win votes by giving away tanks of gas, handing out political pamphlets, and evading electoral officials.[96] And *Carrera Presidencial 2014* was not the only game designed around Panama's 2014 elections. Eduardo Soto and Amado Cerrud, two young Panamanian designers residing in Taiwan and collectively referred to as Amazian Team, designed *Guerra Política* (*Political War*, 2014) as a way of satirizing outgoing president Ricardo Martinelli, whose administration had been racked by a number of political scandals.[97] In the game, a character named "Mentirelli" (a play on words between the president's last name and the Spanish verb *mentir*, "to lie") leaps around among the various electoral candidates seeking to replace him as well as former dictator Manuel Noriega and Venezuelan president Nicolás Maduro, in a race for money and points—the goal is to gather 5,000 Panamanian Balboas in order to earn diplomatic immunity. But what is perhaps most noteworthy about *Guerra Política* is the way it became more than just a satire to be circulated among the general public, entering into the country's political discourse after several opposition candidates played and discussed the game in interviews. Among them was Panama's then-Vice President Juan Carlos Varela, who would eventually win the election to become president of Panama in 2014. Varela commended the designers of *Guerra Política* for including specific elements related to his proposed policies, calling the game "very detail-oriented and creative."[98] The case of *Guerra Política* demonstrates the potential for game designers to develop newsgames, social critiques, and political parodies that not only comment *about* but also actually become a part of the political discourse of their particular time and place.

Educational games, sometimes referred to as "edugames," are also gaining increased attention from Latin American game designers and funding sources alike. Like the Uruguayan developers of the previously discussed RPG *1811*, design teams in several other countries have created games about their respective independence movements. For example, a Dominican team produced *La Trinitaria* (*The Trinity*, Instituto Tecnológico de las Américas 2008), proudly proclaiming it to be a game "by Dominicans and for Dominicans,"[99] while in Mexico, a team of student designers led by Guillermo Medina and Felipe Mandujano developed *Al grito de guerra* (*At the Cry of War*, Máquina Voladora 2013), an FPS based on the Mexican War of Independence. Other design teams throughout the region echoed the call to commemorate major events of national history through games, including Cuba's Youth Computer and Electronics Club (JCCE), the makers of *Gesta Final*, the Cuban Revolution shooter discussed in chapter 2, as well as several educational games that they released simultaneously. Working under the JCCE, a government-supported initiative founded in 1987 with the objective of disseminating information technology among the nation's youth, the Estudio de Videojuegos y Materiales Audiovisuales (Evima, Video Game and Audiovisual Material Studio) developed a series of five games tailor-made to the national population's preferred game genres in 2014.[100] These were publicized as the first games ever fully designed in Cuba, and included the first online game ever published in the country, *Comando Pintura*, a paintball shooting game aimed at fostering nonviolence (figure 3.21). The other games also relate to the official vision of Cuban popular culture and national values: *Beisbolito* (figure 3.22), a learning game for elementary school students, teaches math through the Cuban national sport of baseball; *Boombox* is a 3D puzzle/maze game, one of the country's most popular genres; and *A Jugar* is a collection of mini-games for children that incorporates popular animated characters created by the Cuban Institute for Art and the Cinematic Industry (ICAIC).[101]

These games represent a first for the Cuban game design community, but their efforts mirror those of projects seeking to educate students on issues pertinent to national culture in other countries. For example, the Administration of the Panama Canal published the game *Reto Canal* (*Canal Challenge*, 2013) with the objective of maintaining the waterway's relevance in the minds of Panamanian youth.[102] Likewise, *Súbete al SITP* (*Get on the SITP*, Transmilenio 2014), a bus-driving game sponsored by the Colombian government and aimed at teaching citizens of Bogotá how to safely use public transportation, earned its designers a prize from the organization Games for Change.[103] Like the JCCE's games and those focusing on major historical episodes from Uruguay, the Dominican Republic, and Mexico, games such as *Reto Canal* and *Súbete al SITP*

Figure 3.21
Comando Pintura (JCCE 2014)

fill cultural gaps in the global game industry by providing content produced by designers with a local audience in mind.

Other educational games are supported by a mix of public and private funding, or by nongovernmental philanthropic organizations. The Nicaraguan Zamora Terán Foundation is one such source of financing for game development, having sponsored a "One Laptop Per Child" initiative beginning in 2010 aimed at putting a computer into the hands of every school-age child in Nicaragua. Along with the hardware, the foundation has supported the design of multiple applications to help students and teachers get the most out of the technology at hand, including several video games.[104] All of the applications are freely available, and their source code was released as freeware in order to allow programmers and educators throughout Central and South America to create their own localized versions.[105] One of these games, *Sin Dientes* (*Toothless*, 2011) is a variation on the classic hangman word game, with the difference that incorrect guesses lead to the loss of one of the character's teeth (figure 3.23). Another, *Conozco Nicaragua* (*I Know Nicaragua*, 2011) is an interactive geography game in which players help an explorer find the pieces of a missing ship, discovering the country's different official departments,

Figure 3.22
Beisbolito (JCCE 2014)

rivers, and volcanoes in the process (figure 3.24). In Costa Rica, Nicaragua's neighbor to the south, independent firm Green Lava Studios was contracted by the Pan-American Health Organization to develop the health education game *Pueblo Pitanga: Enemigos Silenciosos* (*Pitanga Town: Silent Enemies*, 2013), a platformer along the lines of *Super Mario Bros.* featuring a protagonist named Fabio who is seeking clues to his sister Luisa's mysterious illness (figure 3.25). As these examples demonstrate, educational games represent a major trajectory in Latin American game design, due in large part to a mixture of support from local, national, and international agencies, entities in the private sector, and forward-thinking governmental administrations and ministries throughout the region.

Game development has also been fueled by the efforts of the private sector, with a corporate tie-ins creating unique opportunities for Latin American game designers in the fields of advergaming, work-for-hire, and outsourced game development. The advergaming and work-for-hire production models involve contractual design for a commercial client, which appeals to game developers seeking to take fewer risks by working on set contracts with predictable rates of return.[106] In addition to being approached by corporate clients, game developers can go looking for business themselves, as in the case of Honduran publisher OK Producciones,

Figure 3.23
Sin Dientes (Fundación Zamora Terán 2011)

Figure 3.24
Conozco Nicaragua (Fundación Zamora Terán 2011)

Figure 3.25
Pueblo Pitanga: Enemigos Silenciosos (Pan-American Health Organization 2013)

who contacted singer-songwriter sensation Polache with a proposal to make a game using him as the protagonist. The result was *Polache Land* (2014), an iOS app in which the singer travels through ten different Honduran settings, singing his hit songs and uttering custom-recorded dialogue in moments of success and failure.[107] Rather than a strict advergaming venture, *Polache Land* is probably better defined as work-for-hire.

The work-for-hire model, in which a game design company uses another company's intellectual property or game concept with the purpose of developing a game from that intellectual property,[108] is an increasingly common approach for Latin American developers seeking to establish stability and a strong track record. A paradigmatic example is *El Chavo Kart* (Televisa 2014), a kart racing game that uses characters (and the characteristic slapstick comedy tone) from the still-popular 1970s Mexican television series *El Chavo del Ocho* (figure 3.26). Colombian Efecto Studios was selected by the game's Mexican developer Slang to design *El Chavo Kart*, which was published by Televisa Home Entertainment in cooperation with Slang.[109] Other examples of work-for-hire from Latin America include games from Frasca's now-defunct commercial design studio Powerful Robot, such as *Legends of Ooo* (Cartoon Network 2012), a video game spinoff of Cartoon Network's *Adventure Time*, and *Cambiemos* (Frente Amplio 2004), which Frasca designed for the political campaign of the leftist coalition Frente Amplio. Paraguayan group Creadores, a two-year-old game design startup with a median worker age of twenty-three, uses a project-by-project business model designing products that can be sold

Figure 3.26
El Chavo Kart (Televisa 2014)

for anywhere from US$500 to US$15,000 depending on the game's complexity.[110] One recent work-for-hire project by Creadores was *Nick Wacky Racers 3D*, a 2013 online game they designed for the television network Nickelodeon.[111] Creadores' model borders on game design outsourcing, which Marisca refers to as the "Peripheral Services Model," that is, "companies providing piecemeal services supporting various stages of game development: motion capture and tracking, digital distribution platforms, platform support and services, cloud services, marketing and advertising, user acquisition, analytics and game data tracking, localisation, and so on."[112] This segment shows a great deal of promise for those working in related industries, or whose firms specialize in specific parts of the design, publication, and distribution process. For example, the Dominican company VAP Dominicana manufactures components of video games that can be exported by request to studios in the United States or Europe, where they are "assembled" into the final product.[113] Outsourcing and peripheral service businesses like VAP are popping up around Latin America, hoping to use their proximity to the United States as a strategic advantage over similar outsourcing efforts in countries like India and China.

In a sense, Latin American game design abroad is the other side of the outsourcing coin, with visionary work coming from designers who have emigrated in search of opportunities to produce their visions. Examples include *Guacamelee!*, a platform brawler that incorporates numerous elements of Mexican culture, which was initially conceived by Mexican animator Augusto "Cuxo" Quijano, a member of the Toronto-based design team at independent Drinkbox Studios[114] (figure 3.27). In this sense, *Guacamelee!* is (at least partially) a product of Latin American game design even though it was developed in Canada by an international team.

Figure 3.27
Guacamelee! (Drinkbox 2013)

Similarly, the fantasy adventure game *Papo & Yo* was developed by Colombian Vander Caballero after he founded Minority Media in Montreal. Quijano and Caballero are but two examples of the enormous number of Latin Americans working in every aspect of game design, production, and distribution today, as major creative centers draw a global talent pool to the game industry. Montreal, for example, is not only home to *Papo & Yo* developer Minority but also to studios of industry giants like Ubisoft, Electronic Arts, Eidos, and Warner Bros. Games, along with startups like Mistic Software, Quazal, and Kutoka Interactive. As David Grandadam, Patrick Cohendet, and Laurent Simon have observed, such an environment is attractive for game development on a multitude of levels: "The video game cluster in Montreal has proven to be one of the most creative clusters worldwide in this specific field," and the firms working in the cluster "have not only benefited from the presence of many organizations in their own sector, they also have nourished themselves from their exchanges with different actors and communities" among the city's more than five thousand video game industry employees.[115] Given the attraction of geographical epicenters of game development like Montreal and Silicon Valley, the trend of Latin American game design abroad is sure to grow in coming years.

However, Latin Americans are not only working in independent design firms in places like Montreal but also, and increasingly, in their own home countries. Independent games have grown considerably as a segment of game development in recent years, due to a number of factors, including growth in the segment of the casual game market and the consequent decline in the required levels of financing, team size, and time from concept to market.[116] In Latin America, the standard for independent game design has been set by the likes of Chile's

Figure 3.28
Abyss Odyssey (ACE Team 2014)

previously mentioned ACE Team, a Santiago-based firm that has produced four games to date for PS3, Xbox 360, and Windows: *Zeno Clash* (2009), a surreal first-person-melee combat game that established ACE Team's imaginative and unconventional style of game design; *Rock of Ages* (2011), which combines a Monty Python-esque medieval environment with the mechanics of *Super Monkey Ball* (Sega 2001); *Zeno Clash 2* (2013), the stylized follow-up to the previous combat hit; and *Abyss Odyssey* (2014), a sci-fi nightmare set in late nineteenth-century Santiago with a blend of mechanics including "a combination of procedurally-generated levels, 2D platforming, intricate combat systems and online, community-driven progression"[117] (figure 3.28). To varying degrees, ACE Team's games have met with considerable critical and commercial acclaim on the global games market, making them an emblem of what many Latin American game designers would like to become. Marisca refers to independent development as "the model most studios aspire to," noting that "[t]here's a fair share of romanticism attached to the idea of the indie: people who are able to get their own ideas out there, work on their own projects, and through sheer willpower and effort manage to produce a massively successful game that will be picked up and celebrated by their peers and thousands of players around the world."[118] In reality, though, working on an independent game based on original intellectual property is a highly risky venture, making it especially difficult to succeed in this segment of game development.

Mitigation of this inherent risk is yet another reason Latin American game developers are paying increased attention to the possibilities opened up by casual gaming. Juul observes that "[b]ecause of their smaller scope, casual games are generally cheaper to develop than the larger hardcore games that have driven the video game industry for so long," and the advent of casual games "shifts the perspective from technical graphical fidelity to more mundane questions such as: how does a game fit into the life of a player, and how much meaning can the game acquire from the context in which it is played?"[119] In Latin America, this means easier access for small designers to local, national, regional, and even global markets. And casual games are indeed booming, as demonstrated by *Mundo Gaturro* (*Gaturro's World*, Clawi 2010), a social game based on a popular Argentine feline comic character that is played by over ten million users.[120] Other independent designers seek to build such massive audiences through a variety of measures: Guatemalan developer OH! promoted its iOS and Android game *CocoMonkeys* (2012) by offering users a monthly chance to win an all-expense-paid trip to the Mayan ruins of Tikal in Guatemala, while using a free-to-play payment model in which users download the app for free, but must pay between US$.50 and US$2 per additional playable level in the game.

The wide variety of game development practices described in this section reflects the rapidly changing climate of the Latin American game industry today. There are Latin American designers pursuing independent development of AAA titles for global distribution both inside the region and abroad, but there are also a growing number of commercial and amateur game design trajectories that are diversifying the region's game design practices. Game developers are working with governmental entities, nongovernmental organizations, private sector investors, and multinational corporations to produce games and game elements that represent an increasingly broad range of production models. These trajectories demonstrate how a supportive environment for game development can produce substantial benefits over a relatively short timespan.

Conclusion: The Next Latin American Boom

As this chapter's introduction explains, the Latin American Boom in literature of the 1960s and 70s was the result of a convergence of a variety of individuals and factors, which included the high-quality novels of a number of talented authors as well as the contributions of literary agents, translators, publishers, academics, journals, literary prizes, and a regional spirit of solidarity brought on by the Cuban Revolution, not to mention the denunciations of the Boom's all-important detractors. Together, these forces created a sort of sociocultural and economic "perfect storm" that provided the ideal conditions for an explosion of cultural production.

Without a doubt, the conditions of Latin American cultural production in the 2010s differ considerably. Nevertheless I would argue that there is substantial evidence of a new confluence of factors promoting the Latin American game industry today, including a growing number of high-quality original games from talented Latin American designers as well as the contributions of incubation and accelerator programs, game jams and design competitions, industry events, development of higher-education programs in game-related fields, an active modding community, and explosive regional growth in casual game development. Together, these factors add up to lay the essential groundwork for a new Latin American Boom in game design and development over the course of the 2010s and 20s.

However, this boom cannot flourish without the continuation and expansion of cultural policy and other initiatives backing Latin American game development. Progressive governmental agencies and individuals are providing models for support throughout the region. The Uruguayan government funded the development of games like *1811* and *D.E.D.* through Ingenio, a state-controlled incubator for startups, while progressive immigration laws assist in attracting talent and investment from abroad, all of which has helped to make the country Latin America's leader for per-capita software exports.[121] The previously mentioned Domaginarium game *Enola* was sponsored by the Salvadoran Ministry of the Economy's Productive Development Fund (Fondepro), which awarded over a quarter-million dollars to seventeen game-related business and design startups in 2013.[122] Colombia's Ministry of Information and Communication Technologies, meanwhile, has instated the Vive Digital plan, "a cross-sector, four-year push to increase Internet adoption and promote the creation of technology-based ventures across the country," which includes "Apps.co, a roving technology development effort designed to support people in coming up with ideas and projects around new technologies, offering different resources and levels of support based on how mature the idea is and what skills the potential entrepreneur has," and the Ministry "has also set up a different partnership with ProExport Colombia (Colombia's export promotion agency) to support the promotion of Colombian game developers at international venues, such as the Game Development Conference (GDC) in San Francisco," covering 50 percent of the costs for attendance at this notoriously pricey but essential industry event, as well as offering assistance in planning and negotiation.[123] Kaxan Media Group, the Guadalajara, Mexico-based creators of the popular iOS and Android app *Taco Master* (Chillingo 2011), developed their game with the support of MexicoFIRST, a program created through a combination of government support and private initiative aimed at increasing Mexico's presence in the information technology field.[124] Honduran firm Oxen Films has received support from the government program known as Honduras Convive! for the development of a series of video game design workshops for at-risk youth, in which attendees participate in courses on narrative, acting, drawing, photography, and video production, allowing them to awaken their creativity and learn a new and valuable skill set.[125]

These and other trailblazing efforts by administrations throughout the region are paving the way for further expansion in regional game development.

Everywhere you look in Latin America today, there is evidence of explosive growth in the game industry and expanding efforts to harness its creative and commercial potential. This eruption is no mistake, but rather is the result of conscious efforts taken by governmental and nongovernmental agencies, multinational game companies, organizers of industry events and design competitions, institutions of higher education, modding communities, and game developers working at all levels of production throughout the region. What's more, these factors are combining amid the shifts in the global geography of the game industry that have accompanied the advent of casual games in recent years, opening up the game market to smaller designers with more modest projects and budgets, and yet offering the potential to make profits on a proportionately higher scale relative to conventional AAA game development. These factors are not just setting the stage—they have already begun to produce tangible results, evidenced time and again in the cases reviewed in this chapter. In light of this evidence, it is safe to say that the next Latin American Boom isn't coming soon: it's already here.

II   HOW GAMES USE CULTURE

4   SEMIOTICS

This chapter explores how cultural meaning is made in the sign systems particular to video games. In games, culture is manifested through images, objects, and signifiers meant to evoke or symbolize the characteristic traits or way of life attributed to a given group of people. This is a departure from Arnold's nineteenth-century characterization of culture as a strictly autonomous sphere dedicated to "the pursuit of light and perfection,"[1] or Bourdieu's description of culture as a category of distinction "predisposed, consciously and deliberately or not, to fulfill a social function of legitimating social differences."[2] Rather, following Latin American cultural critics like Sarlo, García Canclini, and Yúdice, I interpret culture as an always already commodified sphere whose meaning exists through instrumental use and negotiation. Culture is put to work, it is sold in products, it is circulated in intellectual and economic markets. When understood as an expedient, product, resource, or a tangential attempt to metonymically represent of the unrepresentable totality of a given group's contribution to the world, culture garners its particular meaning relative to the context in which it is put to use. This concept in itself is not unique to games, but the idea of culture as something that can be commodified and utilized is that much more relevant in the immersive environments of gamespace, where meaning is actively produced through procedural interaction with culturally coded symbols, sounds, and spaces. While chapter 5 will focus on the latter aspects, space and sound, this chapter examines video games as semiotic systems with unique tools for cultural signification.

Video Games as Semiotic Domains of Culture

As sign systems, video games are distinctive from other forms of cultural production. Just as interpreting the signifiers of a still or moving image requires a different approach than interpreting the signifiers of a written text, the semiotic system at work in a multimodal game environment necessitates certain adjustments. The meaning of a cultural product cannot be deduced without consciousness of how its particular signifying domain functions, as studies in the semiotics of dance, music, and the visual arts have shown. And indeed, as a long history of inquiry attests, no signifier in any semiotic domain of any type is ever capable of directly representing a single, fixed meaning—Ferdinand de Saussure indicated this a century ago in his *Course in General Linguistics*,[3] and with Jacques Derrida's "différance" this polysemy became the key to conveying the ever-differing, ever-deferring relationship among an infinite chain of interconnected signs.[4] Video game semiotics is a relatively new field of inquiry, but one that has provoked strong interest. As Gee explains concisely: "To understand or produce any word, symbol, image, or artifact in a given semiotic domain, a person must be able to situate the meaning of that word, symbol, image, or artifact within embodied experiences of action, interaction, or dialogue in or about the domain."[5] If we take games, then, to be semiotic domains with unique "design grammars," to use Gee's terminology, their difference from other types of semiotic domains is the result of games' nature as coded, interactive environments.

In video games, the signified is even less stably fixed to its signifier than in a text or an image. This is because games transform the relationship between signifier and signified in two important ways: (1) the relationship is made more dynamic by virtue of the sign's inscription in a nonstatic semiotic domain, and (2) a subjective player is capable of acting upon—and therefore changing the meaning of—given signs. I am following N. Katherine Hayles's work *How We Became Posthuman*, in which she, following Lacan, coins the term "flickering signifiers" with regard to electronic media. "In informatics," Hayles argues, "the signifier can no longer be understood as a single marker, for example an ink mark on a page. Rather it exists as a flexible chain of markers bound together by the arbitrary relations specified by the relevant codes."[6] Here, Hayles is referring to the actual inscription of the signifier in electronic form, which is more fleeting, impermanent, and variable than the written word or the photographic image. This is true of any electronic signifier, be it a picture on a website, a menu button in a computer application, or an object in a video game. Equally important is the way video game players create meaning through an active process of negotiation with the obstacles and affordances established by the game's code, described by Galloway as "grammars of action" through which "both the machine and the operator work together in a cybernetic relationship to effect the various actions of the video game in its entirety."[7] Meaning is produced algorithmically in games through the process of interaction between player and code, as in Manovich's dual definition of the algorithm as "the actions the gamer must perform to solve a problem, and the set of computer procedures controlling the representation, responses, rules, and randomness of a game."[8] Because game meaning is algorithmic, players can experiment with and manipulate the structures of signification through gameplay, leading to the "recursive contextualization" of meaning "through which rules are transformed during continuous, repeated, and, most important, recursive reference to those rules."[9] The interactive process of meaning making in a game occurs through these algorithmic and recursive "grammars of action," which are established by the coded software and enacted by the player in order to create signifying experiences.

A game is a discursive field replete with a potentially infinite web of signifiers. These include objects and artifacts representing certain cultures, like Rio de Janeiro's Christ the Redeemer statue; as well as sounds and acts, like the rhythms of hip-hop music thumping far off in the distance, becoming louder as the player approaches a building; or an off-color comment made by a character in a game within the context of a drunken conversation. These are examples of the myriad types of signifying situations that exist within video games (taken from games discussed in this chapter), and none of them—Christ the Redeemer, the diegetic hip-hop music or the off-color joke—has the same meaning it would have at face value, or in the "real world," or outside of its uniquely situated context in a game. All of these examples of "culturally embedded sound and imagery"[10] are also what Lévy refers to as "anthropological objects."[11] Lévy explains that the anthropological object "traces a situation, bears with it the field of a problematic, the knot of tensions or psychic landscape of the group."[12] In short, it is a metonymical stand-in of a sort, a placeholder for the entirety of the culture that it would purport to represent, abstracted from its original context and situated anew in an environment that transforms its signification. For the sake of illustration, we could think of the Christ the Redeemer in this sense (figure 4.1). In *Brasil Quest*, a casual game sponsored by the country's tourist ministry, the

Figure 4.1
Tropico 3 (Kalypso 2009)

monumental statue functions as a picturesque reminder of the setting of Rio; in the combat flight simulator *Tom Clancy's H.A.W.X.* (Ubisoft 2009), the statue stands out as a likely target or obstacle, or both, for the free-roaming player in a fighter jet; in *Call of Duty: Modern Warfare 2* (Activision 2010), seeing Christ the Redeemer on the horizon can help orient the player and thus serve as a navigational tool; in the dictatorially themed management simulation *Tropico 3* (Kalypso 2009), the construction of a Christ the Redeemer-like statue generates tangible effects, boosting the Tropican population's environmental happiness and generating an incremental increase in tourist interest in the island, as well as automatically converting some of the population to the "Religious" faction. This is the process of semiotic redetermination that Manovich has referred to as "transcoding" between the cultural layer and the computer layer of our world,[13] or to borrow Giddens's terminology, the process through which the cultural sign is disembedded and deterritorialized, then virtually reembedded and reterritorialized in a game environment that endows it with new meaning.[14] Such cases demonstrate how a signifier is transformed when it is removed from its conventional context and placed in a game.

This is why scholarship on cultural meaning in video games is so urgent: too often, the meaning of a game has been taken at face value or inferred from screen captures and sound bites without consideration of the signifying system, the semiotic domain, through which that meaning is transmitted. To adapt Barthes's terminology regarding meaning in cinema, analysis of culture in games requires an effort to look beyond the informational level, beyond the symbolic level and on to a "third meaning," the "obtuse meaning."[15] For Barthes, the obtuse meaning of a film sequence "is outside (articulated) language while nevertheless within interlocution" because it signifies through nonlinguistic signs: "For if you look at the images I am discussing, you can see this meaning, we can agree on it 'over the shoulder' or 'on the back' of articulated language. Thanks to the image [...] we do without language yet never cease to understand one another."[16] Barthes's notion of the obtuse meaning is particularly relevant for analyzing video games because of their nature as nonlinguistic sign systems, capable of conveying meaning "'over the shoulder' or 'on the back' of articulated language," but irreducible to the signifying system of language. Along these lines, Mäyrä has described the "silent significance" of a video game for its player by comparing games to orchestral performances: after attending a symphony, for example, how might a concertgoer describe what the concert "was about"?[17] One could certainly articulate many aspects relevant to the meaning of the performance—the size of the orchestra, the tone and tempo of the suites performed, the relative prominence of strings, percussion, woodwinds, or brass—but will never successfully convey the experience felt by the spectator of an act whose meaning exceeds the descriptive capacity of language. The video game, like music, is a nonlinguistic form of cultural production: it does not necessarily use words but nevertheless "regularly succeeds in evoking feelings and sometimes also in conveying more precise ideas."[18] Thus it is important to understand how video games generate meaningful experiences for players using unique, nonlinguistic mechanisms of cultural signification.

As the introduction to this book explains, human history has a longstanding tradition of reducing culture into "symbolic tokens" that can be put into circulation in different cultural environments and markets,[19] or using anthropological objects to convey ideas about the characteristics of a given cultural group.[20] Some in the field of Latin American cultural studies have echoed Benjamin's mourning the loss of the "aura" with regard to video games and other new media technologies, such as when Martín Hopenhayn lamented in 2000 that "[t]he video game, zapping, the shopping centre and feverish consumption have obliterated silence and the fleeting pause, those subtle features that gave so much intensity to modern art."[21] However, García Canclini has examined the specific ways cultural meaning is created and transformed when put into symbolic circulation, referring to the ways the "immaterial cultural heritage" or "oral creations, knowledge, festive rituals and artisanal techniques" passed on in a given cultural group, are made meaningful in different contexts.[22] García Canclini argues that such cultural products and methods are by no means frozen in a single time and place, but rather are part of a living and constantly evolving cultural inheritance: "It is not possible to choose a group of 'authentic' goods, objects and ceremonies, separating them from the social uses that have modified them over the course of history, such as urban development, the communication industries, insertion into commercial networks and mediated representations."[23] Culture is always defined within some type of network of exchange, and it is impossible to separate the "authentic" from the perspective that is imposing the criteria for authenticity. The critical question for García Canclini, then, is how the socially shared meaning of cultural signs comes about, and how that meaning is transformed when it is put to use in diverse spheres and by parties with differing interests and goals.[24]

In game studies, the subject of cultural representation and meaning in games has been approached from a variety of angles. Formalist ludologists like Aarseth are quick to point to the uniqueness of "ergodic" media like games, in which "nontrivial effort is required to allow the reader to traverse the text,"[25] leading to a process in which "[t]he game plays the user just as the user plays the game, and there is no message apart from the play."[26] Mäyrä suggests approaching games' meaning in terms of "core" (gameplay) and "shell" (representational) layers, pertaining to the different structures of signification at work within video game semiotics. Calleja echoes this assertion, adding that in games, "the representational sign might be made of the same code that dictates the behavior of AI agents or the material density of a wooden fence, but for the sake of analysis it makes sense to separate these two configurations of code since they perform very different functions in the game object and process."[27] Therefore we must understand culturally coded signs as simultaneously representational and functional within the game environment. Katie Salen and Eric Zimmerman argue that although the signs used in game worlds "make reference to objects that exist in the real world, they gain their symbolic value or meaning from the relationship between signs within the game."[28] This has complex implications when it comes to the relationship between culture and games. Salen and Zimmerman argue that a term that is racially offensive "*outside* of the context of a game of *Scrabble*," for example, takes on a different meaning in the context of gameplay, mathematically signified by the number of letters and their relative scores.[29] As illustrated in this example, "[t]he meaning of any sign (object, action, or condition) in a game arises from the context of the game itself—from a system of relations between signs," and this contingent and situated way in which meaning is made must be taken into account in order to fully understand games' meaning.[30]

Nevertheless, cultural representation in games is inextricably linked to the traditions of cultural representation in other media. Like film and television before them, video games "are repositories for a range of social-cultural or political-ideological resonances, and for some widely repeated scenarios," and moreover such formats are valuable to game designers for the "very familiarity" of their references and "the extent to which they can readily be drawn upon without needing a great deal of explicit elaboration."[31] Gee argues that games' meaning is dependent upon the "cultural models" employed in game design, that is "images, story lines, principles, or metaphors that capture what a particular group finds 'normal' or 'typical' in regard to a given phenomenon," models that also correspond to longstanding representational traditions.[32] Applying Edward Said's concept of Orientalism to the analysis of games set in the Middle East, Philipp Reichmuth and Stefan Werning explain that game designers "draw from a rich field of Oriental topoi and representations that is well established in Western (and Japanese) culture" when they represent "other" cultural environments, demonstrating "notions of an imagined Orient as a complex cultural metasign that 'is' everything that can be associated with it," including the types of "familiar motifs from popular literature, art, cinema, or even political discourse" that are so common in video games.[33] Moreover, the use of these familiar cultural motifs should not be surprising, as Rachael Hutchinson argues, especially because the simplification of cultural representation can be pragmatically advantageous to game designers by streamlining the design process, making images more easily localizable and making characters and environments more easily and quickly distinguishable.[34] Indeed, simplification is required when culture is represented in any medium or format, and it is particularly unsurprising in the case of video games, a medium whose earliest forms were more metaphorical than representational in their visual displays of culture. This is one reason cultural meaning in video games is so complicated—because it is not only mimetic but also algorithmic, situational, contingent, and activated through procedural gameplay and subjective agency, the parameters that characterize video games as unique semiotic domains of culture.

The Semiotics of Latin American Culture in Video Games

The cultures of Latin America have provided the semiotic foundation for a long history of video games. Elsewhere, I have referred to the categories of "contras," "tomb raiders," and "luchadores" to describe the tropes through which Latin America culture has most frequently been portrayed in video games through the history of the medium, pointing to three among the most commonly used frameworks for this portrayal.[35] This section offers a general historical survey of some of these cultural tropes in game design, looking at games set among the region's ancient cultures, games of exploration and conquest, and military-themed guerrilla warfare games. Any of these cases could be fruitfully explored in much greater depth, as illustrated in the two subsequent sections, which focus on specific ludic interpretations of the Mexican Day of the Dead and the Brazilian favela.

Many of the earliest video games set in Latin America involved the region's ancient cultures as the backdrop for exploration narratives, including the early 1980s games *The Mask of the Sun*, *Aztec*, *Expedition Amazon* (Penguin Software 1983), *Quest for Quintana Roo*, *Montezuma's Revenge* (figure 4.2), and *Amazon* (Telarium 1984). Like Steven Spielberg's blockbuster 1981 film *Raiders of the Lost Ark* and its 1984 sequel *Indiana Jones and the Temple of Doom*, the cultural iconography of these early titles was pseudo-archeological in nature, and these games frequently featured tomb-raiding narratives similar to those featured in the movies. *Aztec*, an early platformer for

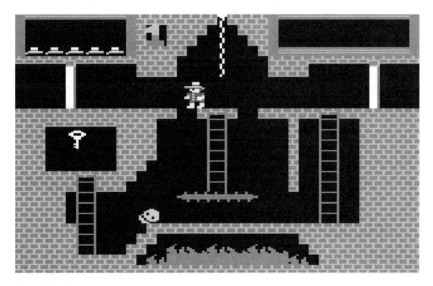

Figure 4.2
Montezuma's Revenge (Parker Brothers 1984)

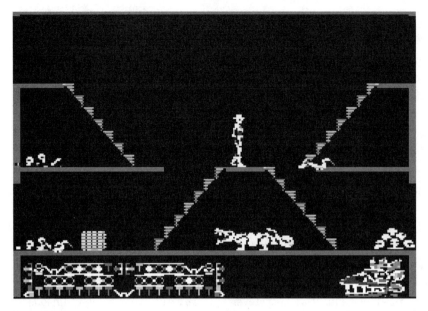

Figure 4.3
Aztec (Datamost 1982)

the Apple II and Commodore 64 home computers, featured an explorer protagonist dodging live jaguars alongside other ludic signifiers of ancient Mesoamerican culture: piles of skulls and bones, slithering serpents and spiders, jaguar heads carved in stone, handwoven baskets, and steep temple stairs (figure 4.3). The text-based adventure game *The Mask of the Sun* also features a Jones-like explorer on a search for a jaguar mask among sacred temples and Mayan pyramids filled with stone urns and altars guarded by skeleton warriors (figure 4.4). *Expedition Amazon* is an educational resource-management game along the lines of the *Oregon Trail* series (MECC 1974); the player excavates clay jaguars, dodges crocodiles, monkeys, and cockroaches, barters with local traders, and avoids dysentery while navigating a river and its surrounding territory (figure 4.5). These games' incorporation of the familiar symbolic repertoire of archeological adventures set in ancient temples is a prime example of remediation, Bolter and Grusin's term for the crossover between different forms of old and new media.

The most enduring video game franchise to use this archeological adventure scenario is *Tomb Raider*, developed by the British firm Eidos Interactive, now a subsidiary of the Japanese game corporation Square Enix. *Tomb Raider* is as much a game about spatial exploration and problem solving as anything else. Therefore, in games in the adventure/puzzle genre that are set in Latin America—from the original 1996 *Tomb Raider* to sequels like *Tomb Raider: Legend* (Eidos 2006), to games from other series like *Uncharted: Drake's Fortune* (Sony 2007)—accuracy

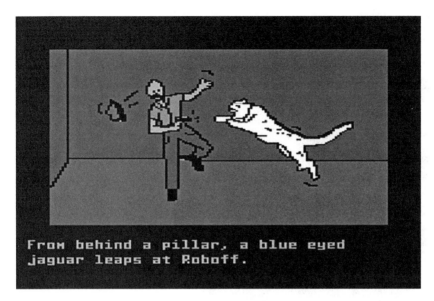

Figure 4.4
The Mask of the Sun (Broderbund 1982)

of cultural signification usually takes a backseat to the demands of gameplay. Marisca has described cultural representation in these types of titles as "the sort of portrayal of Latin American countries typically found in video games: a highly abstracted portrayal of stereotypes from the region's countries, constructed from the outside for the outside."[36] King and Krzywinska echo this assertion, noting that in the *Tomb Raider* games, "indigenous populations are often depicted stereotypically, or are present only tangentially through the material remnants of their culture," reducing the significance of indigenous cultures in the games to "sources of exotic spectacle and artifacts to be stolen for their value to others, rather than [involving] any real engagement with their own qualities."[37] Indeed, while Lara Croft wends her way through a variety of Peruvian settings in *Tomb Raider: Legend*, for example, it is clear that culture is an instrumentalized part of the environment rather than an element oriented toward accuracy of historical representation. The melding of cultural elements from distinct traditions is a trademark of the series: in *Legend*, the Norse god Thor is rendered in the weathered limestone and amethyst crystal outcroppings of Mexico's Yucatán peninsula, while Norse war scenes are depicted in stone reliefs within Mayan temples, making it difficult to take away any clear touchstones of cultural knowledge.

Beyond providing the backdrop for the adventures of Indiana Jones- and Lara Croft-like characters, the ancient cultures of Latin America have been depicted in a broad array of other video game genres and formats. The two-dimensional RPG *Illusion of Gaia* (Nintendo 1994) is

Figure 4.5
Expedition Amazon (Penguin Software 1983)

set among Peru's ancient Nazca lines, while the three-dimensional environments in *Pitfall: The Mayan Adventure* (Activision 1994) or the early advergame *Taco Bell: Tasty Temple Challenge* (BrandGames 2000) are set among the standard indigenous temples (figure 4.6). Game designers from Latin America have also produced a number of games set among the region's ancient cultures referenced in the first half of this book, including *Flappy Quetzal*, *Mayan Pitz*, *Pok ta Pok*, and *Inka Madness*, as well as the Peruvian game *Inkawar* (Luis Grimaldo 2005) (figure 4.7). Likewise, temples and stone reliefs from the region's indigenous empires have been incorporated into the simple tile motifs and navigable environments of casual puzzle games like *Zuma* (PopCap 2003), *Jewel Quest* (iWin 2004), *TiQal* (Microsoft 2008), and *Hamilton's Great Adventure*

Figure 4.6
Taco Bell: Tasty Temple Challenge (BrandGames 2000)

(Fatshark 2011), as well as an ever-expanding and endlessly varied list of other games, includ-
ing the evangelical Christian radio show spinoff *Adventures in Odyssey: The Treasure of the Incas*
(Digital Praise 2005) and the sports/exercise game for the Nintendo Wii *Active Life Explorer*
(Namco Bandai 2010). This spectrum of genres and scenarios demonstrates the versatility that
game designers have developed over decades of variations on the semiotic themes of Latin
America's ancient cultures.

   In addition to scenarios involving modern archeologists raiding ancient Latin American
tombs, the history of the Spanish conquest and colonization of the New World has provided
abundant source material for game developers. A paradigmatic early example, *The Seven Cities
of Gold* (EA 1984) announces that "Adventure awaits any who sail to the New World," then has
the player navigating the Atlantic and discovering the lands of the Americas, eventually going
to war against dark-skinned native people who live in teepees and fight with spears while
searching to bring back "gold and glory for the crown." Though this early example is from
the strategy genre, it is the management simulation genre that has focused with particular
frequency on scenarios of global conquest, as well as on the Latin American case in particular.[38]
Sid Meier's games are probably the most universally familiar management simulation games,
including not only *Sid Meier's Civilization* (MicroProse 1991) and its sequels, but other games

Figure 4.7
Inkawar (Luis Grimaldo 2005)

situated in Latin America like *Sid Meier's Pirates!* (MicroProse 1987) and *Sid Meier's Colonization* (MicroProse 1994). The trope of colonization is deployed in a number of similarly themed games, like *Imperialism II: The Age of Exploration* (SSI 1999) or the *Conquerors* expansion pack released in 2000 for *Age of Empires II: The Age of Kings* (Microsoft 1999). The German-developed *Anno* series includes several games set in the region, such as *Anno 1602: Creation of a New World* (Sunflowers 1998) and *Anno 1503: The New World* (Sunflowers 2003), each of which focuses on development of infrastructure during the colonial period. Other examples of management simulations set against the backdrop of the conquest- and colonial-era history of Latin America include *Gold of the Americas: The Conquest of the New World* (SSG 1989) and *The Gold of the Aztecs* (Kinetica 1989), while *Inca* (Sierra On-Line 1992) and *Inca II: Nations of Immortality* (Sierra On-Line 1994) reimagine the conquest of the Americas as a battle between Spanish conquistador Lope de Aguirre and Incan emperor Huayna Capac, set in outer space 500 years after the actual conquest of Peru. Management simulations have unique ways of representing culture algorithmically. On the one hand, games in the genre require the player to manage economic resources—by cultivating crops, providing housing for the population, and managing international trade. On the other hand, management simulations frequently require the player to make decisions with an *ideological* impact on the populace of the territory being managed. Rebellions must be nullified, populations must be pacified, and leaders must be glorified, all with just the right balance so as not to tilt the scales beyond the level of controllability. In this way, the history of conquest and colonization has appealed to game designers in particular due to simulations' capacity for presenting a dynamic and ever-changing set of variables.

Spain's software industry also showed an early interest in these types of colonial scenarios, as illustrated by the text-based adventure trilogy from design firm Aventuras AD that included *La diosa de Cozumel* (*The Goddess of Cozumel*, 1990), *Los templos sagrados* (*The Sacred Temples*, 1991) and *Chichén Itzá* (1992) (figure 4.8). This trilogy of games involves in-depth narratives of shipwrecks, conquest, and cultural cohabitation in colonial Mexico, and requires the player to use appropriate cultural strategies to maintain equilibrium with the local populations and achieve the tasks at hand. These games of conquest and colonization establish some of the most longstanding semiotic patterns for the representation of Latin American culture, as well as some of the key symbolic tokens or anthropological objects that signify "Latin American culture" within the video game medium: skeletons and temples, exploration and invasion, gold and jungles, serpents and jaguars. Not surprisingly, many of these signifiers correspond to a lengthy tradition of cultural representation in narrative, art, and film predating their use in video games.

Alongside games set among Latin America's ancient cultures and games of conquest and colonization, modern military-themed video games have a long history of using Latin American

Figure 4.8
La diosa de Cozumel (Aventuras AD 1990)

cultural settings and their attendant signifiers. An early example is the 1983 game *Harrier Attack* from British publisher Durell Software, which was inspired by that country's 1982 war with Argentina over the Falkland Islands (Islas Malvinas in Spanish). The Falklands War is just one of many episodes in Latin American military history that have been portrayed in military-themed video games from a number of different genres. Others include the Cuban Revolution, as seen in the 1987 Japanese top-down arcade shooter *Guerrilla War*, which was released in Japan under the title *Guevara*, or the portrayal of the US-led invasion of Cuba at the Bay of Pigs in the flight simulator *A-10 Cuba!* Many massively distributed military video game series feature Latin American storylines tied to real historical events—including Activision's bestselling *Call of Duty* series' own take on the Bay of Pigs in *Black Ops*, or its portrayal of the US-funded Contra war in Nicaragua in *Black Ops II*. In addition to these twentieth-century warfare scenarios, games have taken players to nineteenth-century Latin America in the RPG *The Mexican American War* (HPS Simulations 2008), as well as the previously discussed *Al grito de guerra*, *La Trinitaria*, and *1811*, which commemorate the independence movements of Mexico, the Dominican Republic, and Uruguay in FPS and RPG form.

While many games focus on specific wars and battles from Latin America's military history, others are set in broader, nonspecific scenarios of guerrilla uprisings, foreign intervention, and the US-led "war on drugs" in Latin America. Some, like Konami's 1987 arcade and NES game *Contra*, deal not with specific historical conflicts but with battles between human soldiers and alien invaders against a backdrop rife with iconography of ancient Mesoamerican cultures and Central American flora and fauna. Electronic Arts' 1993 helicopter shoot-'em-up game *Jungle Strike* pits the player as a US Special Forces pilot who must take down the private army of a South American drug lord bent on mass destruction (figure 4.9). If this scenario sounds familiar it is because it corresponds to a long history of representation of the Drug War in Latin America, not only in literature and film but also in mainstream video games like *Code Name Viper* (Capcom 1990), *Call of Juarez: The Cartel*, and *Army of Two: The Devil's Cartel* (EA 2013), as well as independent games like *Narco Terror* (Deep Silver 2013) and the newsgame *NarcoGuerra*, all of which have very different takes on the theme. Beyond those games focusing on drug-related violence, there are games that concentrate on the history of US interventionism in Latin America through fictional scenarios, such as *Battlefield: Bad Company 2* (EA 2010) as well as those mentioned in earlier chapters, *Goldeneye 007*, *Just Cause*, *Conflict: Denied Ops*, and *Mercenaries 2: World in Flames*.

Games set among Latin America's ancient indigenous empires and its history of conquest, colonization, and modern military conflicts represent a significant proportion of the video game depictions of the region's cultures. These games use a symbolic repertoire shared with literature, film, and the visual arts to add familiarity, realism, or depth to the player's experience. The particular characteristics of each of these cultural tropes depend upon the type of

Figure 4.9
Jungle Strike (EA 1993)

semiotic domain in which they are put to use, as can be seen in the wide spectrum of examples already mentioned. This broad view of the dynamics of Latin American cultural portrayal in video games sets the stage for a closer look at the specific types of cultural scenarios we find recreated once and again in video games of different genres, platforms, and formats. For a more in-depth illustration, I turn now to two other common semiotic domains for the representation of Latin American culture, Mexico's Day of the Dead and the urban favela of Brazil, each of which has its own corresponding iconography and associated ludic functions.

Playing the Day of the Dead

Like the narratives of exploration and conquest referenced earlier, the visual signifiers of Mexico's Day of the Dead celebration—laughing *calacas* and *calaveras* (skeletons and skulls), altars covered in burning candles, sugar skulls, flowers, and other offerings to the deceased—enjoys a lengthy history not only in video games but in a variety of other media as well. In *Death and the Idea of Mexico*, Claudio Lomnitz argues that a playful yet unyielding relationship to death is a trademark characteristic of Mexican culture, substantiated by longstanding traditions in

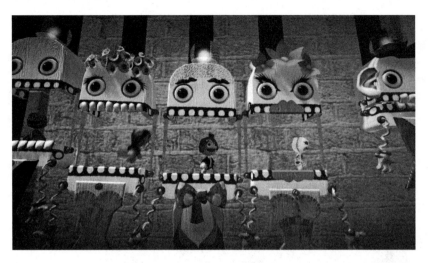

Figure 4.10
Little Big Planet (Sony 2008)

literature, philosophy, and the visual arts.[39] In video games, the symbolic repertoire associating Mexican culture with the dead first appeared in the form of the skulls and skeletons of 1980s titles like *Montezuma's Revenge*, *Aztec*, and *Mask of the Sun*. The essential humor of Mexican cultural depictions of death gradually began to appear in games such as the cult classic *Grim Fandango* (LucasArts 1998), which set the bar for comedic takes on this theme by blending Day of the Dead imagery with film noir tone in a story that follows protagonist Manny Calavera on a detective adventure through the Land of the Dead. This humorous approach to the Day of the Dead has also been pursued by games including *Chili Con Carnage* (Eidos 2007) and *Psychonauts* (Majesco 2009). Another example is *Little Big Planet* (Sony 2008), a console platformer based on a virtual globe featuring ludic interpretations of real-world cultural settings including Japan, India, Russia, and the African savannah. Among these settings is a Mexico-based area replete with sugar skulls, altars, playful skeletons, and characters including Frida the Bride, Don Lu, Sheriff Zapata, and Uncle Jalapeño (figure 4.10). This cultural setting is enhanced by a soundtrack of Mexican pop/alternative music and the option for players to outfit their doll-like avatar in a colorful red serape, a tall sombrero, or skeleton suit fabric while zipping through a lifelike backdrop of a cemetery in the midst of the Day of the Dead celebration. The lighthearted take on death featured in these examples demonstrates the evolution of this trope, with designers bringing games' themes and tone into harmony with their use of the longstanding visual iconography of the Day of the Dead.

The most dynamic uses of the Day of the Dead motif in video games are those that play on the duality of grief and joy and the interplay between the worlds of the living and the dead

Figure 4.11
Mictlan (Phyne 2012)

that characterize the real-life Mexican observation of this holiday. These include games from Mexican game developers like *Mictlan* (Phyne 2012) and the 2013 indie hit *Guacamelee!*. *Mictlan* is a casual game in the wall defense genre in which the character of Luno, "a Mexican boy who has just passed away," must defend himself against other skeletons tossing bones and the like (figure 4.11). Programmer and software developer Arturo Nereu conceived of *Mictlan* with an eye to the international market, incorporating visual elements of Mexican culture (like the cut-out plastic banners used in the game's menu screen) along with an assortment of other international death celebration iconography like Frankenstein masks and jack-o-lanterns. Nereu initially released the game only in English, but *Mictlan* quickly found an audience not only in the English-language market but also in China, Taiwan, and Mexico, leading Nereu to reconsider his assumption that the US market would be more significant than the domestic market as well as others outside the English-speaking world.[40] Nereu also sought to court international players with the visual style of *Mictlan*, which he says was intended to be clearly Mexican in order to appeal to a national audience, but not so locally specific as to alienate players from elsewhere in the world. Nereu explains that his aim was to use elements of Mexican culture in a "subtle" way: "Rather than randomly using elements from the Day of the Dead and the Mexican tradition surrounding that day, the game offers foreigners and locals the opportunity to appreciate death from a different perspective, one that is more active, joyful and humorous."[41] *Mictlan*, then, was designed with an eye to incorporating aspects that would appeal to different audiences—it takes place in a fictionalized Mexico City that will be recognized by residents of that metropolis, but can be equally enjoyed as the great kingdom of Mictlán by a foreign audience.[42] What *Mictlan* gets right is something that game designers outside of Mexico have sometimes missed, an approach to mortality that integrates a sense of humor and envisions life and death as two sides of the same existential coin.

The final example, *Guacamelee!*, incorporates the Day of the Dead procedurally as well as on a symbolic and conceptual level, making it the most remarkable take on the Day of the Dead yet in a video game. This "Metroid-vania" style brawler/platformer is the brainchild of Mexican game designer Augusto Quijano, an illustrator working with around a dozen others at Toronto-based indie developer Drinkbox Studios.[43] *Guacamelee!* is rife with the conventional video game iconography of Mexican culture—the protagonist is a masked *luchador*, enemies include skeletons and laughing skulls, and sacred temples and pyramids dot the map. However, mixed in with these established symbols are images of Mexico that are much less conventional within the game medium—the great *Tule* tree of Oaxaca, the agave fields outside a tequila distillery, a giant stone Olmec head used a teleportation device that transports the player between towns like Santa Luchita and Pueblucho, and a cast of characters including the protagonist Juan Aguacate, a Catholic friar called Fray Ayayay, a goat/god/sensei called Uay Chivo, and the archenemy Juan Calaca. The game's Spanglish dialogue is full of double meanings that the bilingual player will appreciate, and a certain degree of multilingualism is built into the game as well—each time you purchase a "heart chunk" you get a flashy graphic reading "CACHITO DE CORAZÓN," while exclamations like "¡ÓRALE!" and "¡VIENTOS!" are displayed at the top of the screen each time you defeat a series of enemies.

The Day of the Dead altar itself is depicted in *Guacamelee!* as a broad above-ground tomb of carved stone, covered with bright violet and orange silk doilies with an embroidered skull pattern, topped with a large sugar skull decorated with pink accents, a candelabra with three burning blue flames, two vases of flowers, a basket of bread, and some fruit and vegetable *ofrendas* (figure 4.12). Here, the altar is not only representational but also a functional cultural element game—it appears after each major challenge as a checkpoint where the game auto-saves the player's progress and refills his health meter, and offers the menu for the marketplace where Juan can buy further abilities, health, stamina boosts, and other benefits. With the altar checkpoint system as well as the Olmec head that is used as the player's main source of teleportation between areas of the map, *Guacamelee!* incorporates elements of Mexican culture as functional as well as symbolic elements of game design.

But what is most interesting about *Guacamelee!* is the way it incorporates the Day of the Dead in a procedural manner by allowing the player to switch, at the push of a button, between the world of the living and the world of the dead (figure 4.13). This dynamic is key to gameplay, as different obstacles, affordances, enemies, and allies appear in each of these two dimensions. Switching between the living and dead dimensions in *Guacamelee!* has both aesthetic

Figure 4.12
Guacamelee! (Drinkbox 2013)

Figure 4.13
Guacamelee! (Drinkbox 2013)

and functional consequences. Along with visual cues, the game's soundtrack music changes in tone—in the dead world, the score has more echo and reverb and is keyed minor; in the living world, the music is bright and tight, and is keyed major. On an aesthetic level, things that are living change to their dead forms—people and animals become skeletons, living green trees are stripped of their foliage and appear dark and imposing, and the sunlight is replaced with darkness. In another scenario, what appears in the dead world as a Day of the Dead banquet with baskets of food, bowls of fruit, and many bottles of liquor and other drinks set upon a handsomely painted purple table is revealed in the world of the living to be a cemetery, decorated with flowers and altars to loved ones (figure 4.14). On a functional level, certain platforms, walls, and other architectural elements appear only in one world or the other, and likewise certain enemy characters appear only in one dimension or the other, often requiring the player to switch between the living and dead dimensions several times in order to succeed in a single brawl or spatial puzzle. Mastery of the game thus requires dynamic and continuous shifting between the two worlds, a reflection of how game design can offer meaningful insight to what might otherwise be a two-dimensional cultural representation. In *Guacamelee!*, the melding of the worlds of the living and the dead becomes something more than just visual imagery for the player, it becomes an embodied part of the gameplay experience and a reminder of the

Figure 4.14
Guacamelee! (Drinkbox 2013)

interplay between the world of the living and the dead that characterizes the Mexican traditions surrounding the Day of the Dead.

This level of sophistication in cultural representation was first and foremost in the minds of the designers of *Guacamelee!*, who emphasize the harmony between Mexico's intermingling of the worlds of the living and the dead in the Day of the Dead celebration and within the core gameplay mechanic of the light/dark world.[44] Quijano explains that he initially conceived of the idea for the game as an unconventional approach to Mexican culture, due to his dissatisfaction with depictions of the country: "The way that Mexico is portrayed in movies and video games is very shortsighted, and I don't think it does the country justice. With *Guacamelee!* I wanted to portray the richness and the uniqueness, the culture—everything we love about Mexico. [...] The idea was to make a fantastical version of Mexico, not necessarily historically or geographically correct, but definitely genuine."[45] This is another important aspect of this game's design— the "insider perspective" of a Mexican illustrator and conceptual artist who imbued the design team with the confidence to make a product that was culturally different and that approached its subject in unconventional ways, without fear of playing with and sending up stereotypes. *Guacamelee!* shows that there are significant possibilities for cultural representation that can be opened up when games using conventional cultural iconography and tropes are produced by conscientious designers who are familiar with the cultural environments being depicted. This is evidence of an evolution of cultural semiotics in game design with regard to video game representations of the Day of the Dead. Over several decades of development, approaches to this trope have progressed from the use of familiar visual signifiers of the Day of the Dead, to the inclusion of the underlying humor of the relationship between death and Mexican culture in games' narratives, to game design that incorporates important elements of this semiotic domain into the basic procedural dynamics of gameplay.

The Brazilian Favela as Semiotic Domain

There are a number of reasons game designers turn to real-world locations as environments for video games. Some games are set in recognizable cities like New York, Los Angeles, or Chicago, rewarding those acquainted with the real location's geography and landmarks with a sense of familiarity. Others feature "culturally specific locations" aimed at appealing to a broad audience "without the overwhelming expectation of cities known the world over."[46] The sprawling urban favela communities of São Paulo and Rio de Janeiro could be thought of in this way, as the designers of Games like *Call of Duty*, *Max Payne 3* (Rockstar 2012), and even the independent game *Papo & Yo* all sought to appeal to a broad international audience presumed not to know the ins and outs of Brazilian culture and geography. Here it is helpful to borrow a concept from

Misplaced Ideas, Roberto Schwarz's seminal study of *brasilidade* ("Brazilian-ness"), in which he argues that Brazil "unceasingly affirms and reaffirms European ideas, always improperly."[47] Increasingly, video game designers are turning the dynamics Schwarz describes on their head, with game developers located in major production centers of North America now attempting to convey brasilidade, each in their own "improper" ways.

All gamespaces are necessarily reductive environments, in which each element is the result of a design decision aimed at a specific function (even if that function is seemingly "decorative"). Brazilian gamespace is readily characterized by certain signifiers of brasilidade that have been utilized once and again by game designers: soccer, an ethnically diverse population, bossa nova music, a tropical landscape replete with vibrant colors, and, to return to an earlier example, the Christ the Redeemer statue. But the center of this semiotic domain today is the ultimate twenty-first-century sign of Brazil for the outside world—and arguably for Brazilians as well: the favela. The representation of the favela within entertainment is certainly nothing new. As Brazilian film scholar Lúcia Nagib notes, before Fernando Meirelles's 2002 *City of God*, the favela film was already a conventional genre in Brazil, inspiring works such as Walter Salles's *Midnight* (1998), Eduardo Coutinho's documentary *Babilônia 2000* (1999), and João Moreira Salles and Kátia Lund's *News from a Personal War* (1998), as well as numerous works of Brazilian literature, among them the 1997 novel *City of God* by Paulo Lins, the inspiration for the later film version.[48] Symbolically, the favela is frequently employed as a sign of deeply entrenched class divisions, which in Brazil, as in so many other places, represent a structure that "encompasses and organizes all the people, operating as a self-perpetuating system of the social order in force," in the words of Brazilian anthropologist Darcy Ribeiro.[49]

The favela cannot be reduced to any simplistic or unilateral signification: both its cinder-block-and-mortar reality and its mediated representations are complex, contradictory, and polysemic. Beatriz Jaguaribe elaborates: "Cast as both the locus of the 'national imagined community' and as a 'fearful stain' on the landscape of modernity, the favelas [are] often metaphorized as an emblem of Brazil's uneven modernization [...] the favela speaks of a cultural hybridity that bypasses polarities and provides the cities without maps of the twenty-first century."[50] Even before the tourist boom surrounding the 2014 Brazil World Cup and 2016 Summer Olympics in Rio, the favela was not just considered a criminal underworld but a tourist site and a symbolic commodity as well. It is in this form that the favela now enters into mediated representation, qualified by its growing network of semiotic renderings and the fascination it holds for the outside world (including other Brazilians). And indeed, as Schwarz suggests in his review of *City of God*, the viewer's (or the player's) own context is not entirely divorced from the experience of those who live in Brazil's favelas: "Their world is our own. Far from representing anything backward, they are the product of progress—which, naturally, they qualify. Deep inside, the reader is at one with them—and with their regressive fantasy of simply seizing the glittering goods on display."[51] Schwarz's critique of consumer culture's fascination with Brazilian poverty resonates with the characterization of the favela as a space of fantasy and exploration designed for the outsider or tourist-gamer, which is one approach that has been taken in games set entirely or partially in the favela.

The commercial behemoth *Call of Duty: Modern Warfare 2* is a 2009 first-person shooter developed by Infinity Ward, a design studio out of Encino, California, and was published by Activision for PlayStation 3, Xbox 360, and Windows. Since it belongs to the most successful and widely played commercial game series of all time, its portrayal of Brazil has probably been played by more gamers worldwide than any other—to date the game has sold nearly twenty-five million copies globally.[52] *Modern Warfare 2*'s Campaign mode, set seven years into the future in 2016, has players follow a global arms-dealing conspiracy through Russia that eventually leads to a search for intelligence and subsequent battle in the favelas of Rio. The mission is a mad dash over corrugated tin roofs and through the flimsy doorways of the improvised architecture, while the player is assaulted on all sides by members of the mercenary "Brazilian Militia" paid off by the arms trafficker. Most of the favela warriors wear shabby but colorful t-shirts and jeans with bandanas over their faces—clothing colors are used by game designers to visually parallel the tropical tone of the Rio-based map, but also contribute functionally by making the NPCs more easily visible and identifiable to the player. In all, though, the constant barrage of bullets ensures that the player has little time to ponder the nuances of the cultural context in this mission, which is a quick thirty-minute side trip within a Russia-based campaign that takes about twelve hours to complete.

But it is important to remember that many *Call of Duty* players ignore the Campaign mode altogether, concentrating strictly on the online multiplayer mode. Indeed, players from all over the globe can be found shooting it out with one another by the hundreds of thousands at any given moment online. In this regard, while Brazil is a brief distraction for the *Modern Warfare 2* Campaign, it has a heavier presence in the more popular multiplayer arena. Four of the sixteen multiplayer maps are set in Brazil—Quarry, Rundown, Underpass, and of course Favela—meaning that more than 25 percent of the time that millions of players worldwide have spent in the multiplayer arena has been spent playing in a virtual Brazil. After repeated hours interacting with this environment, the complex of cultural signs at play becomes familiar to the committed player. *Call of Duty* games enjoy enormous resources, and their designers put a great deal of work into creating cultural context through a vast array of visual, linguistic, sonic, and spatial signs.

Modern Warfare 2's Favela map reproduces the familiar iconography of the urban shantytown in a broad range of details: rebar reaching skyward from unfinished constructions; lush tropical ferns and banana leaves pushing up through the concrete; TV antennas and loose electrical wires that have been tapped into multiple times; graffiti tags covering exterior walls alongside clotheslines between the ramshackle structures; and of course, the backdrop of Sugarloaf Mountain and Christ the Redeemer looming on the horizon beyond the favela, outside the playable environment. There is even a favela soccer field, basically a set of low cinder-block walls covered in overlapping graffiti tags and a ragtag wooden goal post at either end, riddled with segments of concrete traffic walls, rusted metal barrels, pieces of corrugated iron, drink containers, and a burning tire. In the semiotic domain of video games, the soccer field is second only to the favela itself as a signifier of Brazilian culture. Written language also adds to the cultural context: rock band posters promote "Messias Atômico," while signs identify businesses such as "Mini Mercado Barateiro," "Lavandaria," "Coco Gelado," and "Pelayo's Sorvetes e Lanchonete."

Along with linguistic signs, visual symbols such as the Brazilian national flag add to the cultural context of *Modern Warfare 2*'s Favela map. This is probably not surprising to those familiar with the series, since national flags are a ubiquitous means of cultural contextualization and orientation used by the designers of *Call of Duty* as well as other games, often appearing not only in their conventional form but also as wall paintings or graffiti. In *Call of Duty: Black Ops II*, for example, the medium-sized Panama City-based "Slums" multiplayer map features the same wall painting of the Panamanian flag duplicated in no fewer than nine separate locations, perhaps leading the critical player to wonder why the local vandals are so patriotic. When elements such as the national flag seem redundant, disorienting, or out of place, the devil can be in the very details used to create cultural context in games like *Call of Duty*. Just as the careful player will note the many instances in which particular objects, visual symbols, and written texts are specifically employed to evoke an atmosphere of brasilidade within *Modern Warfare 2*, there are many details that don't quite fit, destabilizing it as a semiotic domain. As players pick around the Brazilian stone quarry, they might begin to note that some of the signs posted in corners of buildings are written in Russian as well as Portuguese; in the same quarry, a "Transportadora" sign that made sense on a body shop in the Favela map is cut and pasted onto a manufacturing building; a fish store in the Brazil-based Rundown is called "Don Pescado" in Spanish and filled with fresh fish and Maine lobsters, with newspapers in Chinese on the walls; among the products on the store shelves are bags marked "Basmati Rice," "Beef Jerky," and "Mint Gum." The explanation for these cultural non sequiturs is fundamentally economic in nature: these are properties created for other culturally coded environments, cut and pasted into these Latin American maps, a reflection of the shortcuts to cultural contextualization necessitated by the development calendar of serial games like *Call of Duty*. A large, neon "DRUGS" sign on a building in the Favela map, for example, can also be found in its original design context on a building in the Los Angeles-based Skidrow map, also featured in *Modern Warfare 2*. Semiotic shortcuts such as these allow game developers to meet their deadlines in a timely fashion, but can also short-circuit the sense of cultural context that those designers seek to convey.

While many big league game companies are driven by deadlines and yearly turnaround in serial franchises, there are also AAA game developers that work with more flexible production schedules, as is the case with *Max Payne 3*, another game portraying the favela. Released in 2012 for PlayStation 3, Xbox 360, and Windows, *Max Payne 3* was developed by Rockstar Vancouver, a division of its publisher, Rockstar Games, the New York- and UK-based company best known for its *Grand Theft Auto* (*GTA*) series. Like that series, *Max Payne 3* is a third-person shooter and is unflinchingly violent—by many measures more so than the *GTA* games, in fact. However *unlike* many of Rockstar's popular "sandbox" or "open world" titles, the game is "on rails," to use game-world terminology: it is narrative-driven and its spatial exploration is heavily restricted, leaving the player relatively little freedom outside of the linear narrative trajectory of the plot. This may make the game less attractive than *GTA* to a general audience—it has sold around four million copies to date, versus twenty-two million copies of *GTA IV* (Rockstar 2008) and over fifty million copies of *GTA V* (Rockstar 2013). This also, incidentally, puts *Max Payne 3*'s playership numbers on par with the total global viewership of the film *City of God*. The game is the third installment in the noir shooter series, after the original *Max Payne* (Rockstar 2001), which was developed by Finland's Remedy Entertainment, and *Max Payne 2* (Rockstar 2003), the first installment in the series designed from the ground up by Rockstar. More than nine years would pass before they released *Max Payne 3*, which melds cinematics with player interaction in a curious blend of episodic narrative and gameplay. Max's noir voiceover advances the plot while the player takes action, and the game is fractured between intense engagement in gunplay and more passive viewing of cinematic sequences.

Rockstar founder Dan Houser describes *Max Payne 3* on the one hand as "a fairly classical noir tale of an ignorant dupe getting in way over his head in a world he does not understand, only with the twist of the dupe being an American in a foreign culture he does not understand," and on the other hand, "a character study of a drunken middle aged man trying to figure out what to do with the second half of his life, having had his delusions firmly beaten out of him by fate."[53] On a narrative level, *Max Payne 3* is indeed the story of a stranger in a strange land, in this case a washed-up failure of a former New York cop who has taken a job as a hired gun for the highest bidder, the wealthy São Paulo-based Branco family. Things quickly go south and Max finds himself doing battle with various government and paramilitary factions within the glitzy high-rise penthouse where the Branco family resides, the soccer stadium of the fictitious soccer club Galatians FC (a reference to the most valuable team in real-world Brazilian soccer, Sport Club Corinthians Paulista), and of course the favelas: both the fictional Favela Nova Esperança (based on the real-world Favela Japiaçu) and the "vertical favela" of the abandoned Hotel Palácio Imperial (based on the real-life Edificio São Vito). This barrage of contrasting Brazilian cultural environments presents challenges to the player at the same time that it parallels the protagonist's loss of control over the situation unraveling before him, as member after member of the Branco family falls victim to violence that Max is unable to prevent. The designers of *Max Payne 3* are sufficiently self-aware to take continuous stabs at Max's attempts to perform as the foreign hero sent in to shoot up Brazil and save the day, a task at which he repeatedly fails, leaving the player wounded but eager for redemption. At one point, the game's dialogue even offers what could be interpreted as a comment on the developers' own variety of favela tourism: stumbling upon a street party in the favela, Max quips, "This was the kind of reality Americans paid top dollar to see. Slums had become tourist attractions, places where yuppies could gawk at the endless spirit of the poor from the inside of their bulletproof buses." *Max Payne 3* offers the player an armchair opportunity to inhabit the favela, but Max's antiheroic experiences offer painful reminders of the importance of maintaining awareness of the cultural cues in the surrounding environment rather than acting like a naïve tourist.

The protagonist's disorientation is echoed by many aspects of *Max Payne 3*'s playable environments, in which a saturated level of cultural detail indicates at every turn that Max is out of his element, in a land that he does not comprehend. A soundtrack replete with Brazilian bossa nova, pop, and hip-hop artists as well as graffiti tags rendered in the style of Brazilian *pichação* demonstrate Rockstar's attempts to create a culturally elaborate—and somewhat disorienting—semiotic domain (figure 4.15). These clues, anthropological objects, or semiotic placeholders for Brazilian culture, of course, do not appear by chance but by design. In a series of blog posts leading up to the game's release, Rockstar explained the research and development process for *Max Payne 3*:

Figure 4.15
Max Payne 3 (Rockstar 2012)

Gathering assets to help accurately inform and create faithful game level environments set in São Paulo, Rockstar game developers and designers took several trips to the area to extensively document everything from the glamour and exclusivity of posh spots like Avenida Morumbi, Avenida Paulista and the Jardins district, to harsh high-crime locales like Favela Japiaçu (Favela do Nove) and the infamous Edificio São Vito (aka Treme Treme or the Vertical Favela). Thousands of pictures were taken for mood and texture, local fashions and outfits were scanned for reference, and a diverse array of Paulistanos from all walks of life—from bossa nova singers to jujitsu champions to favela gang members—were consulted and interviewed to provide thorough background on the dazzling and dangerous world in which the game is set.[54]

The exoticism of these marketing materials notwithstanding, this type of research and development process is extremely rare in the world of video game development. Preparations for *Max Payne 3* included casting hundreds of character roles with local Paulistano talent to record more than ten thousand lines of Portuguese dialogue, contracting musicians for the soundtrack, and using a painstaking image-capture process that involved "scanning local models to serve as the faces and bodies of the game's extras, supporting roles, and Multiplayer character skins," a process that took around thirty minutes for each of the many individuals[55] (figure 4.16). All this detail adds up to what we could call, borrowing Viktor Shklovsky's terminology, a defamiliarizing experience, one that rewards the player with a unique and exotic environment to explore at the same time as it provides gameplay consistent with the narrative.

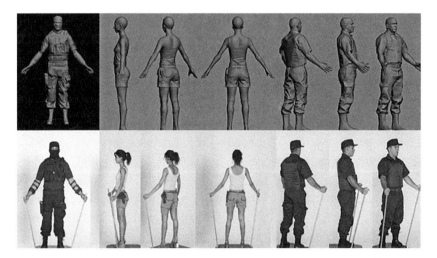

Figure 4.16
Image-capture process, *Max Payne 3* (Rockstar 2012)

The Brazilian cultural environment of *Max Payne 3*, then, functions multimodally to reinforce the game's narrative arc and themes. As Max goes through a midlife crisis in a land beyond his comprehension, the player experiences the many levels of disorientation and defamiliarization that I have discussed: the bedazzlement brought on by a foreign atmosphere, a deeply localized and particular simulation of culture, and a linguistic environment dominated by untranslated Brazilian Portuguese.[56] A final element of this destabilizing vision of the world comes from a particular visual effect used throughout the game that makes the graphics appear "glitchy" like an old television set losing its signal momentarily, an echo of the fact that the protagonist is a recovering alcoholic who keeps falling off the wagon, and hard. In fact, the function of one of the controller's buttons is to make Max pop some painkillers, an action that temporarily boosts his health while briefly imposing a woozy blur over his (and thus the player's) vision. Denial ain't just a river in Egypt, and Max's problems don't all stem from Brazil. Asked if the company was aiming to produce "Rockstar's take on addiction," founder Dan Houser said no, adding, "I'm not sure there is anything quite like addiction. That being said, any medium can find a way to tackle any issue, if that is what the creators want to do, and they can all do so well or badly. All mediums have strengths and weaknesses and advantages and disadvantages. Games are relatively young as a medium, but that does not mean you cannot address any topic you want to, you just have to find the tone and the mechanics to do so, just as you would in music, or film or literature."[57] Rockstar's in-depth research and development process makes for a remarkably immersive world, but can shy away from taking on too strong a message. Curiously enough, although Rockstar's favela foray did not aim to confront the troubled details of living with addiction through a video game, that is exactly the task undertaken by this chapter's final case study in favela semiotics, *Papo & Yo*.

In many ways, *Papo & Yo* stands in stark contrast to the other games discussed in this chapter. As noted in chapter 3, the game was produced by Minority Media, an independent studio based in Montreal that employs some seventeen people in all. This is especially noteworthy since the *Call of Duty* games generally take around a hundred people two years to make, while Rockstar games like *Max Payne 3* take a team of 500 around three years, meaning a sevenfold effort goes into a game like *Max Payne 3* relative to one like *Modern Warfare 2*.[58] *Papo & Yo* is not designed to measure up to these types of competitive metrics, but rather to follow the path of the independent developer, implementing a singular creative vision. The creator and lead designer of *Papo & Yo*, Vander Caballero, is a Colombian-born programmer who worked for several years in the mainstream game industry before going independent to develop this game, his first solo project. *Papo & Yo* was supported with a grant from Sony's "Pub Fund," a program that provides support to small developers, and was initially released in August 2012 as a download-only title through the PlayStation Store, with subsequent releases for home computers through Steam, Mac OS, and Linux.

Figure 4.17
Papo & Yo (Minority 2012)

On the level of gameplay, *Papo & Yo* is a charming and unique puzzle game that employs the architecture of the favela as the building blocks of a series of spatial riddles, all in a ludic realm meant to conjure the tone of Latin American magical realism.[59] This is an environment in which the imagination of the child protagonist, Quico, exercises complete control over his surroundings, turning the favela into a responsive and manipulable space (figure 4.17). An example of this comes early in the game, when the player picks up a series of cardboard boxes, and immediately realizes that as he manipulates the boxes, Quico is also moving individual box-shaped buildings from the favela in the background. Likewise, Quico's chalk drawings magically transform into ropes, staircases, and moving gears capable of altering the surrounding environment. In this way, the protagonist of *Papo & Yo* proceeds to construct a series of increasingly complex bridges, passageways, and mechanisms enabling him to reach new areas in the game.

Throughout the course of *Papo & Yo*, Quico is accompanied by three others. First, he is continually chasing after his runaway sister, who playfully eludes his every attempt, propelling his quest forward. He also has a small, backpack-sized robot named Lula, which functions as a sort of uplifting safety net, using its rocket feet to extend Quico's control to otherwise unreachable heights. Finally, he is accompanied by Monster, a surprisingly imposing presence, all hulking mass and potential for brute force wrapped up in a pale pink reptilian hide. When Monster moves, the ground thunders and shakes, but his presence can also be procedurally advantageous: the player must learn to use coconuts to lure Monster toward switch levers requiring his heavy weight to operate them. While Monster is a protective and enabling presence in Quico's life in this sense, he has a dark secret: he's addicted to eating frogs, and when he eats a frog, he literally bursts into flames, thundering through the area, thrashing everything in sight, and violently tossing around anyone present, even his beloved companion Quico. The game's procedural rhetoric encourages the player to formulate strategies to keep these attacks of Monster's frog-induced rage in check in order to make progress toward the ultimate goal of finding a cure for Monster's affliction.

If *Papo & Yo* sounds like an allegory for a childhood with an abusive and addictive parent that is because that is exactly what it is. Caballero, having grown up with an alcoholic father, and having used video games as a means of escape into a fantasy world, had long sought a way to convey that experience in the form of a game, while simultaneously celebrating the spirit of childhood innocence, optimism, and perseverance. If the array of metamedia surrounding the game—a video trailer featuring a live-action dramatization of Quico seeking refuge from his abusive environment in a fantasy world, or the many interviews in which Caballero has explained the inspiration for the game to the press—had not made this clear enough, there are multiple clues pointing to this allegorical meaning within the game itself. It begins with the dedication, "To my mother, brothers, and sister, with whom I survived the monster in my father." At one point late in the game, Quico feeds whiskey bottles through a tube that leads to Monster's space, where they turn into frogs, creating a ludic parallel between the frog addiction and alcoholism. Toward the game's climax the player experiences an enigmatic journey aboard a ski-lift-like device rising into the skies above the favela, while an oversized human figure—a child's imagined vision of Quico's father—sits pensively with his back to Quico, unapproachable due to the wall that divides them. Eventually, the figure transforms into Monster. The titles of the five checkpoints that are gradually unlocked as the player progresses also indicate phases of the relationship between Quico and Monster, which the game offers up as allegories for the stages in coping with an addicted parent: Discovery, Protection, Friendship, Anger, and finally Liberation. This allegorical meaning gradually develops over the course of *Papo & Yo*'s gameplay, culminating in a scene that manifests Quico's imagination in a constellation of boards and sheets of corrugated metal pulled from his imagined favela and suspended in the air as platforms before him (figure 4.18). Quico's manipulation of the favela buildings is more than just a way to solve his puzzles, it is an allegory for a vulnerable individual's control over his circumstances, a world where Quico can transform his environment at his whim, even if that control can only be exercised through his fleeting flights of fancy. Ultimately, the game suggests that the only real way to take control over a situation like this is to recognize that control is an illusion. At the apex of his quest to find a cure for Monster's addiction, Quico is visited by a presence that tells him the inevitable: "There is no cure for Monster, Quico. You have to let him go." And thus, as the architecture of the favela disintegrates and becomes a

Figure 4.18
Papo & Yo (Minority 2012)

sort of stairway to enlightenment, players are pushed to recognize their own powerlessness to find the cure that would allow Quico to have a conventional final victory in the game, as they come to the simultaneous allegorical realization of the impossibility of exercising control over another individual's addiction.

A comparative analysis of *Modern Warfare 2*, *Max Payne 3*, and *Papo & Yo* demonstrates that while the favela is a frequently employed semiotic domain in video games, this cultural context is symbolized and put to use in vastly different ways depending on the desires and demands of the games' designers. To be sure, game designers in all of these cases use the favela at least partially for the same reasons that have made it such a popular setting for works of literature and film: the setting of the favela is a familiar signifying context that conveys precarious urban existence, entrenched class divisions, and the potential for both danger and thrills. Game designers specifically use the favela for these purposes, but the extent to which they flesh out their depictions and the design practices they use vary widely. For the designers of *Modern Warfare 2*, the cultural context of the favela boiled down to a number of metonymic details meant to represent the broader whole: familiar improvised architecture and outlying land-marks like Christ the Redeemer, as well as written and spoken Brazilian Portuguese, tropical fauna, and other visual and environmental signifiers of *brasilidade* like the soccer field. Rock-star takes this attention to detail several steps further with *Max Payne 3*, adding in complex pro-cesses of motion capture, voice recording, and reconstruction of real-life settings to develop an environment that parallels and enhances the narrative by adding to the player's experience of disorientation, one of the game's central themes. Finally, *Papo & Yo* is a demonstration that using the favela impactfully in a game is not only a matter of more money and more effort on the part of game designers, but also of the underlying vision of how that setting relates to the overall experience of the game, and the messages its designers seek to convey. The architecture of the favela in *Papo & Yo* is not just a symbolic environment rich with the signifying potential it holds in other realms; it is also a functional element of game design. Quico attempts to exercise control over his world emotionally while the player must simultaneously control the world through manipulation of the environment in correspondence with the demands of the game's procedural dynamics. And thus in the most compelling examples of its use in video games, the favela not only has thematic meaning, but ludic meaning as well.

Conclusion: How Cultural Meaning Is Made in Video Games

The diverse approaches to the depiction of culture in games explored in this chapter demonstrate the importance of critical attention to the specific ways culture functions within video games, relative to the particular obstacles and affordances of the games in question. There are certain characteristics that are shared by all video games as semiotic domains. As we have seen, above and beyond their narrative elements, video games generate meaning nonlinguistically in the form of symbolic tokens and anthropological objects that convey cultural context. Moreover, electronic media in general destabilize the relationship between the signifier and the signified, situating flickering signifiers in nonstatic semiotic domains in which their meaning must be activated by a subjective player or actor. Therefore in video games meaning is not static, but unlocked through algorithmic grammars of action in which players harmonize their actions with the coded rules of the software and the physical demands of the hardware. Signifiers take on meaning contextually in video games, and not necessarily in alignment with their "real-world" meaning—Christ the Redeemer is a signifier used in games not (just) as a religious monument but also as a means of ludic advancement.

Cultural representations drawing on symbols and imagery from Latin American cultures span the entire history of the video game medium. Early creators of text-based and graphic adventure games used indigenous temples, skulls, and hidden treasure in their design, initiating a tradition of cultural representation that has endured in major series like *Tomb Raider*, as well as innumerable other examples of games from a spectrum of genres that have drawn on the symbolic archives of the ancient cultures of Latin America to develop and enhance their semiotic domains. The history of conquest and colonization in Latin America has also provided rich source material for the development of management simulation games in particular, which allow for the presentation of a variety of outcomes in dynamic scenarios with ever-changing sets of variables. Likewise, the trope of Latin America as the setting for urban or jungle-based guerrilla warfare reflects the relationship between video games and related traditions of cultural production, such as the popular action films on these same subjects produced contemporaneously with many major video games and series. A closer examination of particular cases of the Day of the Dead and the favela shows the contextual variability in meaning that is possible in video games of different genres, eras, and styles, even when those games are accessing the same symbolic repertoire.

On the one hand culture can be a superficially "skinned" and interchangeable element of game design. Every game involves a representational *skin* overlying the operational mechanics defined by the game's code. Once the rules and basic operations of a game have been programmed, the aesthetic, musical, and representational characteristics can be swapped out, allowing for a single basic game format to be reborn in multiple formats with differing narratives and environmental characteristics. This is known in game design as *skinning*, and is generally thought of negatively, "suggesting commercial exploitation without fundamental innovation"; however, the process of skinning can also be considered a positive for game design insofar as it allows for "the slow refinement of basic ideas toward perfection."[60] Some critics referred to Rockstar's *Red Dead Redemption* as "*Grand Theft Equine*," levying accusations that the game was little more than *GTA* with a Western skin, given that it features many of the same underlying mechanics as the *GTA* series. The "Studio" map in *Call of Duty: Black Ops II* (2012), set in a Hollywood studio back lot, is a skinned version of the "Firing Range" map from the game's 2010 prequel, which was situated in Revolution-era Cuba. The newer version portrays Hollywood through a space filled with varying film sets: a medieval castle, an urban invasion by aliens, and a dinosaur research center with moving animals. These are interchangeable elements of the game's skin used to provide a specific cultural context: the tropical Cuban shooting range, rather than Hollywood props and set pieces, is filled with military barracks, palm trees, and artillery equipment. Skinning shows how a cultural environment can be key to the gameplay experience, at the same time as it demonstrates the potential for cultural portability or modification of gamespace through the manipulation of characteristics on the game's surface. Skinning, of course, has its advantages for designers in terms of code reusability and turnaround time. On the one hand, when another multiplayer map is needed, the makers of *Call of Duty* can reskin an existing map, transforming it through cultural and environmental contextualization without having to build the map from the ground up. On the other hand, culture can be incorporated into game design in ways that goes beyond superficial skinning, such as in the contextual elements paralleling the major themes of the story in *Max Payne 3*, where the environmental defamiliarization experienced by the player echoes the protagonist's misadventures as a stranger in a strange land. And in some of the most ambitious game design visions, as in the use of the living/dead world in *Guacamelee!* or the utilization of favela architecture as a means for ludic and affective advancement in *Papo & Yo*, culture can be fully integrated into the core dynamics of gameplay as well as the game's narrative and environment.

Cases such as these offer clear demonstrations of how cultural meaning can be generated through gameplay in a manner that cannot be reduced to its representational or narrative signification. This is why it is helpful to keep in mind Barthes's critical insistence on seeking out the "third meaning" beyond informational and even symbolic levels of signification, in which meaning is produced in ways that exceed language's capacity to articulate that meaning. Following Barthes, analysts of culture in games must be sensitive to the "obtuse meaning" of cultural signifiers that lies beyond our capacity to decode them in linguistic form. Seeking the obtuse meaning in games demonstrates that the familiar signifiers of the Day of the Dead or the favela are used in video games not just as representational, informational, or anthropological objects, not just as symbols pointing to another truth, but as functional elements that create meaning through contextual use. Cultural signifiers in video games do not simply mean the same thing as those same signifiers mean in a different context, whether in the "real world" or in another mediated form. When we seek out the obtuse meaning of culture in games, the way culture is signified beyond language's grasp, we can begin to accurately account for the particular ways that culture is conveyed through the semiotic systems of video games.

5   SPACE

Space: it was hardly the final frontier for video games. Rather, considerations related to spatiality and environment have been fundamental concerns for game design and analysis from the start. This chapter examines the spatialization of culture in video games, building on the substantial body of existing analysis concerning video game space from the viewpoint of game design or player experience or both, as well as taking into account critical perspectives on the relationship between culture and space in other media traditions. From a game development standpoint, a culturally coded gamespace can add dimension to semiotic and narrative elements by contextualizing them within a specific environment with its own particular manners of conveying meaning. Game designers—working within the parameters of the hardware and software, programming languages, and game engines available to them in a particular place and time—not only adapt settings from real-life spaces with their own cultural connotations, but also make innumerable decisions throughout the design process aimed at augmenting the cultural context of their gamespaces. From the perspective of gameplay, spatial exploration, discovery, and "virtual tourism" are often cited as motivating factors for gamers across the globe. From text-based adventure games to three-dimensional open worlds, culture has been a concern in the development of game interfaces and environments since the onset of the medium, making it crucial to consider the role of culture when seeking to explain how meaning is generated within video game space.

Many game scholars cite spatiality as one of the most significant aspects in distinguishing games from other media, so much so that some see video games as more closely linked to architecture than to film or literature.[1] James Newman argues that "gameplay may not only be seen as bounded in space, but also as a journey through it,"[2] while Henry Jenkins highlights space's relationship to narrative in creating meaning, asserting that "[g]ame designers don't simply tell stories; they design worlds and sculpt spaces."[3] Edvin Babic goes a step further: "More than time, events, and goals, almost all computer games celebrate and explore spatial representation as their central theme."[4] Game spaces are unique because they are spaces that are at once *present in* and *separate from* the spaces of everyday life. In this sense video games can be seen as heterotopias, which Michel Foucault defined as "counter-sites, a kind of effectively enacted utopia in which the real sites, all the other real sites that can be found within the culture, are simultaneously represented, contested, and inverted."[5] And indeed, video games are spaces in which an endless array of "real sites" from known cultural contexts are "represented, contested and inverted," heterotopic locales ritualistically detached from "real life" yet ultimately inseparable from it.

As with narrative techniques, "camera" angles, and game rules, the use of space in video games corresponds to numerous traditions of representation. Most notably, video game spaces appropriate the established techniques of painting, photography, cinema, and just as importantly, those of architecture and computer-aided design, putting them to new uses. Those traditions are never far from hand—referring to their influence on contemporary technology, Manovich goes so far as to argue, "the nineteenth-century panorama can be thought of as a transitional form between classical simulations (wall paintings, human-size sculpture, diorama) and VR [Virtual Reality]."[6] Manovich points to the importance of understanding the ways games relate not just visually or conceptually but also spatially to other forms of representation. Games' fundamental difference from other traditions, as with so many of the other aspects that they remediate, relates to player immersion, embodiment, and interaction with the virtual space, all of which expands games' capacity for conveying cultural experiences. This chapter traces the conceptual progression in the uses of culture in video game space, examining the spatialization of Latin American culture throughout the history of the medium. Ultimately, this chapter demonstrates that no analysis of culture in games is complete without a discussion of space; and likewise a comprehensive analysis of space in video games must take culture into account.

Landscape, Setting, and Environment

The transitions among landscape, setting, and environment in the representational arts are transgenerational as well as transmedial, responding to various technological advances of different historical eras. Video games use space in a way that responds to traditions including nineteenth-century landscape painting and photography, the use of setting by the directors of Hollywood's Golden Age, and contemporary cinematic practices such as the use of computer-generated imagery, computer action modeling, and motion capture. But games fundamentally alter these practices by situating them within a multidimensional and mutable gamespace. This transformation into a multimodal game *environment*, as opposed to a still *landscape* or a narrative *setting*, involves a level of interactivity and responsiveness absent in the prior media. This is the main reason Shoshana Magnet distinguishes pictorial, photographic, and filmic landscapes from interactive "gamescapes," in order "to underline the fact that the virtual landscapes found in video games are not static objects 'to-be-looked-at,' but are dynamic and require the active involvement of the player in their construction."[7] Video games engage players in multisensory and participatory exploration of space, requiring them to interpret input such as on-screen images (both diegetic visual clues as well as nondiegetic health levels and other indicators in the heads-up display),[8] environmental sounds, and physical feedback like controller vibration, all of which distinguishes the medium from other forms of spatial representation.

The study of landscape, unlike that of film or video games, comes from a tradition of the static image, particularly the legacy of nineteenth-century painting and photography. The observer of a landscape is assumed to be situated in "a fixed point of a static scene," while the film viewer takes a "mobile view on a mobile world,"[9] and this mobility is multiplied in the spatialized activity of video game play. Films generally use space as a setting for action—in Martin Lefebvre's terminology, "the place where something happens, where something takes place and unfolds."[10] While video game spaces are certainly frequent sites for action and interaction, they also provide myriad opportunities for players to pause, contemplate, and consider their surroundings. Unbound by the constraints of a ninety-minute narrative arc, video game design opens up landscape in a new way, as an experiential and interactive event within a broader environment. Indeed, in many games there are moments when the action is momentarily halted by something akin to what Lefebvre refers to as the viewer's "landscape gaze" with regard to film—that is, a moment in which "the spectator mentally arrests the unfolding of the film and internally holds the space for contemplation until returning to the narrative mode."[11] Situated within the spatial environment of a video game, such "landscape moments" can enhance the player's experience. "What is attractive" in these moments of pause and contemplation, Calleja explains, "is not only the beauty of the landscape but the element of pleasant surprise at making the discovery."[12] This is one way interactivity fundamentally transforms the ways video games relate to earlier traditions of spatial representation.

Like film and theater, setting is a central consideration in the development of video games, though its uses are also transformed through their adaptation to a different medium. Film directors have long sought to choose a setting that would reflect the overall tone of their works, creating the circumstances in which "[p]lace becomes spectacle, a signifier of the film's subject, a metaphor for the state of mind of the protagonist."[13] Setting is cultural as well, the cinematic "spectacle" being dependent in part on the context in which a film's action takes place. It is in this sense that a film's setting can function as a "symbol that stands for relationships, values and goals of a group of people, e.g. in the form of national attributes,"[14] or more critically as "an ideologically charged cultural creation whereby meanings of place and society are made, legitimized, contested, and obscured."[15] Unlike the single viewpoint offered by the landscape gaze, in cinema setting is a context for metaphorical signification and a space of cultural contestation. Jameson famously referred to space as the "fundamental organizing concern" in the process of cognitive mapping, or "the practical reconquest of a sense of place and the construction or reconstruction of an articulated ensemble which can be retained in memory and which the individual subject can map and remap along the moments of mobile, alternative trajectories."[16] The viewer of a film, like the occupant of a real city, creates a mental depiction of the space they or their narrative occupies, a cognitive map that allows for a sense of spatial context.

Video games allow their players to create ever more complex cognitive maps. Calleja has argued that "[a]s cognitive maps of game environments improve, the player's spatial disposition to them shifts from the conceptual to the inhabited," leading to internalization of a game's spatial architecture and "a stronger sense of inhabiting the game space."[17] This means that as players explore a game's environment, they cease to rely upon guidance mechanisms like maps and radar, turning to their experiential knowledge and the spatial familiarity that supplants the cognitive map with inhabited space. Video game space must be considered in terms of interactivity, responsiveness, and function above and beyond its relationship to traditions of spatial representation in film and the visual arts. If setting is *the space where the story takes place* and landscape is *space freed from eventhood*,[18] the video game environment can be characterized as *evental space*.[19] Video game spaces are virtual environments in which actual events occur: areas are explored, discoveries are made, and gaming literacy is increased. Rather than space in isolation or as the setting for the narration of events, video game space is an environmental context for the active creation of culturally contextualized meaning.

Cultural Considerations for Gamespace

Culture has been incorporated into numerous aspects of gamespace since the inception of the video game medium, and continual advances in design techniques have allowed for simultaneous improvements in the possibilities for the spatialization of culture. In "Space in the Video Game," Mark J. P. Wolf defines eleven different "spatial structures" including entirely text-based games with no visual space, one-screen games, scrolling games, and interactive three-dimensional environments, among others.[20] Examples of Latin American cultural representation can be found for each of Wolf's categories—we could think, for example, of the ways the region's cultures are interpreted in a range of spatial environments including the 1980s text adventures *The Mask of the Sun* and *Amazon*, single-screen games like *Pelé's Soccer* (Atari 1980), flying combat scrollers like *Harrier Attack* or *Jungle Strike*, two-axis scrollers like *Sid Meier's*

Civilization and *Tropico* (Gathering of Developers 2001), or interactive three-dimensional environments in games like *Just Cause*, *Mercenaries 2*, *Tomb Raider*, and *Max Payne 3*. While examples of Latin American cultural representation have existed in all types of spatial frames throughout the history of game design, the relationship between video game space and Latin American culture—and moreover, the relationship between video game space and culture in general—bears substantial further exploration.

Latin America has appeared in video game spaces since the earliest days of the medium, even in games that might appear to be devoid of spatial representation altogether—the types of text-based adventure games Wolf categorizes as having "no visual space." One such example, *Indiana Jones in Revenge of the Ancients* (Mindscape 1987), has Indy traveling through Mexican pyramids and jungles in an effort to recover a key indigenous artifact and, naturally, to keep the Nazis from getting to it first. Though the game is entirely textual in format, it represents Latin America through a narrative focused on exploration of virtual spaces. Consider the centrality of spatial depiction in the game's opening lines:

> With the whine of bullets humming in your ears like annoying mosquitos, you drop through a gaping hole, hoping it will lead to the central chamber of the Tepotzteco Pyramid, and not another Mazatec trap. It's about time you found the power key and got it back to the Army types in D.C. As your boots hit the solid stone floor there is a scraping and sliding noise as a massive stone jams into place above you.
>
> This is a vast, shadowy space. An evil smell mingles with the sound of dripping water. Riverlets [*sic*] of viscous slime run down the eastern wall from an invisible seam far above. Through a door to the south, in the center of a domed room is a golden key, radiant in a shaft of white light. To your north is an open doorway, eighteen feet high, through which a luminous glow emanates. A carved stone panel is centered in the western wall.[21]

As the introductory text of *Indiana Jones in Revenge of the Ancients* makes clear, spatiality prevails even in a game that is devoid of the types of three-dimensional environments to which today's gamers are accustomed. Architectural details (a solid stone floor; a domed room), directional cues (above you; through a door to the south), and sensorial descriptions (a scraping and sliding noise; a vast, shadowy space) provide a sense of spatial orientation, while at the same time cultural cues (the Tepotzteco Pyramid; a carved stone panel) serve as reminders of the Aztec environment that the player inhabits.

In similar ways, other primarily text-based "graphical text adventure" games round out the Latin American cultural spaces depicted in their limited visual imagery with narrative detail. Examples like *The Mask of the Sun* and *Where in the World is Carmen San Diego?* (Broderbund 1985) complement their verbal rendering of Latin American cultural space with images depicting the jungles, temples, and colonial architecture in which the actions take place (figure 5.1). A number of other text-based adventure games carried on the tradition of the explorer/

Figure 5.1
Where in the World Is Carmen San Diego? (Broderbund 1985)

adventure genre, including the early-1990s Spanish games *La diosa de Cozumel, Los templos sagra-dos,* and *Chichén Itzá,* as well as games from the United States such as *Tombs & Treasures* (Infocom 1991). Other graphical text adventure games were situated in the contemporary sociopoliti-cal spaces of Latin America, including Telarium's 1986 PC game *Amazon,* written and partially programmed by bestselling novelist Michael Crichton as an adaptation of his novel *Congo,* then rewritten due to legal concerns, resignifying the African jungle setting as South America in the process. *Hidden Agenda* (Springboard 1988) was a political strategy game set in the fictional Central American nation of Chimerica, which required the player to achieve a sustainable bal-ance in public opinion in a setting highly reminiscent of Nicaragua after the triumph of the Sandinista Revolution in 1979. Graphical text adventure games such as these combined written text and visual elements to create a dynamic and innovative spatial framework for cultural representation.

Though it is by no means all-encompassing, the transition from two-dimensional or tex-tual formats to fully interactive environments seems now to have been an inevitability for game design. Historical signposts signal this transition in games set in Latin America—*Amazon: Guardians of Eden* (Access 1992) still relied upon two-dimensional images, but added animation to its cutscenes, while in *Flight of the Amazon Queen* (Warner 1995), the player moves through two-dimensional space and selects actions from visual menu icons rather than entering textual commands. The transition from a textual to an audiovisual environment is crystallized in *Amazon Trail II* (1996) and *Amazon Trail 3rd Edition* (1999), sequels to developer/publisher MECC's 1994 game *The Amazon Trail*, which first added animation and then real voices and screen-capture acting to the game's audiovisual display. A recent resurgence of two-dimensional and even *non-dimensional* gamespaces rely upon experimentation with innovative game mechanics—British developer Somethin' Else's iOS games *Papa Sangre* (2010) and *Papa Sangre II* (2013) have been respectively described as a "video game with no video" and "a game for your ears," because they are entirely audio-based horror-themed games set in the Mexico-based Kingdom of Papa Sangre. And even in this nonvisual portrayal of culture, spatiality is of the essence, as the game's designers depended upon advances in the generation of 3D binaural audio effects in order to create the sonic illusions of spatial inhabitation necessary to achieve their vision.

In his book *Video Game Spaces*, Michael Nitsche divides his analysis between five spatial planes: rule-based (mathematical programming rules), mediated (presentation on the image plane), fictional (imagined space), play (player and hardware; where play takes place), and social (space affected by interaction with others).[22] While the present analysis touches on aspects of all of these spatial categorizations, the primary concern of this chapter is with the mediated and fictional planes, through which space is represented visually and imagined conceptually. The mediated space, per Nitsche, "consists of all the output the system can provide in order to present the rule-based game universe to the player," while the fictional space is the world the player imagines from the provided information.[23] In the interaction between these two spatial planes, the cultural capacity of video game space is revealed to be both a programmed element of game design and a component of the fictional universe that exists beyond and around a game.

Like other elements of gameplay, the environment can function as an obstacle or an affordance depending on its deployment by the player in relation to the game's rules and coding. As Newman explains: "The player is not merely pitted against the game space but rather is encouraged to think about how the space can be utilized to assist in the attainment of the player's objective."[24] Likewise, it is important to remember that though cultural verisimilitude is an important element of a convincing game environment, its significance is subordinated to the overarching goal of a satisfying gameplay experience, so "while videogames can be said to be spatial, it is their deviation from the patterns of 'real space' that enables them to function as games."[25] And lest we go too far over the edge and fall into the trap of technological determinism, we must weigh player agency as one of the determining factors in creating meaning for game space above and beyond the software's code itself. As Laurie Taylor explains, videogame spaces "are more than simply the sum of their code—they are experiential spaces generated through code and the player's interaction with the execution of that code through the medium of the screen."[26] Thus gamespace can be used to the player's advantage or disadvantage, in ways that go with or against the intentions coded into the games preprogrammed rules, but its meaning is consistently defined through activity.

In other words, culture takes on meaning through use within game environments. In "Game Design as Narrative Architecture," Jenkins emphasizes the role of space in what he calls "environmental storytelling," explaining that "spatial stories can evoke pre-existing narrative associations; they can provide a staging ground where narrative events are enacted; they may embed narrative information within their mise-en-scene; or they provide resources for emergent narratives."[27] This helps explain the associations in game design between space and narrative, and the ways that narrative meaning can be conveyed through culturally coded game spaces in a nonlinear, nontextual fashion. As Jenkins elaborates, "[w]ithin an open-ended and exploratory narrative structure like a game, essential narrative information must be redundantly presented across a range of spaces and artifacts, since one can not assume the player will necessarily locate or recognize the significance of any given element."[28] This is how cultural messages are often communicated in games, as underlying but continuously reiterated elements of the environment that serve to provide an overarching sense of cultural context. Because video games present culture experientially to the player, its means of iteration are also transformed in order to express culture in ways that cannot be captured through language or other systems of representation. Culture is a major element of the environmental contexts of video games, and the possibilities for cultural expression and experience are transformed with each successive technological advance and design breakthrough in the game industry.

Sound and Culture in Gamespace

Sound is an element inseparable from the spatial environment, as well as a key means of cultural signification in gamespace. Like visual and linguistic signs, sounds convey meaning about the cultural space to which they pertain. As Alejandra Bronfman and Andrew Grant Wood argue in their introduction to *Media, Sound, and Culture in Latin America and the Caribbean*, "[s]ound (both natural and mediated) offers us much in the way of content," and moreover, "[i]f sight remains the primary sense by which we constitute and represent our scholarship, then we have marginalized much that is relevant to other sense records potentially rich in information and cultural clues."[29] Michele Hilmes echoes this point, suggesting that "sounds in their creation and in their context are *representations*: the product of a specific communication situation, layered with meaning."[30] Nitsche has noted that sound effects "are part of a virtual world's identity,"[31] with a major impact on the signifying experience of gameplay—for example, "[e]laborate soundscapes can build up a dramatic foreshadowing, provide direct acoustic engagement up to the climax, and mark an end with a cathartic aftermath."[32] Video game sound is carefully crafted to contribute to the overall gameplay experience, including the environmental contextualization of cultural meaning. As Nitsche argues, the "acoustic telling of space in modern video games has become highly elaborate, not to simulate realistic worlds but to evoke dramatic game locations."[33] Furthermore, as others have noted, sounds affect video game meaning by "informing the player about the state of the game world and by cuing emotions that enhance the immersiveness of the game," and "when used effectively can evoke feelings from excitement, to melancholy, to desperation."[34] Every sound in a video game has been carefully selected for a representational purpose by the game's designers, and each sound has the potential to affect the depth and functional meaning of the simulation.

Contextualized within gamespace, all sound—in-game dialogue, ambient noise, sound effects tied to actions, the musical score, and licensed musical tracks—functions as a *feedback system*. Feedback systems in current video games are multiple, pervasive, and increasingly naturalized, not to mention integrated with the cultural environments of present-day games. Feedback systems include not only conventional point tallies and health meters but also environmental cues that indicate player progress as well as missteps. Culturally coded elements are identifiable in all four types of in-game sound identified by the editors of *Understanding Video Games: The Essential Introduction*. These sound categories include (with some examples from games situated in Latin American gamespace): (1) vocalization (spoken dialogue in Spanish or Portuguese); (2) sound effects (footsteps across tin rooftops and plywood buildings of the favela, or echoing through the stone hallways of jungle temples); (3) ambient effects (cheeping frogs and tweeting birds in certain areas, dripping pipes and construction work in others); and (4) music (the Caribbean soundtrack to *Tropico*, or diegetic salsa music playing on a Panamanian yacht in a side mission of *Max Payne 3*).[35] In addition to these *types* of video game sound that can contribute to the conveyance of cultural meaning, there are several *contextual effects* that help shape sounds' meaning relative to gameplay, including effects of: (A) environment, such as "the size of the location, the material of the walls, the characteristics of the carrying medium (air, water, etc.), the weather conditions," and other qualities; (B) spatiality, such as the relative volume of nearby and distant sounds; and (C) physics, as "sound may be affected by relative movement (e.g. it may mimic Doppler shift), etc."[36] Therefore there are not only many reasons to consider the impact of sound on cultural meaning in video games, but there are also many important considerations to take into account when analyzing sound's role in the process of cultural spatialization.

The use of foreign languages in video games is a particularly functional sonic indicator of culture, and in fact foreign language use can relay important information even to players who are not familiar with the language in question. This is because communication occurs on two levels when foreign languages are used in video games, on a narrative (or representational) level and on a ludic level. Take for example the use of Brazilian Portuguese in two of the games discussed in chapter 4, *Call of Duty: Modern Warfare 2* and *Max Payne 3*. In *Modern Warfare 2* the "Brazilian Militia," a playable faction within the game's multiplayer mode, are the primary Portuguese speakers throughout the game. Brazilian Militia members are audible to other players as they communicate among themselves in Portuguese about their actions—"Atirando uma granada de mão," "Apareceu de repente!," "Alvo neutralizado!" or in the campaign, "Tá pensando que invade a minha favela assim?" This type of foreign language communication is a common feature in the *Call of Duty* series, meaning that a hardcore player might know how to say "Enemy down!" or "Throwing frag!" in English, Spanish, Portuguese, Russian, and Arabic. On the one hand, for a player who understands (or learns to understand) the language being spoken, these (foreign-)language phrases retain their representational meaning—they describe the action being taken in throwing a grenade or help to identify a downed target. However, with this type of linguistic usage, it is generally assumed that the player *does not speak the language* in question, and therefore the meaning that is conveyed is not only representational but also ludic, creating a meaning specific to the game environment. These phrases, spoken in Brazilian Portuguese, can offer important ludic information even to the non-Portuguese-speaking player: the sound of spoken language can reveal the location of other players, their relative proximity or distance, and most importantly, whether the person in the next room is a friend or foe. All of this valuable ludic information can be gleaned through a number of game mechanics combined with the fact that Portuguese is being spoken, independent of the linguistic meaning of the words being used.

Language can also be used in other ways to enhance a game's cultural context, as demonstrated by the ubiquitous use of untranslated Portuguese in *Max Payne 3*. During the bulk of the game, both in moments of action and moments of narrative exposition, Max is surrounded by characters speaking a language he does not speak himself. Likewise, the player is constantly exposed to spoken and written Portuguese throughout the game—voiceovers play continually, and almost all of the characters speak Portuguese, at least in background dialogue. Written Portuguese is involved with many of the clues (receipts, letters, files) that must be interpreted visually, as well as being a constant part of the surroundings in the form of advertisements and signage. What is most remarkable about *Max Payne 3*'s employment of Brazilian Portuguese is that the game offers no option for English subtitles for these tens of thousands of lines of foreign-language dialogue. Therefore, only those players fluent in Portuguese will glean the representational meaning communicated by the use of the language, and this definitely works to their advantage within the game, revealing information that remains concealed to other players. In this way, too, the non-Portuguese-speaking player's experience echoes Max's own, as they are immersed together in an environment that is semiotically cryptic and linguistically incomprehensible. These examples reflect how spoken language can be used not only to deepen a game's cultural environment, but to convey important information, whether players are fluent in the language in question or they don't speak a word.

Music, in addition to spoken language and other types of culturally coded sound, can have a major impact on the way culture is conveyed in the gameplay experience. Zach Whalen argues that "music is essential to the semantic operations of a videogame," and that "the musical soundtrack of a game affects the user's experience and creates a seamless impression of game-play,"[37] fluidly combining with other visual and interactive elements to round out the game's environment. Video games' extended periods of gameplay (relative to feature-length films, for example) and variations in level of action (from aimless wandering to brutal confrontation) place unique demands on composers of musical scores as well as curators of video game soundtracks. These demands include not only extending the length and number of tracks included, but also the need to create new approaches to the fusion of music and environment. This has led to the development of *dynamic music generation*, a process through which music files are fragmented into different sections and set to play in loops for given periods of time, after which point "[s]pecific conditions—anything from the protagonist's state of health to the type of on-screen action—may combine to inform the game what music is most appropriate; similarly, built-in rules may tell the game how and when to shift from one composition to another."[38] There are several recent games set in Latin America featuring dynamic music generation as part of their soundscape, including *Tomb Raider: Underworld* and *Red Dead Redemption*, both of which are discussed in detail later in this chapter. Thus, in the most complex of contemporary game environments, score music is not a linear affair along the lines of classical orchestral composition, but rather an active, algorithmic component that is tied through software code to the actions undertaken by the player.

In today's game design world there are several possible approaches to composing the musical score to a game, some more conventional and others more innovative. On the one hand, there are games that rely on a variety of songs from one or two artists to round out the cultural environment, such as *Tropico 3*, which features a brassy jazz soundtrack performed by Miami-based artist Alex Torres, along with a handful of other Caribbean performers. Other games feature original scores written by a single composer. For example, the scores of all of the games in Ubisoft's *Call of Juarez* series have been penned by Polish composer Pawel Blaszczak, who cites the classic film scores of American Westerns by Italian composer Ennio Morricone, as well as "Native American, Mexican, and Gypsy tunes" as influences to the games' musical environment.[39] In this way, composers frequently attempt to incorporate traditional sonic representations associated with a given cultural or historical environment into the musical score, alluding to cultural context through choices in instrumentation, musical genre, and compositional style. Another example is the score of *Papo & Yo*, which was composed by Brian D'Oliveira in collaboration with the game's designer Vander Caballero. D'Oliveira, who "grew up poor in South America," identified with the story of the game's working-class Brazilian child protagonist, and set to work applying his curiosity and passion for the region's music into the game's sonic atmosphere.[40] He incorporated dozens of unique acoustic instruments into the score, many of which struck Caballero as "unnameable, foreign and rare," in an attempt to "create a language ... something that feels familiar internally, something that resonates with your emotions. Something sonic and just as exotic and magical as the game."[41] Cases like *Papo & Yo* show how a composer can specifically aim to complement the vision of the game designers in developing the game's sonic environment.

In addition to (or even in place of) an original musical score, many games use songs by major recording artists on their soundtracks, another way of using music for cultural contextualization. The Mexican-themed levels in *Little Big Planet*, for example, feature songs by popular artists like Mexican Institute of Sound, as well as the song "Volver a comenzar" ("Starting Over Again") by Mexican alternative rock outfit Café Tacuba. These tracks are selected to round out the visual and interactive signifiers of Mexican culture featured in these levels of the game, but they also offer added value for the Spanish-speaking player—for example, the repetitive lyrics and hypnotizing chorus of "Volver a comenzar" represent a clever play on the repetitive starting and restarting of the gameplay, which also restarts the musical track. The game's British developers at Media Molecule also used music to enhance the cultural environment in *Little Big Planet PSP* (Sony 2009), which features songs by Brazilian artists like Astrud Gilberto and Bazeado for the game's climax at a Brazilian carnival parade. The New York-based soundtrack supervision team For *Max Payne 3* took things a step further, increasing the nuance of their portrayal of São Paulo by including recordings by more than a dozen contemporary Brazilian artists and groups, featuring a range of genres from samba and bossa nova to hip-hop. In addition to existing commercial recordings, *Max Payne 3*'s designers enlisted Paulistano rapper Emicida to record several original songs for the soundtrack, demonstrating how cultural context can be effected in part through the musical soundtrack's incorporation into the video game space.

While games like *Little Big Planet* and *Max Payne 3* have original scores in addition to their use of popular music, others have eschewed an original score altogether in favor of prerecorded tracks. Rockstar's *Grand Theft Auto* series has relied entirely upon in-game radio stations to provide its soundtrack up until *GTA V* (2013), the first in the series to feature an original score in addition to in-car radio. In games like the *GTA* series, radio stations are a central component to the multicultural urban environment, offering glimpses of the diverse population of the cities where they broadcast. *GTA V* features seventeen separate radio stations, including those dedicated to hip-hop (West Coast Classics, Radio Los Santos, FlyLo FM), electronica (Soulwax FM, Radio Mirror Park), rock and pop (Los Santos Rock Radio, Non Stop Pop FM), reggae (Blue Ark FM), Latin (East Los FM), alternative/punk (Vinewood Boulevard Radio, Channel X), soul/funk (Lowdown FM, The Space 103.2), international jazz (WorldWide FM), country/western

(Rebel Radio), and talk radio (WCTR, Blaine County Radio). Cultural context is conveyed in multiple ways on each of these radio stations: in the selection of music broadcast, the advertisements and political debates that cut in between songs, and the spoken dialogue of the DJs, who include stars from their respective musical genres such as the hosts of East Los FM, electronic artist Mexican Institute of Sound, and Mexican comic/musician Don Cheto. Latin music and culture have had a longstanding presence on *GTA's* radio dials, starting with Radio Espantoso, the Caribbean jazz, salsa and funk station in *GTA: Vice City* (Rockstar 2002), on which DJs Hector Hernandez and Pepe played hits from Mongo Santamaría, Xavier Cugat, Benny Moré, and Tito Puente, among others. *GTA IV* (2008) introduced San Juan Sounds, a station hosted by reggaeton artist Daddy Yankee, featuring Caribbean artists like Calle 13, Wisin & Yandel, and Don Omar. *GTA V's* East Los FM features a range of Mexican and Latin music including the narcocorridos of Los Tigres del Norte and Los Buitres de Culiacán; 1970s and 80s classics by Sonora Dinamita, Los Ángeles Negros, and Fandango; hip-hop acts like Milkman and La Liga; the quirky electro-pop of Hechizeros Band and Don Cheto; and punk screamers like Jessy Bulbo and La Vida Boheme. Range and diversity like this demonstrates that music is a cultural component of great relevance to the designers of the *GTA* series, a way to add sensorial detail to the diverse cultural environments in which the games take place.

In addition to providing added cultural detail for the player, radio stations are a way of contextualizing the culture of *GTA's* nonplayer characters, as the music choices in a given NPC's vehicle are frequently tied to the culture of the character's neighborhood, which is in turn tied to racial and economic background. A high percentage of residents in *GTA V's* Latin neighborhoods listen to East Los FM, while many African-American residents of Grove Street and Chamberlain Hills prefer one of the hip-hop stations, and the residents of rural Sandy Shores and Blaine County tend to listen to Channel X and Rebel Radio. This correspondence between radio station selection and a character's cultural traits is not consistent, however, nor does it always reinforce stereotypical cultural assumptions. But default radio stations are one way the game demonstrates the potential to convey cultural meaning through environmental cues. For example, all commercial vehicles and helicopters in *GTA V* default to the reggae station, The Blue Ark. In fact, taxi drivers almost universally prefer Latin music in the *GTA* universe, with secondary preferences for hip-hop or public/talk radio, according to the default radio stations in taxi cabs: the taxis in *Vice City* default to Radio Espantoso; in *GTA IV* they default to San Juan Sounds or hip-hop station The Beat 102.7; the cabs in *GTA V* default to East Los FM all the time, except when the cab is hotwired, in which case it defaults to West Coast Talk Radio. Does this imply that all civilian and military transportation workers in *GTA V* have an affinity for Jamaican music, or that all the cabbies in the series are Latin? No, but it demonstrates that music, like spoken language and environmental sound, has the potential to play a significant role in conveying cultural experience through video game sound.

In video games, sound combines with the spatial environment in order to produce a multidimensional cultural context. Sounds are selected, recorded, and integrated by game developers with specific functional purposes in mind, and sound contributes as a feedback system as well as a cultural indicator. Foreign language in games can be used for various purposes, whether to open the game to a different audience through language localization, through communicative meaning, or through ludic meaning conveyed through foreign language's transmission in accordance with a game's particular physics and mechanics. Music, like spoken language, is another major sonic indicator of culture in gamespace. Both musical score and licensed musical tracks contribute meaningfully to a game's cultural context, rounding out narrative, symbolic, and mechanical elements of games' meaning. Music can contribute to a game's representation of a single and specific cultural setting, or it can be used to showcase cultural diversity of the game's environment through the use of different genres of music in different cultural contexts. Because video game spaces are *audio*visual in nature, and because gameplay is a multisensorial experience, the perception of culture in gamespace is affected on myriad levels by sound.

Paradigms of Latin American Gamespace

In a history of development spanning four decades, commercial video games have incorporated culture into an increasingly broad spectrum of spatial environments. A number of typical cultural scenarios for video games now stand out, appearing first in the two-dimensional or textual spaces of late-1970s and early-1980s games, with continual updates including further development of the cultural context in subsequent iterations of games from the same genres and scenarios. With regard to the staging of Latin America in gamespace, there are three spatial paradigms that merit particular attention, each with its own implications for the spatialization of culture: (1) the *recursive space* that is opened up gradually in procedural adventures from *Pitfall!* to *Tomb Raider* to *Uncharted*; (2) the *isometric perspective* of "god games" including *Sid Meier's Civilization* and *Tropico*; and (3) the *open world* or "sandbox" environment of games like *Just Cause* or *Red Dead Redemption*. An examination of each of these prototypical gamespaces will demonstrate the degree to which cultural representation is determined by a game's spatial model.

Tomb Raiding and Recursive Space

As noted in chapter 1 of this book, some of the major motivators for gameplay include exploration, discovery, and acquisition, all of which rely on the player's relationship to space. Aylish

Wood highlights the significance of space to gameplay, describing the latter as "an experience through a combination of engagements with culturally embedded sound and imagery, a physical relation with a game interface, 'imaginative' connections with the game, its rules and objects, as well as the avatars of other players in multiplayer gaming environments."[42] This is why Wood refers to the use of "recursive space" in video games, or "a repeated procedure in which the outcome of each step is defined in terms of the results of previous steps."[43] This procedural conceptualization of video game space can be visualized as the way a player often "opens up" spaces gradually in a game, through a process of trial and error that leads to ways of working around obstacles to spatial advancement. On the most basic level, recursive space is frequently seen in video games that use a black, darkened, or blank map whose content is revealed bit by bit as the player progresses.

While map-based management simulations use recursive space to represent geographical exploration, action/adventure games frequently utilize recursive space to gradually guide the player through complex environmental puzzles. The basic procedural dynamics of the action/adventure genre—explore a new room or screen, discover the necessary clues to reach the next area, perform the series of maneuvers required to navigate the space successfully, and repeat these steps again—were established by text-based adventure games as well as early graphical adventures. The 1979 Atari game *Adventure*, a knights-and-dragons exploration featuring some thirty navigable screens, required the player to procedurally discover space, setting the stage for an enduring tradition in game design. By 1983, *Expedition Amazon* was using a text-based input system to lead to block-by-block revealing of a blacked-out map (figure 5.2), while *Quest for Quintana Roo* contained rooms and areas closed off to the player until necessary tasks had been performed and milestones met. But it was *Pitfall!* that really raised the bar for depth of a game environment in the early 1980s, because of its groundbreaking execution of a circular path of 255 navigable screens.[44] The instruction manual for *Pitfall!* describes the game as "a circular maze" and a "journey" to "encounter all 32 treasures," a spatial framework in which the player accesses the environment's benefits—bags of money, diamond rings, and gold and silver bars—by mastering the navigation of its hazards—rolling logs, scorpions, fires, snakes, crocodiles, swamps, quicksand, and tar pits.[45] The focus on navigation as well as environmental risk and reward would come to typify the action-adventure genre in the following decades.

In 1996, when players walked into the very first mission in the *Tomb Raider* series, they were also entering a relatively early three-dimensional rendering of the adventure genre's typical Latin American cultural setting. Having arrived in the Peruvian Andes, Lara Croft sets out in search of the tomb of the (fictitious) ancient ruler Qualopec. In the narrative cutscene preceding the first mission, a guide wearing a wide-brimmed hat and striped wool cassock guides Lara to a mountain dwelling, where he is suddenly and viciously torn apart by wolves despite Lara's attempt to intervene by gunning down the whole pack. The character has no dialogue in the

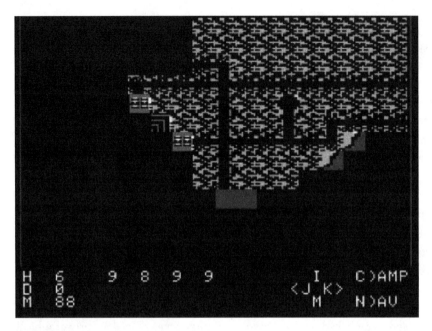

Figure 5.2
Expedition Amazon (Penguin Software 1983)

game, and his passing is merely the next guidepost allowing Lara to move forward. In this way, Lara's unnamed Andean guide embodies the manner in which the Latin American population has frequently been portrayed by games in this and other genres: as a decorative touch or a means to an end for the first-world protagonist. But it must be understood that the reduction of such characters to the level of their objective functionality is not—or at least not entirely—due to shortsightedness in game design. We must remember that nothing in gamespace appears by accident, but rather each element has a function, whether semiotic, procedural, or both. As Barry Atkins explains, "[i]n *Tomb Raider*, if it moves your best option is usually to kill it, and the expectation according to the internal logic of the game is that you should do so," since the real focus of the game is engagement with components of the game's architectural environment: levers, pulleys, ropes, and differently textured surfaces on the walls and ceilings that can be moved, manipulated, or climbed.[46] Christopher A. Paul reiterates the significance of environmental cues, explaining how adventure game environments offer the player "less explicit forms of persuasion" such as falling objects that block off pathways, conveniently colored objects that stand out to indicate an opportunity for interaction, and other elements that "interpolate gamers, encouraging them to pick up and play while offering them the ability to move smoothly without needing too much help."[47] Elements such as these make a functional difference in gameplay through the manipulation of space, demonstrating that the action/ adventure genre is fundamentally based upon the interaction between the lone explorer and an unknown but conquerable environment. Therefore, every element in the gamespace of the action/adventure game, both human and nonhuman, gains significance through its potential as a risk or reward to the player.

This may provide at least a partial explanation for the fact that Latin American locales in adventure games, like others from throughout the globe, are frequently devoid (or practically devoid) of population, with the player more commonly doing battle with spiders and jaguars, or focusing on the other major aspect of *Tomb Raider*'s gameplay: solving spatial puzzles. Though some *Tomb Raider* titles feature more shoot-'em-up action than others, the series focuses primarily upon player interaction with the environment through a series of spatially contextualized puzzles. The navigation and exploration of space by trial and error creates a recursive loop between player and software, requiring the player to make repeated attempts at advancement, each time incorporating the knowledge gleaned from the previous attempt. This recursive process of exploration requires the player to learn through cognitive and muscle response the combinations of buttons and maneuvers required, for example, to make Lara jump upon a ledge, shimmy across it, pull herself up to a standing position, pivot, balance upon a horizontal flagpole, leap to a hanging chandelier, or jump from crumbling rock holds to flimsy boards. Thus the player learns to navigate space through cognition and virtual occupation of the site in question, opening up space recursively with the solution of each consecutive environmental puzzle.

Eidos Interactive, the British design firm (now owned by Japanese publisher Square Enix) that is responsible for the *Tomb Raider* series, has produced more than twenty titles for a multitude of platforms spanning as many years of development. Over this time Eidos designers have taken a variety of approaches to the evocation of culture through space in the series. The 2008 game *Tomb Raider: Underworld* features immersive and responsive, lushly detailed worlds that offer variations on several conventional game scenarios: underwater exploration in the Mediterranean, spelunking in the icy caves of Jan Mayen Island in the Arctic Ocean, and deep jungle quests among the Buddhist temples of Thailand or the Mayan temples and caverns of southern Mexico. The game's depiction of the Mayan temple of Xibalbá—which is the Mayan name for the underworld but does not correspond to a real-world archeological site—is architecturally reminiscent of the seventh-century Mayan constructions at Palenque, Mexico, and abounds with details that help tie the game's virtual space to the real-life cultural environments it portrays. The temple's central ball court offers a 360-degree view of the surroundings, dominated by structures built of large limestone blocks, one of the many material clues that help indicate playable pathways. *Tomb Raider: Underworld* also features multiple environmental feedback systems: when the player is on the right path, colorful clues like parrots or flowers will appear; at each checkpoint a subtle bell rings faintly in the background, indicating progress; small treasures appear occasionally at the sides of the correct pathway; dynamic music generation makes the score's tempo pick up and its tone become more dramatic as the player approaches an objective; and different colors and materials are used for functional objects, such as the handholds on the walls of the Mayan temple of Xibalbá, which consist of sea-weathered limestone and seashells. Each of these elements demonstrates how cultural context can be integrated into persuasive feedback systems. The recursive space model demonstrates that a game's environment can also be procedural, the context for an ongoing trial-and-error process between player and software in which each step builds upon all those that came before. The action/adventure games examined earlier are exemplary of this process, since their players must respond to environmental cues in order to advance, and that advancement is defined in terms of spatial expansion.

God Games and Isometric Perspective

The games sometimes referred to as "god games"—the most ready referents being the *Sid Meier's Civilization* or *The Sims* (EA 2000) series—feature another type of spatial orientation known as isometric perspective. Isometric perspective is a technique borrowed from architectural drawing for the presentation of three-dimensional objects in a two-dimensional form, which unlike the top-down perspective allows the player to inhabit the gamespace in three dimensions.[48] Isometric perspective places the player in the position of looking down from above on a miniature world exposed to her total manipulation. There is a considerable history of resource management simulations and mixed-genre games using isometric perspective that are situated wholly or partially in Latin America, many of them focusing on themes of conquest and colonization. Early examples like *Utopia* (Mattel 1981) and *The Seven Cities of Gold* established enduring patterns carried on by a host of games including *Gold of the Americas: The Conquest of the New World* (figure 5.3), *Inca* and *Inca II: Nations of Immortality*, *Sid Meier's Colonization*, *Conquest of the New World* (Interplay 1996), *Imperialism II: The Age of Exploration*, the *Age of Empires II: The Conquerors* and *Age of Empires III: The War Chiefs* expansions (Microsoft 2000 and 2006), *American Conquest* (CDV 2003), *Anno 1602: Creation of a New World*, *Anno 1503: The New World,* and *Anno 1701* (Sunflowers 2006), all of which focused on management of societies during periods of conquest and colonial rule.

The gamespace of resource management simulations is inhabited by a multitude of manipulable *miniatures* that make up an NPC population to be controlled by the player in a variety of ways. While an avatar is meant to fix the player's identification to a single entity, "miniatures" is the term used to refer to characters that can be fully or partially controlled by the player, but

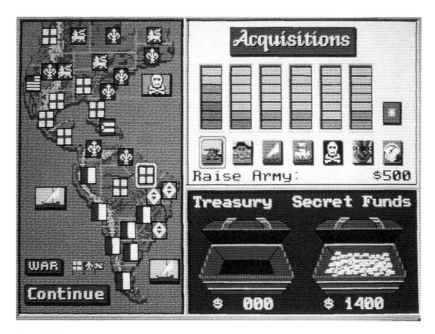

Figure 5.3
Gold of the Americas: The Conquest of the New World (SSG 1989)

do not represent the player.[49] Calleja argues that this dispersion of character identity results in "environmental agency," a form of control that "is not anchored to one particular entity but instead embraces the whole environment."[50] This means that in order to be successful, players of games in the isometric perspective must become one with the game's environment. Some god games are unique in combining the manipulation of miniatures with an identifiable avatar—for example, your choice of an array of real-life and fictional Latin American dictators in *Tropico*, or the Aztec emperor Moctezuma in *Civilization V* (2K Games 2010). The combination of an individual avatar with the distanced manipulation of miniatures further expands and diversifies the player's sense of environmental agency. God games place the player at once above the game space and in the game space, watching over the world that they are free to manipulate and set into action. Friedman refers to simulation games as "maps-in-time, dramas which teach us how to think about structures of spatial relationships,"[51] pointing to the centrality of space to the genre. Isometric perspective can also affect a game's temporal orientation—Juul uses the term "fictional time" to describe the way events such as the establishment of infrastructure or construction of buildings occur at an accelerated pace in the miniature world of simulations.[52] Time, like culture, is ultimately subordinated to the spatial concerns that dominate games using isometric perspective.

This explains why the rendering of culture in management simulations is always dependent upon its environmental and mechanical contributions to gameplay. The gamespace of *Tropico 3*, for example, reflects a process of "high-tech tropicalization"[53] aimed at creating a familiar yet exotic cultural environment for gameplay. Many elements within the space are familiar signifiers of tropical culture in general, and of Caribbean and Cuban culture more specifically—the island's geography contains major sections of coastline, mountains, and forest, which can be used to support agricultural operations like tobacco farms, banana and sugar plantations, and industries producing canned fish, rum, and cigars. Calleja argues that miniature space is a "tactical space" whose functionality is predetermined by the strategic goals of the games' designers.[54] This explains why certain areas in *Tropico 3* are more suited to tobacco production, while in others it is not possible to plant the crop—the player must account for variables like these when making decisions about the development of infrastructure. Playing *Tropico* means internalizing its spatial model, taking into account the environmental obstacles and affordances that affect progress.

Tropico 3 uses isometric perspective in a variety of ways to create a unique spatialized relationship, particularly in the way it bridges the gap between the world of the avatar and the miniature world of the island's inhabitants. At the start of each round of play, the player's view is situated on the ground level of a new Tropican island, putting him on the level of the island's miniature inhabitants, at which point he must zoom back in order to occupy the classic isometric perspective of the god game. This placement of the player at the level of the game's miniatures is a reminder of the uniqueness of the game's NPCs as entities—each character has a series of assigned characteristics that affect its behavior and everyday habits. Clicking on a character will earn the player a quick snippet of dialogue—an older female resident complains, "Los jóvenes de ahora no respetan nada" ("Kids today have no respect"), while an elderly male inhabitant proclaims, "¡Si yo tuviera diez años menos!" ("If only I were ten years younger!"). Clicking a miniature also reveals many culturally relevant attributes of that particular NPC, including its level of religious faith, political orientation, employment, living situation, and family background. Again, these factors are not only cultural but also functional elements of game design, variables that can affect the outcomes of players' decisions. These cultural attributes can have substantial effects on the player's ability to perform the task that is ultimately at hand in a resource management simulation: the manipulation of spatial variables through isometric perspective.

Latin America as Open World

Open world or "sandbox" games, along with those that use recursive and isometric spatial orientations, represent another paradigmatic form of Latin American gamespace. Open world

Figure 5.4
Montezuma's Return! (WizardWorks 1998)

games give the player free reign to explore and interact with a three-dimensional environment without being bound to a linear game narrative, presenting unique opportunities for the development of cultural content. Though there are many precursors and early examples of games with characteristics of the open world, the genre experienced a boom as a result of 3D graphics innovations that allowed for the free-roaming exploration of space, including the groundbreaking open world environments of *Super Mario 64* (Nintendo 1996) and Rockstar's 2001 game *Grand Theft Auto III*. Likewise, representations of Latin America in the open world genre have largely dated from the late 1990s forward. An early example of the 3D rendering of Latin American cultural space is *Montezuma's Return!* (WizardWorks 1998), in which the player embodies a descendent of the Aztec emperor who must solve puzzles and perform tasks within the spatial setting of a pyramid's interior (figure 5.4). The game, a conceptual sequel to the 1984 Parker Brothers game *Montezuma's Revenge!*, allows the player to explore stone temples replete with "ancient" traps and puzzles from the first-person perspective; however, it is bound by a traditional mission-by-mission procedural structure unlike a truly open world or sandbox game. Driving games also frequently feature open world options, for example *Driver 2: Back on the Streets*, which features free-roaming gameplay that allows the player to explore a three-dimensional Havana from behind the wheel of a 1950s sedan, or to barrel through the streets of Rio de Janeiro behind the wheel of a passenger bus.

Since the turn of the millennium, a number of open world third-person shooter games with gameplay mechanics akin to the *GTA* series have been set within the cultural contexts of Latin America. Many of these could be categorized according to Frederick Luis Aldama's distinction between *urban* and *rural* games portraying Latin American culture.[55] Notable examples of open world games set in the region's rural environments include *Just Cause*, situated in the fictitious tropical island of San Esperito; *Call of Juarez: Bound in Blood*, an FPS that features a number of free world areas permitting the player to roam or choose side missions while navigating the Mexican-American border region; and the detailed rendition of the same border region during the early twentieth century in *Red Dead Redemption*. Urban open world games in Latin America are also popular, with examples like the 1950s-era Havana of the video game rendition of *The Godfather II*; contemporary Rio de Janeiro in *Gangstar Rio: City of Saints* (Gameloft 2011); and the colonial-era Havana of *Assassin's Creed IV: Black Flag*. Once again, culture is spatialized in open world games, but as always in ways defined by considerations particular to the genre in question.

Open world game environments are unique contexts for cultural simulation for a number of reasons related to the particularities of the genre. For example, the borders of playable space in open world games are frequently defined by environmental obstacles related to the broader cultural setting, providing a logical explanation for keeping certain areas of the game's map closed off until the player has made a certain degree of progress. In this way, *Red Dead Redemption* begins not as a truly open world, but one whose barriers and barricades are justified through narrative details related to the game's cultural setting: the player cannot explore Mexico until a determined point in the gameplay, due to the fact that the bridge across the San Luis River has been damaged by revolutionary forces and must be repaired. It is necessary to justify these sorts of limitations in order to maintain the illusion of depth of the open world, which is of course not a truly open space, but rather one delimited by the game's underlying code. A major measure of success for open world game design is the ability to maintain the illusion of openness, because once "players realize that there is no opportunity to become lost, the scope for exploration is severely diminished and the environment is perceived for what it is: a multicursal labyrinth (that is, one with branches and dead ends)."[56] Not only that, it is necessary to justify these limitations on a *cultural* level as well, in order to coordinate the player's perception of the open world within the game's broader narrative, lending a sense of openness to the sociocultural situations explored in the plot of games like *Red Dead Redemption*.

Designers of open world games create a sense of openness and limitlessness in a number of different ways. The manner in which Swedish design firm Avalanche Studios went about creating an open world in the 2006 game *Just Cause* is emblematic in this regard, given that they had to overcome hardware and software challenges that required fragmenting the game's narrative and play into different parts of the map and individual mission scenarios, as well as potential disturbances to environmental seamlessness like "loading" screens and narrative cutscenes, while still maintaining the illusion of openness. In spite of the fact that the game's narrative follows a procedural path carved out by the major missions faced by protagonist Rico Rodriguez, the player is free to explore the world outside of the linear narrative of *Just Cause* as well. It is then that the cultural details that define the space of San Esperito as particularly Latin American most clearly emerge on an environmental level. A driving score of guitars, trumpets, and bongos serves as the sonic backdrop to interactions with Spanish-speaking NPCs that greet Rico with short phrases like "¡Hola!," as well as street vendors touting their wares by shouting "¡Aguas frescas!," "¡Coco fresco!," "¡Refrescos!," "¡Cerveza fría!," or "¡Helados, helados, helados!" The soldiers of the presidential regime speak Spanglish—"¡Madre de dios! Get me outta here!" So do those soldiers friendly to Rico's subversive foreign invasion—"Let's go, amigo! ¡Viva la revolución!" The player wanders through palm tree-covered tropical beaches, rural country roads lined with ramshackle buildings, mountainous jungle regions, the haciendas of wealthy land barons, colonial plazas, and rural farms, all of which add breadth and depth to *Just Cause*'s 3D rendition of the geographic and cultural environment of the Spanish-speaking Caribbean.

As evidenced in the preceding section on sound, multicultural open world spaces are key to the success of Rockstar's *Grand Theft Auto* series, considered by many the benchmark of the open world genre. Latin American culture is brought to bear in different ways on all of *GTA*'s gamespaces. Each of the series' major locations—Liberty City (a parodic New York), Vice City (Miami), and Los Santos, San Andreas (Los Angeles, California), established in the first game in the series, *Grand Theft Auto* (BMG Interactive 1997)—is home to a substantial Latino and Latin American NPC population. In addition to the ways that the region is represented in the radio stations and musical soundtracks of these games discussed earlier, cultural space is delineated in *GTA* in uncommonly clear, territorial terms. Since these games center largely on the battles between criminal organizations, particular spaces and areas of the games' maps are frequently dominated by specific criminal (and cultural) groups. Released in 2001, *GTA III* was Rockstar's first open world, three-dimensional title, and was set in Liberty City. Its plot centers on a conflict between Japanese and Italian crime families, but culminates in a conflict with Catalina, one of the series' first major Latin American characters, who is eventually revealed to be associated with a Colombian drug cartel. There are also some early Latino criminal organizations in *GTA III*, such as the street gang Los Diablos.

The gamespace of *GTA: Vice City*, a fictionalized 1980s Miami, is coded Latin at every turn, even from the very moment the player arrives at Escobar International Airport, an obvious reference to the Colombian capo whose cocaine business fueled the real-life 1980s nightlife and underground economy of the cultural setting being parodied in the game. Vice City has a large Caribbean population, and includes a battle for territory between the Haitians, led by the voodoo practitioner Auntie Poulet, and the Cubans, who eventually take control of the city's Little Havana neighborhood. Each of these and other Latin gangs in Vice City—including the Diaz Cartel, the Costa Rican Gang, and the Cortez Crew—occupies a space designated by cultural signifiers specific to that group. For example, the neighborhood known as Little Haiti is occupied by a population of Haitians that all speak patois, wear purple and white, and prefer listening to the radio stations Flash FM and Fever 105 in their favorite car the Voodoo, a two-door low-rider reminiscent of the 1960s Chevy Impala (figure 5.5). Members of the Colombian Diaz Cartel, meanwhile, occupy the area surrounding their leader's mansion, wear crimson and light blue, and can be seen in either of two sedans or a sports car. Groups like these fill the *Vice City*'s space with the visual, linguistic, musical, and dramatic signifiers of the cultures they represent. Such gang rivalries are also prominently portrayed in the next installment in the series, *GTA: San Andreas*, which was released in 2004 and included neighborhoods dominated by various Latin gangs like the Los Santos Vagos, Varrios Los Aztecas, and the Mexican gang San Fierro Rifa. Through the use of audiovisual and behavioral signifiers among the NPC populations of

Figure 5.5
Grand Theft Auto: Vice City (Rockstar 2002)

the *GTA* series, Rockstar creates environments in which culture is not only portrayed but also spatially experienced.

Perhaps more than any previous game in the series, the 2013 blockbuster *GTA V* integrates diverse Latin American cultural elements into its rendering of the open world. Returning to and expanding upon the series' earlier version of Los Santos (the *GTA* version of Los Angeles), *GTA V* features cultural microenvironments ranging from Michael's stylish mansion in the upscale Vinewood Hills neighborhood, to Trevor's trashed trailer in meth-ridden backwoods of Sandy Shores, to urban barrios whose streets resound with Latin music and the Spanish spoken by their primarily Hispanic inhabitants. Transportation offers another environmental reflection of culture as well as socioeconomic class—in the poor, rural area of Sandy Shores in *GTA V*, locals ride dirt bikes, quads, tractors, RVs, and beaters, while in Michael's upscale Vinewood Hills neighborhood residents drive sports cars, luxury SUVs, and high-end sedans. In addition to the neighborhoods where the main characters reside, Los Santos features spaces occupied by the major Latin crews including the return of the Mexican gangs Varrios Los Aztecas and Los Santos Vagos, as well as the first appearance of the Marabunta Grande, a fictionalized version of the real-life Salvadoran-American gang Mara Salvatrucha. As was the case in the series' earlier installments, members' clothing, tattoos, and accessories represent cultural as well as gang identity—the Vagos all wear yellow and black, many feature black bandanas and most have tattoos on their arms, while the Marabunta Grande, like their real-life counterparts, are known for white tank tops and prominent face and neck tattoos in gothic script. Not only these gang members but also Hispanic characters of various ages, nationalities, and backgrounds reside in the neighborhoods of East Los Santos, including La Mesa, El Burro Heights, and Murrieta Heights (in-game equivalents of the East Los Angeles neighborhoods of the Arts District, Signal Hill, and Boyle Heights, respectively). The neighborhoods of East Los Santos are home to many businesses that are coded Latin—like "Auto Re-Perez" and "Attack-A-Taco"—but this working-class area is by no means the only place in the game to feature such cultural signifiers. In fact there are Latin characters at all income levels throughout the game, not only in the barrios of East Los Santos but also in the hilltop mansions of characters like crime kingpin Martin Madrazo. Thus, through the cultural coding of space, *GTA V* attempts to demonstrate the cultural and economic diversity of the populations that inhabit its world.

Culture can also be a functional element of game dynamics in *GTA V*'s open world. For example, each of the game's three protagonists—wealthy Italian-American career criminal Michael de Santa, twenty-something African-American gang member turned mover-and-shaker Franklin Clinton, and loose cannon meth manufacturer Trevor Philips—gets treated differently when approaching the mountain enclave run by the elusive "Altruist Cult." While Michael and Franklin will be relentlessly attacked, Trevor will go unnoticed by the cult members, to whom he refers conversationally as his "friends in the mountains." This is one example of the many ways cultural difference impacts navigation of the game's space: when wandering through El Burro Heights as Franklin, for example, the player will be offered warnings by NPC Vagos gang members, such as "Compadre! It's not safe for you here!" and the more direct, "Get the fuck out of my barrio!" If, on the one hand, examples like these interactions from *GTA V* may strike us as violent trivializations of Latin American culture, on the other hand we must keep in mind that the disposition of the game in question is toward violent interaction with a hostile environment, and that even within this context it is possible to produce a nuanced portrayal of Latin American culture.

Red Dead Redemption (*RDR*), an open world game released by Rockstar in 2010, offers one of the company's most thorough renditions of a Latin American cultural environment to date. *RDR* is the second game in the series after *Red Dead Revolver* (Rockstar 2004), which had been developed by Capcom prior to being sold to Rockstar in 2002. *RDR*, the first game in the series developed entirely by Rockstar, takes place along a fictionalized version of the Texas-Mexico border during the Mexican Revolution. The plot follows the protagonist, John Marston, as he seeks revenge for crimes committed against him and his family, while making his living by wrangling cattle and assisting various lawmen, outlaws, and shysters in the borderlands. Marston (and thus the player) eventually ends up embroiled in the Revolution itself, first on the side of the federal authorities, and later joining the ranks of peasant revolutionaries (figure 5.6). The environment of the game is expansive and richly detailed, and completing its

Figure 5.6
Red Dead Redemption (Rockstar 2010)

main narrative requires more than forty hours of gameplay, though it is highly unlikely that many players would finish the game in that time due to a multitude of digressions that readily derail the game's linear narrative at every turn. When Marston is not corralling steers, he is just as likely to be collecting the herbs of the Sonoran desert for bartering purposes as he is to be learning about the poetry of Mexican *corridos* from revolutionary leaders, or reading a purchasable newspaper's report on the struggle taking place south of the border. In these and myriad other ways, subtle cultural details are conveyed through the mechanisms of *RDR*'s open world.

The environmental detail and cultural contextualization of *Red Dead Redemption* are of course no mistake. Rockstar founder Dan Houser explains that designers strove to imbue the game's spatial environment with cultural reflections of tone, attitude, and atmosphere particular to the border region at the turn of the twentieth century: "You do it in the landscape, you do it in the buildings in the landscape, you do it in the pedestrians, the NPCs, they way they're dressed, the way they behave, the things they're speaking about, their cumbersome interactions with telephones, their talk about mythical technology that we now regard as absurd, their social attitudes, all of these different things, it kind of bleeds into all of them."[57] In *RDR* just as in *GTA*, this means making cultural differences a tangible element of the game's design. The NPC population on either side of the border in *RDR* consists of individuals from a variety of US and Mexican ethnicities. However, population densities as well as the possibilities for interaction with NPCs vary depending on which side of the border the player is occupying. Cultural elements are also incorporated into the game's ethical models. From the start, the player is provided with two meters, one for honor and one for fame, and these meters go up and down depending on the decisions made: steal a horse and kill its owner, and your fame increases; save a horse's owner from having his steed stolen, and your honor increases. It is up to the player to decide which path to take at innumerable points during gameplay, and the relative honor or fame players sustain will profoundly affect the way other characters respond to their actions. The choice of whether to act sympathetically toward the local population or to antagonize them in a sociopathic manner, for example, is not a meaningless or arbitrary decision in this context, but rather such subjective and culturally dependent decisions have ludic consequences. Thus the ability to make choices that are appropriate to the game's cultural context will determine the outcome of any given exchange, requiring the player of *RDR* to adapt culturally in order to advance spatially.

In their own ways, each of the three types of paradigmatic gamespaces discussed in this section require unique considerations of their spatial nature in order to understand the way they incorporate Latin American culture. Recursive space is mechanically oriented toward exploration and discovery through the opening of previously closed-off areas in a game's environment, spatial parameters that have proven attractive to developers of games based on these same themes of exploration and discovery. Games using isometric perspective rely upon environmental agency from a player perched high above the NPC population of miniatures that respond to the player's input, a game mechanic that has been particularly useful to the designers of resource management simulations focused on conquest and colonization. Finally, open world games use detailed and responsive environments with a capacity for producing elaborate simulations of diversity and difference, where cultural awareness can have significant repercussions on the player's progress and experience. Each of these examples demonstrates how the obstacles and affordances particular to a given model of gamespace can set the parameters for particular types of cultural representation.

Conclusion: The Spatialization of Culture in Video Games

Video game spaces are shaped in countless ways by culture. And since spatial exploration and models are key to video games' unique ways of making meaning, the spatialization of culture is an essential consideration for designers and players of all sorts of gamespaces. Players can experience "landscape moments," generate cognitive maps of spaces inhabited, and make discoveries with real-life significance in the eventual space of video games. Moreover, the meaning of cultural artifacts and references within games is determined by their use within the game environment, impacting a game's capacity for environmental storytelling. Culture is spatialized in video games in ways that must be redundant enough for the player to encounter, but not so obvious as to derail the believability of the cultural context. And sound within the game's environment can represent culture in a variety of ways through dialogue, environmental noises, diegetic sound effects, and music. With space as with sound, each genre or type of gamespace endows designers with particular obstacles and affordances to the depiction of culture. Because meaning is spatially situated in video games, cultural portrayal in games must work within the particular parameters of the spatial environment being used.

As the cases in this chapter show, Latin American cultures have been represented in virtually every type of gamespace imaginable, from *Pelé's Soccer* to *GTA V*. When Latin America has been portrayed in games, space has frequently been central to its depiction: ancient indigenous temples, guerrilla war zones, and geographically massive colonial regions seen from a bird's eye view all have their own particular ways of portraying culture spatially. When players explore space recursively, they inhabit cultural spaces defined procedurally: by going back on their previous steps in order to advance a little more with each session of gameplay, replaying difficult sequences of games like *Tomb Raider* or *Uncharted* over and over, the player is rewarded by opening up more space. In the action/adventure genre, the relationship between avatar and environment takes precedence over the characters' relationships with other humans, making space particularly fundamental to the ways culture is evoked in these games. On a different plane altogether, games that use the isometric perspective offer players a top-down view on a miniature world at their behest, allowing them to play god with their own tiny universe but at the same time requiring them to account for the environmental agency dispersed among the NPC population, the balance of which will define their success or failure in games such as *Sid Meier's Civilization* and *Tropico*. Finally, open world games like *Just Cause*, *Grand Theft Auto*, and *Red Dead Redemption* exponentially increase the possibilities for cultural representation in spaces that are expansive, responsive, and filled with interactive cultural details. Within such environments, culture can be conveyed through myriad elements including written and spoken language, the population demographics of different neighborhoods, radio station preferences, quality of available transportation and housing, the relative reaction of NPCs to characters from different backgrounds, and character clothing, tattoos, and hairstyles.

Spaces are culturally coded in video games in order to add dimension to the experience of gameplay, to enhance the game's narrative and procedural meanings, and to offer the player a chance to inhabit an appealing and novel environment. Space is fundamentally related to all sorts of meaning in games, providing the context for semiotic cultural signification as well as the conduit through which a game's narrative or simulated meaning is transmitted. Without a doubt, space has always been a primary consideration for game designers and players alike. As this chapter has shown, game designers have been producing cultural environments of ever-increasing complexity and nuance over the course of the medium's history, making it essential to continue to analyze how culture shapes meaning in gamespace. We cannot realistically explain how culture operates in video games without examining its relationship to space. And at the same time, a rigorous analysis demonstrates that in order to fully understand how space works in video games, we must take into account the multiple and pervasive effects of culture on gamespace.

6   SIMULATION

The final chapter of this book arose from a seemingly straightforward yet ethically complicated question: as a gamer selecting an avatar, why would you choose to play as Augusto Pinochet, one of twentieth-century Latin America's most murderous tyrants, responsible for the torture, imprisonment, killing, and disappearance of thousands of Chileans during his seventeen-year dictatorship? This question resulted from a specific experience I had during the early stages of researching this book. While rereading the essay "Simulation versus Narrative: Introduction to Ludology," one of the foundational texts by Gonzalo Frasca, the Uruguayan game designer and theorist whose work I have referenced throughout this volume, I came across a footnote that at once raised important and timely questions about verisimilitude in cultural representation in video games, and at the same time brought to my mind one of the reasons that the "real" meaning of video games is so difficult to pin down—because of the complicated and culturally contingent role of humor. Frasca's footnote offers a stinging critique of *Tropico*, the resource management simulation game in which the character plays as a recently installed dictator of a fictitious Caribbean island nation—and chooses from avatars including not only fictional characters but also real life despots like Pinochet (figure 6.1), "Papa Doc" Duvalier of Haiti, and Rafael Trujillo of the Dominican Republic. For Frasca, this game is clearly meant to be tongue-in-cheek, but misses its mark: "While this simulation is definitively a parody, its extreme use of clichés and simplification are a clear example of a colonialist attitude in video game design. Having grown up myself during a dictatorship in Uruguay, I find the game insulting. I would not object to a simulation that dealt with issues such as torture or political imprisonment if it aimed at understanding politics and sociology. In this case, however, it is simply used for entertainment, which is nothing short of disgusting. Alas, I guess South American oppressed are not yet a powerful lobby in the land of political-correctness."[1] Whether one has played the games in the *Tropico* series or not, there is certainly much that rings true in Frasca's critique: if a game uses historical tragedy as mere entertainment fodder or as a superficial joke, it will

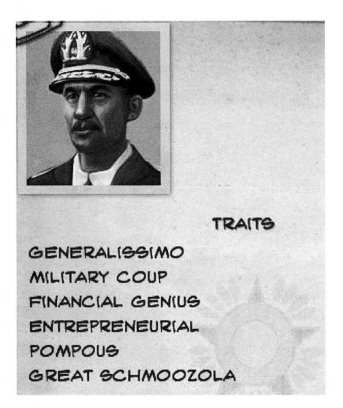

TRAITS

GENERALISSIMO
MILITARY COUP
FINANCIAL GENIUS
ENTREPRENEURIAL
POMPOUS
GREAT SCHMOOZOLA

Figure 6.1
Tropico 3 (Kalypso 2009)

unsurprisingly be regarded as disrespectful to those whose families and friends were affected by such tragedies.

And then I played *Tropico*. And despite the fact that it uses the names and faces of some of the most infamous figures of Latin American history for the purposes of a game, I found it fascinating. Moreover, playing the game destabilized my preconception that its basic framework was "an example of colonialist attitude in video game design," as Frasca had asserted. In fact I believe *Tropico* can be seen as an attempt at the opposite—an example of anticolonialist attitude in game design, precisely because of its nature as a parody, an expressive form whose meaning is never as it appears on the surface. Robert Hariman explains succinctly how meaning works in parodies: "The parody is not what it claims to be, to reveal that the discourse being parodied is what it claims not to be."[2] That is, parody places discourse beside itself in order to reveal its underlying falseness and limitations. "What had seemed to be serious is in fact foolish," Hariman argues, "and likewise the powerful is shown to be vulnerable, the unchangeable contingent, the enchanting dangerous. Parody works in great part by exceeding tacit limits on expression—the appropriate, the rational—but it does so to reveal limitations that others would want to keep hidden."[3] Understood as a parody, *Tropico* can be seen as less a colonialist enterprise than an exposure of US interventionism in Latin America and the atrocities perpetrated by the dictatorships it supported, an attempt to destabilize the imperialist discourse being parodied. Simulation, which Frasca characterizes as "an alternative to representation and narrative,"[4] is both a broad game genre and a software framework in which meaning is made in ways that are nonlinguistic, nonnarrative, and nonrepresentational. However video games often make meaning through representation and narrative as well as simulation, and the effects of games' attempts at realism and verisimilitude, as well as their use of irony, satire, and parody, must be considered when examining games that incorporate Latin American history and cultural heritage into their products. Without taking these factors into account, we cannot offer satisfying answers to some of the most complex questions about cultural representation in video games.

Why would a player choose to play as Pinochet? That simple question can lead down a great many paths. What are the ethical implications of the choice to play as the Spanish in *The Conquerers* expansion of *Age of Empires II*, or any number of other historical factions of ill repute in any number of other historically based simulation games? What makes playing the game as the morally good or bad team a good or bad choice? In short, why would a moral player be compelled to do immoral things in a game, or even to embody the most evil avatars of real history for the purposes of play, and what is the significance of such decisions in the context of a simulation? This chapter aims to provide compelling answers to those questions, by way of a thorough exploration of the ways meaning is conveyed within the framework of video game simulations.

Simulation and Algorithmic Culture

Simulation games revolve around the player's manipulation of a dynamic system to produce a range of possible results. The umbrella simulation genre includes several subgenres: broad-based resource management simulations like those discussed in chapter 5, including *Utopia* and *Sid Meier's Civilization*; business simulations like *Sid Meier's Railroad Tycoon* (MicroProse 1990) and *RollerCoaster Tycoon* (MicroProse 1999); city-building simulations like *SimCity* (Maxis 1989) and *Cities XL* (Monte Cristo 2009); and government simulations such as *Caesar* (Sierra Entertainment 1992) and *Anno 1503: The New World*. In addition to these management simulations, there are open world simulations, those featuring dynamic environments that respond to player decisions and can be explored along multiple paths. Examples of these open world simulations include early titles such as the space simulator *Elite* (Imagineer 1984), 3D "sandbox" games like *Super Mario 64* and *Shenmue* (Sega 1999), and a number of recent examples discussed at different points in this book that are set wholly or partially in Latin America, including *Just Cause, Mercenaries 2: World in Flames, Red Dead Redemption*, and *Grand Theft Auto V*. What these games all share is the underlying coded structure of a simulation, a dynamic system with the potential to produce culturally meaningful experiences in several unique ways. Simulations enable the player to make decisions about consumption and production, political discourse and economic policy, and imperialist expansion or inward-focused nationalism, adopting, building upon, and remediating longstanding dynamics in human society and cultural production. Success in a simulation depends on mastery of its internally coded mechanisms of gameplay, but also requires the player to access skill sets acquired from experience in real-world cultural contexts.

This capacity to make decisions and adjustments that impact progress through the game in different ways is a distinguishing feature of the simulation genre. Unlike linear narratives or two-dimensional images, whose basic content will remain the same upon multiple readings or viewings, simulations offer the capacity to have a new experience each time the game is played, through a novel combination of the adjustable factors at the player's disposal. William Uricchio defines simulation as a "machine for producing speculative or conditional representations,"[5] while Frasca more poetically describes it as "a kaleidoscopic form of representation that can provide us with multiple and alternative points of view."[6] This signifying exchange between subjective player actions and the game software's coded rules is what is often referred to as the algorithmic structure of video games. Therefore Manovich defines the algorithm in procedural terms, as the end goal in a process of discovery on the part of the gamer: "As the player proceeds through the game, she gradually discovers the rules that operate in the universe constructed by the game. She learns its hidden logic—in short, its algorithm."[7] It is this "hidden logic" that players of nearly any game must go about discovering in order to unlock its meaning and ultimately achieve success—step by step, they must discover the best maneuvers in order to clear the obstacles in their path to victory. In simulations, such barriers include both "internal forces" like crime, pollution, and rebellion and "external forces" like natural disasters or military invasions, all of which must be balanced by the player in order to progress.[8] It is through this algorithmic process of trial and error that the player comes to unlock the keys to mastering the internal logic of a simulation.

Due to their algorithmic nature, simulations are fundamentally different from linear narratives because they deal not with historical fact but ahistorical possibility. As Claudio Fogu asserts in "Digitalizing Historical Consciousness," "[d]igital history enters the twenty-first century exclusively under the sign of the possible; we are now interested only in what may happen and are no longer concerned with what had happened."[9] As opposed to linear narratives, simulations are speculative systems offering a chance to carry a single scenario through to several possible outcomes. Simulations do not allow for the types of predetermined, teleological narratives that written histories of human culture tend to privilege. While a cultural object or historical event carries some referential ties to its conventional "real-world" meaning into a simulation, that meaning is transformed within the simulation, subordinated to its significance as a calculable factor within a dynamic system. This recalls Zimmerman's assertion, cited in the introduction to this book, that a football is not a football within the context of a game, but rather a means of scoring points. That is to say, nothing in a video game simulation means what it appears to mean conventionally, or at least it does not mean *only* what it appears to mean conventionally.

To provide an illustration, the player of *Sid Meier's Civilization* must first choose a real-world historical civilization from a predetermined selection of choices. In the most recent iteration from the series, *Civilization V*, the player could choose from eighteen playable civilizations upon the game's release, with an additional twenty-five added as downloadable content in game expansions. The Aztecs are led in the game by Montezuma I (a.k.a. Moctezuma I), the predecessor of Moctezuma II, who was the leader in power when Hernán Cortés arrived at the Aztec capital of Tenochtitlán in 1519. In the *Civilization* universe, Montezuma has appeared as a playable avatar since the very first *Civilization* game in 1991, growing in detail and context with each successive installment in the series. *Civilization V* features animated leaders for each civilization that speak in their native languages, so Montezuma speaks in the Aztec language of Nahuatl, the Incan leader Pachacuti speaks Quechua, Pedro II of Brazil speaks Portuguese, and Queen Isabella and Simón Bolívar speak their own variations of Spanish. The performance of the Aztecs in the game is determined by sixty-three variables, each of which is assigned a numerical value from one to nine. Montezuma (and thus the Aztec civilization) scores high in the areas of "Boldness," "Bullying," and "Conquest of City States," as well as "Likeliness to Declare War." But they also rate highly in historically anachronistic categories like "Nuke Production." The Aztecs are also assigned values for variables such as "Chattiness," "Meanness," and "Military Training Buildings Production." The Aztecs in *Civilization V* have a relatively high emphasis on "Culture," "Wonder," and "Happiness," but a relatively low emphasis on "Science," "Trade," and "Great People." Within the algorithmic structure of *Civilization V*, the cultural traits assigned to the Aztec civilization are calculable variables that affect the way meaning is produced in the simulation, but do not necessarily or accurately reflect real-world traits of the civilizations in question.

Therefore it is problematic to analyze games in ideological terms based strictly on the conventional rather than the algorithmic and contextual meaning of the historical elements they employ. As Galloway argues in *Gaming: Essays on Algorithmic Culture*, attempts to link cultural simulations with real-world entities and events inevitably end in slippage—this is because such elements do not invite a conventional allegorical or metaphorical interpretation. Rather, within a simulation, cultural identity "is a data type, a mathematical variable."[10] Galloway's concept of "algorithmic culture" also points the way toward an answer to my initial question in this chapter, paraphrased here: Why would a player choose to play as a dictator? Because the dictator's identity, like that of Montezuma and any other leader represented in the context of a resource management simulation, is not—or more accurately, is not *only*—a real-world historical figure, but is (primarily) a collection of particular values for a given set of mathematical variables within the game's algorithm.

Realism and Verisimilitude in Video Games

Games are related in innumerable ways to the traditions that have preceded and coincided with them in spheres like literature and film, but games remediate these traditions in important ways. Realism, for example, takes on a different set of meanings in relation to an electronic game than it does with other traditions of cultural production. In literature, realism arises out of the nineteenth-century realist novel in France, which Georg Lukács saw as a superior means of expressing the human condition: "Balzac's many-sided, many-tiered world approaches reality much more closely than any other method of presentation."[11] Of course, the contribution of Honoré de Balzac and his realist contemporaries was not simply offering a *realistic* representation of their world, but rather literary realism has always implied a degree of social critique. In his 1953 analysis of the French realist novel Erich Auerbach enumerates the foundations of nineteenth-century literary realism: the serious treatment of everyday reality, the appearance of previously excluded groups as subjects for problematic-existential representation, the use of a fluid historical background and the embedding of random people and events into the course of history.[12] The same schematic definition basically holds true for cinematic realism, in which persuasion is also privileged over documentary objectivity. In *What Is Cinema?* André Bazin explains that in realist films such as Vittorio De Sica's *The Bicycle Thief* (1948), "the thesis of the film is hidden behind an objective social reality which in turn moves into the background of the moral and psychological drama which could of itself justify the film."[13] Thus nineteenth-century literary realism and the cinematic tradition that followed it are responsible not only for making the quotidian the focus of cultural production, but also for highlighting the role of the underprivileged, underrepresented, and historically marginalized, demonstrating the realist way of critically portraying reality with no pretension of objectivity.

While simulations like *Second Life* (Linden 2003) and *The Sims* follow the literary realists in elevating the everyday into the subject matter of cultural production, realist video games in the conventional sense—those that offer social critiques and highlight the historical role of the marginalized—are relatively few and far between. Some of the best examples from Latin

American designers are highlighted in chapter 2: Rafael Fajardo's *Crosser* and *La Migra*, Coco Fusco and Ricardo Dominguez's *Turista Fronterizo*, and Gonzalo Frasca's *September 12th*. On the one hand, these are realist games because they offer a "serious treatment of everyday reality" in spite of their sometimes-humorous tone, representing the impact of labor, consumption, transit, economics, and politics on the daily lives of their simulated characters. On the other hand they are realist games because of their particular focus on historically marginalized groups—undocumented migrants in *Crosser* and *La Migra*, a domestic worker in *Turista Fronterizo*, and citizens of a Middle Eastern village besieged by assault drones in *September 12th*. These are the rare activist games that, like Bazin's model realist filmmakers, hide their thesis behind representations of objective social and political realities, requiring the player to unlock their meaning procedurally.

But there is another, much more common meaning for *realism* in video games, the one used in promotional materials that advertise games based upon how *realistic* they are in terms of graphic or historical fidelity or both. As Manovich explains, this type of realism is a prevalent measure for success in the game industry: "In media, trade publications, and research papers, the history of technological innovation and research is presented as a progression toward realism—the ability to simulate any object in such a way that its computer image is indistinguishable from a photograph."[14] And while game developers have long sought to create a sense of representational realism in their products, they achieve this effect not through total fidelity to the real world being represented, but rather through the creation of a *sense* of the realistic through design considerations. The "reality effect" or *effet de réel* was Barthes's term for partial realism—he noted that even in the case of the nineteenth-century French literary canon, "its realism is only fragmentary, erratic, restricted to 'details,' "[15] as of course the goal of realism was never really to create a one-to-one equivalent representation of the world, but rather to critically evoke a world through subjectively selected representative elements. The realism that game designers seek to create is also partial, fragmented, and metonymical, with details standing in for the broader cultural and historical elements they represent.

What is most important in a simulation is not necessarily documentary exactitude or attention to minute detail, but rather that all of the components of the game work together to create a sense of harmony for the player. King and Krzywinska use the term "functional realism" to describe the way realistic gameplay can consist of "mechanics of weaponry and vehicles, physics of weather conditions and golf swings, meters covering emotion and other psycho-emotional aspects, etc."[16] For players of video games, the predictable and consistent functioning of gameplay mechanics can contribute as much to a sense of realism as an airtight historical plot. For example, in a flight simulator like *A-10 Cuba!* relatively little in the interface seems to indicate the cultural or historical context of the Bay of Pigs Invasion, however the historical selection of aircraft and equipment available along with the proper functioning of the altimeter and numerous other gauges in the user's heads-up display creates a heightened sense of functional realism for the player. This is why game designers seek to produce "sufficient functional realism to create an impression of 'something like' the real thing,"[17] a context that is believable enough to evoke the real-world location and historical epoch it represents, even if it cannot promise a photorealistic representation.

Verisimilitude is related to functional realism in game design, focusing on the creation of a *feel* or *sense* of overall believability rather than a 1:1 representation of reality. Verisimilitude is required of a video game's cultural context as well, meaning that cultural elements are incorporated into game design only if they can be made to function harmoniously with game mechanics. Take, for example, the differences in the portrayal of the Afro-Brazilian martial art of *capoeira* in *Tekken 3* (Namco 1997) and more than two decades later in the Brazilian-designed *Capoeira Legends: Path to Freedom* (Donsoft 2009). The lone practitioner of capoeira in *Tekken 3* is Eddy Gordo, one of the first Afro-Brazilian characters in video game history. Regarding the depiction of capoeira in *Tekken 3*, Juul suggests that practitioners of the martial art "would undoubtedly feel that the game was an extreme simplification" since "[c]ountless moves have been omitted, and the available moves have been simplified and are only available as either/ or options: perform a handstand or do not perform a handstand," taking away much of the "expressive potential" of this particular style of martial arts.[18] In fact, Juul's hypothesis has been confirmed by none other than the "real-life Eddy Gordo," Marcelo Pereira, the *mestre de capoeira* who provided the motion-capture moves for the character in the game. Asked whether he was pleased with the way Eddy Gordo was represented in *Tekken 3*, Pereira offered the following analysis: "On a scale of 0-10, I give Eddy Gordo a 6. As I mentioned before, tradition is an important fact. Capoeiristas have authentic nicknames such as Ze Faisca ("Joe Spark"), Cobra Verde ("Green Snake"), Gato Preto ("Black Cat"), etc. ... It would be O.K. if the name was in English, but Eddy is not a Brazilian name and Gordo in Portuguese means fat! In the same issue of names, the names chosen for the capoeira movements are pretty off the wall and are not like the traditional names I called the movements as I was motion captured."[19] Pereira adds that Eddy's attire could more accurately reflect realistic capoeira standards of dress, and that a strong drum beat or traditional capoeira music would have added further cultural relevance, though he recognizes that "Namco had to deal with thousands of details for all the characters and strategies of the game."[20] Clearly, for the designers of *Tekken 3*, the functional realism that allows for consistent and predictable manners of interaction between characters trumped the cultural realism that a practitioner of capoeira might desire. More recent titles, like *Martial Arts: Capoeira!* (Libredia 2011) and particularly the 2009 Brazilian game *Capoeira Legends: Path to Freedom*, attempt to merge functional realism with cultural verisimilitude to a greater degree in order to provide the player with both an enjoyable gameplay experience and a sense of cultural authenticity. *Capoeira Legends* is set in 1828 among the outskirts of Rio de Janeiro, with

Figure 6.2
Capoeira Legends: Path to Freedom (Donsoft 2009)

the player operating as Gunga Za, a young slave and capoeira practitioner seeking his freedom (figure 6.2). The game's designers describe *Capoeira Legends* as a way of learning the history of this particularly Brazilian art form, as well as a fundamentally cultural game—"uma incrível experiência cultural" ("an incredible cultural experience").[21]

It is important to remember, of course, that a simplified cultural context is not always the result of oversight on the part of game developers, but rather a factor inherent to all video game simulations. As Kevin Schut has argued, "presenting greater cultural complexity challenges the bias of the medium: Because various cultures have to be turned into an airtight system of programs and game rules, modeling more than a few truly distinct cultures (even if they are greatly simplified) becomes exceptionally difficult."[22] Following this logic, it would be difficult to substantiate the claim that "[b]lackness is erased from the island" in *Tropico*,[23] because *Tropico* is not an island—it is a computer game that simulates an island, which in its every dimension is a constructed, artificial, and coded space. This is not to argue against the need for greater cultural diversity in video games, but rather to recognize that game designers' possibilities for creating cultural context are defined by the parameters of the medium and the genre in question. Therefore not every game provides the opportunity for players to act out every imaginable scenario—a player "may wish for the Zulus in *Civilization* to pursue a different technology tree, for instance, but it is not going to happen because it is simply not part of the game."[24] Cultural environments in video games are built from the ground up, and every element programmed into the game is the result of conscious decision making on the part of the designers. This is why it *is* so important for game designers to continue to expand their efforts in portraying cultural diversity among their characters, making their products more appealing to audiences of different ages, genders, sexual orientations, and racial, national, and socioeconomic backgrounds. Precisely because games are the result of conscious programming and design choices, it is essential to keep in mind the many ways culture can be incorporated into game design in order to create more meaningful experiences for the player.

Games and Empire

It is a commonplace in certain critical circles to refer to video games as part of the "military entertainment complex,"[25] given the historical and ideological links between game design and the defense technology industry. This is due in part to the fact that a number of pioneering early video games were first developed within the context of US military technology, including *Spacewar!* (Steve Russell et al. 1962), widely considered the first video game, which was designed by MIT grad students with funding from the Pentagon. The link between video games and the military has been further established by the government funding of game projects including the *America's Army* series (United States Army 2002). This has led many critics to assert that video games are an essentially imperialistic form of media reflecting a militaristic worldview. For example, building on the work of Michael Hardt and Antonio Negri, Nick Dyer-Witheford and Greig de Peuter argue in *Games of Empire: Global Capitalism and Video Games* that "[v]irtual games are exemplary media of Empire," indeed "*the* media of Empire," since they "originated in the US military-industrial complex, the nuclear-armed core of capital's global domination, to which they remain umbilically connected."[26] Likewise, Nina B. Huntemann asserts that "military-themed games advance a worldview that military intervention and use of force are the only viable responses to global conflict, and that war is inevitable and perpetual, with enemies unmistakably on the side of evil,"[27] echoing other critiques of games' consistent framing of "the 'civilizing mission' as a battle between good and evil,"[28] their reliance on an "us against them" framework that "helps to reinforce simplistic ideas of a collective Self and its hostile Other,"[29] and their overall "function as a 'soft sell' of 'hard power.' "[30] The proponents of this ideological critique argue that video games represent an imperialistic or militaristic worldview, and that players are distanced from engagement with broader issues related to warfare when violence is portrayed in military-themed games. Huntemann explains that the depiction of war in video games is "cleaned up, void of horrific consequences, civilian casualties, and psychic devastation," leading to the "normalization and sanitization of war."[31] Greenfield echoes this assessment, adding that "the histories of oppressed peoples, those who fought on the 'other side' and the victims of war cannot be told" because "[c]ries of 'Stop the killing!' and stories of civilian casualties and immense suffering are not the stuff of entertainment."[32]

The main assertions of the ideological or anti-imperialist critique of military-themed video games are that (1) they are inextricably linked to the military entertainment complex; (2) they justify and normalize a state of permanent warfare as a response to geopolitical problems; (3) they reinforce an "us against them" perspective, emphasizing the division between the self and foreign other; and (4) they sanitize violence, omitting and obscuring morally objectionable issues from their depictions of violence. These points are doubtlessly valid for the analysis of certain military-themed games; however, it is essential to take a closer look at the suggestion that a focus on warfare represents not only these games' content but also their ideological message.

First and foremost, whom do we suppose is playing these games? It seems problematic to assume that players are universally susceptible to the same sorts of ideological manipulations, or that all players interpret games' meaning in a consistent manner. What does it mean when more educated adults are playing video games than innocent schoolchildren? What does it mean for Mexican players to play games based on the contemporary drug war in their own country? Or for a Cuban, Brazilian, or Venezuelan citizen to play games about his or her homeland being invaded by foreign forces? As Galloway argues, in order for a player to experience believability in a video game, "there must be some kind of congruence, some type of *fidelity of context* that transliterates itself from the social reality of the gamer, through one's thumbs, into the game environment and back again."[33] This "congruence requirement" is what enables a gamer to "play along with" the worldview presented by the game. Fidelity of context is a fundamentally cultural concept, meaning that players in different contexts will have opposing ways of reading video games' content. Juxtaposing *America's Army* with *Special Force*, an FPS released by the Lebanese organization Hezbollah in 2003, Galloway explains the relationship between cultural context and the ludic experience of realism: "To put it bluntly, a typical American youth playing *Special Force* is most likely not experiencing realism, whereas realism is indeed possible for a young Palestinian gamer playing *Special Force* in the occupied territories. This fidelity of context is key for realism in gaming."[34] Likewise, US gamers—young and old—may be less likely than Latin American gamers to focus on the details of the cultural depictions of Latin American countries, or may focus on them in different ways. Players familiar with the cultural contexts being represented are likely to be more critical of stereotypical or reductive representations, but this does not mean that players who are not familiar with the cultural contexts represented are necessarily blind to such factors. The danger of exaggerating the imperialist overtones of games is the tendency to assume that games' messages are free from fidelity of context, and that their messages are universally and consistently legible.

The anti-imperialist critique's invocation of a "universal gamer" can lead to critical over-statements regarding factors that may already be self-evident to an increasingly diverse populace of gamers of all ages. To paraphrase Latin American literary critic Brett Levinson, the problem with many of these arguments is not that they are too good to be true, but that they are too true to be good.[35] Levinson criticizes some within the decolonialist vein of Latin American cultural studies (to which he pertains) for overstating the obvious in their critiques, contributing to a "ceaseless unearthing of an already unearthed Eurocentrism" by critics of literary works that themselves offer complex interpretations of the relationship between self and other.[36] Likewise, it is possible that much of what is being criticized with regard to the militaristic frame of video games is readily apparent to anyone who has played the games in question, making it necessary to further problematize our analyses of the ways these games relate to violence and imperialism.

For instance, why should we assume that cries of "Stop the killing!" have no place in video games in particular? Whether in video games or other media, such cries are indeed well estab-lished as the "stuff of entertainment" in a centuries-long literary, artistic, and cinematic tra-dition. To exclude games is to come dangerously close to the oversimplified view that they are—and can only be—child's play. Too often, the anti-imperialist critique of video games suf-fers from what Juul refers to as "video game exceptionalism," which treats games as "more dangerous than other forms of culture" without sufficiently reflecting on the multiple levels they make meaning beyond what is superficially evident.[37] This, I believe, is the root cause of an overstatement on the part of the anti-imperialist critique of the equivalency between games' (military) theme and their (supposedly militaristic) thesis.

Are military games imperialist? Many critics have demonstrated the ways in which they are. But too few have paid attention to the ways in which they are not. Too often it is taken for granted that any game *about* warfare is *in favor of* warfare, another form of video game excep-tionalism. Juul points out that critics are frequently guilty of ignoring the real experience of gameplay, providing narrative-driven analyses that fail to account for the multiple layers of meaning making that we readily accept in literature, the visual arts, and film: "The audience of a movie does not automatically assume that the protagonist *does good*, and neither does the player of a video game believe that the protagonist of the game *does good*. A game is a play with identities, where the player at one moment performs an action considered morally sound and the next moment tries something he or she considers indefensible. The player chooses one mission or another, tries to complete the mission in one way or another, tries to do 'good' or 'evil.' Games are playgrounds where players can experiment with doing things they would or would not normally do."[38] Basing his analysis on the unpredictable and highly variable practices of play, Juul offers a reminder that there are multiple avenues for interpretation of meaning, even in some of the most seemingly straightforwardly imperialist games.

If in fact imperialism is an element within the ideological framework of many games, it can at least be shown that it is not the *only* ideology that these games convey. Indeed, a great many military-themed games can be seen to critique imperialism through their content and the scenarios they portray. When players of *Call of Duty: Black Ops II* participate in a mission that involves illegally framing Panamanian leader Manuel Noriega by planting duffel bags of cocaine in his hotel room, they are not just experiencing the justification of empire, but an implicit critique of its immorality and underhandedness. When players of *Just Cause* witness the US intelligence agents in charge of the invasion of the (fictitious) island of San Esperito whittling away their time gulping down tropical drinks while playing military-themed video games and reading books like *Regime Change in 7 Days*, they are not seeing the legitimization of an imperialist worldview, but its critique through elements of irony, humor, and satire. To truly understand how video games relate to empire, we must steer clear of critiques that are too true to be good, or those that are too straightforward to accurately reflect the complexities of the simulations described. We must recognize that multiple meanings are transmitted in games, above and beyond those that seem most evident on the surface.

On the Ludic Significance of Parody

In *Misplaced Ideas*, his 1992 analysis of literature and society in late nineteenth-century Brazil, literary critic Roberto Schwarz argues that parody "is one of the most combative of literary forms, so long as that is its intention. And anyway," he adds, "a little contemplation never did anyone any harm."[39] Schwarz speaks of the way that cultural standards, when imported to one context from another, undergo a process of mimesis that invariably leads to parodic adaptation, as the importers use and misuse the cultural mechanisms newly placed at their disposal. "In countries where culture is imported," Schwarz explains, "parody is almost a natural form of criticism: it simply makes explicit unintentional parodies which are in any case inevitable."[40] Schwarz's analysis hinges upon the inherent critical capacity of parody, which has been referred to both as the most dangerous form of humor, and an "essential resource for sustaining public culture."[41] In simulations, parody can play an important role in determining the signifying context through which cultural meaning is communicated and interpreted. In order to adequately interpret the cultural messages communicated in video games, it is essential that we consider the tone with which those messages are transmitted. Even humorous games provide real, valid, and culturally contextualized experiences for their players.

Humans have valued games that make us laugh since the dawn of civilization—so what is it that motivates contemporary gamers in particular to play humorous video games? John C. Meyer explains that through "the relaxing elements of humor, parties can lower defenses and be more open to seeing the new perspectives required to appreciate humor," meaning that players can be as receptive—or more receptive—to messages transmitted in "a 'comic frame'" than those in "a rigid 'tragic frame.'"[42] Meyer appeals to the "incongruity theory" of humor, which states that "people laugh at what surprises them, is unexpected, or is odd in a non-threatening way," opening them up to meaningful messages expressed in humorous terms.[43] In this way, players can find as much meaning in humorous simulations of history and culture as they do in games seeking to convey historical gravitas. Certainly, the critical value of satire, irony, and parody can be seen in some of the persuasive games from Latin American designers in chapter 2, such as *Turista Fronterizo*, *Crosser*, and *La Migra*, or the newsgames like *La Mordida*, *Portillo el Tontillo*, and *Guerra Política* discussed in chapter 3. Messages containing sarcasm and irony can offer serious critiques even while they seem diffuse or frivolous.[44] However, it is essential to keep in mind that different individuals have different ways of interpreting messages, regardless of the medium through which they are transmitted. Therefore it is important to take note of what types of messages are procedurally suggested by the experience of gameplay, in order to comprehend what a game *means* above and beyond what it *says* or *portrays*.

Toward that end, there is perhaps no better example on which to focus than Rockstar's *Grand Theft Auto* series, which is both one of the most controversial and one of the most commercially successful game franchises of all time. Chapter 5 discussed the ways culture is incorporated into the spatial and sonic framework of the game's open world environment. In addition to the role of space, it is essential to consider the way that a game's expressive tone affects its meaning. In *Wordplay and the Discourse of Video Games*, Paul offers an analysis of the problematic role of humor in the series: "*GTA* contains heavy touches of irony and satire. Humor changes the dynamics of a text, potentially leading to multiple kinds of readings about what the text 'means.' [...] Within the context of *GTA*, some may appreciate the humor, while others will not. This polarizes the audience; you either laugh with the game or find it even stranger that anyone could like it. For those who laugh, the humor bonds them to the game and becomes memorable, pushing them away from those who just do not get the joke."[45] This is also why Meyer refers to humor as a "double-edged sword," due to its capacity to produce multiple subjective interpretations, and thus the concomitant multiplication of possibilities for (mis)interpretation of the intended message.

As at least a few critics have noted, *Grand Theft Auto* may be the most misunderstood video game series in the history of the medium.[46] The unabashedly graphic series is frequently subjected to moralizing readings of fragments and sound bites extracted from its endless hours of open world gameplay, all of which takes place in an off-color yet thoroughly complex environment. Likewise, although the *GTA* series has had a greater degree of cultural diversity than most, frequently featuring protagonists of diverse cultural backgrounds along with the complex cultural dynamics of the game environment discussed in chapter 5, scholars have characterized the series as racist much more frequently than they have lauded the diversity of its characters and settings. For example, David J. Leonard argues, "*San Andreas* does not merely give life to dominant stereotypes but gives legitimizing voice to hegemonic discourses about race, whether it is 'illegal aliens are invading the country' or that 'Latin America has less culture than a toilet bowl.' "[47] The latter two statements are made by callers on *GTA San Andreas*'s talk radio station, *West Coast Talk Radio*, which perhaps not surprisingly is replete with scathing satire based on exaggerated caricatures of conservatives and liberals alike. In this signifying context, and in the mouths of characters who are supposed to come off as laughably ignorant, these messages are not the sort of straightforward legitimation of hegemonic discourse that Leonard portrays them as, but precisely the opposite: they are elements of a parody meant to destabilize the discourse they appear to represent. To return to Hariman's maxim cited earlier: "The parody is not what it claims to be, to reveal that the discourse being parodied is what it claims not to be." We don't label a film about World War II-era Germany anti-Semitic because its Nazi characters say things that are anti-Semitic, and to characterize *GTA* as straightforwardly racist based on its use of racist characters fails to account for the ways the series really makes cultural meaning.

Other critics of the *GTA* series have looked carefully at the complicated role of humor in its portrayal of race and culture, but have still found plenty to critique. Dyer-Witheford and de Peuter contend that "*GTA* is a cynical game that simultaneously satirizes, indulges, and normalizes individual hyperpossessiveness, racialized stereotypes, and neoliberal violence in a self-cancellation that allows these elements to remain intact, a structure that is, in a very precise way, conservative."[48] Dean Chan echoes their sentiments, arguing that the series is "complicit in the pathologization and fetishization of race" since "there is a fine line to (t)read between parodic critique and discursive reinscription, especially in relation to the deployment of racialized archetypes and the persistent linkage of these archetypes with criminal elements."[49] Taken on its face, it is easy to see Chan's point—a game that consistently portrays black characters as criminals and white characters as police officers, for example, would be highly problematic. But are these "racialized archetypes" truly *persistently* linked to criminality in *GTA*? Or is *GTA* being called racist by virtue of being racial? The *Grand Theft Auto* series features a diverse cast of characters (both playable and nonplayable) from all walks of life. Among the Latin American characters in *GTA V*, for example, there are newly arrived immigrants, both documented and undocumented, as well as second- and third-generation Latinos and Latinas; there are monolingual Spanish and English speakers, bilinguals, and speakers of Spanglish; there are men and women, old and young (though no children); there are gangsters and grandmas, playboys and paupers. Given both the notable cultural diversity and the overall criminal orientation of the *GTA* universe, it is difficult to sustain the argument that the game is racist based upon its representation of any particular racial group as any more criminal than another. In short, if there is an argument that *GTA* is inherently racist, it has yet to be articulated in a way that sufficiently accounts for the complexity of the ways cultural meaning is generated in the series.

An examination of the way Latin American culture relates to the simulated framework of *GTA* helps illustrate the procedural and algorithmic ways that meaning is made in the series. Though they are all based in fictionalized versions of locations in the United States, all of the games in the *GTA* series incorporate significant elements of Latin American culture in a variety of forms. For example, *GTA V* features a number of side missions categorized under "Strangers and Freaks," as well as hidden "Easter egg" characters that pop up when the player randomly approaches them on the map. In one series of Strangers and Freaks missions, Trevor gets involved with a bizarre duo calling themselves the "Civil Border Patrol" and consisting of Joe and Josef, an anti-immigrant "patriot" with a southern accent, and an equally anti-immigrant sidekick who puzzlingly speaks only Russian. They hire Trevor to drive them on absurd hunts for *documented* immigrants including mariachis and cement factory workers, with Trevor growing suspicious of the duo as they use their tasers on victim after innocent victim of their vigilante racial profiling. Eventually, one of the mariachi captives, Manuel, informs Trevor that the Civil Border Patrol has been harassing Mexican-American citizens of the area for years, and challenges him to quit supporting them and to make things right. The player, as Trevor, then encounters Joe and Josef in the midst of an attack on a Mexican family's farm, and in a characteristic fit of rage resolves the situation by slaying the Civil Border Patrol members in an act of vengeance for their years of racist persecution of the local population.

Another of *GTA V*'s Easter egg characters, referred to online as the "Secret Mexican Mariachi Easter Egg" or "El mexicano desesperado" ("The Desperate Mexican"), is an actor who complains in vibrant detail about being assigned the same stereotypical acting roles in Vinewood movies over and over again, among the many other injustices he faces as a Mexican in Los Santos. This desperately overqualified thespian, who explains that he is handicapped only by his lack of English-speaking abilities, proclaims, "¡Este país es el país de las mentiras, y la mentira más grande es que todos somos iguales! No hay ni un caso en el que seamos iguales—ni en ingresos, ni en impuestos, ni en derechos, ¡ni en nada! ¡Es una mentira a la cual se pueden adherir los idiotas!" ("This country is the country of lies. And the biggest lie of all is this—we are all equal! There is not one single area in which we are equal—not income, not taxes, not rights, not anything! It's a big lie for the idiots to cling to!"). In addition to offering a biting social critique about discrimination against Mexicans in the United States, this mariachi/actor brings us back around once again to the role of humor in negotiating cultural meaning in video games, as he exclaims, "¡He estudiado Lope de Vega! ¡Aquí tengo suerte si juego el papel de cartero en el rodaje de una película porno!" ("I studied Lope de Vega! Here I'm lucky if I get to play the mailman on a porn shoot!"). If the ironic Civil Border Patrol missions left any doubt, this pointed piece of satire demonstrates the difficulty of reading *GTA* as a simplistic or unilateral reinforcement of conventional discriminatory attitudes. If we understand *GTA* as a parody and account for the significance of that fact with sufficient critical rigor, it becomes clear that, while the game may appear to be a culturally conservative reinforcement of hegemonic cultural attitudes on its surface, it is not that—or at the very least, it is never *only* that. As a parody, the discourse of *GTA* is often the opposite of what it claims, in order to reveal that, in fact, hegemonic attitudes about culture and race are not as all-encompassing and universal as their defenders would like them to appear.

A critical reader may argue that I am not approaching *Grand Theft Auto* like a normal player, but rather as an academic, using theory and criticism to make an argument in favor of cultural relativism. Surely there are those players not sophisticated enough to pick up on the multiple layers of meaning at work in a parody like *GTA*, those who "don't get" its jokes and those who are simply turned off by its (at times outrageously crude) attempts at humor. But at the same time, one should not assume that players are blind to the way that a complex game like *GTA* plays with meaning. A 2008 study of "at risk" youth gamers playing *GTA: San Andreas* noted that the players saw the game as "a satire of media representations," and even concluded that "there was some evidence that a gaming disposition, when activated around a game with such deep social satire, opened space for these marginalized kids to critique contemporary social structure."[50] This study is a reminder of players' capacity for what Sicart calls "ludic practical judgment" and "ludic maturity," even while engaging in actions that may or may not adhere to real-world ethics "because those actions have meaning within the game for the player-subject."[51] At the same time, it offers a reminder of the increasing diversity and complexity of the game-playing populace, as well as the role of contextual fidelity in defining the meaning of video game simulations.

Parody is a potentially productive means of transmitting cultural meaning in video games due to the ways subversive and satirical representations can expose cultural fallacies for what they are. When analyzing a game's ways of representing culture, it is important to remember that, as much literature on games and education has suggested, video games teach the player on multiple levels. In particular, humor in games "can work in support of social or emotional results," meaning "that humor can enhance persuasion" in video games by combining these results with cognitive functions in the player including attention, recognition, awareness, stimulation, clarification, differentiation, problem solving, retention, creativity, and divergent thinking.[52] In fact, Claire Dormann and Robert Biddle argue that "[s]erious games are often too serious, and the ability of humor to mediate learning suggests that the best games will be both serious and funny."[53] Dormann and Biddle's critique offers a reminder that intentionally "serious" or "persuasive" games on political topics are not the only games that have cognitive influence on players. This illustrates the need to intensify our critical examinations of the simulation of race and culture in video games, in order to more realistically assess how tone and other components of communication can affect games' meaning.

Tropico: Why Would You Play as Pinochet?

Having surveyed examples of the ways realism and verisimilitude, as well as irony, humor, and parody, affect video games' meaning, I would like to return now to the question with which this chapter began: Why would a player choose to play as Chilean dictator Augusto Pinochet in *Tropico*? Like most management simulations, *Tropico* is a game that revolves around decision making and its repercussions. At the beginning of a game session, the player chooses one of several scenarios, each of which places relative value on a different factor, for example, avoiding invasion by the US or USSR, or a revolution from within the country, or both, or achieving a certain percentage of "Happiness"—as a calculable variable—among the island's population. Based on the task at hand, the player then selects an avatar for that round of play, choosing from a pantheon of famous dictators, revolutionaries, and other leaders—Anastasio Somoza, Manuel Noriega, Fidel Castro, Che Guevara, Juan Perón, Eva Perón, and Pinochet among them—as well as several fictitious characters. Each of these avatars is described in terms of their title, how they came to power ("Bought Election," "Elected as Socialist," etc.), two positive qualities ("Hardworking," "Patriot," etc.), and two negative qualities ("Lazy," "Paranoid," etc.). As with the example of Montezuma in *Civilization* examined earlier, these characteristics and attributes do not add up to a historically accurate portrayal of the leaders in question, but rather their meaning in the game hinges upon their ludic value. For example, a leader's manner of coming to power—through democratic means or corruption, whether it accurately reflects the history of that particular figure or not—affects the Tropican population's level of trust in the leader, as well as their own sense of "Liberty," factors which can lead to stability or revolution, depending on the avatar the player chooses.

While the variables attributed to the avatar continue to have calculable effects on gameplay, the name and face of the particular dictatorial avatar that the player has chosen fade quickly into the background, as all leaders are addressed simply as the character of "El Presidente" within the game's ongoing satirical dialogue. The specificity of historical characters is fleeting in a framework that ultimately is less about history than it is about the conventional stuff of the resource management simulator—building industry and infrastructure with the right balance—as well as the political simulator, which requires the player to balance public opinion. After the opening moments, then, gameplay is only vaguely related to the embodiment of a particular personality, with the player's control over environmental agency being measured in the output of their island's cigar factories and rum distilleries, levels of education and employment, the population's government approval rating, and a number of other factors with varying repercussions depending on the particular scenario being played out.

Notwithstanding these algorithmic considerations as well as a lengthy tradition of "playing dictator" in other forms of media (like the well-established genre of the dictator novel in Latin America),[54] *Tropico*'s scenario positing the player as the recently installed autocrat of a fictitious Caribbean island makes it an apt target for the ideological critique. First and foremost, there is the lengthy footnote from Frasca with which I began this chapter, a condemnation of the game that I take very seriously. Though he recognizes that the game is a parody, Frasca argues that *Tropico*'s "extreme use of clichés and simplification" represent a "colonialist attitude in video game design," concluding that the game is "insulting" and even "disgusting." Building upon Frasca's critique of the game's apparent colonialist overtones, Magnet argues that the game functions as "a landscape of colonization for players who would be kings"[55] in an analysis that offers significant insight into the trope of *tropicalization* and its implications for the game's meaning. Magnet chose *Tropico* as the object of her analysis "because of the interest some players have shown in using Tropico as an educational instrument to teach American children about governance," finding it noteworthy that "the Tropican gamescape is so effective in concealing the underlying assumptions of the game, many of which are intimately tied to ideas about US imperialist expansion, that it could be posited as a useful education tool."[56] Magnet's analysis is a critique of the hypothetical possibility of the game being used "unreflexively as an educational tool," as she explains in her conclusion:

> Caution must be exercised in thinking about the educational possibilities for *Tropico*. In an article on the potential of using video games to teach kids, Squire (2002) suggested that games such as *Tropico* could serve an instructional purpose with respect to teaching children about "island governance." Given the ways in which *Tropico* represents a gamescape of colonization, careful consideration as to the kind of cultural and capitalist messages that the game articulates would have to be an essential part of the educational process. It is frightening to imagine that a game such as *Tropico*, which represents essentialist stereotypes about Latina/os and Latinidad, could be used unreflexively as an educational tool.[57]

The reasons *not* to play as Pinochet, then, are all too clear from the perspective of the ideological critique: the game is colonialist and demeaning, and its veiled essentialism contributes to the hegemony of imperialist discourse. So why, then, would educators advocate using this "frightening" colonialist simulation as a way of teaching governance without any further critical reflection in the classroom?

As it turns out, the answer is simple: they wouldn't, and they weren't. The basis for Magnet's argument—the assertion that "some players" had sought to use the game as a straightforward (yet unconsciously colonialist) educational tool—was actually aimed at the same text mentioned in the above quote from her conclusion, namely a 2002 article by Kurt Squire in the academic journal *Game Studies* titled "Cultural Framing of Computer/Video Games." In that article, Squire in fact argues *against* using any of these games as a straightforward political text in the classroom in any "unreflexive" manner, primarily focusing on the importance of exploring the pedagogical implications of games including *SimCity* and *Civilization*, with *Tropico* thrown in as one of several minor examples.[58] In a speculative article about how management simulations *might possibly* be used in future educational settings after their pedagogical potential is better understood, Squire suggests that "students might spent 25 percent of their time playing the game, and the remainder of the time creating maps, historical timelines, researching game concepts, drawing parallels to historical or current events, or interacting with other media, such as books or videos," so that "the educational value of the game-playing experiences comes not from just the game itself, but from the creative coupling of educational media with effective pedagogy to engage students in meaningful practices."[59] Just as importantly, Squire raises questions about how these games might be used and misused: he asks whether games such as these "impact players' conceptions of politics or diplomacy," making the critical suggestion that students "be required to critique the game and explicitly address built-in simulation biases" as part of using a simulation like *Tropico* within a pedagogical framework.[60]

These details reveal the problem that all too frequently afflicts the application of the ideological critique to complex cultural products like *Tropico*. Such a critique comes from the perspective of the informed player, but is built on the normative assumption of a "naïve" player, uninformed and incapable of interpreting irony, satire, or parody. This player is akin to what Levinson describes as the "subject-supposed-not-to-know" by the postcolonial critique in Latin American literary studies.[61] For a player who has spent significant time with the game, however, it is difficult to accept the argument that "the user is unconsciously incorporated into the game ideology and, as a result, unproblematically reproduces a particular kind of colonial landscape without being aware that *Tropico*'s game rules naturalize certain historical specificities—such as a US-centric worldview."[62] Indeed, for any mature individual who has played *Tropico*, it should be no revelation to say that it somehow reflects imperialism—that is exactly what the game is about. It is a broad parody on the theme of imperialism and revolution in the Cold War, with two main targets: propagandistic utopian regimes like that of Fidel Castro (represented by the paternalistic and all-powerful El Presidente), and the imperialist interventionism of the United States in twentieth-century Latin America, a threat of which the player is constantly reminded as leader of their island nation. Once again, to say that the game somehow supports the ideology of any one of these leaders over the other, or that it is in favor of totalitarianism because the player embodies a dictator, is to equate theme to thesis, and to set aside the significance of simulation and parody in favor of a straightforward answer to a question that is anything but.

So what are acceptable reasons for a player to play a game as Pinochet, or as Hernán Cortés, or Moctezuma, or any other historical figure responsible for the deaths of many? My answers, perhaps not surprisingly, are more ludic than ideological. In *Gamer Theory*, McKenzie Wark offers an antidote to the view of games as spaces where colonialist players who would be kings play out their imperialist pretensions, explaining why good people do bad things in games:

> Gamers are not always good Gods. It's such a temptation to set up a Sim to suffer. Deprive them of a knowledge of cooking and pretty soon they set fire to themselves. Build a house without doors or windows and they starve. Watch as the algorithm works itself out to its terminal state, the bar graphs sliding down to nothing. This violence is not "real." Sims are not people. They are images. They are images in a world that appears as a vast accumulation of images. Hence the pleasure in destroying images, to demonstrate again and again their worthlessness. They can mean anything and nothing. They have no saving power. But even though the images are meaningless, the algorithm still functions. It assigns, if not meaning, if not veracity, if not necessity, then at least a score to representations.[63]

This is what is too frequently forgotten or set aside by the ideological critique: the player is not a dictator, and she is not participating in the assassination of real people any more than she is participating in the cultivation of real crops. Rather, the player is learning to read the game's algorithm by playing with variables that can frequently be reduced to numerical factors.

This leads me to a dirty little secret that helps destabilize a strictly ideological critique of the way this particular game represents history and makes meaning: *Tropico* is really just *Railroad Tycoon II* (Gathering of Developers 1997) with a skinned veneer of political parody (figure 6.3).The *Tropico* series was the brainchild of Phil Steinmeyer, a programmer and designer who had done prior work on the *Sid Meier's Civilization* series. Steinmeyer founded Missouri-based PopTop Software in 1993, releasing *Railroad Tycoon II* as its first major title in 1997, and the original *Tropico* in 2001. Steinmeyer says that he had mulled over the idea of *Tropico* for years, and that it was "a nice coincidence that the *Railroad Tycoon II* engine happened to be a fairly close fit for what *Tropico* needed" in terms of a software framework capable of running the game's operations. The combination of a resource management simulation with a political simulation has its roots in a lengthy tradition of games, but Steinmeyer also had a specific inspiration: "The idea for a game where you're the ruler of your own island, for better or worse, is one I've been thinking about for a long time. Waaaaay back, there was a game for the old Intellivision console called *Utopia*, where you ruled an island, built farms, hospitals and housing and fought rebels. It was arguably the first graphical strategy game ever and a favorite of mine, and obviously, we're touching on a lot of those same elements in *Tropico*"[64] (figure 6.4). In the beginning, work focused primarily on software functionality—after a year of development, Steinmeyer

Figure 6.3
Railroad Tycoon II (PopTop 1997)

explains, "the engine was working, the people moved about and behaved fairly realistically, the building interactions worked. ... Then we had about seven months to mold these basics into a finished game, layering in politics, balancing things, etc.," an order of operations that reflects the primacy of simulation over narrative for the game's designers.[65]

One implication of the *Railroad Tycoon II* framework is that the player's avatar is ultimately of much less significance than the NPC "miniatures" that make up the Tropican population. Steinmeyer was particularly proud of the way NPCs were diversified in the original game of the series, explaining that in order for the "political and social elements to work we needed deep, realistic people," which meant coding each NPC in *Tropico* with "over 50 unique characteristics—from innate qualities, like their intelligence and courage, to their immediate needs like their hunger and rest level, to things like their political views and level of religious belief, to family relationships."[66] While the attributes of the player's avatar affect the way the game plays out, those of the multitudinous population can be of even greater significance in determining success or failure, meaning that the particular despot chosen by the player

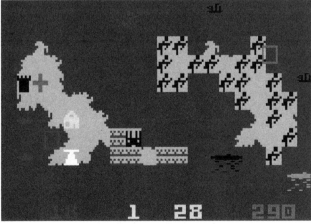

Figure 6.4
Utopia (Mattel 1981)

is ultimately of less relative weight in the game than the ideological critique would seem to suggest.

So what exactly is the significance of the player's choice of avatar in *Tropico*? The answer depends on the demands of the situation. Each avatar within the game is assigned certain characteristics. Take, for example, how this plays out in *Tropico 3* (Kalypso 2009), an installment in the series that returned to its parodic roots and that clearly evidences the algorithmic analysis I wish to carry out here. In *Tropico 3*, each avatar is attributed with a leadership style, a means of coming to power, two of thirteen available positive traits, and two of fifteen available negative traits or flaws (see table 6.1).

In turn, each of these qualities is assigned a value that has an impact on the population's attitudes about the leader. Compare, for example, the relative profiles of Castro and Pinochet in the game:

Fidel Castro

- Background: Man of the People (+20 Communist faction respect, −5 Religious faction respect)
- Rise to Power: Communist Rebellion (Low democratic expectations, +10 Communist faction respect, +25 USSR relations, +10 percent farmers' production)
- Positive Traits:
  - Charismatic (+5 all Tropican factions respect, +50 percent radio/TV dogma effectiveness)
  - Patriot (+20 Nationalist respect, +10 Tropico born citizens respect)
- Flaws:
  - Short-tempered (−15 Intellectual faction respect, −10 Militarist faction respect)
  - Paranoid (−10 all Tropican factions respect, +10 Militarist faction respect)

Augusto Pinochet

- Background: Generalissimo (+20 Militarist faction respect, +20 Nationalist faction respect, −20 percent Liberty, +15 percent soldiers' experience)
- Rise to Power: Military Coup (Very low democratic expectations, +20 Militarist faction respect, −20 percent Crime, −20 percent Liberty, −25 percent military building costs)
- Positive Traits:
  - Financial Genius (+10 Capitalist faction respect, +20 percent factory workers production, −25 percent cost of banks, marketplaces, souvenir shops)
  - Entrepreneurial (+10 percent export prices)

- Flaws
  - Pompous (−20 US respect, +30 percent edict costs; can only praise yourself in election speeches)
  - Great Schmoozola (−25 percent Intellectual faction respect, −10 US relations, −10 USSR relations, +10 percent respect of least-intelligent citizens)

As might have been predicted from previous examples, these assigned characteristics offer a nod to reality from time to time—Castro rises to power through communist rebellion, and Pinochet through a military coup, for example. However, whether they are accurate or not, these historical details are subjugated to *Tropico*'s algorithm, meaning that they are ultimately placeholders for a number of underlying mathematical equations that have little or no correspondence to historical reality. Did Cuban communists gain 10 percentage points of respect when the real-life Castro declared himself a communist? Did farm production increase by exactly or approximately 10 percent? Of course not: these are factors that produce rippling algorithmic effects that make the game interesting as a product of play, not a simulation focused on verisimilitude or accuracy in any "real" sense. In short, these seemingly ideological factors are in fact the superficial skinning over a coded framework: vis-à-vis the context of *Railroad Tycoon II*, for example, *Tropico*'s rebels replace train robbers, while intervention by the World Bank replaces a stock market crash. Considered this way, the real-world referents are nothing more than the superficial décor overlying the code.

But what about players who really do have colonialist fantasies, or perhaps even worse, sadistic dreams of being tyrants who torture, murder, and disappear scores of individuals in their country's population? Quite simply, those players' fantasies have no chance of being fulfilled by a game like *Tropico*. As King and Krzywinska note, the player "is far from entirely free to determine policy in *Tropico* [...] and can face interventions from the game that mirror real-world constraints; the player who runs up too great a budget deficit, for example, faces intervention from the game's version of the World Bank, an enforced capping of wages of the workforce."[67] Likewise, if the player starts to assassinate members of the NPC population, the NPCs' family members and friends will grow increasingly oppositional to the player's rule and will eventually spark a revolution. As much as a player—or a critic—might want *Tropico* to be a game about "playing dictator" and carrying out imperialist fantasies, this is ultimately not a satisfying characterization of the possibilities opened up in this particular simulation. Instead, *Tropico* is a resource and political management simulation whose satirical surface narrative conceals a critique of colonialism that exposes the inherent fallaciousness of a would-be hegemonic discourse.

Our critiques of games' meanings will be more accurate if we do not base them on the presumption of player naïveté, or the straw man of a subject-supposed-not-to-know. We are

Table 6.1

Mapping *Tropico 3*'s Dictatorial Algorithm

Character	Administrator	Alcoholic	Charismatic	Cheapskate	Compulsive Gambler	Compulsive Liar	Coward	Diplomatic	Entrepreneurial	Financial Genius	Flatulence
Fidel Castro			X								
Che Guevara		X	X								
Hernandez Martinez											
"Papa Doc" Duvalier	X		X			X					
Juan Peron									X		X
Augusto Pinochet									X	X	
Antonio Salazar				X						X	
Anastasio Somoza, Sr				X				X		X	
Manuel Noriega									X	X	
Rafael Trujillo				X				X	X		
Eva "Evita" Peron			X		X				X		
Marie Gomez								X			
Isabela Llorando			X				X				
Gabriela Maria Jose		X									
El Pollo Diablo				X	X				X		
El Septimo	X									X	
Oscar Malasuerte							X			X	
Voodoo Pizzaman										X	

	Trait														
Great Schmoozola	Green Thumb	Hardworking	Jingo	Lazy	Moronic	Paranoid	Patriot	Pompous	Propaganda Specialist	Religious Zealot	Scholarly	Short Tempered	Ugly	Well-Travelled	Womanizer
						X	X					X			
		X										X			
	X	X	X					X							
X															
		X			X										
X								X							
		X								X					
								X							
						X							X		
					X										
				X								X		X	
		X													
							X	X	X						
											X				
			X								X				
		X										X			
										X				X	X

better off assuming that players of games like *Tropico* are, in fact, capable of ludic practical judgment and a nuanced understanding of the multiple levels on which the game produces meaning. As Beth Simone Noveck argues, the player, under the auspices of his avatar, "may act in antisocial and even pathological ways—ways in which the 'real' person never would," because the avatar "is a citizen—a legal and moral personage distinct from the private individual—who acts in a social capacity" determined by the particular rules of the game in question.[68] This is why a player exercising ludic maturity can undertake actions that would be ethically questionable in the real world. It is also why we should recognize that many, if not most, players "get" the jokes made by a game like *Tropico* (or at the very least, they get that a joke is being made), and therefore they are able to move past the game's superficial imperialist discourse to the underlying ideological critique that was always already contained within its parodic frame. Contra the naïve player of *Tropico*, I advocate for an analysis of how a historically themed parodic simulation like *Tropico* makes meaning for mature and experienced players of video games, the individuals most likely to play a complex resource management simulation like the one in question. Mature players, as we know, do not simply do "what is right" in a real-world moral sense when they play games, but base their in-game behavior on the specific demands of the particular coded environment with which they are interacting.

For a player with ludic maturity, *Tropico*'s parody is not just apparent but all-encompassing, impossible to miss. For example, as El Presidente, you are guided through the world by your "enthusiastically loyal" servant, Penúltimo, who mentions early on that he's working on a project of his own, asking if El Presidente knows a good pharmacy that sells cheap poison (wink, wink). When not pumping the Caribbean rhythms that drive gameplay along, the game's radio broadcasts are dominated by two competing satirical voices: revolutionary radio host Betty Boom and El Presidente's lapdog DJ Juanito. Betty Boom vociferously condemns the player's every move in a hilarious parody of over-the top rhetoric—build a wind turbine, and she will take to the airwaves to provide a vitriolic denunciation of El Presidente's false environmentalism and ignorance of the real problems of the island (complaints that sometimes have the ludic effect of directing the player's attention to neglected factors and variables). Juanito, meanwhile, is basically an adoring microphone for his leader, in everything from political reportage to meteorology: "And for our evening forecast," Juanito explains at a random point over the radio, "El Presidente predicts the weather will be fair, clear and sunny. Remember, El Presidente is right, *even when he's wrong!*" I do not believe that any critic could realistically conclude that players are taking messages like Juanito's at face value. Rather, players of *Tropico* know that leaders are not right even when they are wrong, and therefore probably find some humor in this parodic piece of dialogue. Critically, we can't have it both ways—we can't posit a player capable of engaging in a complex parodic environment that is clearly couched in humor and satire, and at the same time argue that the player is incapable of seeing past the game's colonialist surface.

If we do take players seriously and assume that they are capable of critically assessing the way a game deals with historical representation, we can envision a scenario in which players could not only succeed in certain scenarios in *Tropico 3* more efficiently by playing as Pinochet, they could also benefit from playing as Pinochet by finding the motivation to further explore the history of violence and exploitation. In such a case, a passing familiarity with the darkest reaches of Latin America's history could lead a player to learn more about that history, even going on to make a difference in the world, or at least in their own personal worldview. If that sounds overly idealistic, I would like to at least offer one small piece of anecdotal evidence to the contrary. When I first purchased *Tropico 3* online through Amazon.com, that website used its own algorithms to provide marketable answers to the question, "What Other Items Do Customers Buy After Viewing This Item?" The first item recommended, surprisingly, was not a video game, as it almost always is when a customer is browsing games on the site. Rather, it was a regional historical survey by Peter Bakewell that belongs to the Blackwell History of the World series: the most purchased item for *Tropico 3* buyers was *A History of Latin America*.

Conclusion: Simulation and Culture in Video Games

In the best of cases, culturally and historically contextualized video games can serve as a springboard to player interest in the subject matter at hand. Galloway argues that identity in *Sid Meier's Civilization*, the flagship of the management simulation genre, "is modular, instrumental, typed, numerical, algorithmic," and that "the more one begins to think that *Civilization* is about a certain ideological interpretation of history (neoconservative, reactionary, or what have you), or even that it creates a computer-generated 'history effect,' the more one realizes that it is about the absence of history altogether, or rather, the transcoding of history into specific mathematical models."[69] This "absence of history" evokes some familiar ideological modes, political perspectives, and cultural tendencies, but does not put them into an order that coincides with real-world history, creating a meaningful void that the player may indeed seek to fill. This is evidenced in a number of phenomena, for example the *Civilization Wiki*, an open-source site that goes into depth about the playable civilizations and other mechanics of the game series. This Wiki, and many others like it centered on other games, go into detail that far surpasses what is necessary for playing the game, informing the player about real-world events and cultural traditions that fall outside of the would-be magic circle of gameplay.

So, once and for all, why would you choose to play as Pinochet? I hope that this chapter's discussion of the multiple and coinciding roles of realism, verisimilitude, irony, satire, and parody in generating the meaning of video games has offered sufficient explanation. In short, games are not a form of narrative history—or at least they are not primarily that—and they are of course not real, but rather a means for playing with different factors in order to see the different possible outcomes to a situation. Therefore gamers are not so much "playing dictator" as they are choosing a set of variables—it makes sense to play as Pinochet if the scenario calls for support from the "Militarists" and "Nationalists" for example, but it would be a bad ludic decision to play as Pinochet if the scenario were to involve high democratic expectations on the part of the population or a need to praise others in speeches (as Pinochet, in the game, can only praise himself). In a ludic framework like that of *Tropico*, it makes little sense to make decisions based on real-world ideology, because they will not allow the player to make progress. Engaging in play requires the player to do things that they cannot or would not do in the real world, including taking actions that would be considered questionable or even reprehensible by real-world cultural standards of morality or decision making. And even still, such actions embody good ludic decision making, because they make sense within the logic of a simulation's algorithm.

Of course my algorithmic interpretation of cultural meaning in *Tropico* is not the only one that is possible. Others may interpret it as the opposite of what I have suggested, and this is an inherent quality of works of parody and satire. "One risk for the satirist," Lisa Gring-Pemble and Martha Solomon Watson have explained, "is that a reader may find the satire amusing, especially when it involves *reductio ad absurdum*, without sharing the author's attitudes or viewpoints."[70] This is true of *Grand Theft Auto*, it is true of *Tropico*, and it is also true of scores of other video games from throughout the history of the medium. But when we examine this body of cultural production, which is ever-diversifying in its means of conveying meaning and experience, we must not abandon the critical sensibilities that have guided us through the interpretation of centuries of human civilization that came before. As critics, we have much to say about the way history is conveyed, but up to now we have been too quick to apply incompatible frameworks when explaining how history works in the systems of meaning making particular to video games. Likewise, we must not abandon critical distance and sensitivity when we look at games, but show an understanding of how tone affects meaning. Being too serious can lead to taking games' messages at face value as if they were expressing their ideological arguments in every snippet of dialogue, and in order to comprehend games in all their dimensions, one of our responses has got to be laughter. In other words, to truly understand the way meaning is made in many video games, we must not lose our sense of humor.

AFTERWORD: DECODING CULTURE

At this relatively early point in the evolution of the medium, would it be possible to play every video game ever set in Latin America? That is a question I posed to myself a few years ago, probably knowing somewhere within that I was opening up a much larger Pandora's box. Indeed, that question quickly led to others. Would it be possible to play every video game ever *made* in Latin America? Would it be possible to play every video game with a Latin American character, setting (such as a race track, fighting locale, or sports arena), or national/regional team or identity (in sports games and *Civilization*-type games)? To tell the truth, I am no longer interested in answering those questions. This is in part because I now realize that the deeper one goes down the rabbit hole of game design and development, the harder it is to believe in totalizing concepts like playing *every* game of a specific kind. While I used to think of video games in terms of the relatively small number of titles published for major home consoles and computer platforms on cartridge or disc, I have come to recognize a much more expansive world of games that not only includes downloadable software but also web games, mobile applications, art games, and software modifications. Likewise, I have moved on from those initial questions because of the fact that the journey they initiated has been so unpredictably and remarkably rewarding on so many levels.

At the same time as I began to perceive an ever-greater number of unturned stones and critical possibilities for future developments in cultural ludology, a variety of intersecting paths and passageways were leading me toward what would eventually become *Cultural Code*. One of these trajectories was my relationship with Latin American culture, which began when I arrived in Costa Rica as a sixteen-year-old ready to work on a summer public health project. That experience led to an enduring personal relationship and intellectual fascination with Latin America and its cultural production, inspiring me to pursue studies in the Spanish language and Latin American history and culture first at the undergraduate level, and eventually for my Ph.D. In the meantime, I had opportunities to live, work, study, or pursue research in countries including Mexico, Cuba, the Dominican Republic, Puerto Rico, Venezuela, Ecuador, Chile, Uruguay, and Argentina, diversifying and deepening my relationship with Latin American culture on a personal level while my academic interests advanced simultaneously. Looking back, I can see how certain episodes contributed to a path that has led to this book. I can remember specific times playing games with friends in arcades, cybercafés, and living rooms in locations across Latin America, without realizing that those games might become part of my academic interests as well. The first academic talk I ever presented at a major conference was on Ricardo Dominguez, whose work I also discuss in this book, though I didn't think of it as a game studies project at the time. And back in my first year of graduate school, as my academic trajectory was really just beginning to take shape, when one of my more experienced peers, Justin Crumbaugh, advised me that it was important to let my personal and academic interests bleed over into one another, I could not have imagined then just how meaningful that advice would be for me. Over the course of my graduate studies, my intellectual pursuits expanded from Latin American literature and poetry into the broader realm of cultural production including film, the visual arts, and new media, sowing the seeds that would eventually lead to my research on video games and Latin America.

In fact, the entire time I have been developing my personal and intellectual relationship with Latin American culture, there has been another relationship active in the background, a simultaneous but only occasionally intersecting trajectory: my development as a gamer and video game enthusiast. When I was not traveling throughout Latin America (and sometimes when I was), I was also obsessively playing games like *Driver 2*, *Goldeneye*, *Call of Duty*, and *Grand Theft Auto*, increasing my experiences inhabiting Latin America as a gamespace at the same time that I was getting to know and appreciate real places throughout the region. For a long time, I was interacting with Latin American culture on a ludic level as well as a personal level, but without stopping to think of video games in terms of their crossover with my real-life cultural experiences.

By the time I began teaching at the University of Delaware in 2010, I had begun to pursue research on subjects including cultural representation in film and new media. Shortly thereafter, my old friend and gaming buddy Matt Harrington wrote to tell me about a new game he had played, *Red Dead Redemption*, which he thought I might like because he knew I had lived in Mexico and that I had an enduring interest in Mexican culture. That provocative suggestion, along with the financial constraints faced in the first semester of my first long-term job out of grad school, led me to wonder whether I might be able to use some of my startup research funds to purchase not just books but other forms of cultural production ... like video games. When I checked with the administrators in my department, I was surprised and pleased to hear that one of my new colleagues, Japanese professor Rachael Hutchinson, did research on video games and had used research funds for their purchase. When I talked to Rachael, I discovered that she taught classes on Japanese language and culture including manga, anime, and video games, but that her research focused entirely on games. This was a revelation to me, and as I quickly purchased then played *RDR*, I was also beginning to devour the substantial body of high-quality game studies research in academic journals and research publications. This highly stimulating archive added wind to my sails. At the 2012 International Congress of the Latin American Studies Association in Toronto, I excitedly announced to my colleague and friend Nicolas Poppe that I was positioning myself as the "video games guy" within our shared field of contemporary Latin American cultural studies. He told me it was either the stupidest thing or the coolest thing that he had ever heard. It was around this time that I realized I really had a new book project on my hands.

As I began the research process for what would eventually become *Cultural Code* several years ago, I came to a final realization that would shape the trajectory of my research. I had begun thinking of my analysis in terms of the ways game developers in North America, Europe, and Asia depict Latin American culture in their games. But I quickly began to discover games from Latin American designers like Gonzalo Frasca and Daniel Benmergui, as well as the makers of commercial games such as *Lucha Libre AAA: Héroes del Ring*. Eventually, I dug deeper and became aware of the rich history of game design in the region, examining cases like TEG's software modification practices in 1990s Peru and Enrique and Ariel Arbiser's wonderful game *Truco*, first released on the Argentine market in 1982. These discoveries eventually led to the first half of this book, as I became familiar with not only the history of game design in the region, but also the growing and expanding trajectories that have led to the current boom in regional game development. As I have contacted and gradually come to know so many game designers and developers from throughout Latin America, I have become increasingly aware of both my debt and my responsibility to this community. It is my greatest hope that this book does justice to the incredibly diverse body of game production that has come out of Latin America and that continues to be produced throughout the region today.

With all that said, I am now asking myself a new set of questions. What does it mean to decode culture in video games? And how can we continue to decode games' relationship to daily life in human society? Today it is ever clearer that games impact cultural spheres including economics, politics, aesthetics, education, entertainment, and cultural production in other types of media. This is true the world over, but each cultural environment and microenvironment has its own ways of consuming, producing, politicizing, and otherwise putting games to use. Therefore I see a great need for innovative work on the intersections between games and culture, particularly from perspectives looking beyond the much-discussed mainstream game markets like Western Europe, the United States, and Japan. This is why I perceive an ever-increasing urgency to cultural ludology, to broaden and deepen our understanding of how video games can be useful for human culture, and how cultures are put to use in games in different contexts across the globe. For my part, there is much more that I would have liked to have done in *Cultural Code*, and there are surely elements within that will draw criticism from some readers—if so, I will be grateful that this work has found an audience and generated enough interest to provoke a response. As I look forward into a hopeful future for my own and others' research on the relationship between video games and Latin America in particular, and on cultural aspects of ludology more generally, I hope that the groundwork I have laid in *Cultural Code* at the very least provides the basis for discussions that will expand and grow in years to come. There is much work to be done; let us continue to decode culture together.

NOTES

Introduction

1. As a result of this dual focus on uses, there is an intentional duality in the book's use of the term "culture," which is further explained later in the introduction.

2. Frans Mäyrä, "Getting into the Game: Doing Multidisciplinary Game Studies," in *The Video Game Theory Reader 2*, ed. Bernard Perron and Mark J. P. Wolf (New York: Routledge, 2009), 319.

3. Larissa Hjorth and Dean Chan, "Locating the Game: Gaming Cultures in/and the Asia-Pacific," in *Gaming Cultures and Place in Asia-Pacific*, ed. Larissa Hjorth and Dean Chan (New York: Routledge, 2009), 2–5.

4. Gonzalo Frasca, "Simulation versus Narrative: Introduction to Ludology," in *The Video Game Theory Reader*, ed. Wolf and Perron, 222.

5. Steven E. Jones, *The Meaning of Video Games: Gaming and Textual Strategies* (New York: Routledge, 2008), 5.

6. Tara McPherson, "Self, Other and Electronic Media," in *The New Media Book*, ed. Dan Harries (London: British Film Institute, 2002), 183–194.

7. Gonzalo Frasca, "Ludologists Love Stories Too: Notes from a Debate that Never took Place," *Level Up*, Digital Games Research Association Conference Proceedings, accessed 30 June 2015, http://www.ludology.org/articles/Frasca_LevelUp2003.pdf, 1–2.

8. Johan Huizinga, *Homo Ludens: A Study of the Play Element in Culture* (Boston: Beacon Press, 1955 [1944]), 8.

9. Ibid., 10.

10. Roger Caillois, *Man, Play and Games*, trans. M. Barash (Urbana: University of Illinois Press, 2001 [1958]), 7.

11. Ibid., 6.

12. Edward Castronova, *Synthetic Worlds: The Business and Culture of Online Games* (Chicago: University of Chicago Press, 2005), 147–148.

13. Jones, *The Meaning of Video Games*, 69.

14. Celia Pearce, *Communities of Play: Emergent Cultures in Multiplayer Games and Virtual Worlds* (Cambridge, MA: MIT Press, 2009), 178.

15. For a discussion of the term "gamespace," see, among others, McKenzie Wark, *Gamer Theory* (Cambridge, MA: Harvard University Press, 2007), sect. 66. With regard to space in games, Wark concludes: "What topology yields is not a cyberspace but a gamespace. The idea of cyberspace is still too linked to images from the world of radio and television, of flow and 'seamless' movement, of access and excess, of lines running anywhere and everywhere. Topology is experienced more as a gamespace than a cyberspace: full of restrictions and hierarchies, firewalls and passwords. It is more like a bounded game than a free space of play. Once again: If it is free, it is valueless. Those odd lines within topology where anything goes are the ones of no consequence."

16. Markku Eskelinen, "The Gaming Situation," *Game Studies* 1, no. 1 (2001), accessed 9 July 2015, http://www.gamestudies.org/0101/eskelinen/.

17. Espen J. Aarseth, "Genre Trouble: Narrativism and the Art of Simulation," in *First Person: New Media as Story, Performance, and Game*, ed. Noah Wardrip-Fruin and Pat Harrigan (Cambridge, MA: MIT Press, 2004), 47.

18. Eric Zimmerman, "Jerked Around by the Magic Circle: Clearing the Air Ten Years Later," *Gamasutra*, 7 February 2012, accessed 10 July 2015, http://www.gamasutra.com/view/feature/135063/jerked_around_by_the_magic_circle_.php.

19. Frans Mäyrä, *An Introduction to Game Studies: Games in Culture* (London: Sage, 2008), 14.

20. Jesper Juul, *Half-Real: Video Games between Real Rules and Fictional Worlds* (Cambridge, MA: MIT Press, 2005), 6–7, 36. Juul offers the following definition: "A game is a rule-based system with a variable and quantifiable outcome, where different outcomes are assigned different values, the player exerts effort in order to influence the outcome, the player feels emotionally attached to the outcome, and the consequences of the activity are negotiable" (36).

21. Aarseth, "Genre Trouble," 47–48.

22. Alexander R. Galloway, *Gaming: Essays on Algorithmic Culture* (Minneapolis: University of Minnesota Press, 2006), 1.

23. Unless otherwise noted, all emphasis in textual citations is from the original text. Jane McGonigal, *Reality Is Broken: Why Games Make Us Better and How They Can Change the World* (New York: Penguin, 2011), 21.

24. Néstor García Canclini, *Consumers and Citizens*, trans. G. Yúdice (Minneapolis: University of Minnesota Press, 2001 [1995]), 15.

25. Unless otherwise noted, all translations from Spanish and Portuguese to English in this book are my own. Néstor García Canclini, *Cultura y comunicación: Entre lo global y lo local* (La Plata, Argentina: Periodismo y Comunicación, 1997), 37.

26. George Yúdice, "New Social and Business Models in Latin American Musics," in *Consumer Culture in Latin America*, ed. John Sinclair and Anna Cristina Pertierra (New York: Palgrave Macmillan, 2012), 17.

27. Theodor W. Adorno, "Culture Industry Reconsidered," in *The Culture Industry: Selected Essays on Mass Culture* (New York: Routledge, 1991 [1963]), 103.

28. Walter Benjamin, *Illuminations*, trans. H. Zohn (New York: Schocken Books, 2007 [1955]), 221.

29. Fredric Jameson, *The Cultural Turn: Selected Writings on the Postmodern, 1983-1998* (London: Verso, 1998), 144.

30. Fredric Jameson, *The Geopolitical Aesthetic: Cinema and Space in the World System* (Bloomington: Indiana University Press, 1992), 212–213.

31. Anthony Giddens, *The Consequences of Modernity* (Stanford: Stanford University Press, 1990), 22.

32. Pierre Lévy, *Becoming Virtual: Reality in the Digital Age* (New York: Plenum, 1998), 162.

33. Arjun Appadurai, *Modernity at Large: Cultural Dimensions of Globalization* (New York: Routledge, 1996), 48.

34. Manuel Castells, *The Rise of the Network Society* (Cambridge, MA: Blackwell, 1996), 375.

35. Lev Manovich, *The Language of New Media* (Cambridge, MA: MIT Press, 2001), 46.

36. Mäyrä, *Introduction to Game Studies*, 13–14.

37. James Paul Gee, *What Video Games Have to Teach Us About Learning and Literacy*, 2nd ed. (New York: Palgrave Macmillan, 2007), 17.

38. Mäyrä, *Introduction to Game Studies*, 21.

39. *Popol Vuh*, English version by Delia Goetz and Sylvanus G. Morley, from the Spanish translation by Adrián Recinos (Norman: University of Oklahoma Press, 1950 [1701]), 79–84.

40. Jesper Juul, *A Casual Revolution: Reinventing Video Games and Their Players* (Cambridge, MA: MIT Press, 2010), 5.

41. "Jóvenes guatemaltecos lanzan videojuego," *Ministerio de Cultura y Deportes del Gobierno de Guatemala*, 29 May 2013, accessed 30 June 2015, http://mcd.gob.gt/jovenes-guatemaltecos -lanzan-videojuego/.

42. "Guatemaltecos lanzarán videojuego sobre juego de pelota maya," Taringa.net, 17 January 2012, accessed 30 June 2015, http://www.taringa.net/comunidades/chapines/4541679/ Guatemaltecos-lanzaran-videojuego-sobre-juego-de-pelota-may.html.

43. Bernardino de Sahagún, *General History of the Things of New Spain*, trans. A. Anderson and C. Dibble, part 9, book 8, chapter 10 (Santa Fe, NM: School of American Research, 1954 [1577]), 29–30.

44. Francisco López de Gómara, *La conquista de México* (2012 [1552]), Red Ediciones, accessed 30 June 2015, https://books.google.com/books?id=XSW-AoMiueIC&pg=PA148&lpg=PA148&dq=, 148.

45. Sahagún, *General History*, 29.

46. Felipe Guaman Poma de Ayala, *First New Chronicle and Good Government* (1615), accessed 30 June 2015, http://www.kb.dk/permalink/2006/poma/390/en/text/, 390.

47. Ibid., 243.

48. Ibid., 780.

49. Jorge Luis Borges, *Ficciones* (Buenos Aires: Emecé, 1996 [1944]).

50. Janet H. Murray, *Hamlet on the Holodeck: The Future of Narrative in Cyberspace* (Cambridge, MA: MIT Press, 1998), 30.

51. Janet H. Murray, "Inventing the Medium," in *The New Media Reader*, ed. Noah Wardrip-Fruin and Nick Monfort (Cambridge, MA: MIT Press, 2003), 3.

52. Manovich, *The Language of New Media*, 225.

53. Espen J. Aarseth, *Cybertext: Perspectives on Ergodic Literature* (Baltimore: Johns Hopkins University Press, 1997), 8.

54. Gordon Calleja, *In-Game: From Immersion to Incorporation* (Cambridge, MA: MIT Press, 2011).

55. Nick Montfort, "Introduction: The Garden of Forking Paths," in *The New Media Reader*, ed. Wardrip-Fruin and Monfort, 29.

56. Julio Cortázar, *Hopscotch*, trans. G. Rabassa (New York: Pantheon, 1966 [1963]).

57. Montfort, "Introduction," 29.

58. Nick Montfort, *Twisty Little Passages* (Cambridge, MA: MIT Press, 2003), 71.

59. David Alfaro Siqueiros, Antonio Berni, Lino Eneas Spilimbergo, Juan C. Castagnino, and Enrique Lázaro, "Ejercicio plástico" (1933), in Mari Carmen Ramírez and Héctor Olea, *Heterotopías: Medio siglo sin lugar, 1918/1968* (Madrid: Museo Nacional Centro de Arte Reina Sofía, 2000), 477.

60. Augusto Boal, *Theater of the Oppressed* (London: Pluto, 2000 [1979]), xx–xxi.

61. Jay David Bolter, "Digital Media and the Future of Filmic Narrative," in *The Oxford Handbook of Film and Media Studies*, ed. Robert Kolker (New York: Oxford University Press, 2008), 25.

62. Juul, *Half-Real*, 72–73.

63. Ibid., 73.

64. Jay David Bolter and Richard Grusin, *Remediation* (Cambridge, MA: MIT Press, 1999), 15.

65. "Cámara de Comercio de Bogotá presenta exposición con videojuegos representativos de Colombia," *Universia.net.co*, 9 July 2014, accessed 30 June 2015, http://noticias.universia. net.co/en-portada/noticia/2014/07/09/1100286/camara-comercio-bogota-presenta -exposicion-videojuegos-representativos-colombia.html; "Una muestra para conocer toda la historia de los videojuegos," *La Nación* (Buenos Aires, Argentina), 7 January 2014, accessed 6 July 2015, http://www.lanacion.com.ar/1653368-una-muestra-para-conocer-toda-la-historia -de-los-videojuegos.

66. Fernando Chaves Espinach, "Orquesta Sinfónica Nacional deleitó con música de video-juegos," *La Nación* (San José, Costa Rica), 26 September 2013, accessed 17 July 2014, http:// www.nacion.com/ocio/musica/Orquesta_Sinfonica_Nacional-videojuegos-Emanuel_Olivieri _0_1368463337.html.

67. Tom Boellstorff, "A Ludicrous Discipline? Ethnography and Game Studies," *Games and Culture* 1, no. 1 (2006): 31–32.

68. McPherson, "Self, Other and Electronic Media," 192.

69. David Golumbia, "Computers and Cultural Studies," in *The Oxford Handbook of Film and Media Studies*, ed. Kolker, 509.

70. Larissa Hjorth, *Games and Gaming: An Introduction to New Media* (New York: Berg, 2011), 6.

71. Mäyrä, *Introduction to Game Studies*, 24.

72. Stuart Hall, "Cultural Identity and Cinematic Representation," in *Film and Theory: An Anthology*, ed. Robert Stam and Toby Miller (Oxford: Blackwell, 2000), 714.

73. See, for example, Tom Boellstorf, Bonnie Nardi, Celia Pearce, and T. L. Taylor, eds., *Ethnography and Virtual Worlds: A Handbook of Method* (Princeton: Princeton University Press, 2012).

74. See, for example, Henry Jenkins, *Fans, Bloggers, and Gamers: Exploring Participatory Culture* (New York: New York University Press, 2006); and Pearce, *Communities of Play*.

75. See, for example, Jesús Martín-Barbero, *Communication, Culture and Hegemony: From the Media to Mediations*, trans. E. Fox and R. A. White (London: Sage, 1993 [1987]); García Canclini, *Consumers and Citizens*; Beatriz Sarlo, *Scenes from Postmodern Life*, trans. J. Beasley-Murray (Minneapolis: University of Minnesota Press, 2001 [1994]); George Yúdice, *The Expediency of Culture: Uses of Culture in the Global Era* (Durham: Duke University Press, 2003); Rubén Gallo, *Mexican Modernity: The Avant-Garde and the Technological Revolution* (Cambridge, MA: MIT Press, 2005).

76. See, for example, Beth E. Kolko, Lisa Nakamura, and Gilbert B. Rodman, eds., *Race in Cyberspace* (New York: Routledge, 2000); Lisa Nakamura, *Cybertypes: Race, Ethnicity, and Identity on the Internet* (New York: Routledge, 2002); Christopher McGahan, *Racing Cyberculture: Minoritarian Art and Cultural Politics on the Internet* (New York: Routledge, 2008).

77. Anthony Sze-Fai Shiu, "What Yellowface Hides: Video Games, Whiteness, and the American Racial Order," *Journal of Popular Culture* 39, no. 1 (2006): 109.

78. Nakamura, *Cybertypes*, 40.

79. Ibid., 3.

80. Ibid., 99.

81. McGahan, *Racing Cyberculture*, 83–84.

82. Dean Chan, "Playing with Race: The Ethics of Racialized Representations in E-Games," *International Review of Information Ethics* 4 (2005): 25.

83. Vit Sisler, "Digital Arabs: Representation in Video Games," *European Journal of Cultural Studies* 11, no. 2 (2008): 205.

84. Manovich, *The Language of New Media*, 333.

85. Jon Dovey and Helen W. Kennedy, *Game Cultures: Computer Games as New Media* (Maidenhead, UK: Open University Press, 2006), 147.

86. Yuri Takhteyev, *Coding Places: Software Practice in a South American City* (Cambridge, MA: MIT Press, 2012), 2.

87. McGahan, *Racing Cyberculture*, 76.

88. Sarlo, *Scenes from Postmodern Life*, 40.

89. Ibid., 43.

90. Beatriz Sarlo, *La ciudad vista: Mercancías y cultura urbana* (Buenos Aires: Siglo Veintiuno, 2009), 90.

91. García Canclini, *Consumers and Citizens*, 95–96.

92. Néstor García Canclini, *Hybrid Cultures: Strategies for Entering and Leaving Modernity*, trans. R. Rosaldo (Minneapolis: University of Minnesota Press, 1995 [1990]), 65.

93. Martín Hopenhayn, "Globalization and Culture: Five Approaches to a Single Text," in *Cultural Politics in Latin America*, ed. Anny Brooksbank Jones and Ronaldo Munck (New York: St. Martin's Press, 2000), 154.

94. Jesús Martín-Barbero, "Pensar nuestra globalizada modernidad. Desencantos de la sociedad y reencantamientos de la identidad," *Iberoamericana* 8, no. 30 (2008): 149.

95. Gareth Williams, *The Other Side of the Popular: Neoliberalism and Subalternity in Latin America* (Durham: Duke University Press, 2002), 131.

96. Shirin Shenassa, "The Lack of Materiality in Latin American Media Theory," in *Latin American Literature and Mass Media*, ed. Edmundo Paz-Soldán and Debra A. Castillo (New York: Garland, 2001), 265.

97. Diana Taylor, *The Archive and the Repertoire: Performing Cultural Memory in the Americas* (Durham: Duke University Press, 2003), 277.

98. Heidi Tinsman and Sandhya Shukla, eds., *Imagining Our Americas: Toward a Transnational Frame* (Durham: Duke University Press, 2007).

99. José David Saldívar, *Trans-Americanity: Subaltern Modernities, Global Coloniality, and the Cultures of Greater Mexico* (Durham: Duke University Press, 2012).

100. Néstor García Canclini, *Latinoamericanos buscando lugar en este siglo* (Buenos Aires: Paidós, 2002), 61.

101. Ibid., 69.

102. John Beverley, *Latinamericanism after 9/11* (Durham: Duke University Press, 2011), 71.

Chapter 1

1. Johan Huizinga, *Homo Ludens: A Study of the Play Element in Culture* (Boston: Beacon Press, 1955 [1944]), 173.

2. Ibid., 25.

3. Roger Caillois, *Man, Play and Games*, trans. M. Barash (Urbana: University of Illinois Press, 2001 [1958]), 59.

4. Roland Barthes, *Image, Music, Text*, trans. S. Heath (New York: Hill and Wang, 1977), 162.

5. Miguel Sicart, "Against Procedurality," *Game Studies* 11, no. 3 (2011).

6. Janet H. Murray, *Hamlet on the Holodeck: The Future of Narrative in Cyberspace* (Cambridge, MA: MIT Press, 1998), 153.

7. Néstor Garcia Canclini, *Lectores, espectadores e internautas* (Barcelona: Gedisa, 2007), 32.

8. Lev Manovich, *The Language of New Media* (Cambridge, MA: MIT Press, 2001), 210.

9. Alexander R. Galloway, *Gaming: Essays on Algorithmic Culture* (Minneapolis: University of Minnesota Press, 2006), 2.

10. Gordon Calleja, *In-Game: From Immersion to Incorporation* (Cambridge, MA: MIT Press, 2011), 55.

11. Martti Lahti, "As We Become Machines: Corporealized Pleasures in Video Games," in *The Video Game Theory Reader*, ed. Mark J. P. Wolf and Bernard Perron (New York: Routledge, 2003), 158.

12. Ibid., 166.

13. Galloway, *Gaming*, 4.

14. Ibid.

15. J. L. Austin, "How to Do Things with Words (Lecture II)," in *The Performance Studies Reader*, 2nd ed., ed. Henry Bial (New York: Routledge, 2007), 177.

16. J. R. Searle, "What Is a Speech Act?," in *The Philosophy of Language*, ed. J. R. Searle (Oxford: Oxford University Press, 1971), 39.

17. Judith Butler, "Performative Acts and Gender Constitution: An Essay in Phenomenology and Feminist Theory," in *The Performance Studies Reader*, ed. Bial, 197.

18. Ibid., 188.

19. Mia Consalvo, *Cheating: Gaining Advantage in Video Games* (Cambridge, MA: MIT Press, 2007), 95.

20. James Paul Gee, *What Video Games Have to Teach Us about Learning and Literacy* (New York: Palgrave Macmillan, 2007), 83.

21. Richard Schechner, *Performance Studies: An Introduction*, 3rd ed. (New York: Routledge, 2013), 89.

22. Diana Taylor, "Translating Performance," in *The Performance Studies Reader*, ed. Bial, 382.

23. Murray, *Hamlet on the Holodeck,* 143.

24. Jane McGonigal, *Reality Is Broken: Why Games Make Us Better and How They Can Change the World* (New York: Penguin, 2011), 4.

25. Schechner, *Performance Studies*, 290.

26. Calleja, *In-Game*, 1.

27. Ibid., 73.

28. Simon Egenfeldt-Nielsen, Jonas Heide Smith, and Susana Pajares Tosca, eds., *Understanding Video Games: The Essential Introduction*, 2nd ed. (New York: Routledge, 2013), 140.

29. Ibid., 74.

30. Geoff King and Tanya Krzywinska, *Tomb Raiders and Space Invaders: Videogame Forms and Contexts* (New York: I. B. Tauris, 2006), 76.

31. Alison Gazzard, "Unlocking the Gameworld: The Rewards of Space and Time in Videogames," *Game Studies* 11, no. 1 (2011), accessed 20 May 2013, http://gamestudies.org/1101/articles/gazzard_alison.

32. Gee, *What Video Games Have to Teach Us about Learning and Literacy*, 142.

33. Ibid., 223.

34. Calleja, *In-Game*, 181. For further discussion of cognitive mapping in video games, see chapter 5.

35. Mark Prensky, "Computer Games and Learning: Digital Game-Based Learning," in *Handbook of Computer Game Studies*, ed. Joost Raessens and Jeffrey Goldstein (Cambridge, MA: MIT Press, 2005), 107.

36. Ibid.

37. Simon Romero, "Pastoral Uruguay Yields a Crop of Digital Yetis and Adventures," *New York Times*, 21 February 2013, accessed 6 July 2015, http://www.nytimes.com/2013/02/22/world/americas/uruguays-video-game-start-ups-garner-attention.html?_r=0.

38. Brandon Sheffield, "Q&A: Frederico [*sic*] Beyer on Targeting Latino Market with Slang, *Lucha Libre*," *GamaSutra*, 9 June 2010, accessed 6 July 2015, http://www.gamasutra.com/view/news/119723/QA_Frederico_Beyer_On_Targeting_Latino_Market_With_Slang_Lucha_Libre.php.

39. Ibid.

40. Ibid.

41. See chapters 3 and 4 for discussions of *Papo & Yo* as an example of independent Latin American game design abroad and the use of the favela as a gamespace, respectively.

42. Mark Griffiths, "The Therapeutic Value of Video Games," in *Handbook of Computer Game Studies*, ed. Raessens and Goldstein, 165.

43. Ibid., 167–168.

44. Larissa Hjorth, *Games and Gaming: An Introduction to New Media* (New York: Berg, 2011), 103.

45. Héctor Óscar González Seguí, "Veinticinco años de videojuegos en México. Las mercancías tecnoculturales y la globalización económica," *Comunicación y Sociedad* 38 (2000): 105–106. See also Daniel Madrid and Jonathan Valenzuela, *Chile Game*, YouTube video, 00:02:51. Posted 2 March 2013, https://www.youtube.com/watch?v=vKESbojym5k.

46. González Seguí, "Veinticinco años," 105–106.

47. "A história dos video games no Brasil–ACIGAMES," YouTube video, 00:02:06. Posted by "Canal de ACIGAMES," 20 October 2012, accessed 6 July 2015, https://www.youtube.com/watch?v=OkHB8zVLhdk.

48. Eduardo Marisca, "Buscando un *gamer*: Reconstruyendo la historia del videojuego peruano," *Pozo de letras* 11, no. 11 (2013): 20–21.

49. Ibid.

50. "A história dos video games no Brasil–ACIGAMES."

51. Gonzalo Frasca, "Latin America," in *Encyclopedia of Video Games: The Culture, Technology, and Art of Gaming*, ed. Mark J. P. Wolf (Santa Barbara, CA: Greenwood, 2012), 355–356.

52. Ibid.

53. Madrid and Valenzuela, *Chile Game*, 00:03:04.

54. Ibid.

55. Ibid., 00:05:01; piracy is further discussed later in this chapter.

56. Néstor García Canclini, *Consumers and Citizens*, trans. G. Yúdice (Minneapolis: University of Minnesota Press, 2001 [1995]), 100.

57. Jesús Martín-Barbero, *Communication, Culture and Hegemony: From the Media to Mediations*, trans. E. Fox and R. A. White (London: Sage, 1993 [1987]), 183.

58. Madrid and Valenzuela, *Chile Game*, 00:12:27.

59. González Seguí, "Veinticinco años," 117.

60. Ibid.

61. Ibid., 123.

62. Ibid.

63. Ibid.

64. Jacob Mazel, "An Introduction to the Video Game Market in Mexico," *VGChartz*, 9 March 2011, accessed 6 July 2015, http://www.vgchartz.com/article/84570/an-introduction-to-the-video-game-market-in-mexico/.

65. Luis Wong, "Feeling Blue," *Killscreendaily.com*, 5 August 2011, accessed 6 July 2015, http:// killscreendaily.com/articles/feeling-blue/.

66. Mark Stanley, "Gamers Brasileiros, Nós Ouvimos Vocês," *PlayStation Blog*, 21 October 2013, accessed 6 July 2015, http://blog.br.playstation.com/2013/10/21/gamers-brasileiros-nos -ouvimos-voces/.

67. Frasca, "Latin America," 356. Game production in Latin America, rather than consumption, is discussed in chapter 3.

68. Madrid and Valenzuela, *Chile Game*, 00:04:37.

69. "Los *gamers*, cosa de adultos," *El Tiempo* (Bogotá, Colombia), 4 August 2010, accessed 6 July 2015, http://www.eltiempo.com/archivo/documento/MAM-4082286.

70. Wong, "Feeling Blue."

71. Ibid.

72. Ibid.

73. Robert Levitan, "What You Might Not Know about the Latin American Games Industry," *Gamasutra*, 18 October 2011, accessed 6 July 2015, http://www.gamasutra.com/blogs/ RobertLevitan/20111018/90160/What_You_Might_Not_Know_About_the_Latin_American _Games_Industry.php.

74. Ibid.

75. Viviana Celso, "El lenguaje de los videojuegos: Sus pliegues y recortes en las prácticas sociales," *Novedades Educativas* 185 (2006): 75.

76. Ibid.

77. Eduardo Marisca, "Developing Game Worlds: Gaming, Technology and Innovation in Peru," master's thesis, Massachusetts Institute of Technology, Cambridge, MA, June 2014, 62–63, accessed 16 July 2014, http://marisca.pe/files/EM-DGW-Final.pdf.

78. Ibid., 64.

79. Guillermo Gómez-Peña, "Culturas-in-Extremis: Performing Against the Cultural Backdrop of the Mainstream Bizarre," in *The Performance Studies Reader*, ed. Bial, 348.

80. Miguel Sicart, *The Ethics of Computer Games* (Cambridge, MA: MIT Press, 2009), 62.

81. Jacob Mazel, "PES 2010 Sold 600,000 Copies in Growing Latin American SW Market," *VGChartz*, 15 July 2010, accessed 6 July 2015, http://www.vgchartz.com/article/80883/pes-2010 -sold-600000-copies-in-growing-latin-america-sw-market/.

82. King and Krzywinska, *Tomb Raiders and Space Invaders*, 172.

83. Néstor García Canclini, *Diferentes, desiguales y desconectados. Mapas de la interculturalidad* (Barcelona: Gedisa, 2004), 161.

84. Ibid.

85. Javier Jerjes Loayza, "Los videojuegos on-line en Latinoamérica: impacto en las redes sociales y de consumo," *Icono 14* 8, no. 11 (2009): 170.

86. Ibid., 173.

87. Global Collect, "The Changing Payment Landscape in LATAM: Payments, Intelligence and Trends," August 2014, accessed 6 July 2015, http://www.globalcollect.com/ changing-payment-landscape-in-latin-america.

88. Ibid.

89. New Zoo, "Infographic: The Brazilian Games Market," 10 December 2013, accessed 6 July 2015, http://www.newzoo.com/infographics/infographic-the-brazilian-games-market/.

90. Ibid.

91. Arturo Peña, "El mercado de los videojuegos está mirando hacia América Latina," *La Nación* (Buenos Aires, Argentina), 11 July 2012, accessed 16 July 2014, http://www.lanacion .com.py/articulo/80406-el-mercado-de-los-videojuegos-esta-mirando-hacia-america-latina .html.

92. "Los *gamers*, cosa de adultos."

93. Ibid.

94. New Zoo, "Infographic: The Brazilian Games Market."

95. Helena Lozano Galarza, "La industria de los videojuegos en América Latina," *Newsweek en Español*, 4 October 2012, accessed 25 April 2013, http://www.newsweek.mx/index.php/ articulo/615#.UXlibit34t0. See also Peña, "El mercado de los videojuegos."

96. Global Collect, "The Changing Payment Landscape in LATAM."

97. Entertainment Software Association, "Essential Facts about the Computer and Video Game Industry," 2014, accessed 6 July 2015, http://www.theesa.com/wp-content/uploads/2014/10/ESA_EF_2014.pdf,10.

98. Francisco Rubio, "'Gamers' latinos impulsan a Konami," *CNN Expansión*, 27 August 2012, accessed 10 April 2013, http://www.cnnexpansion.com/negocios/2012/08/27/konami-se-la-juega-con-mercado-de-la.

99. Ibid.

100. "Fútbol y 'Call of Duty' dominaron videojuegos en Paraguay," *ABC* (Asunción, Paraguay), 4 January 2013, accessed 17 July 2014, http://www.abc.com.py/ciencia/futbol-y-call-of-duty-dominaron-videojuegos-en-paraguay-524197.html.

101. New Zoo, "Infographic: The Brazilian Games Market."

102. New Zoo, "Global Games Market Report Infographics," 15 July 2013, accessed 6 July 2015, http://www.newzoo.com/infographics/global-games-market-report-infographics/.

103. New Zoo, "Infographic: The Global Mobile Landscape Reloaded," 22 July 2014, accessed 6 July 2015, http://www.newzoo.com/infographics/infographic-global-mobile-landscape-reloaded/.

104. Ibid.

105. Alison Cathles, Gustavo Crespi, and Matteo Grazzi, "The Region's Place in the Digital World: A Tale of Three Divides," in *Development Connections: Unveiling the Impact of New Information Technologies*, ed. Alberto Chong (New York: Palgrave Macmillan, 2011), 31.

106. Judith Mariscal, Carla Bonina, and Julio Luna, "New Market Scenarios in Latin America," in *Digital Poverty: Latin American and Caribbean Perspectives*, ed. Hernan Galperin and Judith Mariscal (Ottawa: International Development Research Center, 2007), 76.

107. Ibid., 62.

108. Cathles, Crespi, and Grazzi, "The Region's Place," 48.

109. Inter-American Development Bank, "Bridging Gaps, Building Opportunity: Broadband as a Catalyst of Economic Growth and Social Progress in Latin America and the Caribbean," March 2012, accessed 6 July 2015, http://publications.iadb.org/bitstream/handle/11319/5475/Bridging%20Gaps%2c%20Building%20Opportunity%3a%20Broadband%20as%20a%20catalyst%20of%20Economic%20Growth%20and%20Social%20Progress%20in%20Latin%20America%20and%20the%20Caribbean%20-%20RG-T2051.pdf?sequence=1, 16 (emphasis added).

110. Samuel Berlinski, Matías Busso, Julian Cristiá, and Eugenio Severín, "Computers in Schools: Why Governments Should Do Their Homework," in *Development Connections*, ed. Chong, 183.

111. Antonio García Zaballos and Rubén López-Rivas, "Socioeconomic Impact of Broadband in Latin American and Caribbean Countries," Inter-American Development Bank, 2012, accessed 25 April 2013, http://publications.iadb.org/bitstream/handle/11319/5754/Socioeconomic%20Impact%20of%20Broadband%20in%20Latin%20America%20and%20Caribbean%20Countries.pdf?sequence=1, 15.

112. International Telecommunication Union, "Internet Users (per 100 People)," *WorldBank.org*, accessed 6 July 2015, http://databank.worldbank.org/data//reports.aspx?source=2&country=BRA&series=&period=.

113. Kelly Samara Silva et al., "Changes in Television Viewing and Computers/Videogames Use Among High School Students in Southern Brazil between 2001 and 2011," *International Journal of Public Health* 59, no. 1 (2014): 79–85.

114. Ibid.

115. Manuel Castells, *Communication Power* (Oxford: Oxford University Press, 2009), 63.

116. Lozano Galarza, "La industria."

117. Kirk Hamilton, "Global Gaming Grows in Leaps and Bounds, Especially in Developing Nations," *Kotaku*, 15 December 2011, accessed 6 July 2015, http://kotaku.com/5868509/global-gaming-grows-by-leaps-and-bounds-especially-in-developing-nations.

118. Superdata, "Brazil Online Games Market: Introduction," 2011, accessed 27 May 2013, http://www.superdataresearch.com/wp-content/uploads/2011/01/LatinAmericaMapPic.jpg.

119. Global Collect, "The Changing Payment Landscape in LATAM."

120. Ibid.

121. Ibid.

122. New Zoo, "Global Monetization of Games: Emerging Markets as Drivers of Growth," 15 May 2013, accessed 6 July 2015, http://www.newzoo.com/keynotes/global-monetization-of-games-emerging-markets-as-drivers-of-growth/, 24.

123. New Zoo, "Global Games Market Report Infographics," 15 July 2013, accessed 6 July 2015, http://www.newzoo.com/infographics/global-games-market-report-infographics/.

124. New Zoo, "Towards the Global Games Market in 2017: Casual Games Sector Report," June 2014, accessed 6 July 2015, http://www.newzoo.com/trend-reports/free-casual-games -association-sector-report-towards-global-games-market-2017/.

125. Castells, *Communication Power*, 414.

126. McGonigal, *Reality Is Broken*, 226.

127. *Brasil Game Show 2014*, mobile application, 16 September 2014, accessed 6 July 2015, https:// play.google.com/store/apps/details?id=me.doubledutch.brasilgameshow&hl=en.

128. Róger Almanza G., "Juegos que controlan," *La Prensa* (Managua, Nicaragua), 16 September 2012, accessed 17 July 2014, http://www.laprensa.com.ni/busqueda.php?cx=00597725947541 8635108%3Arwlxrw1v5gm&ie=UTF-8&cof=FORID%3A10&q=juegos+que+controlan&sa.x=0&sa .y=0&sa=Buscar.

129. Alex Wawro, "Major League Gaming Goes International with MLG Brasil," *Gamasutra*, 14 February 2014, accessed 16 July 2014, http://gamasutra.com/view/news/210869/Major _League_Gaming_goes_international_with_MLG_Brasil.php.

130. "Bolivia va al mundial de videojuegos," *El Sol de Santa Cruz* (Santa Cruz, Bolivia), 3 October 2011, accessed 17 July 2014, http://elsol.com.bo/index.php?c=tecnolog%EDa&articulo =Bolivia-va-al-mundial-de-videojuegos&cat=182&pla=3&id_articulo=21515.

131. "Gamers panameños están participando en el EVO 2014," *Freax-tv.com*, 11 July 2014, accessed 17 July 2014, http://www.freax-tv.com/gamers-panamenos-estan-participando-en -el-evo-2014/.

132. "Opinión: Boricuas rumbo al torneo de videojuegos más importante del mundo," *Metro* (San Juan, Puerto Rico), 30 June 2014, accessed 17 July 2014, http://www.metro.pr/ blogs/opinion-boricuas-rumbo-al-torneo-de-videojuegos-mas-importante-del-ano/pGXnfD !ItzfD9HmbkJgM/.

133. Huizinga, *Homo Ludens*, 173.

Chapter 2

1. Jesper Juul, *A Casual Revolution: Reinventing Video Games and Their Players* (Cambridge, MA: MIT Press, 2010), 151.

2. Jay David Bolter and Richard Grusin, *Remediation* (Cambridge, MA: MIT Press, 1999), 99–100.

3. Christopher A. Paul, *Wordplay and the Discourse of Video Games: Analyzing Words, Design, and Play* (New York: Routledge, 2012), 98–99.

4. Theodor W. Adorno, "Culture Industry Reconsidered," in *The Culture Industry: Selected Essays on Mass Culture* (New York: Routledge, 1991 [1963]), 85.

5. Alexander R. Galloway, *Gaming: Essays on Algorithmic Culture* (Minneapolis: University of Minnesota Press, 2006), 71.

6. Judd Ethan Ruggill and Ken S. McAllister, *Gaming Matters: Art, Science, Magic, and the Computer Game Medium* (Tuscaloosa: University of Alabama Press, 2011), 63.

7. Matthew Thomas Payne, "Marketing Military Realism in Call of Duty 4: Modern Warfare," *Games and Culture* 7, no. 4 (2012): 310.

8. Daniel Borunda, "Juárez Mayor Calls New Video Game 'Despicable,'" *El Paso Times* (El Paso, Texas), 9 March 2007, accessed 27 May 2013, http://www.elpasotimes.com/news/ci_5390403.

9. "Game Set on Mexican Border Draws Ire," *New York Times*, 20 February 2011, accessed 6 July 2011, http://www.nytimes.com/2011/02/21/world/americas/21mexico.html?_r=0.

10. Claire F. Fox, *The Fence and the River: Culture and Politics at the U.S.-Mexico Border* (Minneapolis: University of Minnesota Press, 1999), 92.

11. Fernando Romero/Lar, *Hyperborder: The Contemporary U.S.-Mexico Border and Its Future* (New York: Princeton Architectural Press, 2008), 143.

12. Ibid., 76.

13. Ubisoft, *Call of Juarez: The Cartel—Launch Trailer*, YouTube video, 00:01:27, posted 19 June 2011, accessed 10 July 2015, https://www.youtube.com/watch?v=YdHVBhc0RB0.

14. "Game Set on Mexican Border."

15. Constantine Von Hoffman, "Why We Need a Sensationalized Bloody Video Game about the Mexican Drug War," CBS News, 16 June 2011, accessed 6 July 2011, http://www.cbsnews.com/news/why-we-need-a-sensationalized-bloody-video-game-about-the-mexican-drug-war/.

16. Unless otherwise noted, estimates of specific games' sales numbers are cited from the website VGChartz, accessed 7 July 2015, http://www.vgchartz.com/.

17. "Juego sobre invasión a Venezuela repercute en política," Terra (Uruguay), 25 May 2006, accessed 7 July 2011, http://www.uy.terra.com/copa2006/interna/0,,OI1020760-EI4134,00.html.

18. Hugo Chávez,"Aló, Presidente No. 348," Transcripciones del Aló Presidente, 17 January 2008, accessed 7 July 2011, http://www.alopresidente.gob.ve/materia_alo/25/8507/?desc=348_alopresidentefilas_de_ma.pdf.

19. See for example, coverage by the Honduran newspaper El Heraldo, which inaccurately reports: "The controversy arises when the player must kill Hugo Chávez, the leader of that nation absorbed in violence, according to Pandemic Studios, creator of the game." "PlayStation es un 'veneno': Hugo Chávez," El Heraldo (Tegucigalpa, Honduras), 18 January 2010, accessed 7 July 2011, http://blogs.elheraldo.hn/bloqueinteractivo/2010/01/18/playstation-es-un-veneno-hugo-chavez/.

20. Christopher Toothaker, "Venezuela to Outlaw Violent Video Games, Toys," NBC News, 4 October 2009, accessed 6 July 2011, http://www.nbcnews.com/id/33165079/ns/technology_and_science-games/t/venezuela-outlaw-violent-video-games-toys/.

21. Asamblea Nacional de la República Bolivariana de Venezuela, "Ley para la prohibición de videojuegos bélicos y juguetes bélicos," 3 December 2009, accessed 6 July 2011, http://www.asambleanacional.gov.ve/uploads/leyes/2009-10-29/doc_2ee23380d32975c898c352c12106fd34548142ba.pdf.

22. Secretaría General de la Asamblea Nacional de Panamá, "Ley que prohíbe los videojuegos bélicos o de violencia y los juegos bélicos y se dictan otras disposiciones," 12 January 2011, accessed 17 July 2014, http://www.asamblea.gob.pa/actualidad/anteproyectos/2010_2111/2011_A_111.pdf; see also Luis Miranda, "Ahora Panamá busca regular la venta de videojuegos," Niubie.com, 28 January 2011, accessed 7 July 2015, https://www.niubie.com/2011/01/ahora-panama-busca-regular-la-venta-de-videojuegos/.

23. "Ley Número 20.756 REGULA LA VENTA Y ARRIENDO DE VIDEOJUEGOS EXCESIVAMENTE VIOLENTOS A MENORES DE 18 AÑOS Y EXIGE CONTROL PARENTAL A CONSOLAS," May 2014, accessed 17 July 2014, http://www.leychile.cl/Navegar?idNorma=1063104.

24. Alejandra Di Brino, "La cosa de los videojuegos venezolanos," Tendencia.com, 23 April 2014, accessed 17 July 2014, http://www.tendencia.com/2014/la-cosa-de-los-videojuegos-venezolanos/.

25. Gregory David Escobar, "Mercenaries 2: El polémico juego incomprendido que nadie jugó," Aporrea.org, 7 November 2011, accessed 22 November 2011, http://www.aporrea.org/actualidad/a133087.html.

26. Ibid.

27. Ibid.

28. J. Javier Martín, "El gobierno venezolano critica abiertamente a Mercenaries 2," Meri-Station, 26 May 2006, accessed 22 November 2011, http://www.meristation.com/xbox-360/noticias/el-gobierno-venezolano-critica-abiertamente-a-mercenaries-2/1520819/1638642.

29. "Venezuelan Anger at Computer Game," BBC News.com, 25 May 2006, accessed 6 July 2011, http://news.bbc.co.uk/2/hi/business/5016514.stm.

30. In video games, the concept of "skinning" refers to changing the aesthetic or presentational image of a game, while maintaining its essential underlying code and functions intact. See Nick Montfort and Ian Bogost, *Racing the Beam: The Atari Video Computer System* (Cambridge, MA: MIT Press, 2009), 104–105. Skinning is further discussed in chapter 5.

31. Robert Kahn, "Manuel Noriega Sues Video Game Maker for Using Him in a Game," Courthouse News Service, 15 July 2014, accessed 16 July 2014, http://www.courthousenews.com/2014/07/15/69523.htm.

32. For further discussion of the portrayal of Cuban culture in *Ghost Recon: Island Thunder*, see Rafael Miguel Montes, "*Ghost Recon: Island Thunder*: Cuba in the Virtual Battlescape," in *The Players' Realm: Studies on the Culture of Video Games and Gaming*, ed. J. Patrick Williams and Jonas Heide Smith (Jefferson, NC: McFarland, 2007), 154–170.

33. "Nueva operación contra Cuba: EEUU lanza videojuego cuyo objetivo es asesinar a Fidel," Cubadebate, 9 November 2010, accessed 7 July 2011, http://www.cubadebate.cu/noticias/2010/11/09/nueva-operacion-contra-cuba-eeuu-lanza-videojuego-cuyo-objetivo-es-asesinar-a-fidel/#.VZv_MRNViko.

34. New Zoo Games Market Research, "Infographic: PC/MMO Gaming Revenues to Total $24.4Bn in 2014," 17 November 2014, accessed 7 July 2015, http://www.newzoo.com/infographics/infographic-pcmmo-gaming-revenues-to-total-24-4bn-in-2014/.

35. Miguel Sicart, *The Ethics of Computer Games* (Cambridge, MA: MIT Press, 2009), 198–199.

36. "Crean videojuego sobre la revolución cubana," Noticieros Televisa, 28 March 2013, accessed 7 July 2015, http://noticierostelevisa.esmas.com/especiales/577377/crean-videojuego-sobre-revolucion-cubana/.

37. Ibid.

38. Rui Ferreira, "Un videojuego recrea el enfrentamiento entre las tropas de Castro y Batista," *El Mundo* (Madrid, Spain), 29 March 2013, accessed 7 July 2015, http://www.elmundo.es/america/2013/03/29/cuba/1364580039.html.

39. Ian Bogost, *Unit Operations: An Approach to Videogame Criticism* (Cambridge, MA: MIT Press, 2006), 120.

40. Néstor García Canclini, *Consumers and Citizens*, trans. G. Yúdice (Minneapolis: University of Minnesota Press, 2001 [1995]), 15.

41. Miguel Sicart, "Values between Systems: Designing Ethical Gameplay," in *Ethics and Game Design: Teaching Values through Play*, ed. Karen Schrier and David Gibson (New York: Information Science Reference, 2010), 7.

42. Ibid., 7–8.

43. Ian Bogost, *Persuasive Games: The Expressive Power of Videogames* (Cambridge, MA: MIT Press), 3.

44. Gonzalo Frasca, "Videogames of the Oppressed: Critical Thinking, Education, Tolerance, and Other Trivial Issues," in *First Person: New Media as Story, Performance, and Game*, ed. Noah Wardrip-Fruin and Pat Harrigan (Cambridge, MA: MIT Press), 88.

45. *Newsgaming*, 2003, accessed 7 July 2015, http://www.newsgaming.com/.

46. Sicart, *The Ethics of Computer Games*, 43.

47. Bogost, *Unit Operations*, 119.

48. Bogost, *Persuasive Games*, 88.

49. Patrick Crogan, *Gameplay Mode: War, Simulation, and Technoculture* (Minneapolis: University of Minnesota Press, 2011), 152.

50. OnRamp Arts, accessed 7 July 2015, http://www.onramparts.org/.

51. Ibid.

52. Ibid.

53. Nick Montfort, *Twisty Little Passages* (Cambridge, MA: MIT Press, 2003), viii–xi.

54. Espen J. Aarseth, *Cybertext: Perspectives on Ergodic Literature* (Baltimore: Johns Hopkins University Press, 1997), 1–5.

55. OnRamp Arts, *Tropical America* (2002), accessed 7 July 2015, http://www.tropicalamerica.com/.

56. Henry Jenkins, *Fans, Bloggers, and Gamers: Exploring Participatory Culture* (New York: New York University Press, 2006), 220.

57. inSite Archive, UC San Diego Libraries, 1992–2006, accessed 7 July 2015, http://libraries
.ucsd.edu/speccoll/findingaids/mss0707.html.

58. Osvaldo Cleger, "Procedural Rhetoric and Undocumented Migrants: Playing the Debate
over Immigration Reform," *Digital Cultures and Education* 7, no. 1 (2015): 21–22.

59. Ricardo Dominguez and Coco Fusco, *Turista Fronterizo* (2005), accessed 7 July 2015, http://
www.thing.net/~cocofusco/choose.html.

60. Claire Taylor, "Monopolies and Maquiladoras: The Resistant Re-encoding of Gaming in
Coco Fusco and Ricardo Domínguez's *Turista Fronterizo*," *Journal of Iberian and Latin American
Research* 18, no. 2 (2012): 163.

61. Rita Raley, "Border Hacks: The Risks of Tactical Media," in *Risk and the War on Terror*, ed.
Louise Amoore and Marieke de Goede (New York: Routledge, 2008), 212.

62. Bogost, *Persuasive Games*, 340.

Chapter 3

1. José Donoso, *Historia personal del Boom* (Barcelona: Anagrama, 1972), 11–15.

2. Raymond Leslie Williams, *The Twentieth-Century Spanish American Novel* (Austin: University
of Texas Press, 2003), 126.

3. Jean Franco, *The Decline and Fall of the Lettered City: Latin America in the Cold War* (Cambridge,
MA: Harvard University Press, 2002), 159.

4. Espen J. Aarseth, "The Game and Its Name: What Is a Game Auteur?," in *Visual Authorship: Creativity and Intentionality in Media*, ed. Torben Grodal, Bente Larsen, and Iben Thorving Laursen
(Copenhagen: Museum Tusculanum Press, 2004), 268–269.

5. See, for example, "Los videojuegos argentinos conquistan el mundo con goles y héroes vir-
tuales," *Clarín* (Buenos Aires, Argentina), 18 September 2011, accessed 10 April 2013, http://www
.clarin.com/sociedad/titulo_0_556744441.html; or "NicaBird te invita a volar," Radionicaragua
.com, 10 May 2014, accessed 17 July 2014, http://www.radionicaragua.com.ni/noticias/ver/
titulo:8423-nicabird-te-invita-a-volar-.

6. "La industria de videojuegos en Argentina: Un análisis en base a la Segunda Encuesta Nacional
a empresas desarrolladoras de videojuegos," Centro de Estudios para el Desarrollo Económico
Metropolitano (2010), accessed 11 July 2015, http://comex.mdebuenosaires.gov.ar/contenido/
objetos/inforvj.pdf, 7.

7. In a 2007 study based on data gathered in 2003, Roxana Barrantes found that nearly three-quarters of Peruvian households were "Extremely Digitally Poor" (as opposed to 18.1 percent economically categorized as "Extremely Poor"). See Roxana Barrantes, "Analysis of ICT Demand: What Is Digital Poverty and How to Measure It?," in *Digital Poverty: Latin American and Caribbean Perspectives*, ed. Hernan Galperin and Judith Mariscal (Ottawa: International Development Research Center, 2007).

8. María Silvia Duarte Acha, "El juego paraguayo que mejora la vista," Ejempla, 10 July 2014, accessed 17 July 2014, http://ejempla.com/futuro/el-juego-paraguayo-que-mejora-la-vista.

9. Eduardo Marisca, "Developing Game Worlds: Gaming, Technology and Innovation in Peru," master's thesis, Massachusetts Institute of Technology, Cambridge, MA, June 2014, accessed 16 July 2014, http://marisca.pe/files/EM-DGW-Final.pdf, 213.

10. Jesús Martín Barbero, "Between Technology and Culture: Communication and Modernity in Latin America," in *Cultural Agency in the Americas*, ed. Doris Sommer (Durham: Duke University Press, 2006), 43.

11. Yuri Takhteyev, *Coding Places: Software Practice in a South American City* (Cambridge, MA: MIT Press, 2012), 42–43.

12. Ibid.

13. Ibid., 43.

14. Larissa Hjorth, *Games and Gaming: An Introduction to New Media* (New York: Berg, 2011), 6, 103.

15. Marisca, "Developing Game Worlds," 167.

16. "Videojuego argentino ganó el premio de la innovación en el Festival de Videojuegos Independientes," Ecetia, 8 March 2012, accessed 16 July 2014, http://ecetia.com/2012/03/videojuego-argentino-gana-premio-a-la-innovacion-en-el-festival-de-videojuegos-independientes. For further analysis of Benmergui's games, see Phillip Penix-Tadsen, "Latin American Game Design and the Narrative Tradition," in *Technology, Literature, and Digital Culture in Latin America: Mediatized Sensibilities in a Globalized Era*, ed. Matthew Bush and Tania Gentic (New York: Routledge, 2015).

17. Nicolás Rueda, "¿Cómo va Colombia en la industria de los videojuegos?," Enter.co, 10 February 2014, accessed 16 July 2014, http://www.enter.co/cultura-digital/colombia-digital/como-va-colombia-en-la-industria-de-los-videojuegos/.

18. Jorge Luis Borges, "The Argentine Writer and Tradition," in *Jorge Luis Borges: Selected Nonfictions*, trans. and ed. Eliot Weinberger (New York: Viking, 1999 [1951]), 427.

19. Ibid., 424.

20. Marie Custodio Collazo, "Desarrolladores de videojuegos nativos apuestan al potencial económico de esa industria," *El Nuevo Día* (San Juan, Puerto Rico), 24 May 2014, accessed 17 July 2014, http://www.elnuevodia.com/desarrolladoresdevideojuegosnativosapuestanalpotencial economicodeesaindustria-1779546.html.

21. Cited in Marisca, "Developing Game Worlds," 134.

22. Ibid., 142.

23. Fabiola Chambi, "'Hooligan Alone,' un videojuego boliviano de exportación," *Los Tiempos* (Cochabamba, Bolivia), 18 June 2014, accessed 17 July 2014, http://www.lostiempos.com/diario/actualidad/vida-y-futuro/20140618/hooligan-alone-un-videojuego-boliviano-de_263179_576062.html.

24. Jairo Lugo, Tony Sampson, and Merlyn Lossada, "Latin America's New Cultural Industries Still Play Old Games: From the Banana Republic to Donkey Kong," *Game Studies* 2, no. 2 (2002), accessed 9 July 2015, http://www.gamestudies.org/0202/lugo/.

25. Ibid.

26. "Top 100 Countries Represent 99.8% of $81.5Bn Global Games Market," Newzoo.com, 23 June 2014, accessed 16 July 2014, http://www.newzoo.com/insights/top-100-countries-represent-99-6-81-5bn-global-games-market/.

27. "Industry Profile: Creative Industries in Mexico," PROMÉXICO Trade and Investment, 2013, accessed 10 April 2013, http://mim.promexico.gob.mx/wb/mim/ind_perfil_del_sector.

28. Jairo Lugo-Ocando, ed., *The Media in Latin America* (New York: McGraw-Hill, 2008), 1.

29. D'Angelo, William, "Microsoft to Build 17,000 Xbox 360's per week in Brazil with Price Cut," VGChartz, 29 September 2011, accessed 10 April 2013, http://www.vgchartz.com/article/3013/sony-starts-shipping-to-latin-america/.

30. "Top 100 Countries."

31. "La industria de los videojuegos nacional lidera el ranking de América Latina," MinutoUno, 21 September 2012, accessed 10 April 2013, http://www.minutouno.com/notas/263031-la-industria-los-videojuegos-nacional-lidera-el-ranking-america-latina.

32. "La industria de videojuegos en Argentina" (2010), 31.

33. "La industria de videojuegos en la Argentina: Tercera Encuesta nacional a Empresas Desarrolladoras de Videojuegos: un diagnóstico en base a 26 empresas encuestadas," Centro de Estudios para el Desarrollo Económico Metropolitano (July 2012), accessed 11 July 2015, http://www.buenosaires.gob.ar/areas/hacienda/sis_estadistico/desarrollo_videojuegos_julio_2012.pdf, 15.

34. "La industria de videojuegos en Argentina" (2010), 6, 11.

35. Ibid., 18.

36. Ibid., 22.

37. "La industria de videojuegos en la Argentina" (2012), 5, 14.

38. "La industria de videojuegos en Argentina" (2010), 8, 25, 36.

39. "La industria de videojuegos en la Argentina" (2012), 22.

40. "La industria de videojuegos en Argentina" (2010), 6.

41. Ibid., 8.

42. Ibid., 31.

43. Ariel and Enrique Arbiser, email message to the author, 25 February 2015.

44. Ariel and Enrique Arbiser, *Página del TRUCO Arbiser*, accessed 7 July 2015, http://www-2.dc.uba.ar/charlas/lud/truco/.

45. Ricardo Vinicius Ferraz de Souza, "Video Game Localization: The Case of Brazil," *TradTerm, São Paulo*, 19 (2012): 305.

46. "Tec Toy mostra cem produtos," *Folha de São Paulo* (São Paulo, Brazil), 23 March 1995, accessed 7 July 2015, http://www1.folha.uol.com.br/fsp/1995/3/23/dinheiro/21.html.

47. "Estrela e Gradiente trazem jogos Nintendo," *Folha de São Paulo* (São Paulo, Brazil), 18 March 1993, accessed 7 July 2015, http://acervo2.folha.com.br/7/61/8/78/4780861/1024/4780861.png.

48. "El juego del Chapulín Colorado," YouTube video, 00:06:09, uploaded by "PakomixVG" on 4 August 2008, accessed 7 July 2015, https://www.youtube.com/watch?v=ehPPX4c_8sQ.

49. For a thorough discussion of localization practices, see Miguel Á. Bernal-Merino, *Translation and Localization in Video Games: Making Entertainment Global* (New York: Routledge, 2014).

50. Marisca, "Developing Game Worlds," 52–53. Advergaming is further discussed later in this chapter.

51. Luis Wong, "Mr Byte: The 'Gang' Leader of Gaming in Peru," *Polygon*, 10 February 2014, accessed 14 July 2014, http://www.polygon.com/features/2014/2/10/5373586/mr-byte-indie-king -of-peru.

52. Eduardo Marisca, "Buscando un *gamer*: Reconstruyendo la historia del videojuego peruano," *Pozo de letras* 11, no. 11 (2013): 24.

53. Ibid., 21.

54. Ibid.

55. Wong, "Mr Byte."

56. Ibid. See also Marisca, "Buscando un *gamer*," 23–24.

57. Ibid.

58. Tanja Sihvonen, *Players Unleashed! Modding* The Sims *and the Culture of Gaming* (Amsterdam: Amsterdam University Press, 2011), 12.

59. Henry Jenkins, *Convergence Culture: Where Old and New Media Collide* (New York: New York University Press, 2006), 137.

60. Marisca, "Buscando un *gamer*," 29.

61. Alberto Moreiras, *The Exhaustion of Difference: The Politics of Latin American Cultural Studies* (Durham: Duke University Press, 2001), 64.

62. Marisca, "Buscando un *gamer*," 22.

63. Alex Wawro, "Crafting *To Leave*, an Autobiographical Indie Game from Ecuador," *Gamasutra*, 14 April 2014, accessed 16 July 2014, http://www.gamasutra.com/view/news/215248/Crafting _To_Leave_an_autobiographical_indie_game_from_Ecuador.php.

64. Sihvonen, *Players Unleashed!*, 12–13.

65. Tristan Donovan, *Replay: The History of Video Games* (Lewes, England: Yellow Ant, 2010), 328.

66. Jenkins, *Convergence Culture*, 164–165.

67. Sihvonen, *Players Unleashed!*, 37.

68. Owen Good, "Modders Keep *MVP Baseball 2005* Alive with the World Baseball Classic," *Kotaku*, 10 March 2013, accessed 7 July 2015, http://kotaku.com/5989832/modders-keep-mvp-baseball-2005-alive-with-the-world-baseball-classic.

69. Owen Good, "An MVP Hangs In There with *Los Muchachos Del Verano*," *Kotaku*, 31 July 2010, accessed 14 July 2014, http://kotaku.com/5601435/an-mvp-hangs-in-there-with-los-muchachos-del-verano.

70. Ibid.

71. Doris Ajin, "Lanzan el videojuego guatemalteco 'Flappy Quetzal,'" Soy502.com, 21 February 2014, accessed 17 July 2014, http://www.soy502.com/articulo/lanzan-el-videojuego-guatemalteco-flappy-quetzal.

72. "NicaBird te invita a volar," Radionicaragua.com, 10 May 2014, accessed 17 July 2014, http://www.soy502.com/articulo/lanzan-el-videojuego-guatemalteco-flappy-quetzal.

73. Marisca, "Developing Game Worlds," 209.

74. Leonel Fernández, "La agenda digital de República Dominicana," *El Periódico* (Santo Domingo, Dominican Republic), 14 July 2014, accessed 17 July 2014, http://www.elperiodico.com.do/2014/07/14/la-agenda-digital-de-republica-dominicana/.

75. Jesús Martín-Barbero, "Medios y culturas en el espacio latinoamericano," *Iberoamericana* 2, no. 6 (2002): 104.

76. Devworks, accessed 7 July 2015, http://www.devworks.com.br/principal/site.asp?val=1.

77. Luis Wong, "The Argentinian Arcade Cabinet *Nave* Turns Play into a Performance," Kill Screen Daily, 15 July 2014, accessed 16 July 2014, http://killscreendaily.com/articles/argentinian-arcade-cabinet-nave-turns-play-performance/.

78. Marisca, "Developing Game Worlds," 94.

79. Captain Mike, "'Rundown del Global Game Jam donde los Puertorriqueños ¡brillaron!,'" Yosoyungamer.com, 28 January 2014, accessed 17 July 2014, http://yosoyungamer.com/2014/01/rundown-del-global-game-jam-donde-los-puertorriquenos-brillaron/.

80. "Industria del videojuego da sus primeros frutos bolivianos," *Opinión* (Cochabamba, Bolivia), 12 October 2013, accessed 17 July 2014, http://www.opinion.com.bo/opinion/vida_de_hoy/2013/1012/vidadehoy.php?id=1494.

81. Marisca, "Developing Game Worlds," 200.

82. Mark Lennon and Christine Magee, "Startups Surge in South America," *Tech Crunch*, 1 July 2014, accessed 16 July 2014, http://techcrunch.com/2014/07/01/startups-surge-in-south-america/.

83. "Video Games 'Made in Mexico,' A Serious Bet," PROMÉXICO Trade and Investment, December 2009, accessed 7 July 2015, http://negocios.promexico.gob.mx/english/12-2009/art05.html.

84. Hugo Juárez, "Entrevista con Mark Stanley, Director General para América Latina de Sony Computer Entertainment America," *Psicodiarrea*, 27 October 2008, accessed 7 July 2015, http://psicodiarrea.blogspot.com/2008/10/entrevista-con-mark-stanley-director.html.

85. Kyle Orland, "Sony Offers New Hardware Bundles, First PlayStation Ads for Latin America," *Gamasutra*, 10 November 2014, accessed 7 July 2015, http://www.gamasutra.com/view/news/122108/Sony_Offers_New_Hardware_Bundles_First_PlayStation_Ads_For_Latin_America.php.

86. "Programa de incubación de desarrolladores de Sony PlayStation," Sony Computer Entertainment America LLC, 2014, accessed 7 July 2015, http://latam.playstation.com/corporativo/incubationprogram/.

87. Daniela Zárate G., "Juego chileno se convierte en el primer título latinoamericano en ser publicado por Sony," Emol.com (Chile), 16 June 2014, accessed 17 July 2014, http://www.emol.com/noticias/tecnologia/2014/06/13/665088/juego-chileno-se-convierte-en-el-primer-titulo-latinoamericano-en-ser-publicado-por-sony-domingo.html.

88. Wawro, "Crafting *To Leave*."

89. Ibid.

90. Adriana Molano, "Square Enix y el futuro de los videojuegos en América Latina," ColombiaDigital, 22 May 2012, accessed 10 April 2013, https://www.colombiadigital.net/entorno-tic/item/1818-square-enix-y-el-futuro-de-los-videojuegos-en-am%C3%A9rica-latina.html.

91. "Videojuegos hechos por colombianos," Cámara de Comercio de Bogotá, July 2014, accessed 5 July 2015, http://www.ccb.org.co/Cree-su-empresa/Sectores-estrategicos/Industrias-Culturales-y-Creativas-ICC/Artecamara/Exposiciones-pasadas/Ano-2014/Videojuegos-hechos-por-colombianos.

92. Andrés Tovar, "Venezolano crea juego 'para vengarse' de la delincuencia," *Últimas Noticias* (Venezuela), 21 November 2012, accessed 17 July 2014, http://www.ultimasnoticias.com.ve/noticias/chevere/espectaculos/venezolano-crea-videojuego-para-vengarse-de-la-del.aspx.

93. Ibid.

94. *La Mordida* (LEAP Games 2014), accessed 7 July 2015, http://lamordidagame.com/.

95. "Lanzan videojuego para reírse de la ignorancia de Portillo," *Ñandutí*, 5 July 2014, accessed 17 July 2014, http://www.nanduti.com.py/v1/noticias-mas.php?id=87922.

96. "La política panameña ya tiene su 'Mario Bros': se trata de un videojuego," Telemetro. com (Panama City, Panama), 4 May 2013, accessed 7 July 2015, http://www.telemetro.com/ voto2014/politica-panamena-Mario-Bros-videojuego_0_584941559.html.

97. "Videojuego satírico de Martinelli, furor en candidatos opositores panameños," *El Espectador* (Panama City, Panama), 30 March 2014, accessed 17 July 2014, http://www.elespectador.com/ tecnologia/juegos/videojuego-satirico-de-martinelli-furor-candidatos-opos-articulo-483862.

98. Ibid.

99. "Lanzan primer videojuego educativo dominicano," *Hoy* (Santo Domingo, Dominican Republic), 1 March 2008, accessed 17 July 2014, http://hoy.com.do/lanzan-primer-videojuego -educativo-dominicano/.

100. "Se inserta Cuba en la industria de videojuegos." *Auca en Cayo Hueso*, 2 May 2014, accessed 14 July 2014, https://aucaencayohueso.wordpress.com/2014/05/02/se-inserta-cuba -en-la-industria-de-videojuegos/.

101. Ibid.

102. "Lanzan juego educativo en línea sobre operación del Canal de Panamá," *América Economía*, 7 February 2013, accessed 17 July 2014, http://www.americaeconomia.com/ negocios-industrias/lanzan-juego-educativo-en-linea-sobre-operacion-del-canal-de-panama.

103. María Alejandra Medina C., "La empresa que le puso ruedas al barril del Chavo del 8," *El Espectador* (Bogotá, Colombia), 4 July 2014, accessed 17 July 2014, http://www.elespectador .com/tecnologia/empresa-le-puso-ruedas-al-barril-del-chavo-del-8-articulo-502480.

104. Byron Corrales, "Aplicaciones para laptops XO desarrolladas en Nicaragua," Servicio de Información Mesoamericano sobre Agricultura Sostenible (SIMAS), 21 July 2011, accessed 17 July 2014, http://www.simas.org.ni/tic-y-sl/articulo/aplicaciones-para-laptops-xo -desarrolladas-en-nicaragua.

105. Ibid.

106. Marisca, "Developing Game Worlds," 161.

107. "Polache ya tiene su propio videojuego," *La Noticia* (Tegucigalpa, Honduras), 21 April 2014, accessed 21 July 2014, http://lanoticia.hn/cultura/polache-ya-tiene-su-propio-videojuego/.

108. Marisca, "Developing Game Worlds," 159.

109. Medina, "La empresa."

110. Ibid.

111. Miguel Benítez, "Videojuego paraguayo conquista emblemático canal infantil de EE.UU.," *Última Hora* (Asunción, Paraguay), 24 July 2013, accessed 17 July 2014, http://www.ultimahora.com/videojuego-paraguayo-conquista-emblematico-canal-infantil-ee-uu-n706765.html.

112. Marisca, "Developing Game Worlds," 164.

113. Daryelin Torres, "Los videojuegos 'made in' la República Dominicana," *Listin Diario* (Santo Domingo, Dominican Republic), 20 February 2008, accessed 17 July 2014, http://www.listin.com.do/economia-and-negocios/2008/2/19/48685/Los-videojuegos-made-in-la-Republica-Dominicana.

114. For further discussion of *Guacamelee!*, as well as *Papo & Yo*, see chapter 5.

115. David Grandadam, Patrick Cohendet, and Laurent Simon, "Places, Spaces and the Dynamics of Creativity: The Video Game Industry in Montreal," *Regional Studies* 47, no. 10 (2013): 1705.

116. Simon Egenfeldt-Nielsen, Jonas Heide Smith, and Susana Pajares Tosca, eds., *Understanding Video Games: The Essential Introduction*, 2nd ed. (New York: Routledge, 2013), 19.

117. Alasdair Duncan, "Review: Abyss Odyssey," Destructoid.com, 15 July 2014, accessed 7 July 2015, http://www.destructoid.com/review-abyss-odyssey-277987.phtml.

118. Marisca, "Developing Game Worlds," 162.

119. Jesper Juul, *A Casual Revolution: Reinventing Video Games and Their Players* (Cambridge, MA: MIT Press, 2010), 148.

120. "Reconocen a Nik como personalidad destacada de la cultura," *La Nación* (Buenos Aires, Argentina), 7 November 2014, accessed 7 July 2015, http://www.lanacion.com.ar/1741933-reconocen-a-nik-como-personalidad-destacada-de-la-cultura.

121. Simon Romero, "Pastoral Uruguay Yields a Crop of Digital Yetis and Adventures," *New York Times*, 21 February 2013, accessed 16 July 2014, http://www.nytimes.com/2013/02/22/world/americas/uruguays-video-game-start-ups-garner-attention.html.

122. "El Salvador venderá video juego a mercados estadounidense, europeo y asiático," Government of El Salvador, Ministry of the Economy, *Noticias*, 11 March 2014, accessed 16 July 2014,   http://www.minec.gob.sv/index.php?option=com_content&view=article&id=2563:el -salvador-vendera-video-juego-a-mercados-estadounidense-europeo-y-asiatico-&catid =1:noticias-ciudadano&Itemid=77.

123. Marisca, "Developing Game Worlds," 202–203.

124. "Convierten tradición mexicana en aplicaciones telefónicas y videojuegos," Informador.com.mx, 7 April 2013, accessed 16 July 2014, http://www.informador.com.mx/ tecnologia/2013/449411/6/convierten-tradicion-mexicana-en-aplicaciones-telefonicas-y -videojuegos.htm.

125. "Jóvenes hondureños crean sus propios videojuegos animados," Universia, 17 September 2013, accessed 21 July 2014, http://noticias.universia.hn/en-portada/ noticia/2013/09/17/1049965/jovenes-hondurenos-crean-propios-videojuegos-animados .html.

Chapter 4

1. Matthew Arnold, *Culture and Anarchy: An Essay in Political and Social Criticism* (London: Smith, Elder & Co., 1869), 81.

2. Pierre Bourdieu, *Distinction: A Social Critique of the Judgment of Taste* (New York: Routledge, 2013 [1979]), xxx.

3. Ferdinand de Saussure, *Course in General Linguistics*, trans. W. Baskin (New York: Columbia University Press, 2013 [1916]), part 1, chapter 1.

4. Jacques Derrida, "Différance," *Margins of Philosophy* (Chicago: University of Chicago Press, 1982), 1–28.

5. James Paul Gee, "Semiotic Domains: Is Playing Video Games a 'Waste of Time?,'" *The Game Design Reader: A Rules of Play Anthology*, ed. Katie Salen and Eric Zimmerman (Cambridge, MA: MIT Press, 2006), 240.

6. N. Katherine Hayles, *How We Became Posthuman: Virtual Bodies in Cybernetics, Literature, and Informatics* (Chicago: University of Chicago Press, 1999), 30–31.

7. Alexander R. Galloway, *Gaming: Essays on Algorithmic Culture* (Minneapolis: University of Minnesota Press, 2006), 5.

8. Dominic Arsenault and Bernard Perron, "In the Frame of the Magic Cycle: The Circle(s) of Gameplay," in *The Video Game Theory Reader 2*, ed. Bernard Perron and Mark J. P. Wolf (New York: Routledge, 2009), 111.

9. David Myers, *Play Redux: The Form of Computer Games* (Ann Arbor: University of Michigan Press, 2010), 21.

10. Aylish Wood, "Recursive Space: Play and Creating Space," *Games and Culture* 7, no. 1 (2012): 90.

11. Pierre Lévy, *Becoming Virtual: Reality in the Digital Age* (New York: Plenum Press, 1998), 162.

12. Ibid.

13. Lev Manovich, *The Language of New Media* (Cambridge, MA: MIT Press, 2001), 47.

14. Anthony Giddens, *The Consequences of Modernity* (Stanford: Stanford University Press, 1990), 21–22.

15. Roland Barthes, *Image, Music, Text*, trans. S. Heath (New York: Hill and Wang, 1977), 52–54.

16. Ibid., 61.

17. Frans Mäyrä, *An Introduction to Game Studies: Games in Culture* (London: Sage, 2008), 14.

18. Ibid.

19. Giddens, *The Consequences of Modernity*, 22.

20. Lévy, *Becoming Virtual*, 162.

21. Martín Hopenhayn, "Globalization and Culture: Five Approaches to a Single Text," in *Cultural Politics in Latin America*, ed. Anny Brooksbank Jones and Ronaldo Munck (New York: St. Martin's Press, 2000), 146.

22. Néstor García Canclini, *La sociedad sin relato. Antropología y estética de la inminencia* (Buenos Aires and Madrid: Katz, 2010), 67.

23. Ibid., 73.

24. Ibid., 127.

25. Espen J. Aarseth, *Cybertext: Perspectives on Ergodic Literature* (Baltimore: Johns Hopkins University Press, 1997), 1.

26. Ibid., 162.

27. Gordon Calleja, *In-Game: From Immersion to Incorporation* (Cambridge, MA: MIT Press, 2011), 12.

28. Katie Salen and Eric Zimmerman, "Game Design and Meaningful Play," in *Handbook of Computer Game Studies*, ed. Joost Raessens and Jeffrey Goldstein (Cambridge, MA: MIT Press, 2005), 63–64.

29. Ibid., 64.

30. Ibid., 66.

31. Geoff King and Tanya Krzywinska, *Tomb Raiders and Space Invaders: Videogame Forms and Contexts* (New York: I. B. Tauris, 2006), 172–173.

32. James Paul Gee, *What Video Games Have to Teach Us about Learning and Literacy* (New York: Palgrave Macmillan, 2007), 149.

33. Philipp Reichmuth and Stefan Werning, "Pixel Pashas, Digital Djinns," *ISIM Review* 18 (2006): 46–47.

34. Rachael Hutchinson, "Performing the Self: Subverting the Binary in Combat Games," *Games and Culture* 2, no. 4 (2007): 286.

35. Phillip Penix-Tadsen, "Latin American Ludology: Why We Should Take Video Games Seriously (and When We Shouldn't)," *Latin American Research Review* 48, no. 1 (2013): 181–184.

36. Eduardo Marisca, "Developing Game Worlds: Gaming, Technology and Innovation in Peru," master's thesis, Massachusetts Institute of Technology, Cambridge, MA, June 2014, accessed 16 July 2014, http://marisca.pe/files/EM-DGW-Final.pdf, 110.

37. King and Krzywinska, *Tomb Raiders and Space Invaders*, 174.

38. For further discussion of the portrayal of Latin American culture in resource management simulations, see chapter 6.

39. Claudio Lomnitz, *Death and the Idea of Mexico* (Cambridge, MA: Zone, 2005).

40. Karen E. Skoog, "Insights Learned from Indie Game Developers in Latin America & the Middle East," *Gamasutra*, 8 September 2012, accessed 25 April 2013, http://www.gamasutra.com/blogs/KarinESkoog/20120908/177354/Insights_Learned_from_Indie_Game_Developers_in_Latin_America__the_Middle_East.php.

41. Arturo Nereu, "Mictlan Postmortem," Phyne Games Blogs, 17 May 2012, accessed 25 April 2013, http://www.blogs.phynegames.com/?p=13.

42. Ibid.

43. See also chapter 3. "Metroid-vania" is a portmanteau of the titles of *Metroid* (Nintendo 1986) and *Castlevania* (Konami 1986).

44. Rory McCarty, "Discussing Mexican Wrestlers and Day of the Dead with *Guacamelee*'s Chris McQuinn," VentureBeat, 10 March 2013, accessed 25 April 2013, http://venturebeat .com/community/2013/03/10/platforming-with-an-exclamation-point-a-guacamelee -interview-with-drinkbox-studios-chris-mcquinn/. The light/dark world dynamic had been seen in previous game series, for instance in the "dark" character of Shadow the Hedgehog, who first appeared as the Sonic's dark side in *Sonic Adventure 2* (Sega 2001).

45. "TierraGamer entrevista a DrinkBox Studios," TierraGamer, 16 April 2013, accessed 17 May 2013, http://www.tierragamer.com/especial-tierragamer-entrevista-a-drinkbox-studios/.

46. Ian Bogost, *How to Do Things with Videogames* (Minneapolis: University of Minnesota Press, 2011), 28.

47. Roberto Schwarz, *Misplaced Ideas*, trans. J. Gledson (London: Verso, 1992), 29.

48. Lúcia Nagib, *Brazil on Screen: Cinema Novo, New Cinema, Utopia* (New York: I. B. Tauris, 2007), 101.

49. Darcy Ribeiro, *The Brazilian People: The Formation and Meaning of Brazil*, trans. G. Rabassa (Gainesville: University of Florida Press, 2000 [1995]), 147.

50. Beatriz Jaguaribe, "Favelas and the Aesthetics of Realism: Representations in Film and Literature," *Journal of Latin American Cultural Studies* 13, no. 3 (2004): 327.

51. Roberto Schwarz, "*City of God*," trans. J. Gledson, *New Left Review* 12 (2001), 112.

52. VGChartz, accessed 8 July 2015, http://www.vgchartz.com/gamedb/?name=modern +warfare+2.

53. "Max Payne 3 Dan Houser Interview: On Redefining a Genre," *Polygon*, 9 May 2012, accessed 2 may 2013, http://www.polygon.com/2012/11/14/3550224/max-payne-3-dan -houser-interview-on-redefining-a-genre.

54. "Rockstar Research: The Weapon-Wielding Gangsters and Special Police Comman- dos of Max Payne 3," Rockstar Newswire, 9 January 2012, accessed 2 May 2013, http://www .rockstargames.com/newswire/article/20011/rockstar-research-the-weaponwielding -gangsters-and-special-polic.html.

55. "From NYC to São Paulo: Behind the Scenes of Max Payne 3's Voiceover, Mo-Cap & Scanning Sessions," Rockstar Newswire, 29 May 2012, accessed 2 May 2013, http://www.rockstargames .com/newswire/article/34991/from-nyc-to-so-paulo-behind-the-scenes-of-max-payne -3s-voiceover.html.

56. See chapter 5 for further discussion of the use of Portuguese in *Modern Warfare 2* as well as *Max Payne 3*.

57. "Max Payne 3 Dan Houser Interview."

58. Ben Fritz, "Red Dead Redemption Brings the Western to Video Games," *Los Angeles Times*, 25 April 2010, accessed 1 May 2013, http://articles.latimes.com/2010/apr/25/entertainment/ la-ca-reddead-20100425.

59. "*Papo & Yo* Dev. Diary 1," 8 May 2012, accessed 11 July 2015, http://www.weareminority .com/just-released-papo-yo-dev-diary-1/.

60. Nick Montfort and Ian Bogost, *Racing the Beam: The Atari Video Computer System* (Cambridge, MA: MIT Press, 2009), 104–105.

Chapter 5

1. Philipp Reichmuth and Stefan Werning, "Pixel Pashas, Digital Djinns," *ISIM Review* 18 (2006): 46.

2. James Newman, *Videogames* (New York: Routledge, 2004), 108.

3. Henry Jenkins, "Game Design as Narrative Architecture," in *The Game Design Reader: A Rules of Play Anthology*, ed. Katie Salen and Eric Zimmerman (Cambridge, MA: MIT Press, 2006), 674.

4. Edvin Babic, "On the Liberation of Space in Computer Games," *Eludamos* 1, no. 1 (2007), accessed 9 July 2015, http://www.eludamos.org/index.php/eludamos/article/view/vol1no1-3/6.

5. Michel Foucault, "Of Other Spaces," trans. J. Miskowiec, *diacritics* 16, no. 1 (1986): 24.

6. Lev Manovich, *The Language of New Media* (Cambridge, MA: MIT Press, 2001), 114.

7. Shoshana Magnet, "Playing at Colonization: Interpreting Imaginary Landscapes in the Video Game *Tropico*," *Journal of Communication Inquiry* 30 (2006): 142.

8. My usage here follows Galloway, who adopts the terminology of film critics to distinguish between "diegetic" and "nondiegetic" acts, keeping in mind that the "diegesis of a video game

is the game's total world of narrative action," and that on-screen acts that do not correspond to that narrative (such as pausing the game or interacting with the menu) are nondiegetic, though they are still on-screen elements of the game. See Alexander R. Galloway, *Gaming: Essays on Algorithmic Culture* (Minneapolis: University of Minnesota Press, 2006), 7–8.

9. Tim Cresswell and Deborah Dixon, "Introduction: Engaging Film," in *Engaging Film: Geographies of Mobility and Identity*, ed. Tim Cresswell and Deborah Dixon (Lanham, MD: Rowman & Littlefield, 2002), 4.

10. Martin Lefebvre, "Between Setting and Landscape in the Cinema," in *Landscape and Film*, ed. Martin Lefebvre (New York: Routledge, 2006), 24.

11. Ibid., 52.

12. Gordon Calleja, *In-Game: From Immersion to Incorporation* (Cambridge, MA: MIT Press, 2011), 74.

13. Stuart C. Aitken and Leo E. Zonn, "Re-Presenting the Place Pastiche," in *Place, Power, Situation, and Spectacle: A Geography of Film*, ed. Stuart C. Aitken and Leo E. Zonn (London: Rowman & Littlefield, 1994), 17.

14. Anton Escher, "The Geography of Cinema—A Cinematic World," *Erdkunde* 60, no. 4 (2006): 310.

15. Jeff Hopkins, "A Mapping of Cinematic Places: Icons, Ideology, and the Power of (Mis)representation," in *Place, Power, Situation, and Spectacle*, ed. Aitken and Zonn, 47.

16. Fredric Jameson, *Postmodernism, or, The Cultural Logic of Late Capitalism* (Durham: Duke University Press, 1991), 50–51.

17. Calleja, *In-Game*, 87.

18. Lefebvre, "Between Setting and Landscape," 22.

19. Here I follow Bogost's adoption of Alain Badiou's term "eventalsite," which Badiou characterizes as "an entirely abnormal multiple" that "is on the edge of the void, or foundational," and which Bogost refers to as "the place where current practice breaks down." See Alain Badiou, *Being and Event* (London: Continuum, 2005), 175; and Ian Bogost, *Persuasive Games: The Expressive Power of Videogames* (Cambridge, MA: MIT Press), 332.

20. Mark J. P. Wolf, "Space in the Video Game," *The Medium of the Video Game*, ed. Mark J. P. Wolf (Austin: University of Texas Press, 2001), 53–54.

21. "Indiana Jones in Revenge of the Ancients for the Apple II," YouTube gameplay video, 00:09:00, posted by "Highretrogamelord," 5 April 2011, accessed 8 July 2015, https://www .youtube.com/watch?v=h-SszjGcWhs.

22. Michael Nitsche, *Video Game Spaces: Image, Play, and Structure in 3D Worlds* (Cambridge, MA: MIT Press, 2008), 15–16.

23. Ibid., 16.

24. Newman, *Videogames*, 117.

25. Ibid., 122.

26. Laurie Taylor, "When Seams Fall Apart: Video Game Space and the Player," *Game Studies* 3, no. 2 (2003), accessed 20 May 2013, http://www.gamestudies.org/0302/ taylor/.

27. Jenkins, "Game Design as Narrative Architecture," 676–677.

28. Ibid., 681.

29. Alejandra Bronfman and Andrew Grant Wood, "Introduction: Media, Sound, and Culture," in *Media, Sound, and Culture in Latin America and the Caribbean*, ed. Alejandra Bronfman and Andrew Grant Wood (Pittsburgh: University of Pittsburgh Press, 2012), xvi.

30. Michele Hilmes, "Postscript: Sound Representation: Nation, Translation, Memory," in *Media, Sound, and Culture*, ed. Bronfman and Wood, 122–123.

31. Nitsche, *Video Game Spaces*, 133.

32. Ibid., 142.

33. Ibid., 143–144.

34. Simon Egenfeldt-Nielsen, Jonas Heide Smith, and Susana Pajares Tosca, eds., *Understanding Video Games: The Essential Introduction*, 2nd ed. (New York: Routledge, 2013), 148.

35. Ibid., 145–146.

36. Ibid., 147.

37. Zach Whalen, "Play Along—An Approach to Videogame Music," *Game Studies* 4, no. 1 (2004), accessed 20 May 2013, http://www.gamestudies.org/0401/whalen/.

38. Egenfeldt-Nielsen, Smith, and Tosca, eds., *Understanding Video Games*, 147.

39. Chris Greening, "Interview with Pawel Baszczak," *SEMO*, March 2012, accessed 18 April 2013, http://www.squareenixmusic.com/features/interviews/pawelblaszczak.shtml.

40. Alexa Ray Corriea, "Papo & Yo Composer Brian D'Oliveira Melds Sentiment with Sound," Dual Shockers, 22 March 2012, accessed 18 April 2013, http://www.dualshockers.com/2012/03/22/papo-yo-composer-brian-doliveira-melds-sentiment-with-sound/.

41. Ibid.

42. Aylish Wood, "Recursive Space: Play and Creating Space," *Games and Culture* 7 (2012): 90.

43. Ibid., 91.

44. Nick Montfort and Ian Bogost, *Racing the Beam: The Atari Video Computer System* (Cambridge, MA: MIT Press, 2009), 110.

45. *Pitfall!* instruction manual, accessed 8 July 2015, http://atariage.com/manual_html_page.html?SoftwareLabelID=360.http://atariage.com/manual_html_page.html?SoftwareLabelID=360.

46. Barry Atkins, *More than a Game: The Computer Game as Fictional Form* (Manchester, UK: Manchester University Press, 2003), 41.

47. Christopher A. Paul, *Wordplay and the Discourse of Video Games: Analyzing Words, Design, and Play* (New York: Routledge, 2012), 26.

48. Egenfeldt-Nielsen, Smith, and Tosca, eds., *Understanding Video Games*, 129.

49. Calleja, *In-Game*, 60.

50. Ibid.

51. Ted Friedman, "*Civilization* and Its Discontents," in *Discovering Discs: Transforming Space and Genre on CD-ROM*, ed. Greg Smith (New York: New York University Press, 1998).

52. Jesper Juul, *Half-Real: Video Games between Real Rules and Fictional Worlds* (Cambridge, MA: MIT Press, 2005), 143.

53. Magnet, "Playing at Colonization," 154. For further discussion of *Tropico 3*, see chapter 6.

54. Calleja, *In-Game*, 92.

55. Frederick Luis Aldama, "Latinos and Video Games," in *Encyclopedia of Video Games: The Culture, Technology, and Art of Gaming*, ed. Mark J. P. Wolf (Santa Barbara, CA: Greenwood, 2012), 356.

56. Calleja, *In-Game*, 75–76.

57. Charles Onyett, "Red Dead Redemption: A Man and His Horse," IGN, 8 May 2009, accessed 1 May 2013, http://www.ign.com/articles/2009/05/09/red-dead-redemption-a-man-and-his -horse.

Chapter 6

1. Gonzalo Frasca, "Simulation versus Narrative: Introduction to Ludology," in *The Video Game Theory Reader*, ed. Mark J. P. Wolf and Bernard Perron (New York: Routledge, 2003), 234–235.

2. Robert Hariman, "Political Parody and Public Culture," *Quarterly Journal of Speech* 94, no. 2 (2008): 260.

3. Ibid., 251.

4. Frasca, "Simulation versus Narrative," 222–223.

5. William Uricchio, "Simulation, History, and Computer Games," in *Handbook of Computer Game Studies*, ed. Joost Raessens and Jeffrey Goldstein (Cambridge, MA: MIT Press, 2005), 333.

6. Gonzalo Frasca, "Videogames of the Oppressed: Critical Thinking, Education, Tolerance and Other Trivial Issues," in *First Person: New Media as Story, Performance, and Game*, ed. Noah Wardrip-Fruin and Pat Harrigan (Cambridge, MA: MIT Press, 2004), 93.

7. Lev Manovich, *The Language of New Media* (Cambridge, MA: MIT Press, 2001), 222.

8. Mark J. P. Wolf, "Genre and the Video Game," in *Handbook of Computer Game Studies*, ed. Raessens and Goldstein, 113–134.

9. Claudio Fogu, "Digitalizing Historical Consciousness," *History and Theory* 48, no. 2 (2009): 121.

10. Alexander R. Galloway, *Gaming: Essays on Algorithmic Culture* (Minneapolis: University of Minnesota Press, 2006), 102.

11. Georg Lukács, "Georg Lukács on Balzac's *Lost Illusions*" (1957), in *Realism*, ed. Lilian R. Furst (London: Longman, 1992), 107.

12. Erich Auerbach, "Erich Auerbach on Stendhal, Balzac, and Flaubert" (repr. from "In the Hotel de la Mole" in *Mimesis* [1953]), in *Realism*, ed. Furst, 86.

13. André Bazin, *What Is Cinema?*, 2 vols., ed. and trans. H. Gray (Berkeley: University of California Press, 1994 [1971]), 2: 53.

14. Manovich, *The Language of New Media*, 184.

15. Roland Barthes, "The Reality Effect in Descriptions" (1968), trans. R. Howard, in *Realism*, ed. Furst, 140.

16. Geoff King and Tanya Krzywinska, *Tomb Raiders and Space Invaders: Videogame Forms and Contexts* (New York: I. B. Tauris, 2006), 143.

17. Ibid., 150.

18. Jesper Juul, *Half-Real: Video Games between Real Rules and Fictional Worlds* (Cambridge, MA: MIT Press, 2005), 172.

19. "Meet the Real Eddy Gordo! Scary Larry Interviews Capoeira Artist Marcel Pereira—the Man Who Gave Tekken 3's Eddy Gordo His Moves," GamePro, 9 February 1998, accessed 9 July 2015, http://web.archive.org/web/20001016024720/www.gamepro.com/exclusives/exclusives115 .html.

20. Ibid.

21. Donsoft Entertainment, accessed 9 July 2015, http://www.capoeiralegends.com/Site/CL/.

22. Kevin Schut, "Strategic Simulations and Our Past: The Bias of Computer Games in the Presentation of History," *Games and Culture* 2, no. 3 (2007): 225.

23. Shoshana Magnet, "Playing at Colonization: Interpreting Imaginary Landscapes in the Video Game *Tropico*," *Journal of Communication Inquiry* 30 (2006): 155.

24. Schut, "Strategic Simulations and Our Past," 229.

25. Among others, see Nina B. Huntemann and Matthew Thomas Payne, "Introduction," in *Joystick Soldiers*, ed. Huntemann and Payne (New York: Routledge, 2010), 1–18.

26. Nick Dyer-Witheford and Greig de Peuter, *Games of Empire: Global Capitalism and Video Games* (Minneapolis: University of Minnesota Press, 2009), xxix.

27. Ibid., 231–232.

28. Gerard Greenfield, "Writing the History of the Future: The Killing Game," *Z Magazine* 6, no. 17 (2004), accessed 5 July 2011, http://zcombeta.org/znetarticle/writing-the-history-of-the -future-by-gerard-greenfield/.

29. Vit Sisler, "Digital Arabs: Representation in Video Games," *European Journal of Cultural Studies* 11, no. 2 (2008): 204.

30. Joel Penney, "No Better Way to 'Experience' World War II: Authenticity and Ideology in the *Call of Duty* and *Medal of Honor* Player Communities," in *Joystick Soldiers*, ed. Huntemann and Payne, 204.

31. Nina B. Huntemann, "Playing with Fear: Catharsis and Resistance in Military-Themed Video Games," in *Joystick Soldiers*, ed. Huntemann and Payne, 232.

32. Greenfield, "Writing the History of the Future."

33. Galloway, *Gaming*, 77.

34. Ibid., 84.

35. Brett Levinson, *The Ends of Literature* (Stanford: Stanford University Press), 110.

36. Ibid.

37. Jesper Juul, *A Casual Revolution: Reinventing Video Games and Their Players* (Cambridge, MA: MIT Press, 2010), 151.

38. Juul, *Half-Real*, 193.

39. Roberto Schwarz, *Misplaced Ideas*, trans. J. Gledson (London: Verso, 1992), 40.

40. Ibid., 127.

41. Hariman, "Political Parody and Public Culture," 248.

42. John C. Meyer, "Humor as a Double-Edged Sword: Four Functions of Humor in Communication," *Communication Theory* 10, no. 3 (2000): 313.

43. Ibid.

44. Joshua M. Averbeck and Dale Hample, "Ironic Message Production: How and Why We Produce Ironic Messages," *Communication Monographs* 75, no. 4 (2008): 397.

45. Christopher A. Paul, *Wordplay and the Discourse of Video Games: Analyzing Words, Design, and Play* (New York: Routledge, 2012), 89.

46. See, for example, Judd Ethan Ruggill and Ken S. McAllister, *Gaming Matters: Art, Science, Magic, and the Computer Game Medium* (Tuscaloosa: University of Alabama Press, 2011), 63.

47. David J. Leonard, "Not a Hater, Just Keepin' It Real: The Importance of Race- and Gender-Based Game Studies," *Games and Culture* 1, no. 1 (2006): 85.

48. Dyer-Witheford and de Peuter. *Games of Empire*, 181.

49. Dean Chan, "Playing with Race: The Ethics of Racialized Representations in E-Games," *International Review of Information Ethics* 4 (2005): 28.

50. Ben DeVane and Kurt D. Squire, "The Meaning of Race and Violence in Grand Theft Auto: San Andreas," *Games and Culture* 3 (2008): 281.

51. Ibid., 196.

52. Claire Dormann and Robert Biddle, "A Review of Humor for Computer Games: Play, Laugh and More," *Simulation and Gaming* 40, no. 6 (2009): 815–817.

53. Ibid., 820.

54. For a discussion of the relationship between the *Tropico* series and the Latin American dictator novel, see Daniel Chávez, "El coronel no tiene con quien jugar: representaciones latinoamericanas en la literatura y el videojuego," *Arizona Journal of Hispanic Cultural Studies* 14 (2010): 164–172.

55. Magnet, "Playing at Colonization," 142.

56. Ibid., 143.

57. Ibid., 157.

58. Kurt Squire, "Cultural Framing of Computer/Video Games," *Game Studies* 2, no. 1 (2002), accessed 15 July 2014, http://www.gamestudies.org/0102/squire/.

59. Ibid.

60. Ibid.

61. Levinson, *The Ends of Literature*, 109.

62. Magnet, "Playing at Colonization," 150.

63. McKenzie Wark, *Gamer Theory* (Cambridge, MA: Harvard University Press, 2007), sect. 36.

64. Tom Bridge, "Tropico Interview: Phil Steinmeyer," Inside Mac Games, 16 May 2001, accessed 1 May 2013, http://www.insidemacgames.com/features/view.php?ID=35.

65. Ibid.

66. Ibid.

67. King and Krzywinska, *Tomb Raiders and Space Invaders*, 195.

68. Beth Simone Noveck, "Democracy—The Video Game: Virtual Worlds and the Future of Collective Action," in *The State of Play: Law, Games, and Virtual Worlds*, ed. Jack M. Balkin and Beth Simone Noveck (New York: New York University Press, 2006), 270.

69. Galloway, *Gaming*, 102–103.

70. Lisa Gring-Pemble and Martha Solomon Watson, "The Rhetorical Limits of Satire: An Analysis of James Finn Garner's Politically Correct Bedtime Stories," *Quarterly Journal of Speech* 89, no. 2 (2003): 138.

REFERENCES

Games

1811 (Trojan Chicken 2011)

1812 (Trojan Chicken 2015)

A Jugar (Joven Club de Computación y Electrónica [JCCE] 2014)

A Ponte (Devworks 2003)

A-10 Cuba! (Activision 1996)

Abyss Odyssey (ACE Team 2014)

Act of War: High Treason (Atari 2006)

Active Life Explorer (Namco Bandai 2010)

Adventure (Atari 1979)

Adventures in Odyssey: The Treasure of the Incas (Digital Praise 2005)

Age of Empires II: The Age of Kings (Microsoft 1999)

Age of Empires III (Microsoft 2005)

Al grito de guerra (Máquina Voladora 2013)

Amazon (Telarium 1984)

Amazon: Guardians of Eden (Access 1992)

The Amazon Trail (MECC 1994)

Amazon Trail II (MECC 1996)

Amazon Trail 3rd Edition (MECC 1999)

America's Army (United States Army 2002)

American Conquest (CDV 2003)

Angry Birds Rio (Rovio 2011)

Anno 1503: The New World (Sunflowers 2003)

Anno 1602: Creation of a New World (Sunflowers 1998)

Anno 1701 (Sunflowers 2006)

Argentum Online (NGD Studios 2001)

Army of Two: The Devil's Cartel (EA 2013)

Assassin's Creed IV: Black Flag (Ubisoft 2013)

Atrévete a soñar (Televisa 2011)

Aventuras D'Onofrio (SISTAP 1987)

Aztec (Datamost 1982)

Battlefield: Bad Company 2 (EA 2010)

Beisbolito (JCCE 2014)

Boombox (JCCE 2014)

Brasil Quest (Embratur 2012)

Breach (Space Rhino 2014)

Caesar (Sierra Entertainment 1992)

Call of Duty (Activision 2003)

Call of Duty: Black Ops (Activision 2010)

Call of Duty: Black Ops II (Activision 2012)

Call of Duty: Modern Warfare 2 (Activision 2009)

Call of Juarez (Ubisoft 2006)

Call of Juarez: Bound in Blood (Ubisoft 2009)

Call of Juarez: Gunslinger (Ubisoft 2013)

Call of Juarez: The Cartel (Ubisoft 2011)

Cambiemos (Frente Amplio 2004)

Capoeira Legends: Path to Freedom (Donsoft 2009)

Carrera Presidencial 2014 (Cerdipuerca Studios 2013)

Castlevania (Konami 1986)

Cazaproblemas (Trojan Chicken 2011)

Chapolim x Dracula: Um Duelo Assustador (Tectoy 1989)

Chichén Itzá (Aventuras AD 1992)

Chili Con Carnage (Eidos 2007)

Cidade Maravilhosa Rio (Mentez 2011)

Cities XL (Monte Cristo 2009)

Clash of the Olympians (Ironhide 2010)

Coca Kolector (Bujllai 2013)

CocoMonkeys (OH! 2012)

Code Name Viper (Capcom 1990)

Colheita Feliz (Mentez 2009)

Comando Pintura (JCCE 2014)

Command & Conquer: Red Alert 2 (EA 2000)

Command & Conquer: Red Alert 3 (EA 2008)

Conflict: Denied Ops (Eidos 2008)

Conozco Nicaragua (Fundación Zamora Terán 2011)

Conquest of the New World (Interplay 1996)

Contra (Konami 1987)

Corrida da pesada (Devworks 2003)

Crosser (Rafael Fajardo 2000)

Cuban Missile Crisis: The Aftermath (G5 Software 2005)

D.E.D. (Trojan Chicken 2010)

Desert Strike: Return to the Gulf (EA 1992)

Driver 2: Back on the Streets (Infogrames 2000)

Druids, the Epic (CPoint 2002)

E.T. (Atari 1982)

El Chavo Kart (Televisa 2014)

Elite (Imagineer 1984)

Enola (Domaginarium 2014)

Expedition Amazon (Penguin Software 1983)

Fenix Rage (Reverb Triple XP 2014)

FIFA (EA 1993)

FIFA 12 (EA 2011)

Final Fantasy (Square Enix 1987)

Flappy Bird (Dong Nguyen 2013)

Flappy Quetzal (Carlos Villagrán 2014)

Flight of the Amazon Queen (Warner 1995)

Frogger (Konami 1981)

Front Mission 4 (Square Enix 2004)

Fútbol Deluxe (Evoluxion 2004)

Fútbol Excitante (TEG 1997)

Gangstar Rio: City of Saints (Gameloft 2011)

Gesta Final (JCCE 2014)

Ghost House (Sega 1986)

God of War (Sony 2005)

The Godfather II (EA 2009)

Gold of the Americas: The Conquest of the New World (SSG 1989)

Gold of the Aztecs (Kinetica 1989)

Goldeneye 007 (Nintendo 1997)

Grand Theft Auto (Rockstar 1997)

Grand Theft Auto III (Rockstar 2001)

Grand Theft Auto IV (Rockstar 2008)

Grand Theft Auto V (Rockstar 2013)

Grand Theft Auto: San Andreas (Rockstar 2004)

Grand Theft Auto: Vice City (Rockstar 2002)

Grim Fandango (LucasArts 1998)

Guacamelee! (Drinkbox 2013)

Guerra Política (Amazian Team 2014)

Guevara, a.k.a. *Guerrilla War* (SNK 1987)

Gunbee F-99 (APC & TCP 1998)

Halo (Microsoft 2001)

Hamilton's Great Adventure (Fatshark 2011)

Harrier Attack (Durell 1983)

Hidden Agenda (Springboard 1988)

Hooligan Alone (Island of the Moon 2014)

I Wish I Were the Moon (Daniel Benmergui 2008)

Illusion of Gaia (Nintendo 1994)

Imperialism II: The Age of Exploration (SSI 1999)

Inca (Sierra On-Line 1992)

Inca II: Nations of Immortality (Sierra On-Line 1994)

Indiana Jones in Revenge of the Ancients (Mindscape 1987)

Inka Madness (Magia Digital 2013)

Inkawar (Luis Grimaldo 2005)

International Superstar Soccer (Konami 1995)

Jewel Quest (iWin 2004)

Jungle Strike (EA 1993)

Just Cause (Eidos 2006)

The King of Peru 2 (TEG 2001)

Kingdom Rush (Ironhide 2011)

Kingdom Rush: Frontiers (Ironhide 2013)

Kingdom Rush: Origins (Ironhide 2014)

La diosa de Cozumel (Aventuras AD 1990)

La Migra (Rafael Fajardo 2001)

La Mordida (LEAP 2014)

La Trinitaria (Instituto Tecnológico de las Américas 2008)

The Last of Us (Sony 2013)

League of Legends (Riot 2009)

Legends of Ooo (Cartoon Network 2012)

The Legend of Zelda (Nintendo 1986)

Little Big Planet (Sony 2008)

Little Big Planet PSP (Sony 2009)

Los templos sagrados (Aventuras AD 1991)

Lucha Libre AAA: Héroes del Ring (Konami 2010)

Madrid (Newsgaming.com 2004)

Malvinas 2032 (Sabarasa 1999)

Martial Arts: Capoeira! (Libredia 2011)

The Mask of the Sun (Broderbund 1982)

Max Payne (Rockstar 2001)

Max Payne 2 (Rockstar 2003)

Max Payne 3 (Rockstar 2012)

Mayan Pitz (Calidá 2013)

Mercenaries: Playground of Destruction (LucasArts 2005)

Mercenaries 2: World in Flames (EA 2008)

Metal Gear Solid (Konami 1998)

Metroid (Nintendo 1986)

The Mexican American War (HPS Simulations 2008)

Mictlan (Phyne 2012)

Monster Bag (Sony 2015)

Mônica no Castelo do Dragão (Tectoy 1991)

Montezuma's Return! (WizardWorks 1998)

Montezuma's Revenge (Parker Brothers 1984)

Mr. Patch (Gabriela Galilea 2014)

Mundo Gaturro (Clawi 2010)

MVP Baseball 2005 (EA 2005)

MVP Caribe (mod of *MVP Baseball 2005*, 2007)

Nación Motorizada (Ciro Durán 2012)

Narco Terror (Deep Silver 2013)

NarcoGuerra (GameTheNews 2013)

NAVE (Hernán Sáez and Máximo Balestrini 2012)

NicaBird (Ninfusds Estudio 2014)

Nick Wacky Racers 3D (Nickelodeon 2013)

Oregon Trail (MECC 1974)

Papa Sangre (Somethin' Else 2010)

Papa Sangre II (Somethin' Else 2013)

Papo & Yo (Minority 2012)

Pelé's Soccer (Atari 1980)

Pentagon (NGD Studios 1998)

Phantasy Star (Sega/Tectoy 1991)

Pitfall! (Activision 1982)

Pitfall: The Mayan Adventure (Activision 1994)

Pok ta Pok (Lion Works 2012)

Polache Land (OK Producciones 2014)

Portillo el Tontillo (Groupweird 2014)

Pro Evolution Soccer (Konami 2001)

Pro Evolution Soccer 2012 (Konami 2011)

Psychonauts (Majesco 2009)

P.T. (Konami 2014)

Pueblo Pitanga: Enemigos Silenciosos (Pan-American Health Organization 2013)

Quest for Quintana Roo (Telegames 1983)

Raiders of the Lost Ark (Atari 1982)

Railroad Tycoon II (Gathering of Developers 1997)

Red Dead Redemption (Rockstar 2010)

Red Dead Revolver (Rockstar 2004)

Regnum (NGD Studios 1995)

Regnum 2 (NGD Studios 1996)

Regnum Online (NGD Studios 2007)

Reto Canal (Canal de Panamá 2013)

Rock of Ages (ACE Team 2011)

RollerCoaster Tycoon (MicroProse 1999)

Samba de Oruga (TEG 2003)

Save the Turtles (Sabarasa 2012)

Second Life (Linden 2003)

September 12th: A Toy World (Newsgaming.com 2003)

The Seven Cities of Gold (EA 1984)

Shenmue (Sega 1999)

Sid Meier's Civilization (MicroProse 1991)

Sid Meier's Civilization V (2K Games 2010)

Sid Meier's Colonization (MicroProse 1994)

Sid Meier's Pirates! (MicroProse 1987)

Sid Meier's Railroad Tycoon (MicroProse 1990)

SimCity (Maxis 1989)

The Sims (EA 2000)

Sin Dientes (Fundación Zamora Terán 2011)

Soccer (Telematch 1978)

Sonic Adventure 2 (Sega 2001)

Space Invaders (Taito/Midway 1978)

Spacewar! (Steve Russell et al. 1962)

Special Force (Hezbollah 2003)

SpongeBob Skate & Surf Roadtrip (THQ 2011)

Squares (LEAP 2015)

Storyteller (Daniel Benmergui 2008 alpha, 2012 beta)

Street Fighter II (Capcom 1991)

Súbete al SITP (Transmilenio 2014)

Super Mario 64 (Nintendo 1996)

Super Mario Bros. (Nintendo 1985)

Super Monkey Ball (Sega 2001)

Taco Bell: Tasty Temple Challenge (BrandGames 2000)

Taco Master (Chillingo 2011)

Tekken 3 (Namco 1997)

This War of Mine (11 bit 2014)

TiQal (Microsoft 2008)

To Leave (Sony 2013)

Today I Die (Daniel Benmergui 2010)

Tom Clancy's Ghost Recon (Ubisoft 2002)

Tom Clancy's Ghost Recon: Advanced Warfighter 2 (Ubisoft 2007)

Tom Clancy's H.A.W.X. (Ubisoft 2009)

Tom Clancy's Rainbow Six 3: Raven Shield (Ubisoft 2003)

Tomb Raider (Eidos 1996)

Tomb Raider: Legend (Eidos 2006)

Tomb Raider: Underworld (Eidos 2008)

Tombs & Treasures (Infocom 1991)

Tropical America (OnRamp Arts 2002)

Tropico (Gathering of Developers 2001)

Tropico 3 (Kalypso 2009)

Truco (Ariel and Enrique Arbiser 1982)

Truco (Devworks 2003)

Turista Fronterizo (Ricardo Dominguez and Coco Fusco 2006)

Ultra Street Fighter IV (Capcom 2014)

Uncharted: Drake's Fortune (Sony 2007)

Urban Strike (EA 1994)

Utopia (Mattel 1981)

Where in the World is Carmen San Diego? (Broderbund 1985)

Wonder Boy in Monster Land (Sega 1988)

Zeno Clash (ACE Team 2009)

Zeno Clash 2 (ACE Team 2013)

Zuma (PopCap 2003)

Print

Aarseth, Espen J. *Cybertext: Perspectives on Ergodic Literature.* Baltimore: Johns Hopkins University Press, 1997.

Aarseth, Espen J. "The Game and Its Name: What Is a Game Auteur?" In *Visual Authorship: Creativity and Intentionality in Media*, ed. Torben Grodal, Bente Larsen, and Iben Thorving Laursen, 261–269. Copenhagen: Museum Tusculanum Press, 2004.

Aarseth, Espen J. "Genre Trouble: Narrativism and the Art of Simulation." In *First Person: New Media as Story, Performance, and Game*, ed. Noah Wardrip-Fruin and Pat Harrigan, 45–55. Cambridge, MA: MIT Press, 2004.

Adorno, Theodor W. "Culture Industry Reconsidered" (1963). In *The Culture Industry: Selected Essays on Mass Culture*, 98–106. New York: Routledge, 1991.

Aitken, Stuart C., and Leo E. Zonn. "Re-Presenting the Place Pastiche." In *Place, Power, Situation, and Spectacle: A Geography of Film*, ed. Stuart C. Aitken and Leo E. Zonn, 3–25. London: Rowman & Littlefield, 1994.

Aldama, Frederick Luis. "Latinos and Video Games." In *Encyclopedia of Video Games: The Culture, Technology, and Art of Gaming*, ed. Mark J. P. Wolf, 356. Santa Barbara, CA: Greenwood, 2012.

Appadurai, Arjun. *Modernity at Large: Cultural Dimensions of Globalization.* New York: Routledge, 1996.

Arnold, Matthew. *Culture and Anarchy: An Essay in Political and Social Criticism.* London: Smith, Elder & Co, 1869.

Arsenault, Dominic, and Bernard Perron. "In the Frame of the Magic Cycle: The Circle(s) of Gameplay." In *The Video Game Theory Reader 2*, ed. Bernard Perron and Mark J. P. Wolf, 109–131. New York: Routledge, 2009.

Atkins, Barry. *More than a Game: The Computer Game as Fictional Form.* Manchester, UK: Manchester University Press, 2003.

Auerbach, Erich. "Erich Auerbach on Stendhal, Balzac, and Flaubert." In *Realism*, ed. Lilian R. Furst, 53–86. London: Longman, 1992 [1953].

Austin, J. L. "How to Do Things with Words (Lecture II)." In *The Performance Studies Reader*, 2nd ed., ed. Henry Bial, 147–153. New York: Routledge, 2007 [1962].

Averbeck, Joshua M., and Dale Hample. "Ironic Message Production: How and Why We Produce Ironic Messages." *Communication Monographs* 75, no. 4 (2008): 369–410.

Babic, Edvin. "On the Liberation of Space in Computer Games." *Eludamos* (Göttingen) 1, no. 1 (2007). Accessed 9 July 2015, http://www.eludamos.org/index.php/eludamos/article/view/vol1no1-3/6.

Badiou, Alain. *Being and Event*. London: Continuum, 2005.

Barrantes, Roxana. "Analysis of ICT Demand: What Is Digital Poverty and How to Measure It?" In *Digital Poverty: Latin American and Caribbean Perspectives*, ed. Hernan Galperin and Judith Mariscal, 29–53. Ottawa: International Development Research Center, 2007.

Barthes, Roland. *Image, Music, Text*. Trans. S. Heath. New York: Hill and Wang, 1977.

Barthes, Roland. "The Reality Effect in Descriptions." Trans. R. Howard. In *Realism*, ed. Lilian R. Furst, 135–141. London: Longman, 1992 [1968].

Bazin, André. *What Is Cinema?* 2 vols. Ed. and trans. H. Gray. Berkeley: University of California Press, 1994 [1971].

Benjamin, Walter. *Illuminations*. Trans. H. Zohn. New York: Schocken Books, 2007 [1955].

Berlinski, Samuel, Matías Busso, Julian Cristiá, and Eugenio Severín. "Computers in Schools: Why Governments Should Do Their Homework." In *Development Connections: Unveiling the Impact of New Information Technologies*, ed. Alberto Chong, 169–212. New York: Palgrave Macmillan, 2011.

Bernal-Merino, Miguel Á. *Translation and Localisation in Video Games: Making Entertainment Global*. New York: Routledge, 2014.

Beverley, John. *Latinamericanism after 9/11*. Durham: Duke University Press, 2011.

Boal, Augusto. *Theater of the Oppressed*. London: Pluto, 2000 [1979].

Boellstorff, Tom. "A Ludicrous Discipline? Ethnography and Game Studies." *Games and Culture* 1, no. 1 (2006): 31–32.

Boellstorff, Tom, Bonnie Nardi, Celia Pearce, and T. L. Taylor, eds. *Ethnography and Virtual Worlds: A Handbook of Method*. Princeton: Princeton University Press, 2012.

Bogost, Ian. *How to Do Things with Videogames*. Minneapolis: University of Minnesota Press, 2011.

Bogost, Ian. *Persuasive Games: The Expressive Power of Videogames*. Cambridge, MA: MIT Press, 2007.

Bogost, Ian. *Unit Operations: An Approach to Videogame Criticism*. Cambridge, MA: MIT Press, 2006.

Bolter, Jay David. 2008. "Digital Media and the Future of Filmic Narrative." In *The Oxford Handbook of Film and Media Studies*, ed. Robert Kolker, 21–37. New York: Oxford University Press.

Bolter, Jay David, and Richard Grusin. *Remediation*. Cambridge, MA: MIT Press, 1999.

Borges, Jorge Luis. "The Argentine Writer and Tradition." In *Jorge Luis Borges: Selected Nonfictions*, trans. and ed. Eliot Weinberger, 420–427. New York: Viking, 1999 [1951].

Borges, Jorge Luis. *Ficciones*. Buenos Aires: Emecé, 1996 [1944].

Bourdieu, Pierre. *Distinction: A Social Critique of the Judgment of Taste*. New York: Routledge, 2013 [1979].

Bronfman, Alejandra, and Andrew Grant Wood. "Introduction: Media, Sound, and Culture." In *Media, Sound, and Culture in Latin America and the Caribbean*, ed. Alejandra Bronfman and Andrew Grant Wood, ix–xvi. Pittsburgh: University of Pittsburgh Press, 2012.

Butler, Judith. "Performative Acts and Gender Constitution: An Essay in Phenomenology and Feminist Theory." In *The Performance Studies Reader*. 2nd ed., ed. Henry Bial, 154–166. New York: Routledge, 2007.

Caillois, Roger. *Man, Play and Games*. Trans. M. Barash. Urbana: University of Illinois Press, 2001 [1958].

Calleja, Gordon. *In-Game: From Immersion to Incorporation*. Cambridge, MA: MIT Press, 2011.

Castells, Manuel. *Communication Power*. Oxford: Oxford University Press, 2009.

Castells, Manuel. *The Rise of the Network Society*. Cambridge, MA: Blackwell, 1996.

Castronova, Edward. *Synthetic Worlds: The Business and Culture of Online Games*. Chicago: University of Chicago Press, 2005.

Cathles, Alison, Gustavo Crespi, and Matteo Grazzi. "The Region's Place in the Digital World: A Tale of Three Divides." In *Development Connections: Unveiling the Impact of New Information Technologies*, ed. Alberto Chong, 29–68. New York: Palgrave Macmillan, 2011.

Celso, Viviana. "El lenguaje de los videojuegos: Sus pliegues y recortes en las prácticas sociales." *Novedades Educativas* 185 (2006): 74–76.

Chan, Anita Say. *Networking Peripheries: Technological Futures and the Myth of Digital Universalism.* Cambridge, MA: MIT Press, 2013.

Chan, Dean. "Playing with Race: The Ethics of Racialized Representations in E-Games." *International Review of Information Ethics* 4 (2005): 24–30.

Chávez, Daniel. 2010. "El coronel no tiene con quien jugar: representaciones latinoamericanas en la literatura y el videojuego." *Arizona Journal of Hispanic Cultural Studies* 14: 159–176.

Chiado, Marcus Vinicius Garrett. *1983 + 1984: E mais! O livro digital.* São Paulo: Self-published, 2013.

Cleger, Osvaldo. "Procedural Rhetoric and Undocumented Migrants: Playing the Debate over Immigration Reform." *Digital Culture & Education* 7, no. 1 (2015): 19–39.

Consalvo, Mia. *Cheating: Gaining Advantage in Video Games.* Cambridge, MA: MIT Press, 2007.

Cortázar, Julio. *Hopscotch.* Trans. G. Rabassa. New York: Pantheon, 1966 [1963].

Cresswell, Tim, and Deborah Dixon. "Introduction: Engaging Film." In *Engaging Film: Geographies of Mobility and Identity,* ed. Tim Cresswell and Deborah Dixon, 1–10. Lanham, MD: Rowman & Littlefield, 2002.

Crogan, Patrick. *Gameplay Mode: War, Simulation, and Technoculture.* Minneapolis: University of Minnesota Press, 2011.

Derrida, Jacques. *Margins of Philosophy.* Chicago: University of Chicago Press, 1982.

DeVane, Ben, and Kurt D. Squire. "The Meaning of Race and Violence in Grand Theft Auto: San Andreas." *Games and Culture* 3 (2008): 264–285.

Donoso, José. *Historia personal del Boom.* Barcelona: Anagrama, 1972.

Donovan, Tristan. *Replay: The History of Video Games.* Lewes, England: Yellow Ant, 2010.

Dormann, Claire, and Robert Biddle. "A Review of Humor for Computer Games: Play, Laugh and More." *Simulation and Gaming* 40, no. 6 (2009): 802–824.

Dovey, Jon, and Helen W. Kennedy. *Game Cultures: Computer Games as New Media.* Maidenhead, UK: Open University Press, 2006.

Dyer-Witheford, Nick, and Greig de Peuter. *Games of Empire: Global Capitalism and Video Games.* Minneapolis: University of Minnesota Press, 2009.

Egenfeldt-Nielsen, Simon, Jonas Heide Smith, and Susana Pajares Tosca, eds. *Understanding Video Games: The Essential Introduction.* 2nd ed. New York: Routledge, 2013.

Escher, Anton. "The Geography of Cinema—A Cinematic World." *Erdkunde* 60, no. 4 (2006): 307–314.

Eskelinen, Markku. "The Gaming Situation." *Game Studies* 1, no. 1 (2001). Accessed 9 July 2015, http://www.gamestudies.org/0101/eskelinen/.

Ferraz de Souza, Ricardo Vinicius. "Video Game Localization: The Case of Brazil." *TradTerm, São Paulo* 19 (2012): 289–326.

Fogu, Claudio. "Digitalizing Historical Consciousness." *History and Theory* 48, no. 2 (2009): 103–121.

Foucault, Michel. "Of Other Spaces." Trans. J. Miskowiec. *diacritics* 16, no. 1 (1986): 22–27.

Fox, Claire F. *The Fence and the River: Culture and Politics at the U.S.-Mexico Border.* Minneapolis: University of Minnesota Press, 1999.

Franco, Jean. *The Decline and Fall of the Lettered City: Latin America in the Cold War.* Cambridge, MA: Harvard University Press, 2002.

Frasca, Gonzalo. "Latin America." In *Encyclopedia of Video Games: The Culture, Technology, and Art of Gaming*, ed. Mark J. P. Wolf, 355–356. Santa Barbara, CA: Greenwood, 2012.

Frasca, Gonzalo. "Ludologists Love Stories Too: Notes from a Debate that Never Took Place." Level Up, Digital Games Research Association Conference Proceedings, 2003. Accessed 30 June 2015, http://www.ludology.org/articles/Frasca_LevelUp2003.pdf.

Frasca, Gonzalo. "Simulation versus Narrative: Introduction to Ludology." In *The Video Game Theory Reader*, ed. Mark J. P. Wolf and Bernard Perron, 221–235. New York: Routledge, 2003.

Frasca, Gonzalo. "Videogames of the Oppressed: Critical Thinking, Education, Tolerance and Other Trivial Issues." In *First Person: New Media as Story, Performance, and Game*, ed. Noah Wardrip-Fruin and Pat Harrigan, 85–94. Cambridge, MA: MIT Press, 2004.

Friedman, Ted. "*Civilization* and Its Discontents." In *Discovering Discs: Transforming Space and Genre on CD-ROM*, ed. Greg Smith. New York: New York University Press, 1998.

Gallo, Rubén. *Mexican Modernity: The Avant-Garde and the Technological Revolution.* Cambridge, MA: MIT Press, 2005.

Galloway, Alexander R. *Gaming: Essays on Algorithmic Culture.* Minneapolis: University of Minnesota Press, 2006.

García Canclini, Néstor. *Consumers and Citizens.* Trans. G. Yúdice. Minneapolis: University of Minnesota Press, 2001 [1995].

García Canclini, Néstor. *Cultura y comunicación: Entre lo global y lo local*. La Plata, Argentina: Periodismo y Comunicación, 1997.

García Canclini, Néstor. *Diferentes, desiguales y desconectados. Mapas de la interculturalidad*. Barcelona: Gedisa, 2004.

García Canclini, Néstor. *Hybrid Cultures: Strategies for Entering and Leaving Modernity*. Trans. R. Rosaldo. Minneapolis: University of Minnesota Press, 1995 [1990].

García Canclini, Néstor. *Latinoamericanos buscando lugar en este siglo*. Buenos Aires: Paidós, 2002.

García Canclini, Néstor. *Lectores, espectadores e internautas*. Barcelona: Gedisa, 2007.

García Canclini, Néstor. *La sociedad sin relato. Antropología y estética de la inminencia*. Buenos Aires, Madrid: Katz, 2010.

Gazzard, Alison. "Unlocking the Gameworld: The Rewards of Space and Time in Videogames." *Game Studies* 11, no. 1 (2011). Accessed 20 May 2013, http://gamestudies.org/1101/articles/gazzard_alison.

Gee, James Paul. "Semiotic Domains: Is Playing Video Games a 'Waste of Time?" In *The Game Design Reader: A Rules of Play Anthology*, ed. Katie Salen and Eric Zimmerman, 228–267. Cambridge, MA: MIT Press, 2006.

Gee, James Paul. *What Video Games Have to Teach Us About Learning and Literacy*. 2nd ed. New York: Palgrave Macmillan, 2007.

Giddens, Anthony. *The Consequences of Modernity*. Stanford: Stanford University Press, 1990.

Golumbia, David. "Computers and Cultural Studies." In *The Oxford Handbook of Film and Media Studies*, ed. Robert Kolker, 508–526. Oxford: Oxford University Press, 2008.

Gómez-Peña, Guillermo. "Culturas-in-Extremis: Performing Against the Cultural Backdrop of the Mainstream Bizarre." In *The Performance Studies Reader*. 2nd ed., ed. Henry Bial, 287–298. New York: Routledge, 2007.

González Seguí, Héctor Óscar. "Veinticinco años de videojuegos en México. Las mercancías tecnoculturales y la globalización económica." *Comunicación y Sociedad* 38 (2000): 103–126.

Grandadam, David, Patrick Cohendet, and Laurent Simon. "Places, Spaces and the Dynamics of Creativity: The Video Game Industry in Montreal." *Regional Studies* 47, no. 10 (2013): 1701–1714.

Greenfield, Gerard. "Writing the History of the Future: The Killing Game." *Z Magazine* 6, no. 17 (2004). Accessed 5 July 2011, http://zcombeta.org/znetarticle/writing-the-history-of-the-future-by-gerard-greenfield/.

Griffiths, Mark. "The Therapeutic Value of Video Games." In *Handbook of Computer Game Studies*, ed. Joost Raessens and Jeffrey Goldstein, 161–170. Cambridge, MA: MIT Press, 2005.

Gring-Pemble, Lisa, and Martha Solomon Watson. "The Rhetorical Limits of Satire: An Analysis of James Finn Garner's Politically Correct Bedtime Stories." *Quarterly Journal of Speech* 89, no. 2 (2003): 132–153.

Guaman Poma de Ayala, Felipe. *First New Chronicle and Good Government*. 1615. Trans. R. Adorno. Accessed 9 July 2015, http://www.kb.dk/permalink/2006/poma/390/en/text/, 390.

Hall, Stuart. "Cultural Identity and Cinematic Representation." In *Film and Theory: An Anthology*, ed. Robert Stam and Toby Miller, 210–222. Oxford: Blackwell Publishers, 2000.

Hariman, Robert. "Political Parody and Public Culture." *Quarterly Journal of Speech* 94, no. 2 (2008): 247–272.

Hayles, N. Katherine. *How We Became Posthuman: Virtual Bodies in Cybernetics, Literature, and Informatics*. Chicago: University of Chicago Press, 1999.

Hilmes, Michele. "Postscript: Sound Representation: Nation, Translation, Memory." In *Media, Sound, and Culture in Latin America and the Caribbean*, ed. Alejandra Bronfman and Andrew Grant Wood, 122–126. Pittsburgh: University of Pittsburgh Press, 2012.

Hjorth, Larissa. *Games and Gaming: An Introduction to New Media*. New York: Berg, 2011.

Hjorth, Larissa, and Dean Chan. "Locating the Game: Gaming Cultures in/and the Asia-Pacific." In *Gaming Cultures and Place in Asia-Pacific*, ed. Larissa Hjorth and Dean Chan, 1–14. New York: Routledge, 2009.

Hopenhayn, Martín. "Globalization and Culture: Five Approaches to a Single Text." In *Cultural Politics in Latin America*, ed. Anny Brooksbank Jones and Ronaldo Munck, 142–157. New York: St. Martin's Press, 2000.

Hopkins, Jeff. 1994. "A Mapping of Cinematic Places: Icons, Ideology, and the Power of (Mis)representation." In *Place, Power, Situation, and Spectacle: A Geography of Film*, ed. Stuart C. Aitken and Leo E. Zonn, 47–65. London: Rowman & Littlefield.

Huizinga, Johan. *Homo Ludens: A Study of the Play Element in Culture*. Boston: Beacon Press, 1955 [1944].

Huntemann, Nina B. "Playing with Fear: Catharsis and Resistance in Military-Themed Video Games." In *Joystick Soldiers*, ed. Nina B. Huntemann and Matthew Thomas Payne, 223–236. New York: Routledge, 2010.

Huntemann, Nina B., and Ben Aslinger. *Gaming Globally: Production, Play, and Place*. New York: Palgrave Macmillan, 2013.

Huntemann, Nina B., and Matthew Thomas Payne. "Introduction." In *Joystick Soldiers*, ed. Nina B. Huntemann and Matthew Thomas Payne, 1–18. New York: Routledge, 2010.

Hutchinson, Rachael. "Performing the Self: Subverting the Binary in Combat Games." *Games and Culture* 2, no. 4 (2007): 283–299.

Jaguaribe, Beatriz. "Favelas and the Aesthetics of Realism: Representations in Film and Literature." *Journal of Latin American Cultural Studies* 13, no. 3 (2004): 327–342.

Jameson, Fredric. *The Cultural Turn: Selected Writings on the Postmodern, 1983-1998*. London: Verso, 1998.

Jameson, Fredric. *The Geopolitical Aesthetic: Cinema and Space in the World System*. Bloomington: Indiana University Press, 1992.

Jameson, Fredric. 1991. *Postmodernism, or, The Cultural Logic of Late Capitalism*. Durham: Duke University Press.

Jenkins, Henry. *Convergence Culture: Where Old and New Media Collide*. New York: New York University Press, 2006.

Jenkins, Henry. *Fans, Bloggers, and Gamers: Exploring Participatory Culture*. New York: New York University Press, 2006.

Jenkins, Henry. "Game Design as Narrative Architecture." In *The Game Design Reader: A Rules of Play Anthology*, ed. Katie Salen and Eric Zimmerman, 670–689. Cambridge, MA: MIT Press, 2006.

Jones, Steven E. *The Meaning of Video Games: Gaming and Textual Strategies*. New York: Routledge, 2008.

Juul, Jesper. *A Casual Revolution: Reinventing Video Games and Their Players*. Cambridge, MA: MIT Press, 2010.

Juul, Jesper. *Half-Real: Video Games between Real Rules and Fictional Worlds*. Cambridge, MA: MIT Press, 2005.

King, Geoff, and Tanya Krzywinska. *Tomb Raiders and Space Invaders: Videogame Forms and Contexts*. New York: I. B. Tauris, 2006.

Kolko, Beth E., Lisa Nakamura, and Gilbert B. Rodman, eds. *Race in Cyberspace*. New York: Routledge, 2000.

Lahti, Martti. "As We Become Machines: Corporealized Pleasures in Video Games." In *The Video Game Theory Reader*, ed. Mark J. P. Wolf and Bernard Perron, 157–170. New York: Routledge, 2003.

Lefebvre, Martin. "Between Setting and Landscape in the Cinema." In *Landscape and Film*, ed. Martin Lefebvre, 19–59. New York: Routledge, 2006.

Leonard, David J. "Not a Hater, Just Keepin' It Real: The Importance of Race- and Gender-Based Game Studies." *Games and Culture* 1, no. 1 (2006): 83–88.

Levinson, Brett. *The Ends of Literature*. Stanford: Stanford University Press, 2001.

Lévy, Pierre. *Becoming Virtual: Reality in the Digital Age*. New York: Plenum Press, 1998.

Loayza Javier, Jerjes. "Los videojuegos on-line en Latinoamérica: impacto en las redes sociales y de consumo." *Icono 14* 8, no. 1 (2009): 59–74.

Lomnitz, Claudio. *Death and the Idea of Mexico*. Cambridge, MA: Zone, 2005.

López de Gómara, Francisco. *La conquista de México*. 1552. Red Ediciones. Accessed 30 June 2015, https://books.google.com/books?id=XSW-AoMiueIC&pg=PA148&lpg=PA148&dq=.

Lugo-Ocando, Jairo, ed. *The Media in Latin America*. New York: McGraw-Hill, 2008.

Lugo, Jairo, Tony Sampson, and Merlyn Lossada. "Latin America's New Cultural Industries Still Play Old Games: From the Banana Republic to Donkey Kong." *Game Studies* 2, no. 2 (2002). Accessed 9 July 2015, http://www.gamestudies.org/0202/lugo/.

Lukács, Georg. "Georg Lukács on Balzac's *Lost Illusions*." In *Realism*, ed. Lilian R. Furst, 98–109. London: Longman, 1992 [1957].

Madrid, Daniel, and Jonathan Valenzuela. "Chile Game." YouTube video, 00:47:17. Posted 2 March 2013. Accessed 9 July 2015, https://www.youtube.com/watch?v=vKESbojym5k.

Magnet, Shoshana. "Playing at Colonization: Interpreting Imaginary Landscapes in the Video Game *Tropico*." *Journal of Communication Inquiry* 30 (2006): 142–162.

Manovich, Lev. *The Language of New Media*. Cambridge, MA: MIT Press, 2001.

Marisca, Eduardo. "Buscando un gamer: Reconstruyendo la historia del videojuego peruano." *Pozo de letras* 11, no. 11 (2013): 17–30.

Marisca, Eduardo. "Developing Game Worlds: Gaming, Technology and Innovation in Peru." Master's thesis, Massachusetts Institute of Technology, Cambridge, MA, 2014. Accessed 16 July 2014, http://marisca.pe/files/EM-DGW-Final.pdf.

Mariscal, Judith, Carla Bonina, and Julio Luna. "New Market Scenarios in Latin America." In *Digital Poverty: Latin American and Caribbean Perspectives*, ed. Hernan Galperin and Judith Mariscal, 55–77. Ottawa: International Development Research Center, 2007.

Martín-Barbero, Jesús. "Between Technology and Culture: Communication and Modernity in Latin America." In *Cultural Agency in the Americas*, ed. Doris Sommer, 37–51. Durham: Duke University Press, 2006.

Martín-Barbero, Jesús. *Communication, Culture and Hegemony: From the Media to Mediations*. Trans. E. Fox and R. A. White. London: Sage, 1993 [1987].

Martín-Barbero, Jesús. 2006. "Medios y culturas en el espacio latinoamericano." *Iberoamericana (Madrid, Spain)* 2 (6): 89–106.

Mateas, Michael, and Andrew Stern. "Interaction and Narrative." In *The Game Design Reader: A Rules of Play Anthology*, ed. Katie Salen and Eric Zimmerman, 642–669. Cambridge, MA: MIT Press, 2006.

Mäyrä, Frans. "Getting into the Game: Doing Multidisciplinary Game Studies." In *The Video Game Theory Reader 2*, ed. Bernard Perron and Mark J. P. Wolf, 313–329. New York: Routledge, 2009.

Mäyrä, Frans. *An Introduction to Game Studies: Games in Culture*. London: Sage, 2008.

McGahan, Christopher. *Racing Cyberculture: Minoritarian Art and Cultural Politics on the Internet*. New York: Routledge, 2008.

McGonigal, Jane. *Reality Is Broken: Why Games Make Us Better and How They Can Change the World*. New York: Penguin, 2011.

McPherson, Tara. "Self, Other and Electronic Media." In *The New Media Book*, ed. Dan Harries, 183–194. London: British Film Institute, 2002.

Medina, Eden. *Cybernetic Revolutionaries: Technology and Politics in Allende's Chile*. Cambridge, MA: MIT Press, 2012.

Meyer, John C. "Humor as a Double-Edged Sword: Four Functions of Humor in Communication." *Communication Theory* 10, no. 3 (2000): 310–331.

Montes, Rafael Miguel. "*Ghost Recon: Island Thunder*: Cuba in the Virtual Battlescape." In *The Players' Realm: Studies on the Culture of Video Games and Gaming*, ed. J. Patrick Williams and Jonas Heide Smith, 154–170. Jefferson, NC: McFarland, 2007.

Montfort, Nick. "Introduction: The Garden of Forking Paths." In *The New Media Reader*, ed. Noah Wardrip-Fruin and Nick Monfort, 29–30. Cambridge, MA: MIT Press, 2003.

Montfort, Nick. *Twisty Little Passages*. Cambridge, MA: MIT Press, 2003.

Montfort, Nick, and Ian Bogost. *Racing the Beam: The Atari Video Computer System*. Cambridge, MA: MIT Press, 2009.

Moreiras, Alberto. *The Exhaustion of Difference: The Politics of Latin American Cultural Studies*. Durham: Duke University Press, 2001.

Murray, Janet H. *Hamlet on the Holodeck: The Future of Narrative in Cyberspace*. Cambridge, MA: MIT Press, 1998.

Murray, Janet H. "Inventing the Medium." In *The New Media Reader*, ed. Noah Wardrip-Fruin and Nick Monfort, 3–11. Cambridge, MA: MIT Press, 2003.

Myers, David. *Play Redux: The Form of Computer Games*. Ann Arbor: University of Michigan Press, 2010.

Nagib, Lúcia. *Brazil on Screen: Cinema Novo, New Cinema, Utopia*. New York: I. B. Tauris, 2007.

Nakamura, Lisa. *Cybertypes: Race, Ethnicity, and Identity on the Internet*. New York: Routledge, 2002.

Newman, James. *Videogames*. New York: Routledge, 2004.

Nitsche, Michael. *Video Game Spaces: Image, Play, and Structure in 3D Worlds*. Cambridge, MA: MIT Press, 2008.

Noveck, Beth Simone. "Democracy—The Video Game: Virtual Worlds and the Future of Collective Action." In *The State of Play: Law, Games, and Virtual Worlds*, ed. Jack M. Balkin and Beth Simone Noveck, 257–282. New York: New York University Press, 2006.

Paul, Christopher A. *Wordplay and the Discourse of Video Games: Analyzing Words, Design, and Play*. New York: Routledge, 2012.

Payne, Matthew Thomas. "Marketing Military Realism in Call of Duty 4: Modern Warfare." *Games and Culture* 7, no. 4 (2012): 305–327.

Pearce, Celia. *Communities of Play: Emergent Cultures in Multiplayer Games and Virtual Worlds*. Cambridge, MA: MIT Press, 2009.

Penix-Tadsen, Phillip. "Latin American Game Design and the Narrative Tradition." In *Technology, Literature, and Digital Culture in Latin America: Mediatized Sensibilities in a Globalized Era*, ed. Matthew Bush and Tania Gentic, 205–230. New York: Routledge, 2015.

Penix-Tadsen, Phillip. "Latin American Ludology: Why We Should Take Video Games Seriously (and When We Shouldn't)." *Latin American Research Review* 48, no. 1 (2013): 174–190.

Penney, Joel. 2010. "'No Better Way to "Experience" World War II': Authenticity and Ideology in the *Call of Duty* and *Medal of Honor* Player Communities." In *Joystick Soldiers*, ed. Nina B. Huntemann and Matthew Thomas Payne. New York: Routledge.

Popol Vuh. English trans. D. Goetz and S. G. Morley, from Spanish trans. A. Recinos. Norman: University of Oklahoma Press, 1950. [1701].

Prensky, Mark. "Computer Games and Learning: Digital Game-Based Learning." In *Handbook of Computer Game Studies*, ed. Joost Raessens and Jeffrey Goldstein, 97–122. Cambridge, MA: MIT Press, 2005.

Raley, Rita. "Border Hacks: The Risks of Tactical Media." In *Risk and the War on Terror*, ed. Louise Amoore and Marieke de Goede, 197–217. New York: Routledge, 2008.

Reichmuth, Philipp, and Stefan Werning. "Pixel Pashas, Digital Djinns." *ISIM Review* 18 (2006): 46–47.

Ribeiro, Darcy. *The Brazilian People: The Formation and Meaning of Brazil.* Trans. G. Rabassa. Gainesville: University of Florida Press, 2000 [1995].

Romero/Lar, *Fernando. Hyperborder: The Contemporary U.S.-Mexico Border and Its Future.* New York: Princeton Architectural Press, 2008.

Ruggill, Judd Ethan, and Ken S. McAllister. *Gaming Matters: Art, Science, Magic, and the Computer Game Medium.* Tuscaloosa: University of Alabama Press, 2011.

Sahagún, Bernardino de. *General History of the Things of New Spain.* Trans. A. Anderson and C. Dibble. Santa Fe, NM: School of American Research, 1954 [1577].

Saldívar, José David. *Trans-Americanity: Subaltern Modernities, Global Coloniality, and the Cultures of Greater Mexico.* Durham: Duke University Press, 2012.

Salen, Katie, and Eric Zimmerman. "Game Design and Meaningful Play." In *Handbook of Computer Game Studies*, ed. Joost Raessens and Jeffrey Goldstein, 59–79. Cambridge, MA: MIT Press, 2005.

Samara Silva, Kelly, Adair da Silva Lopes, Samuel Caravalho Dumuth, Leandro Martin Totaro Garcia, Jorge Bezerra, and Markus Vinicius Nahas. "Changes in Television Viewing and Computers/Videogames Use Among High School Students in Southern Brazil between 2001 and 2011." *International Journal of Public Health* 59, no. 1 (2014): 77–86.

Sarlo, Beatriz. *La ciudad vista: Mercancías y cultura urbana.* Buenos Aires: Siglo Veintiuno, 2009.

Sarlo, Beatriz. *Scenes from Postmodern Life.* Trans. J. Beasley-Murray. Minneapolis: University of Minnesota Press, 2001 [1994].

de Saussure, Ferdinand. *Course in General Linguistics.* Trans. W. Baskin. New York: Columbia University Press, 2013 [1916].

Schut, Kevin. 2007. "Strategic Simulations and Our Past: The Bias of Computer Games in the Presentation of History." *Games and Culture* 2 (3): 215–235.

Schechner, Richard. *Performance Studies: An Introduction.* 3rd ed. New York: Routledge, 2013.

Schwarz, Roberto. "*City of God.*" Trans. J. Gledson. *New Left Review* 12 (2001): 102–112.

Schwarz, Roberto. *Misplaced Ideas.* Trans. J. Gledson. London: Verso, 1992.

Searle, J. R. "What Is a Speech Act?" In *The Philosophy of Language*, ed. J. R. Searle, 39–53. Oxford: Oxford University Press, 1971.

Shenassa, Shirin. "The Lack of Materiality in Latin American Media Theory." In *Latin American Literature and Mass Media*, ed. Edmundo Paz-Soldán and Debra A. Castillo, 249–269. New York: Garland, 2001.

Shiu, Anthony Sze-Fai. "What Yellowface Hides: Video Games, Whiteness, and the American Racial Order." *Journal of Popular Culture* 39, no. 1 (2006): 109–125.

Sicart, Miguel. "Against Procedurality." *Game Studies* 11, no. 3 (2011). Accessed 20 May 2013, http://gamestudies.org/1103/articles/sicart_ap.

Sicart, Miguel. *The Ethics of Computer Games.* Cambridge, MA: MIT Press, 2009.

Sicart, Miguel. "Values Between Systems: Designing Ethical Gameplay." In *Ethics and Game Design: Teaching Values through Play*, ed. Karen Schrier and David Gibson, 1–15. New York: Information Science Reference, 2010.

Sihvonen, Tanja. 2011. *Players Unleashed! Modding The Sims and the Culture of Gaming.* Amsterdam: Amsterdam University Press.

Siqueiros, David Alfaro, Antonio Berni, Lino Eneas Spilimbergo, Juan C. Castagnino, and Enrique Lázaro. "Ejercicio plástico." In *Heterotopías: Medio siglo sin lugar, 1918/1968*, ed. Mari Carmen Ramírez and Héctor Olea, 476–478. Madrid: Museo Nacional Centro de Arte Reina Sofía, 2000 [1933].

Sisler, Vit. "Digital Arabs: Representation in Video Games." *European Journal of Cultural Studies* 11, no. 2 (2008): 203–220.

Squire, Kurt. "Cultural Framing of Computer/Video Games." *Game Studies* 2, no. 1 (2002). Accessed 9 July 2015, http://www.gamestudies.org/0102/squire/.

Takhteyev, Yuri. *Coding Places: Software Practice in a South American City*. Cambridge, MA: MIT Press, 2012.

Taylor, Claire. "Monopolies and Maquiladoras: The Resistant Re-encoding of Gaming in Coco Fusco and Ricardo Domínguez's *Turista Fronterizo*." *Journal of Iberian and Latin American Research* 18, no. 2 (2012): 151–165.

Taylor, Diana. *The Archive and the Repertoire: Performing Cultural Memory in the Americas*. Durham: Duke University Press, 2003.

Taylor, Diana. "Translating Performance." In *The Performance Studies Reader*. 2nd ed., ed. Henry Bial, 44–50. New York: Routledge, 2007.

Taylor, Laurie. "When Seams Fall Apart: Video Game Space and the Player." *Game Studies* 3, no. 2 (2003). Accessed 20 May 2013, http://www.gamestudies.org/0302/taylor/.

Tinsman, Heidi, and Sandhya Shukla, eds. *Imagining Our Americas: Toward a Transnational Frame*. Durham: Duke University Press, 2007.

Tinsman, Heidi, and Sandhya Shukla. "Introduction: Across the Americas." In *Imagining Our Americas: Toward a Transnational Frame*, ed. Sandhya Shukla and Heidi Tinsman, 1–33. Durham: Duke University Press, 2007.

Uricchio, William. "Simulation, History, and Computer Games." In *Handbook of Computer Game Studies*, ed. Joost Raessens and Jeffrey Goldstein, 327–338. Cambridge, MA: MIT Press, 2005.

Wark, McKenzie. *Gamer Theory*. Cambridge, MA: Harvard University Press, 2007.

Whalen, Zach. "Play Along—An Approach to Videogame Music." *Game Studies* 4, no. 1 (2004). Accessed 20 May 2013, http://www.gamestudies.org/0401/whalen/.

Williams, Gareth. *The Other Side of the Popular: Neoliberalism and Subalternity in Latin America*. Durham: Duke University Press, 2002.

Williams, Raymond Leslie. *The Twentieth-Century Spanish American Novel*. Austin: University of Texas Press, 2003.

Wolf, Mark J. P. "Genre and the Video Game." In *Handbook of Computer Game Studies*, ed. Joost Raessens and Jeffrey Goldstein, 113–134. Cambridge, MA: MIT Press, 2005.

Wolf, Mark J. P. "Space in the Video Game." In *The Medium of the Video Game*, ed. Mark J. P. Wolf, 51–75. Austin: University of Texas Press, 2001.

Wolf, Mark J. P., ed. 2015. *Video Games around the World*. Cambridge, MA: MIT Press.

Wood, Aylish. "Recursive Space: Play and Creating Space." *Games and Culture* 7, no. 1 (2012): 87–105.

Yúdice, George. *The Expediency of Culture: Uses of Culture in the Global Era.* Durham: Duke University Press, 2003.

Yúdice, George. "New Social and Business Models in Latin American Musics." In *Consumer Culture in Latin America*, ed. John Sinclair and Anna Cristina Pertierra, 17–34. New York: Palgrave Macmillan, 2012.

INDEX